The Economics of Staging the Olympics

The Economics of Staging the Olympics

A Comparison of the Games 1972–2008

Holger Preuss

*Professor of Sport Economics and Sportmanagement,
Johannes Gutenberg-University Mainz, Germany and
member of the Research Team Olympia*

Edward Elgar
Cheltenham, UK • Northampton, MA, USA

Published by
Edward Elgar Publishing Limited
Glensanda House
Montpellier Parade
Cheltenham
Glos GL50 1UA
UK

Edward Elgar Publishing, Inc.
136 West Street
Suite 202
Northampton
Massachusetts 01060
USA

A catalogue record for this book
is available from the British Library

ISBN 1 8 4376 893 3

Printed and bound in Great Britain by MPG Books Ltd, Bodmin, Cornwall

Contents

List of figures

List of tables

List of abbreviations

ABC	American Broadcasting Companies
ACOG	Atlanta Organizing Committee of the Olympic Games
ACOP	Atlanta Centennial Olympic Properties
AOB	Athens Olympic Broadcasting
AOC	Australian Olympic Committee
ARD	Arbeitsgemeinschaft der öffentlich-rechtlichen Rundfunkanstalten der Bundesrepublik Deutschland
ATC	Australian Tourist Commission
BBC	British Broadcasting Corporation
BOB	Beijing Olympic Broadcasting
BOBICO	Beijing Olympic Bidding Committee
BOCOG	Beijing Organising Committee of the Olympic Games
CBA	Cost Benefit Analysis
CHN	China
COC	Chinese Olympic Committee
COJO	Calgary Organizing Committee of the Olympic Games
CPI	Consumer Price Index
DOZ	Deutsches Olympia Hörfunk- und Fernsehzentrum
EBU	European Broadcasting Union
ECU	European Currency Unit
EDP	Electronic Data Processing
FIFA	International Football Federation
FIP	Fédération Internationale de Philatélie
GDP	Gross Domestic Product
GDR	German Democratic Republic
GER	Germany
GNP	Gross National Product
HCC	Host City Contract
HDTV	High Definition Television
HKG	Hong Kong
IBC	International Broadcasting Centre
IF	International Federation
INA	Indonesia
IND	India
IOC	International Olympic Committee
ISL	International Sport and Leisure (agency)

ITVR	International Television and Radio Signal
JPN	Japan
KBC	Korean Broadcasting Commission
KBS	Korean Broadcasting Systems
KOR	Korea
MAS	Malaysia
MBC	Mun-Hwa Broadcasting Corporation
MICE	Meetings, Incentives, Congresses, Exhibitions
MPC	Main Press Centre
NBA	National Basketball Association
NBC	National Broadcasting Corporation
NFL	National Football League
NOC	National Olympic Committee
NSW	New South Wales
NZL	New Zealand
OBI	Name of German sponsor
OBO	Olympic Broadcasting Organization
OBS	Olympic Broadcasting Service
OCA	Olympic Co-ordination Authority
OCOG	Organising Committee of the Olympic Games
OECD	Organisation for Economic Co-operation and Development
OIRT	Organization internationale de radiodiffusion et de télévision
OIT	Organización de Television Iberoamericanas
ORTA	Olympic Road and Transport Authority
PPP	Purchasing Power Parities
PR	Public Relations
SIN	Singapore
SOCOG	Sydney Organizing Committee of the Olympic Games
SOBO	Sydney Olympic Broadcasting Organization
SRi	SRi International: Non-profit Research Institute
TFC	Tourism Forecasting Council
THA	Thailand
TMOP	Team Millennium Olympic Partners
TPE	Chinese Taipee
TOP	The Olympic Programme / The Olympic Partner
UNESCO	United Nations Educational, Scientific, and Cultural Organization
URTNA	Union for Radio and Television Networks for Africa
USOC	United States Olympic Committee
VIK	value in kind
WADA	World Anti Doping Agency
WINS	Wide Information Network Service
WTO	World Trade Organization
ZDF	Zweites Deutsches Fernsehen

Preface

The Olympic Games are the most prestigious sports event that a city can organize. They are the dream and fulfilment of young athletes. They also represent an extraordinary sporting, social, cultural and environmental legacy for the host city, the region and the country. The International Olympic Committee is dedicated and committed to ensuring that its legacy is the best possible one.

With the new edition of the book *The Economics of Staging the Olympics: A Comparison of the Games 1972–2008*, Professor Holger Preuss highlights the beneficial impact of the Olympic Games, financially and socially. Nowadays, hosting the Olympic Games can act as a catalyst for urban redevelopment, enabling changes, which might normally take several decades, to be completed over a seven-year cycle.

This work, which highlights macroeconomic and business analysis related to over 30 years of Olympic Games' history, will certainly be useful to share the knowledge and the various experiences in this field and prove a valuable tool for students and researchers who are interested in the Olympic Movement.

It is through similar publications that the complexity of the Olympic Games and their economic impact can be further understood by the generations to come.

I trust that each of you will enjoy reading this book and appreciate the work of its author.

Jacques Rogge
President of the International Olympic Committee
12 June 2004

Foreword

This book arises from the need to analyse, in detail, the various economic aspects that the Olympic Games mean for host cities. Since 1984 increasingly more cities in the world have announced their interest in staging the Olympic Games, making it a festival with significant economic dimensions. What followed have been economic triumphs and tragedies, glories and fiascos – all are included in the 36 years of Olympic history reviewed in this book.

In the libraries of the world are thousands of sources on the economics of the Olympic Games, but only a few try to compare the economic effects of the world's largest peaceful gathering of humanity. Only a long-term comparison can give a host city, or potential bid city, an idea of the economic size and complexity of the Games today. Therefore, it is time to find a way to convert data from different time periods (1972–2008) and different macro economies to analyse the economics and commercialization of the Olympic Games over the past three decades.

My previous books on this topic that were published in Germany (1999) (Agon Verlag), Australia (2000) (Walla Walla Press), form the bases for this book, but did not cover the variety of the economic influences this work examines. Over ten years of Olympic archival research in Munich, Montreal, Los Angeles, Seoul, Barcelona, Atlanta, Sydney and Athens, as well as visits to Olympic study centres in Los Angeles, Barcelona, London (Ontario), Olympia and Lausanne provide the basis for this book. More than a thousand sources completed the picture. However, it is the many interviews with Olympic experts consulted for this book that offers unique and valuable insight missing in other publications.

I would like to express my sincere gratitude to my wife Sonja and my children Merle and Finja for their patience, to the 'Research Team Olympia', especially Professor Müller and Professor Messing and to my father for their discussions, to my student helpers for the layout and finally all the Olympic experts around the world for their willingness to provide the data I needed.

Holger Preuss, 7 July 2004

1. Introduction: the situation of modern cities and the Olympic Games

During the past 108 years, the Olympic Games have developed into an event which, every four years, offers the host city the opportunity to become the centre of global interest. There are numerous reasons that motivate cities to stage the Olympic Games. For one, the Games are the biggest, most prestigious, peaceful multi-sport event of the world. In addition, the Games provide a unique opportunity for politicians and industry to move hidden agendas such as the improvement of infrastructure for sport, housing, communication, traffic and other sectors. Furthermore there are a number of political, cultural, ecological and social issues related to the Olympic Games thus making their organizations a multidimensional complex project. While many of these issues have non-economic aims, they remain closely related to economic issues: for example, the motivation of the host population to practise active sports themselves results in lower health costs. New political relations can increase the national trade balance (for example, Seoul 1988) as well as reaching greater consensus of politicians regarding decisions for infrastructure construction (for example, Athens 2004 and Barcelona 1992). Ecological sustainability of Games-related structure can showcase newly developed technology (for example, Sydney 2000) and cultural presentation can increase post-Olympic tourism, such as in Sydney 2000 and Barcelona 1992.

When one considers the gigantic scale of the Olympic Games and the money required to stage them, it is reasonable to assume that only the largest cities in the world are equipped to act as hosts. Smaller cities often have budgets that are strained and are unable to provide sufficient Olympic infrastructure without public investment.

The lack of public money makes it difficult to trigger huge impacts that can re-urbanize or restructure a city. Therefore recent trends suggest that large events such as world exhibitions, continental games or world championships are used to attract visitors and investors to a city (Garcia, 1993). However, this 'festivalization of city politics' carries the inherent risk of false development and therefore may not be an appropriate strategy for each city.

Since Munich 1972, the Olympics have experienced great changes. Economic interests have become very important in public debate. There is much discussion about the International Olympic Committee's (IOC) ability to market the Games efficiently. Other concerns include: (1) the interests of organizing committees (OCOG) to produce a financial surplus; (2) the interests of politicians to develop the infrastructure and image of the host city; (3) the interests of sponsors to link their image to sport and the uniqueness of the Olympic Games; (4) the interests of the media to broadcast the Games to increase viewing rates and to sell commercial times at the highest prices; and (5) the interests of businesses within a host region to claim a fraction of the immense monetary sums involved.

Those responsible for the health of the Olympic Movement fear the consequences of 'over-commercialization' and the loss of Olympic ideals. Furthermore, Olympic opponents advocate the likelihood of increased debt and the unjust distribution of public money where certain groups will be disadvantaged and denied funds. Together, such factors place the Olympic Games in a questionable light. In Atlanta, journalists who coined the phrases, 'Coca-Cola Games' and 'Fair of the century' legitimized such criticisms. A closer economic investigation of the above problems will help to correct misguided ideas about the development of the Olympic Movement and to present them in a more objective light in order to make imminent dangers obvious.

Today, economic and political interests are prime concerns when bidding for the Olympic Games. So far, organizers have assessed the positive effects of Olympic Games primarily by the officially stated profit margin. This can clearly be seen by the increased number of bids – there are nine for the 2012 Games. However, OCOG profits are calculated in very different ways, and sometimes, the figures are incomprehensible.

This book will show new methods to assess how the economic balance of the Games can be calculated more precisely. In order to make a successful comparison of host countries, it is necessary to homogenize the calculation methods employed to determine the final balance. It is only in this way that a comprehensive economic evaluation of the Olympic Games can be made. This work could serve both future hosts as well as potential bid cities. It will enlighten the decision-making processes in managing the Olympic Games and provide information which is paramount to its organization.

It must not be ignored that the size and importance of the Olympic Games also affects the political, sociocultural, ecological and technological areas of the host city. This book will be limited to the economic subsystems without implying that economic aspects alone would suffice to describe the complexity of the system of 'Olympic Games' as a whole. To be precise, it is not possible to investigate the economic field in isolation from other areas. The fact that non-economic topics are permanently touched upon reflects the strong interrelation of the various aspects, which cannot be ignored when dealing with the Olympic Games.

The main intention of this work is to show the manifold economic relations referring to the staging of Olympic Games, especially by looking at Beijing 2008. The investigation of several subsequent Olympics is given special importance. If regionally based economic particularities, which are dependent on a specific region are eliminated, then general developments can be recognized. Results, which do not change over a number of Olympic Games, prove an economic aspect to be independent in a geopolitical way. Variations in the significance of an economic aspect display the existing potential, which can be activated according to the host region/nation. This is the basis for the superordinate nomothetic approach in this work: that is, isolating individual macroeconomic effects on the host city and individual revenue/cost positions of an OCOG over a longer period of time as well as their homogenization could make general principles obvious.

So far, it has seemed impossible to compare Olympic Games because they have been staged at different times in different countries where the financing and organizational structures have strongly differed. Using special conversion methods for the data, which were compiled by analysing documents combined with the interviewing of experts, it was possible to greatly eliminate these differences. The investigation will necessarily deal with a variety of topics ranging from macroeconomic to business-economic considerations.

2. Methodology: justifications for use

2.1 STATE OF RESEARCH AND OBJECTIVES

From the OCOG's viewpoint, the Olympic Games have only a short life. It is difficult to compare the various Games with each other because they are affected by changing variables of economics, organization, time and space. These factors have, thus far, impeded research work with regards to the economic impacts of staging the Olympic Games. It has, therefore, seemed impossible to compare the Games (Los Angeles OCOG, 1984). Economic impacts also became a matter of interest for future bidders only after the 1976 Olympics, with its allegedly substantial deficit for the city and the citizens of Montreal. Furthermore, with Los Angeles 1984 the Olympics assumed such financial pressure that new financing sources had to be opened up. In view of the rapid development and the deep changes, several Olympiads have to be investigated in order to make general statements.

Lee (1989), Hall (1992), Brunet (1993), Landry and Yerlès (1996) and Toohey and Veal (2000) compiled tables to compare revenues and expenditures, as they were stated in the official reports, and converted the figures into one currency but did not provide further interpretations. These investigations are, therefore, very superficial. As shown subsequently, the conversion methods are inaccurate and thus weaken their credibility. Maennig (1997) is the only author who provides an approach on the comparison of Olympic Games.

Other investigations are limited to individual Olympic Games. With the increasing economic significance of the Games as it relates to the host, economic analyses have recently become more important. It must, however, be kept in mind that pre-Olympic analyses were mostly linked to the ordering body while post-Olympic analyses were frequently compiled by OCOG staff. Therefore, most analyses cannot claim to be neutral.

From 1896, the financing of the Olympic Games has been a controversial subject (Brill, 1996; Philemon, 1996 [1896]; Müller and Gieseler, 1996). Considering the growth of the Games during the past few years and the complexity to organize them, it becomes clear that staging this mega-event bears a financial risk for all hosts. Nevertheless, the number of cities bidding for the Olympic Games has increased since 1977.

Today, the impact of Olympic Games amounts to up to US\$$_{00}$ 5 billion depending on the size of restructuring the city. From the business-economic point of view, with regard to the OCOG it amounts to US\$$_{00}$ 2 billion. Those interested in hosting the Olympics will have to answer the following questions before submitting their bid:

- What are the benefits and costs for the citizens of the host city?
- What are the financing sources available to the OCOG? What is the approximate amount of the revenues?
- What are the expenditures of the OCOG? Will it be able to organize the Games without a deficit?

The major investigations of the past were restricted to the economic impacts of individual Games. The prime objective was to show both a surplus by subtracting expenditures from revenues and a macroeconomic success by measuring benefits against costs. This objective might be justified as a means to promote the acceptance of the Games in the host country and a way to give information to the decision-makers. Apart from the economic effects, future bidders are also interested in the variables and the risks affecting them. Both are specifically emphasized in this book. In addition, the interrelations of the economic effects are investigated in order to show mutual interdependencies of the variables. Developments can only be shown and phenomena can only be categorized by analysing and evaluating several Olympic Games in sequence.

Individual data, minutes, reports, proceedings and publications of various institutions are condensed and substantiated by expert interviews. The aim of this book is to reduce the stated lack of research by finding the answers to questions such as:

- What is the share of the public and private interests when financing the Olympic Games?
- How were the Games from Munich 1972 to Sydney 2000 financed and what is planned for Athens 2004 and Beijing 2008?
- What is the economic benefit of the Games? Is it transitory or lasting? Is there any Olympic economic legacy?
- How reliable are data on the costs of past Games?
- How did the various financing sources develop and how are they interrelated?
- What costs must be covered by an OCOG and what factors determine them?

2.2 AREA OF INVESTIGATION

The area of investigation is delimited according to institutions, topics, space and time. From an institutional point of view, the Olympic Movement consists of many subsystems. Each of the subsystems in turn acts and reacts autonomously. This makes the Olympic Movement an extremely sensitive system, which changes during the course of time whenever one of its subsystems changes.

The OCOG and host city are investigated under economic aspects exclusively. Although this study concentrates on economic aspects, references to other disciplines are often necessary and cannot be avoided.

In general, the Olympic Games are organized and staged by an OCOG in cooperation with the host city. The Games are a festival with sporting competitions, which are staged every four years. The OCOG and host city of modern times enter the Olympic Movement only temporarily because of the permanently changing location of the host site. This is a direct contrast to the ancient Olympics where the competitions were staged in Olympia, the original location of the Games from 776 BC to AD 393.

Olympic Winter Games have been staged since 1924. Until 1992, they were hosted in the same year as the Olympic Games. In 1994, they were separated from the Olympic Games and hosted in the second year of each Olympiad. This decision was based on the fact that television networks were no longer willing to pay the high sums for television rights in the Olympics and Winter Olympics in the same year. In addition, the sponsors' advertising budgets were not large enough. However, the Winter Olympics are also staged every four years (IOC, 2003d, Rule 9, para. 4); they are an independent event and, in this book, are considered only occasionally.

The Paralympics, World Games for disabled athletes, have their origin in Stoke Mandeville, England. They have been staged in the Olympic year since 1960 (Guttman, 1979). The delimitation problem is their financial link to the OCOG balance sheet. Thus far, independent organizing committees have organized almost all Paralympics, although they are included in the Bid books for Olympic Games. Their finances are included in the Olympic balance sheet. The IOC recognized the Paralympics and since 1997 a city can only bid for Olympic Games and Paralympics together. For Barcelona 1992, Lillehammer 1994 and Sydney 2000, there was a single organizing committee for both Olympics and Paralympics, but still with different departments. The Paralympics of Atlanta 1996 saw a special organizing committee. However, it acted in close cooperation with the OCOG (interview, Price, 1997). In Athens 2004 for the first time the same departments and staff organize both the Olympic Games and Paralympics. In this book the Paralympics are not considered.

In 1894, Baron Pierre de Coubertin founded the IOC as the umbrella organisation of the Olympic Movement. The first Olympic Games of modern times were staged in Athens in 1896. Since then, they have taken place every four years corresponding to the period of an Olympiad in ancient times. Under the presidency of J.A. Samaranch, the financial situation of the IOC has steadily improved and it has been successful in expanding its powers repeatedly (IOC, 2001c; Landry and Yerlès, 1996). Today, the IOC oversees the negotiations of almost half of an OCOG's budget. On the one hand, this ensures the lasting existence of the Movement and on the other hand, it justifies its paramount position in the Olympic Movement. IOC financing will be reviewed in this study only where it is directly linked to OCOG financing.

National Olympic Committees (NOC) and International Federations (IF) are independent of and only partially financed by the Olympic Movement. Apart from their relationships to the OCOG, their economic links to the Olympic Movement are not considered in detail.

From a time point of view, the number of Olympic Games under detailed review here delimits the book. They are the ten Olympics from Munich in 1972 to Beijing in 2008. The story of the modern Olympic Games can be divided into four periods. The individual periods are formed according to the groupings made in this investigation and according to the economic aspects of the Olympic Games. The investigation mainly concentrates on periods II (1969–80) and III (1981–2003). However, period I (1896–1968), in particular, is examined with regards to the history of individual financing sources and period IV (2004–08) with regards to the chances and risks for the Olympic Movement that can be foreseen today.

Period I

Period I (1896–1968) is characterized by the financing problems of many OCOGs. It is conspicuous that new financing sources were developed whenever a government tried to avoid financial obligations. Some sources were used only once, others have been used until today. In this period, the economic impacts of the Olympic Games were given almost no attention at all. The effects were either rarely documented at the time or they were minimal on the host city because of their small size. The references made in this book to the Games of this period with regards to the origins of individual financing sources serve to clarify and evaluate the importance of the respective source. They do not claim to summarize the complete history of the modern Olympic Games as far as economics are concerned.

Period II

In period II (1969–80), the urgency to open up financing sources increased because of the growing gigantism of the Olympics. In this period, the selling of television rights and sponsoring, which are the most important sources today, grew to a considerable extent. Munich 1972 is of interest, since it is important in regard to public financing. After the 1976 Olympics caused a tremendous deficit for the City of Montreal, no city dared to bid for the 1984 Games due to the fact that they no longer seemed to be financially bearable. The Olympic Games of Moscow 1980 receive little consideration due to the lack of available information. Therefore, this period is mainly defined by the publicly financed Games of Munich 1972 and Montreal 1976.

Period III

Period III (1981-2003) starts with the Olympiad of Los Angeles 1984. When the host for the 1984 Olympic Games had to be decided upon on 1 July 1978, there were no candidates except for Los Angeles, which had failed in its bid for the Games of both 1980 and 1976. This unique situation allowed the OCOG to push through conditions the IOC would not otherwise have conceded (Hill, 1992; Reich, 1986). After long negotiations, stipulations in the Olympic Charter were eventually declared void, thereby allowing the City of Los Angeles to decline any financial obligations for the Games (IOC, 1978b; 1979b).

    This period is also characterized by the IOC presidency of J.A. Samaranch (1980–2001). It was Samaranch who promoted the commercialization of the Olympics by liberalizing the amateur regulations. This fundamental change secured the financial independence of the Olympic Movement. Results, such as the surplus of the Los Angeles

1984 Olympics and the development of worldwide Olympic sponsoring, which is linked to the name of H. Dassler, characterize the true beginning of the commercialization that can be seen today (Barney et al., 2002; for critics on Dassler, see Jennings and Sambrook, 2000; Kistner and Weinreich, 1996; Simson and Jennings, 1992). These results once again attracted the interest of many cities in staging the Olympics – a fundamental requirement for the permanent existence of the Games. However, this also caused over-commercialization and corruption, which finally ended in the IOC crisis of 1999. The large financial burden of the cities led to the need for cost–benefit analyses that were used to investigate the economic impacts of the Olympics and to justify them politically.

Period IV

Period IV (2004–08) refers to future Olympics. For nearly 25 years, commercialization has had a decisive influence on the success of the Olympic Movement. However, the strong dependency on industry could force a radical change if the Olympic ideals lose their power. It is possible to continue the successful development of the Olympic Movement if industry makes certain concessions and the Olympic ideals are better protected. The economic gigantism and the related risks, as well as the significance of the Olympic aura, which is basically fed by the Olympic ideals, will frequently be focused on in this book. Therefore, two interpretations of the Olympic ideals will be given. First, how they are investigated by Olympic researchers and then how they are seen today by consumers. Olympic researchers identified the following Olympic ideals:

> The cultural and religious celebration, artistic and spiritual training, the idea of elite and equal chances, competition and contest, sportsmanship, fair play, and the spirit of chivalry, the regular staging of the Games, tradition and armistice, internationalism and nationalism, mutual understanding and cultural pluralism, community of all sports, amateurism, independence, ancient model and the modern form. (Müller and IOC, 1986; Lenk, 1972)

These briefly stated ideals play an important role in the subsequent economic review since they are the element that makes the Games unique, defines their intrinsic value, and opens up marketing opportunities.

Understanding this, the IOC commissioned a global brand assessment to develop a strategy to protect, build, and leverage the Olympic Movement and Brand Olympic. During 1998/99 a broad sample of consumer research and interviews was used to identify unique aspects of Brand Olympic and its power. This represents the largest, most wide-ranging data sample ever gathered on the Olympic Brand. The strongest Brand attributes 'go beyond sport' to feature the Olympic values. Two sets of values were identified: a peaceful and festive forum for cultural exchange and fair play, and ideals of equality, tradition, honour and excellence.

This benefit hierarchy translates into four strong positioning options with which corporate partners can align their own brands.

- Hope: the Olympics transcend time, and thus offer hope for a better world using sport competition for all without discrimination as an example and lesson for humanity.
- Dreams and inspiration: the Olympics provide humanity with the inspiration to achieve personal dreams through the lessons of athletes' striving, sacrifice, and determination.
- Friendship and fair play: the Olympics provide tangible examples of how humanity can overcome political, economic, religious and racial prejudices through the values inherent in sport.
- Joy in effort: the Olympics celebrate the universal joy in effort through sport competition that is always intense, friendly and fair.

2.3 TRANSFORMATION OF DATA

In the following, the problems in collecting and evaluating the economic data are shown and the difficulties of comparing them to each other are explained. A distinction is made between tangible and intangible effects through their measurability in monetary units. Using the conversion parameters μ or ß all tangible values are expressed in US$ based on prices in 2000. It is only in this way that data from different Olympic Games can be compared sensibly with each other.

When comparing tangible effects of the Olympic Games since Munich 1972, two basic problems arise: first, Olympic Games are staged in different countries and consequently in different economies and, secondly, they take place in different years.

The data will be made comparable using purchasing power parities *PPP*(c/o) or if not available by the average yearly exchange rate in US$. For Athens 1896 gold parities were used to calculate the exchange rate. This does away with any territorial distortion. In a second step, the original data *A*(c/o) are adapted to the basic year 2000. Using the USA Consumer Price Index (CPI) all data are inflation adjusted. The CPI from 2002 to 2008 is estimated (average 2 per cent). Each original economic unit A is multiplied by the conversion factor μ (in case PPP are available) or ß (in case the exchange rate *Ex* was used), to eliminate distortions of territory and time and then transferred to the uniform value in US$ at the basic year 2000. All data of the Olympic Games are transformed in order to appear as if all Games had taken place in the USA in 2000. The USA was chosen as the basic country because the Games were hosted there twice during the period under review. This reduces possible distortions caused by the conversion with purchasing power parities. Apart from that, many invoices are balanced in US$ (selling of television rights, insurance fees and so on) which must simply be inflation adjusted. In Barcelona 1992, for example, more than 40 per cent of the revenues were made in US$ (Barcelona OCOG, 1992).

$$N_{(USA/2000)} = A_{(c/o)} \cdot I_{(2000)} \cdot ppp_{(c/o)} \tag{2.1}$$

$$N_{(USA/2000)} = A_{(c/o)} \cdot \mu \tag{2.2}$$

or

$$N_{(USA/2000)} = A_{(c/o)} \cdot I_{(2000)} \cdot Ex_{(c/o)} \tag{2.3}$$

$$N_{(USA/2000)} = A_{(c/o)} \cdot ß \tag{2.4}$$

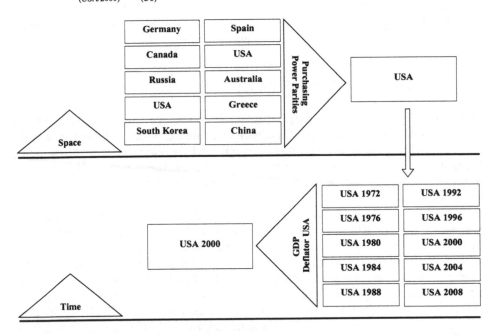

Figure 2.1 Methodology of data transformation

The fact that many payments were made in pre-Olympic years can be ignored. Since the chronological distribution of payments received and payments made was similar for all Olympic Games this small inaccuracy will not distort a comparison of the Games.

The data required to derive the conversion factors μ or $ß$ are listed in Table 2.1. All data used in this book are converted and marked with the currency and year of value such as US\$.$_{00}$ for American dollars in real value of the year 2000. A detailed description of the methodology can be found in Preuss (2000a).

$$N_{(USA/2000)} = A_{(c/o)} / \mu \tag{2.5}$$

$$N_{(USA/2000)} = A_{(c/o)} / ß \tag{2.6}$$

Formular (2.5) and (2.6) can be used to recalculate the original figures.

Table 2.1 Data for calculating the parameter μ and β

	A (c/o)	Ix (2000)	Exchange rate (c/o)	PPP (c/o)	μ (based on PPP)	β (based on exchange rate)
Greece	A(GRD/1896)	20.410	5.180	N/A	---	3.9398
France	A(FRF/1900)	20.410	5.16351	N/A	---	3.95238
USA	A(USD/1904)	19.230	1.000	N/A	---	19.230
Great Britain	A(GBP/1908)	19.230	0.20519	N/A	---	0.01067
Sweden	A(SEK/1912)	17.240	3.74165	N/A	---	4.60796
Belgium	A(BEF/1920)	8.621	8.04587	N/A	---	1.07144
France	A(FRF/1924)	9.804	19.0131	N/A	---	0.51564
Netherlands	A(Florint/1928)	9.804	2.48623	N/A	---	3.94331
USA	A(USD/1932)	12.500	1.000	N/A	---	12.500
Germany	A(RM/1936)	12.350	2.487	N/A	---	4.96408
Great Britain	A(GBP/1948)	7.143	0.24795*	N/A	---	28.8077
Finland	A(FIM/1952)	6.494	227.316	N/A	---	0.02857
Australia	A(AUD/1956)	6.329	0.90575	N/A	---	6.98767
Sweden	A(SEK/1956)	6.329	5.19654	N/A	---	1.21795
Italy	A(ITA/1960)	5.814	620.6876	N/A	---	0.009367
Japan	A(JPY/1964)	5.556	360.00	N/A	---	0.01543
Mexico	A(MXP/1968)	4.950	12.4905	N/A	---	0.39634
Germany	A(DEM/1972)	4.115	3.180	3.160	1.302	---
Canada	A(CAD/1976)	3.030	0.980	1.240	2.444	---
Russia	A(RUB/1980)	2.088	0.637**	N/A	---	3.27737
USA	A(USD/1984)	1.658	1.000	1.000	1.658	---
South Korea	A(KRW/1988)	1.456	734.760	722.700	0.00201	---
Spain	A(ESP/1992)	1.227	102.400	113.300	0.0108	---
USA	A(USD/1996)	1.098	1.000	1.000	1.098	---
Australia	A(AUD/2000)	1.000	1.730	1.330	0.752	---
Greece***	A(GRD/2004)	0.924	N/A	0.754	1.225	---
China***	A(CNY/2008)	0.853	N/A	N/A	---	---
N/A***	A(N/A/2012)	0.787	N/A	N/A	---	---

Notes:
*   Average rate from 21 June to 31 December.
**   Average rate from 1 August to 16 August 1980.
***   Inflation rate 2002–04/2008/2012 of 2 per cent p.a. is estimated, PPP from 2002.

Sources: International Monetary Fund (1996); Oanda (2002); OECD (1996; 2003).

3. Financing of the Games: interests, winners and losers

This chapter concentrates on the origin of the means necessary to finance the Olympic Games. Starting from the restrictions stated in the Olympic Charter, which affects the financing of Olympic Games, the financing of the Games from Munich 1972 to Beijing 2008 will be presented. Then it becomes obvious which financing model was used for the respective Games. Finally, the interests in the Games will show who are the winners and losers of Olympic Games.

3.1 DEMANDS STATED IN THE OLYMPIC CHARTER

Due to the increasing size of the Games it ultimately became necessary for the IOC to secure its influence on the Olympic Movement by obtaining financial guarantees from the organizers. Therefore, the basic demands of the IOC regarding the financing of Olympic Games which, in the end, can be summarized in two main points were incorporated in the Olympic Charter.

3.1.1 Staging the Games in One City and Co-operating with the OCOG

The IOC awards the Olympic Games only to a city and not to a private institution: 'The honour of hosting the Olympic Games is entrusted by the IOC to a city, which is designated as the host city of the Olympic Games' (IOC, 2003d, Rule 36, para. 3). Thus, demands are placed on the city when it comes to hosting the Games. Therefore, the Olympic Charter had to be adjusted to address the rising costs of the Games in order to regulate the financing of the Olympics. A major cost factor is the construction of sports facilities and the Olympic Village. This has to be qualified by the fact that the IOC can agree to stage individual events in the region or even in the host country. That often is the case for football and sailing, due to the need for huge stadiums and the sea. It remained a necessity that 'the opening and closing ceremonies must be organized in the host city itself' (IOC, 2003d, Rule 38, para. 1).

With the bidding for the Games in 1992, contracts were signed with all bid cities in the run-up repeating the exclusive rights of the IOC to the Olympic Games and pinpointing the promises of the bidders as being binding. Since 1996, the following has applied to the Olympic Games. 'All representations, warranties and covenants contained in the city's bid documents as well as other commitments made, either in writing or orally, by the city's candidature committee, the city or the NOC to the IOC ... shall be binding' (IOC, 1997d). Pre-contracts of this kind became necessary because many OCOGs did not live up to the promises they had made during the bid or they interpreted them in a way the IOC could not accept (Hill, 1996; Waldbröl, 1996b).

When a city is elected, the Host City Contract is signed in a ceremony. It legally regulates all financial relations between the IOC and the host. 'The IOC enters into a written agreement with the host city and the NOC of its country ... Such agreement is signed immediately upon the election of the host city' (IOC, 2003d, Rule 37, para. 8). The Olympic Charter, valid at the time the contract was signed, applies for the Games. If there are major changes to the Olympic Charter shortly before the Games are awarded renegotiations are the consequence. All Host City Contracts contain very high demands but during the preparatory phase of the Games compromises have frequently been agreed upon (interview, DeFrantz, 1997).

Whereas the NOC, OCOG and the city are jointly and severally liable for organizing and staging the Games, the IOC stipulation in regard to financial responsibility states: 'excluding the financial responsibility for the organization and staging of such Games, which shall be entirely assumed jointly and severally by the host city and the OCOG, without prejudice to any liability of any other party, particularly as may result from any guarantee' (IOC, 2003d, Rule 40). This exempts the NOC from any financial responsibility for the Games. The city and OCOG are jointly and severally liable. However, contracts were possible which exempted the city from a great portion of its financial obligations. Los Angeles 1984, for example, evaded any responsibility. On 27 October 1978 an agreement was signed which freed the City of Los Angeles from any liability which might occur due to organizing or staging the Games. Furthermore on 7 November 1978 the city electorate voted for a ban of any municipal investment for the Olympic Games (Los Angeles OCOG, 1984). At that time it was allowed to organize privately financed Games. However, when Atlanta was elected in 1990, a different Olympic Charter was valid which fixed the 'complete financial responsibility for the organization of the Olympic Games ... jointly and severally' to the NOC and the city (IOC, 1989, Rule 4). However, again a contract was signed which transferred the financial responsibility to the OCOG (interview, De Frantz, 1997; IOC, 1979).

Immediately after the Olympic flame of Atlanta extinguished, there were loud demands not to award Games again without a governmental warranty declaration. 'The down-to-the-wire finances ... have convinced the IOC of one thing: We're never going through this again ... the IOC ... now plans to look more favourably on those bids that have the backing, ideally, of the state or federal government' (Ruffenach, 1996a). Although the Charter was not supposed to be changed after Atlanta 1996, A. DeFrantz emphasized that in future there would be no Games again which were completely financed by private bodies (interview, DeFrantz, 1997). The 'Sydney 2000 model' seemed to have the right solution. It had the following key elements: a games financially underwritten by the Government of the State of New South Wales; a formal and explicit relationship between the Organizing Committee, the New South Wales government and the Commonwealth of Australia, and strong state and Commonwealth Government coordination mechanisms, backed as far as possible by legislation.

This model was highly appreciated by the IOC. Both, Athens 2004 and Beijing 2008 involved their government in the financing and organization of the Games.

3.1.2   Financial Guarantees and IOC Protection against Deficit

Apart from a precise regulation of the financial responsibilities, the IOC demands a guarantee in order to avoid a financial failure of the Games.

> Since the events of 1901 and 1905 (the transfer of the 1904 and 1908 Games from Chicago to St. Louis and from Rome to London), the IOC had decided to consider only applications that were backed by an already soundly prepared organisation and by serious financial guarantees. Such had been the case with Stockholm, Berlin and Antwerp; and would be for Amsterdam too. (Coubertin, 1936, p. 182)

The recent Olympic Charter states: 'Any candidate city shall offer such financial guarantees as considered satisfactory by the IOC Executive Board. Such guarantees may be given by the city itself, local, regional or national public collectives, the State or other third parties' (IOC, 2003d, Rule 38, para. 1).

The responsibility of the guarantee giver is restricted solely to the case of a Games deficit. A financial guarantee of any Beijing OCOG 2008 revenue shortfalls (Bidding Committee Beijing 2008, 2001) has been given by the Chinese Central and Beijing Municipal Governments.

The Olympic Charter still allows for private guarantee givers apart from public ones. A consequence of the demand stated after Atlanta 1996 not to organize Games again on a merely private basis was that the private bid committee of Salt Lake was awarded the Winter Olympics 2002 only when the city had submitted a financial guarantee (NN, 1996o). Theoretically, this would allow Olympics without public funds if the OCOG accepts the sole financial responsibility and a private guarantee giver could be found. However, the regulations in the Host City Contract and the demand in the Olympic Charter that the 'government guarantees to the IOC that the country will respect the Olympic Charter' (IOC, 2003d, Rule 37, para. 4), require the involvement of the government in the organization of the Games.

It is incontestable that the IOC is exempted from any financial obligation since the Olympic Charter states: 'The IOC shall have no financial responsibility whatsoever in respect thereof' (IOC, 2003d, Rule 40). Thus, the organizer of the Olympic Games is like a franchisee: the IOC awards the rights, pays attention to the corporate design and participates in the revenues to a certain extent whereas the organizer bears the risk alone. However, in case of a profit, the IOC usually gets 20 per cent, which is fair due to the high financial support the IOC gives during the preparation for the Games.

3.2 EVOLUTION OF FINANCING FROM MUNICH 1972 TO BEIJING 2008

For a better understanding of the models developed in this section an overview of the Olympic Games from 1972 to 2008 is given. This review includes all 'Games-related' expenditures.

Munich 1972

The Munich 1972 Olympics were mostly financed by 'Special financing means'. These are all OCOG revenues, which are linked to government approval. They include the issuing of Olympic coins and stamps as well as the sharing in the revenues of an Olympic lottery. Apart from the revenues of the OCOG itself (approximately 19 per cent), the Games were financed by special financing means (approximately 50 per cent) and by the federal government, federal state and the city (approximately 31 per cent). The remaining deficit of US$$_{00}$ 893.1 million was covered by the federal government (50 per cent), by the federal states (25 per cent) and by the cities of Munich and Kiel respectively (25 per cent) (Munich OCOG, 1974a; Weber, 1994).

Montreal 1976

For the 1976 Olympics a 'written guarantee that the federal government would not be called upon to absorb the deficit nor to assume interim financing for organization' left the OCOG and the city of Montreal with the sole responsibility to finance the staging of the Games (Montreal OCOG 1976, p. 55). At the conclusion of the Games the private revenues generated by the OCOG amounted to a mere 5 per cent of the funds required. The remaining 95 per cent was provided by special financing means and by the public sector (Montreal OCOG 1976, p. 59). When including the interest paid on the debt over the years and the additional US$$_{00}$ 537 million required completing the facilities after the Games, the Olympic debt totalled US$$_{00}$ 2,729 million (Levesque, 2001). Municipal and provincial tax dollars eased the burden of the debt, with final payment scheduled for the 2005/06 financial years by a special tobacco tax.

It should be noted that the deficit was not the result of low revenues. It was caused by large investment in infrastructure, mismanagement, strikes by construction workers and on imbalance in the market (Commission of Inquiry, s.t., p. 314). After the experience of Montreal, cities were reluctant to bid for the 1984 Games because the cost was no longer considered bearable.

Moscow 1980

There is a lack of financial information concerning the Moscow Games, although it is safe to assume that they were financed overwhelmingly by state subsidy due to the political aim to demonstrate the superiority of the communist system (Killanin, 1983, p. 146; Ueberroth et al., 1985, pp. 55–9).

Los Angeles 1984

These lessons learnt encouraged the citizens of Los Angeles to vote against public financial support of the 1984 Olympics since they feared deterioration in their quality of life. The local protest movements caused the state of California and the city of Los Angeles not to invest public funds in the Games (Hill, 1996; IOC, 1978b; Koar, 1993). The OCOG promised to pay the city the costs of security, transportation and other expenditures unless they were covered by the 0.5 per cent hotel tax and 6 per cent surcharge on the tickets (NN, 1984a). Despite the regulations in the Olympic Charter, the United States Olympic Committee (USOC) was successful in evading a financial responsibility (Barney et al., 2002; IOC, 1979b). These Games were the first in history without organizational links to the host city and the first to be financed from purely private sources. Very little public money was invested in the traffic infrastructure and sports facilities. Therefore, the overall costs of the Games amounted to a mere US$$_{00}$ 683.9 million, which were covered by the OCOG revenues. There was even an official surplus of US$$_{00}$ 380.6 million that was distributed amongst the USOC, the Amateur Athletic Foundation and towards the support of national institutions of Olympic sports (Taylor and Gratton, 1988). With the Games of Los Angeles 1984, private financing increased and publicly financed Games became history. The Olympic Movement started to receive high revenues from selling Olympic rights to television networks and sponsors.

Seoul 1988

The Korean Olympics 1988 covered their Olympic-related costs by 53 per cent of public money, 25 per cent from the OCOG and 22 per cent from private bodies (Kim et al., 1989). The alleged surplus of approximately US$$_{00}$ 192 million must be qualified in view of the high share of public means (Hill, 1992; NN, 1989).

Barcelona 1992

Barcelona used the 1992 Olympics to reurbanize the city and to present itself, next to Madrid, as an international site for industry and tourism. This was the reason why there were large public investments during the Olympiad. They actually brought the city and the province of Catalonia the desired impetus to develop. Despite public investments amounting to US$$_{00}$ 6.95 billion the share of privately financed Games-related expenditures amounted to 38 per cent. The official profit of only US$$_{00}$ 3.3 million must also be qualified (Brunet, 1993).

Atlanta 1996

When the city declined to financially participate, the Atlanta 1996 OCOG organized a privately financed Olympics. Compared to previous Games, these Atlanta Olympics were characterized by a relatively small budget. The overall Games-related expenditures amounted to US$$_{00}$ 2.22 billion. The city infrastructure hardly changed but some new sports facilities were built. With the exception of the publicly financed rowing facility, all sports facilities were financed by the OCOG. As a result, the Olympics did wind up with a financial surplus (Sydney OCOG, 2001, p. 27).

Sydney 2000

The Olympic Co-ordination Authority (OCA) Act 1995 merged five governmental departments into one statutory authority. With the establishment of the Sydney Organizing Committee of the Olympic Games (SOCOG) and OCA Sydney had two cornerstone organizations. The OCA was entrusted to deliver venues and facilities for use during the Olympics and Paralympics as well as the co-ordination of all aspects of the government involvement in the Games. The SOCOG was solely responsible to stage and market the Games (Sydney OCOG, 2001, p. 27). The overall costs of the Games were split between SOCOG (US$$_{00}$ 2,071.5 million), private sector (US$$_{00}$ 832.5 million), the New South Wales (NSW) Government (US$$_{00}$ 997.2 million), the Commonwealth Government (US$$_{00}$ 186 million) and others. In total, the Games cost US$$_{00}$ 4,788.2 million (Olympic Co-ordination Authority, 2002, pp. 12–13). Officially the Games ended with a small deficit of US$$_{00}$ 45 million. This has to be qualified because payments have been made to the NSW Government and the Australian Olympic Foundation as legacy contributions (Olympic Co-ordination Authority, 2002, p. 25).

Athens 2004

The Athens OCOG is in charge of the entire Games organization, while the Greek government takes care of the required infrastructure. As in Barcelona, the Games are being used to reurbanize the city and solve major traffic problems. Not only has Athens acquired a new airport and major new roads, but also a new underground railway. The costs of the Games has been calculated to reach US$$_{00}$ 5.3 billion. However, the Greek construction industry is overstretched. Speculation is that the cost of preparing for the Games will reach up to US$$_{00}$ 10 billion (Scott, 2002, p. 7). Disregarding the calculation of Games-related and non-Games-related costs of infrastructure upgrades the OCOG budget is approximately US$$_{00}$ 2,404 million (Athens OCOG 2003b, p. 22). There is no calculated profit.

Beijing 2008

The construction of the infrastructure and sports facilities to support and host the Games is financially guaranteed by the Chinese Central and Beijing Municipal Government. The Bid book forecasts an OCOG budget of only US$$_{.00}$ 1.6 billion. This is very conservative, which is usual for bid cities in order to not overestimate revenues (interview, Payne, 2004). The city, region, state and private sector are expected to invest US$$_{.00}$ 14.3 billion. From this portion the total investment in sports facilities is estimated to be US$$_{.00}$ 2.1 billion, of which 90.8 per cent will be spent by the government and other sectors (Bidding Committee Beijing 2008, 2001).

3.3   INTERESTS IN FINANCING THE OLYMPICS

In all past host countries several bodies have been involved in financing the Olympic Games. In general, there are four bodies that can be involved in different fields: government of the host country, region/province/federal state, city/community and the private sector economy. Each body provides different resources (Figure 3.1).

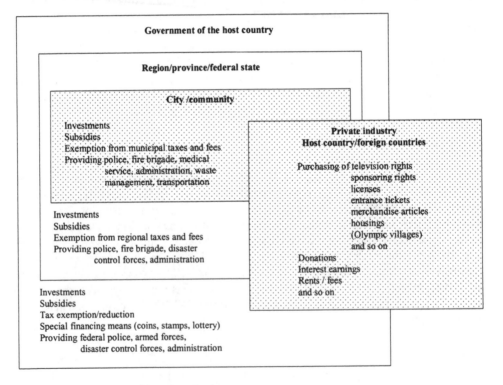

Figure 3.1   Resources of various bodies

All these different interests cause different bodies to invest in Olympic Games. The different bodies are the basis for the model in Figure 3.2. All means provided by the government, the province and the city are accumulated, forming the public share in the financing of the Olympic Games. All means that originate from privately owned corporations form the private share.

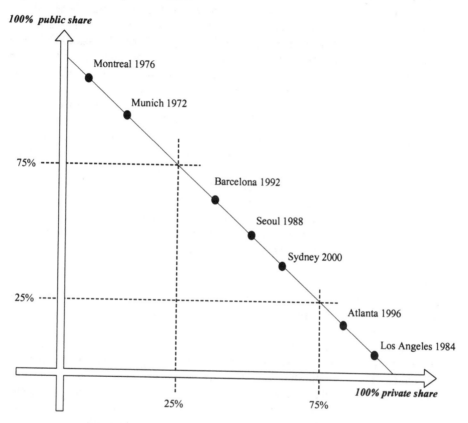

Sources: German Bundestag (1975); Montreal OCOG (1976); Los Angeles OCOG (1984); Kim et al. (1989); Park (1991); Hill (1992); Brunet (1993); Weber (1994); Atlanta OCOG (1998), The Audit Office (1999); Olympic Co-ordination Authority (2002).

Figure 3.2 Financing models of the Games from Munich 1972 to Sydney 2000

Figure 3.2 reveals that the financing of the Munich 1972 and Montreal 1976 Games was public, that of Seoul 1988, Barcelona 1992 and Sydney 2000 was mixed and that of Los Angeles 1984 and Atlanta 1996 was private.

The extent to which the systems from Figure 3.1 participate financially in the Olympic Games depends on the specific objectives the individual bodies have. The range of interests involved in the staging of the Olympic Games is wide and differs from host to host. To identify the interested parties, and especially to identify 'winners', we have to look at the pattern of financial and ideological support at the bidding stage of the process of host selection. All interests that are mentioned here are drawn from specific Games and, while some common patterns emerge, caution is required regarding generalization because of the distinctive sociocultural, political, historical and economic circumstances of each country.

The first interest is that of the regional groupings of IOC members whose cultural identity is, according to Huntington (1996, pp. 315–16), an important factor in determining how their vote is cast (see Persson, 2000, pp. 157–61; Preuss, 2000b). The second interest is that of the host governments who recognize the value of the Games in three particular areas, international relations, national morale and public relations. As regards international relations the Seoul Games, for example, were an opportunity for the government to attempt to improve relations with North Korea and other socialist countries as well as raise international awareness of Korean manufactured products (Kim et al., 1989, pp. 48–66; Kramar, 1994, pp. 141–84). The extra resources which are usually invested in developing the country's high-performance athletes prior to the Games provides a useful diplomatic resource as the athletes give the country a higher profile at international sports events (Bernard and Busse, 2000). In addition, the host nation stages more international sports events before and after the Olympic Games, which provide further opportunities for strengthening links with foreign nations. Prior to the Sydney Games almost every member of the Olympic squad competed internationally between September 1999 and March 2000, which included participation in seven World Cups (Sydney OCOG, 2000, p. 75).

As regards improvements to national morale the Seoul Olympics created 'a national perspective, a feeling of vitality, taking part, being recognized, modern and technologically up-to-date' (Denis et al., 1988, p. 229). However, in addition to feelings of enhanced national pride the effects of hosting the Games can also lead to a deeper understanding of disability through hosting of the Paralympics or a greater motivation to participate in sport as a result of watching the Games. Finally, the Games also provide important public relations opportunities. In earlier times one motivation to stage the Games was to demonstrate the superiority of a political system. The communist regimes of the 1970s and 1980s as well as the German Reich in 1936 saw the Games as a chance to prove the superiority of their systems. More recently, the motivation has been to announce or demonstrate to the world major changes in the host country. For example, Munich wanted to show that West Germany had rid itself of its Nazi past (interview, Hattig, 2001). South Korea wanted to showcase its modern, high-technology national industries and replace its image as a developing country. Australia used the Games to enhance the tourist image of Australia and not just Sydney (Morse, 2001) and wanted to develop an international Australian profile as more than merely 'a good source for raw material' (Parker, 2001, p. 9). Finally, Beijing, which is to host the 2008 Games, is demonstrating the growing importance of China to the world economy.

In general, the Olympic Games are the biggest advertising opportunity that a city and a country can hope for. Years before the Games, companies will promote their association with the event; in the months before the opening ceremony reporters will write stories about the country; and in the weeks prior to the Games, the torch relay generates further media attention. The Opening Ceremony, which showcases the culture of the host, is worldwide watched by at least 3 billion people, while the Games themselves are watched by 92.5 per cent of all adults who have access to a television. The number of hours of Games coverage and the number of countries that broadcast the Games has increased at every Olympics (IOC, 2000e, p. 5). The type and intensity of the promotion depends on the hosts and the media. In Sydney the Australian Tourist Commission (ATC) developed a strategy with well over 1000 individual projects and provided not only good working conditions for the media, but also much additional information about Australia and Sydney (ATC, 2001, p. 3).

The third interest is that of the politicians of the host city. One of their aims is to achieve a lasting increase in general tourist arrivals, and in congress and convention business in particular (Dunn and McGuirk, 1999, p. 20; Hall, 1992, p. 17; Persson, 2000). This was a clear aim for both Barcelona and Sydney, and is often also the case for cities hosting Olympic Winter Games. A second common objective of local politicians is to promote their city as a 'global city' with the ambition to generate international investment (Weirick, 1999, p. 70). At present there is evidence of the development of a network of 'global cities' based on a combined global and transnational-regional level in which 'global cities' establish important links through which the international economic relations of industry are coordinated. Olympic hosts develop the factors that are important to become a 'global city' such as new office accommodation, improvements in telecommunications, gentrification of parts of the city, first class tourist facilities and an international airport (Sassen, 1996, p. 123). In Seoul the increased awareness of the host city and its improved infrastructure both stimulated the location of foreign industry and increased the sales of national products on foreign markets (Roulac, 1993, p. 18). A third, and related, objective of local politicians is to help host cities that are not the capital of a country to be better recognized nationally. Scott (interview, 1997) admitted that one objective of the Manchester bid was to project a sharper profile by comparison to other second-rank cities in the UK. Other examples include Barcelona establishing itself as a second centre of economic growth after Madrid, or Munich improving its status prior to the Games of 1972.

Local politicians are also concerned to stimulate the local economy. This can be done by attracting funding which does not come from the city itself or which otherwise would have left the city thus creating an economic impact. In a country staging the Olympics such external or 'autonomous' money stems from the financial support of the state government and the OCOG. Most revenues of the OCOG are autonomous because they are from sponsors and television networks that are not from the host city. Therefore, the argument of Olympic opponents that public funds used for the Olympic Games could be better spent on other projects has to be qualified (Preuss, 1998b, p. 201). For example, when the Winter Games 1994 were staged in Lillehammer, Norway, local politicians aimed to improve the long-term employment situation by creating an autonomous economic impact through the Games in 1994 (correspondence, Spilling, 2001). However, the assumption of a positive economic impact must be qualified. For a city the impact may be large because most money is autonomous, but for a nation the impact will be much smaller. In addition, the economic situation at the time of investment has to be considered, as Olympic-related investment can lead to 'crowding out' of other possible investment. Therefore, it should not be assumed that hosting the Games is always the best way to stimulate the local or national economy (Baade and Matheson, 2002). The Games are often used as an instrument to solve urban problems. When a city is elected host city the time pressures that it experiences frequently lead to the breaking of deadlocks in urban planning. The Games offer the chance of achieving an acceleration of development and is thus a further motive of local politicians. Finally, association with the Games can positively affect the image of politicians. In the media the names of politicians involved in the Games are often mentioned, allowing them to 'bask in the reflected glory' (Snyder et al., 1986) as was clearly evident during Sydney 2000.

A fourth set of interests is that of the local/regional construction industry, which benefits most obviously from the building of infrastructure and sports facilities. During an economic boom, the prices paid for building work increase, which means that builders earn more money for the same work, and during a recession companies receive additional orders. Moreover, the companies also gain publicity. Multiplex, for example, which constructed Stadium Australia, has used its Olympic credentials to win large contracts overseas, such as a contract to build Britain's new Wembley stadium (Parker, 2001, p. 9). Other local businesses may be Olympic 'partners' and also see the Games as an important, though unique, opportunity to initiate business, develop contacts, and promote their image internally and externally.

The final interest group is the television network. Not only is broadcasting the Games a source of prestige, but it is also the case that the networks can generate profit from the sale of advertising provided the Games can be broadcast during network 'prime time'. The National Broadcasting Corporation (NBC) bought the American rights to the Games for 2010 and 2012 for US$3.5 billion, but due to the time difference the viewing figures during the Sydney Games were much lower than anticipated (NN, 2000b). The 2004 Games as well as the 2008 Olympics again will not be staged during American prime time. Consequently, there was a strong preference among American broadcasters to have the 2012 Games in New York or at least in Rio de Janeiro or Havana.

The analysis indicates that it is possible to identify those social groups or interests that receive a net increase in benefits from the hosting of the Olympic Games, the winners (Figure 3.3), and that these can be distinguished from those with a decrease in net benefits level, the losers (Figure 3.4). However, owing to the complexity of the interrelationships the effects can only be described on a relatively abstract level.

It is assumed that the Olympics have had a positive effect on the image of the city that stages them and that there was a financial surplus. The first group of 'winners' is the local politicians who have been able to use the external resources flowing into the city – such as government subsidies – and make the reallocations within the city budget to change the structure of the city according to their political priorities. Frequently, their arguments for implementing certain projects are justified by claims that the Olympic Games 'demand' a certain structure or certain facilities within the city. The second group of 'winners' is the construction industry, which can confidently expect to receive contracts for extensive projects including parks, hotels, roads, sports facilities, housing and, sometimes, convention and trade fair centres. Many of these construction projects contribute to the gentrification of areas of the city, a process which benefits higher income groups and constitutes the third set of 'winners'. The fourth group is tourists who benefit from an improved tourism infrastructure and additional attractions in the host city.

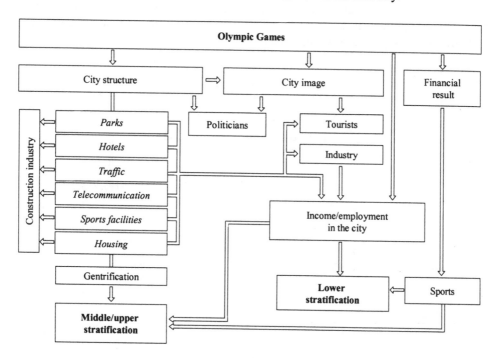

Figure 3.3 'Winners' of the overall economic effects of the Olympic Games

A further group of 'winners' is the city's general population, many of whom benefit from the general upswing in economic activity produced by the improvements to the urban infrastructure and, consequently, to the image of the city. Although the extent of Games-related economic activity differs greatly between the host cities reviewed here, the improved structure, the better image and the higher expenditures produced higher income and additional employment in all host cities. The frequently made criticism that additional income and employment only benefit members of the middle and upper classes must be rejected. Even if unskilled workers were underpaid, they did have work and their income was improved, irrespective of the duration of their employment. The capacity of the Games to create jobs and protect existing jobs is frequently overlooked. The generality of the city's population may also benefit if the Games produces a surplus. Normally, any surplus is distributed between the IOC, the NOC of the host country and various institutions that promote sport in the city. The last mentioned recipients have the potential to use the income for the benefit of citizens irrespective of their social status. The city can maximize its financial benefit if it can persuade the OCOG to invest an anticipated surplus before the final balance is compiled, thus avoiding the risk of money being siphoned out of the city to the host country NOC or, via the IOC, to the NOCs of other countries and the international federations.

Turning attention to the 'losers' Figure 3.4 identifies the groups negatively affected by the Olympic Games. In this scenario it is assumed that the Games negatively affected the image of the city and that they were run at a financial deficit. The fact that even this scenario will produce winners is not ignored.

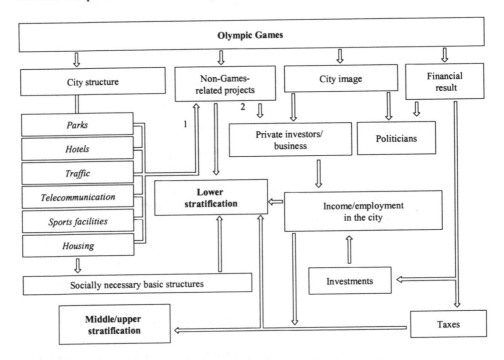

Figure 3.4   'Losers' of the overall economic effects of the Olympic Games

It is not surprising that many negative effects have the greatest impact on the poor given the obvious priority within the low income group for employment, affordable housing, adequate medical care and social integration. Hosting the Games means that other projects in the city are crowded out (1 in Figure 3.4). Prior to the Games, the sites of newly erected Olympic facilities were often housing areas of the poor (former workers' areas in the vicinity of industrial enterprises). It is exactly this part of the population which suffers from expropriation and relocation caused by the construction activities and which leads to a loss of their social environment. Without doubt some municipal authorities tried to use the opportunity of the Olympics to expel from the area socially marginal groups, such as the homeless, street traders and prostitutes who, in the opinion of the authorities, contradict the image of a modern city open to tourism that they are attempting to manufacture (for Los Angeles and Seoul: NN, 1996h; for Barcelona: Garcia, 1993, pp. 260–1; for Atlanta: Gladitz and Günther, 1995; in general: Lenskyj,

1996, p. 395). It must also be noted that the poor are forced out of their residential areas not just by major construction projects, but also by the subsequent gentrification of areas (Cox et al., 1994, p. 75).

In cases where the Olympics worsens the image of the host city or prevents investment in non-Games-related projects because of a strong reallocation of resources, general economic activity in the host city (**2** in Figure 3.4) is negatively affected. Local enterprises in the city will not expand nor will businesses be encouraged to relocate to the city. The reduced economic activity has a negative effect on income and employment with consequences for all citizens. Should the Olympics produce a deficit which has to be covered by the city then there are consequences for future public investment and the level of municipal taxes which may well have to rise – thus again producing negative effects for all citizens. Roaf et al. (1996, p. 31) suggest that the lessons from previous Games are clear in so far as they stress that those who pay for the Games do not necessarily profit from the Games and that the poor are more affected by capacity constraints and, therefore, are far more vulnerable to eviction and displacement than are middle-income groups.

When bidding for the Olympics, the risk of possible negative effects and whether they can be borne from an economic point of view must be measured. This review has shown that hosting the Games runs the risk of deepening the social polarization in the city.

3.4   THE IMPACTS OF OLYMPIC GAMES

'The best Games ever', was the remark IOC President J.A. Samaranch liked to make at the conclusion of 'successful' Games. But how could he measure the success of the Olympic Games? Did he mean the financial, social, organizational or sportive success? And from what point of view did he measure the success? From that of politicians – of the construction industry – of medal winners – of the prosperous citizens or of the IOC? In other words from the winners' point of view? Even if it were possible to answer these questions a central problem remains, namely that of comparing the recently completed Games with previous Games.

The above remarks have shown why it is so difficult to compare previous Games with each other – even from a financial point of view. The various motives of those bodies participating in financing the Games imply different levels of investment. Without considering these differences, privately financed Games with their objective of maximizing short-term profit cannot be compared to Games with a mixed or public financing which emphasize the structural change of the city.

Regarding the press which frequently writes about surplus or deficit after the Games it remains to be mentioned that, considering the three situations outlined above, the

- different number of bodies involved in the financing, the
- different interests of the bodies in a financial involvement, and the
- different financial dimension of the Games,

it is impossible and even wrong to state the overall effect of different Olympics with a single surplus or deficit.

The true outcome is measured in the infrastructural, social, political, ecological and sporting impacts a city and a country receive from the Games and not in a simple subtraction of the expenditures from the revenues. Even if this difference was only used to express the economic impact of Olympic Games, ignoring macroeconomic and intangible effects would lead to a result with a very limited meaning.

Every impact a city or country wants to create for its region costs in one way or another and therefore makes this single-value 'financial surplus' unimportant.

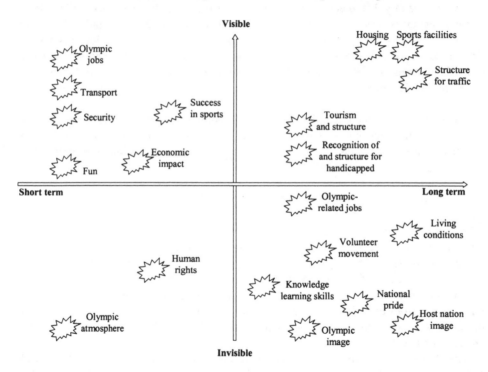

Source: Preuss (2002c).

Figure 3.5   Impactmatrix of the Sydney 2000 Olympic Games

The figure shows both the estimated duration of the most important impacts of Olympic Games and the complexity of the impacts created. Certainly the position of impacts in this matrix is different for each Olympics related to the intended impacts.

In future, the Games will be financed neither with a completely public share nor with a completely private share. There are two objections to public financing: on the one hand, the private financing sources of an OCOG (selling of television rights, sponsoring), apart from private investors, have become much more important compared with the past. On the other hand, the rising costs of the Games will cause more severe protests by Olympic opponents if the Games are financed exclusively by tax revenues. But even the purely private share, which would de facto be possible according to the Olympic Charter, is not the model for the future either. A private financing of Olympic Games allows, on the one hand, for flexibility, quick reactions to new situations and political independence. It can thus facilitate many preparatory processes. On the other hand, the support of and cooperation with the city and the government can be equally helpful, which says C. Battle (Vice President OCOG Atlanta, interview 1998), have more advantages than disadvantages in a municipal participation in the Games. Besides, the IOC has clearly spoken out against Games which are financed purely privately and has established this demand in the Host City Contract. Thus, in future there will be mixed financing. Beijing 2008 definitely plans to stress the public share. Vice-major Liu Jingmin even said that they will not accept donations from their citizens. However the Bid book did mention donations from individuals (NN, 2001b; Bidding Committee Beijing 2008, 2001).

4. Growth and financial gigantism: the scale of the Olympic Games

4.1 GROWTH OF THE GAMES

Throughout its history the Games increased in tandem with the expansion of organizational variety. Although only 13 IOC members are mentioned in the first Bulletin of the IOC, that number increased over time to a total of 69 in 1925, 81 in 1980, 113 in 2000 (IOC, 2000d, p. 71) and 124 in 2004. In Athens 2004, the whole Olympic system comprises 202 NOCs, 28 International Summer Sport Federations (IFs), and the entire structure of the Paralympics and the Olympic Winter Games (www.olympic.org).

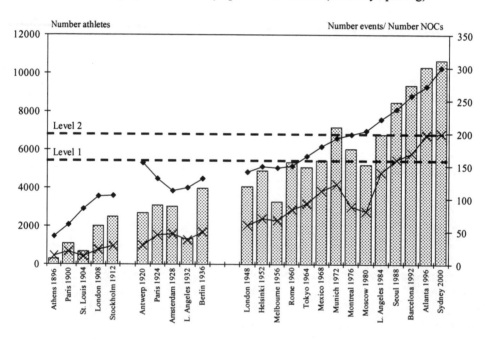

Source: IOC (2000d).

Figure 4.1 Developments and number of athletes, events and NOCs from 1896 to 2000

Figure 4.1 shows the growth of the Olympic Games in terms of both the number of athletes and events associated with the Games and the number of NOCs associated with the Olympic organization. The growth results mainly from the mechanization (transport, communication) that, in turn, brought a complexity that could no longer be handled by the IOC members and their few part-time employees. Thus, a rational and bureaucratic structure had to be created in order to address the fact that legal, informal and subjectively fair decisions had become impossible to make in many cases. As the need for rationalisation increased, the basis for the start of legal ruling structures in the IOC was built. This rationalization can be seen in the specialization and differentiation of positions in the IOC. It can also be seen even more clearly in the evidence of the extensive legalisation and "de-emotionalization" of the Olympic Charter that serves as the formalized constitution of the IOC and gives the Committee its legal power. It is interesting to note that until 1952 the charter did not experience significant change, but that from 1953 it has been changed on a yearly basis.

The first level in Figure 4.1 was reached in the mid-1960s. This is in line with the mechanization (communication technology) that has made worldwide live television coverage possible since the 1964 Tokyo Games. The next level was reached in 1972 and again in the mid-1980s. This shift was caused through new Olympic financing sources and the exchange ability of capital of the formerly politically blocked east-west borders. This shift, in turn, supported worldwide sponsorship. These respective periods are ones in which the IOC included elements of legal ruling.

4.2   GROWTH OF THE IOC

Until 1965, the administrative demands of the IOC were such that only two part-time staff members were needed to carry out the work. The Dutch secretary-general, General Johann Westerhoff, however, stated that the IOC was in need of 10 to 15 employees in order to cope with the IOC's growing requirements (Schantz, 1995). The need to add to the number of staff members occurred, once again, in the mid-1960s when the workload increased and it became evident that the introduction of a bureaucratic structure was required. In 1969, Brundage was not satisfied with Westerhoff's work. 'He found him neither sufficiently capable nor sufficiently industrious' (Schantz, 1995, p. 147). Brundage's assessment of Westerhoff's inabilities serve as proof of the fact that there was a need for position-centred and performance-orientated placements in the IOC administration. At this time the steadily increasing number of NOCs and the rapidly growing Games overtaxed the administrative structure of the IOC.

Figure 4.2 reflects the increase of work due to the introduction of administrative structures in the 1960s. In the early 1970s the number of employees rose to Level 1, which exactly corresponds with Level 2 in Figure 4.1 (1972–84). During this same period the size of the Games remained relatively unchanged. In addition, a differentiation and objectification of the Olympic Charter occurred. It is a change that now appears to indicate the increasing bureaucracy and the corresponding elements of legal ruling.

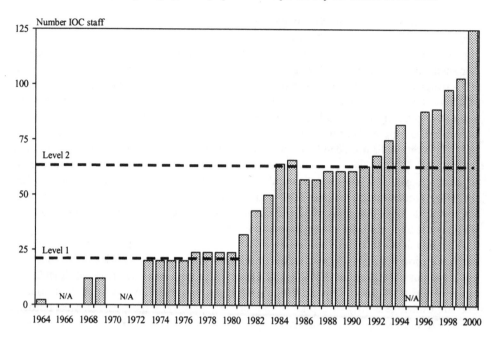

Note: Staff includes only IOC administration and not the Olympic Museum or Olympic Solidarity.

Sources: IOC (1998b, p. 20); Landry and Yerlès (1996, p. 69); `Schantz (1995, pp. 145–8); Wheeler, (correspondence, 2001)

Figure 4.2   Development of the number of employees in the IOC administration

Until '1972, the Olympic Charter was clearly not up to date with the reality of marketing and sponsorship in the Olympic world itself' (Landry and Yerlès, 1996, p. 143). In the years that followed, however, many paragraphs relating to the commercial aspects of the Games were either added to or more precisely worded in the Charter. Level 2 (Figure 4.2) and Level 3 (Figure 4.3) were reached at the Games in Los Angeles 1984. In the mid-1980s the worldwide sponsorship was successfully introduced.

> The ... IOC had to continue developing and adapting its policies in the heat of the action. ... The IOC also took measures to avoid abuse, particularly the pirating of the Olympic symbol and emblems. Amendments to all sorts of rules, byelaws and instructions appeared in the Charter. These amendments dealt with increasingly varied aspects of marketing. (Landry and Yerlès, 1996, p. 145)

Certainly the acceptance of the legal personality as an international non-profit organisation in 1981 has brought elements of "legal power" (Weber, 1922) into the IOC.

Prior to 1981 there were only three divisions within the IOC: the Directorate, the Sports division and the Olympic Solidarity division. Most of the work was done by commissions (Figure 4.3). Since 1985, however, there has been both an addition to the number of commissions as well as the successive creation of several departments. By 1998 13 departments were established at the IOC headquarter in Lausanne.

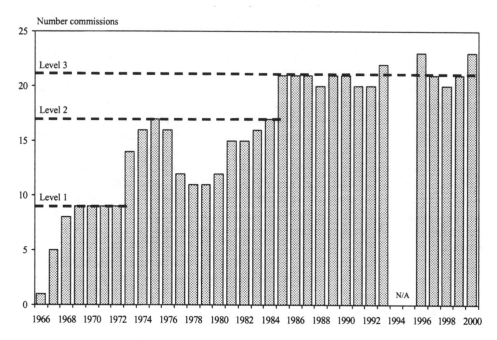

Note: Without Council of the Olympic Order, sub-commissions except for those of coordination of the Olympic Games.

Sources: IOC (1998a, p. 18; 1999f, pp. 19–28); Landry and Yerlès (1996, p. 72)

Figure 4.3 Development of the number of commissions in the IOC

Figure 4.3 shows the number of IOC commissions. The first was established in 1966. In 1967 four more followed. Three out of these five initial commissions were related to the economic system. More specifically, these three were the commissions 'Press and Public Relations', 'Protection of the Olympic Emblems' and 'Finances'.

In Figure 4.3, Level 2 is first reached in the middle of the 1970s, because since 1972 the IOC has received a substantial share of the revenues from the sale of television rights. Due to the financial crisis in the Olympic Movement that followed the 1976 Montreal Games, the total number of commissions was reduced for a short period of time. In 1985, Level 2 was reached for the second time. This time around it also marked the beginning of the IOC-owned worldwide sponsoring programme. The rationalization push that began in the mid-1980s and leads in Figures 4.1, 4.2 and 4.3 to the next higher level can certainly be connected with the separation of high-performance sport from the traditional amateur idea of the Olympic Games. The specific impact of this change will be seen more often in the following chapters.

4.3 GROWTH AND FINANCIAL GIGANTISM

The economic dimension of the Olympic Games can neither be determined by a single figure nor by comparing several Games, depending as it does on both the economic intention of the politicians and the development level and size of the city. Smaller and/or less industrialized cities must invest much more in their infrastructure than larger cities. Therefore 'expensive' and 'cheap' Games can be distinguished.

Games are 'expensive' if they require extensive investments in traffic infrastructure, communication systems, housing and sports facility construction. Sydney, Barcelona, Seoul, Montreal and Munich invested a lot in the construction of sports facilities. Barcelona and Seoul used the Games for extensive improvements to the city infrastructure. Munich, Montreal but also the Games in Athens and Beijing developed or are developing parts of their city, mainly the traffic infrastructure. These organizers saw the basic maxim in compensating short-term Olympic expenditures with long-term benefits.

Games were 'cheap' if costs were largely limited to organizing and staging the Games. Los Angeles and Atlanta only built a few sports facilities while maximizing the use of their existing infrastructures. Their basic maxim was maximizing short-term profit or avoiding any deficit.

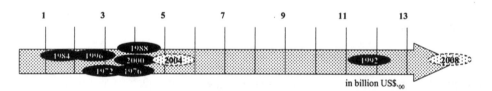

in billion US$

Sources: German Bundestag (1975); Montreal OCOG (1976); Los Angeles OCOG (1984); Kim et al. (1989); Park (1991); Hill (1992); Brunet (1993); Weber (1994); Atlanta OCOG (1998); The Audit Office (1999); Kynge et al. (2001); Katalis (2002); Olympic Co-ordination Authority (2002).

Figure 4.4 Financing of Games from Munich 1972 to Beijing 2008 related to their financial dimension

The past decades have shown that the Olympic Games did not only grow on the cost and revenue side but also on the structural and organizational side. 'Because ever upward is the Olympic creed – that is citius, altius, fortius – the recent Olympic Games experiences have enlighten some limits. These are e.g. negative external effects of oversized sport facilities and ecological effects' (DaCosta, 2002, p. 80). Owing to the gigantic construction in Athens and Beijing, the IOC wants to make the Games more streamlined and efficient in future. The IOC Olympic Games Study Commission recommended: 'Maximize temporary installations over permanent construction especially where legacy requirements are lower than Games requirements' (IOC, 2003a, p. 44).

The comparison of some national economic indicators with the costs of hosting the Olympic Games illustrates the economic dimension of the Olympic Games for a country (Table 4.1).

Table 4.1   Games costs in relation to indicators of national accounts

Games	Costs in million US$	In % of GDP	In % of government consumption
	6 years prior to Games	6-year period	6-year period
Olympic Games			
Atlanta 1996	2021	0.006	0.026
Sydney 2000	3438	0.102	0.553
Olympic Winter Games			
Lillehammer 1994	1511	0.245	1.154
Nagano 1998	3412	0.015	0.156

Sources: International Monetary Fund (2000); Preuss (2002a).

Figure 4.5 compares the economic dimension of the Sydney 2000 Olympic Games with those of the Nagano 1998 Olympic Winter Games and the 2002 Commonwealth Games in Manchester, England. Revenues from ticket sales, sponsorship, television rights and licensing were chosen to display the business economic dimensions. Macroeconomic dimensions are represented by the number of athletes and events, which indicate costs related to investments in sports facilities and the organization. Additionally, the number of tickets is related to spectators (Olympic tourists) who spent their money in the host city. However, this figure does not distinguish between spectators who are citizens and tourists. Citizens just reallocate their money, while tourists bring additional money into the city. This distinction is important when calculating the size of the true economic impact on a city.

The economic indicators in Figures 4.5 and 4.6 solely represent those of the organizing committees. However, it can be seen that the Olympic Games are a much bigger event than the other multi-sports events – at least from an economic point of view.

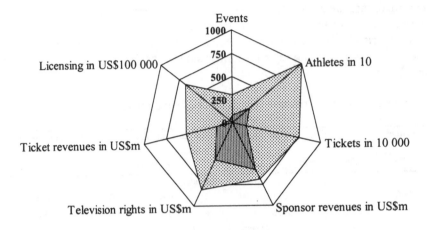

Sources: Preuss (2000c); IOC (2001b); Barney et al. (2002).

Figure 4.5   Nagano 1998 in comparison to the Sydney 2000 Olympic Games

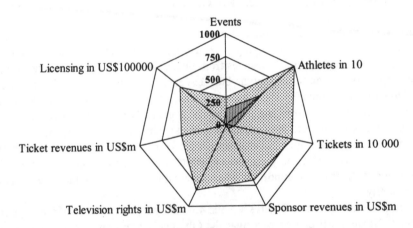

Sources: Preuss (2000c); IOC (2001b); Barney et al. (2002).

Figure 4.6   Commonwealth Games Manchester 2002 in comparison to the Sydney 2000
*   Olympic Games*

5. Technique of measuring: the economic impact of Olympic Games

The good methodology of evaluating macroeconomic effects of mega-events is a cost-benefit analysis. However, numerous inherent shortcomings and a lack of data on previous Games force the display of only elements of cost-benefit analysis in this book.

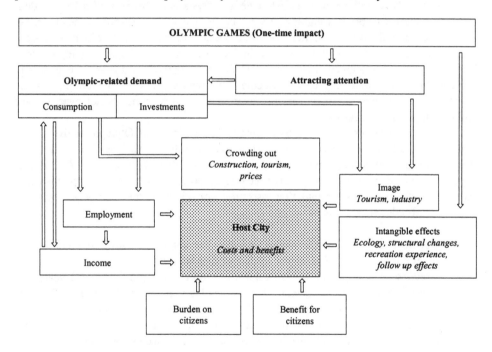

Figure 5.1   Economic effects of Olympic Games on the host city

First, the Games increase the demand for consumption (Chapter 6) and investments (Chapter 7), which form a 'one-time' Games-related economic impact (Figure 5.1). Increased demand leads to additional jobs (Chapter 10), but also to a so-called crowding out. On the one hand, public projects, which are financed without any effect on the budget, will reallocate other public projects. On the other hand, they also crowd out private projects if prices rise due to additional demand. The charge of increased inflation in the host city, which is frequently mentioned by opponents of the Olympic Games, will be examined in Chapter 11. The worldwide interest in the Games indirectly increases the demand if a better image attracts tourists (Chapter 6) and foreign investments (Chapters 7 and 11) to the city after the Games. Frequently, the intangible impacts of Olympic Games are reviewed.

5.1   ANALYSIS METHOD IN THIS BOOK

In this book, the macroeconomic impacts of the past ten Olympics are reviewed in order to evaluate both general effects and extent. The export of the service 'Olympic Games' causes an inflow of funds to the host city, resulting in additional production which, in turn, leads to income and employment effects.

However, there will be no full cost–benefit analysis done because of a lack of data. Therefore there will be no weighing of whether alternative investments in the respective city/regions would have been better, nor will there be a judgement as to which Games had been the best. On the other hand, to calculate the economic impact an input-output analysis is too shortsighted. However, it is the best method to analyse the economic impact for studies that only aim to calculate the tangible effects of Olympic Games. Intangible effects would not be sensibly expressed, pecuniary effects not overseen and indirect impacts not measured.

The source basis proved to be problematic. The majority of Olympic analyses were linked to the client and carried out a priori. It could hardly be expected that the data was empirically backed or objective. T. Slagel (interview, 1994) said to me: 'We can only give you the analyses which carry a positive image. Other analyses remain unpublished so as not to make the Atlanta population insecure.' For this book the following procedures are aimed at reducing the risk of misinterpretations:

- A critical reflection of the method used in the analyses relating to literature can reveal possible calculation errors made by other authors.
- A review or new partial interpretation of 'neutral' data from statistical yearbooks helps to verify or falsify statements in past analyses. However this data is often very global on the overall economy of the host country and can only be used with reservations as a proof of changes caused by the Olympics in a city/region. Baade and Matheson (2002) interpret the effect of the Los Angeles and Atlanta Games by these indicators.
- A comparison of several Olympic Games analyses should reveal possible analytic errors. This comparison can even reveal errors in the data used or factors of uncertainty.

5.2   THE ECONOMIC IMPACT OF OLYMPIC GAMES

The central question of this book is the amount of the economic primary and induced benefit in a host city in return for exporting the service 'Olympic Games'. To measure the economic impact of Olympic Games it is important to determine both the size of the region under consideration and the time. The city, state or country border naturally gives the region. The time is difficult to determine. Nowadays Olympic Games create impacts as early as at least 11 years before the Games to several years after the Games. The post-Games phase very much depends on the Olympic legacy of the Games – for example, St Moritz, 1928 and 1948, still profits from its image gained through hosting the Olympic Winter Games 76 and 56 years ago respectively. On the cost side, Munich 1972 and Montreal 1976 will soon have to redevelop their Olympic parks, which are now 30 years old.

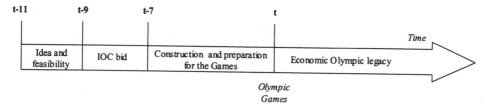

Figure 5.2   Phases of economic activities through Olympic Games

The 'Idea and feasibility' phase can take much longer than shown in Figure 5.2. Olympic cities such as Athens and Beijing often had to bid twice before they won. That increases the first phase to ten years. The 'IOC bid' phase is split in two stages and takes nearly two years. The first year is called 'applicant stage' which is used by the IOC to evaluate the physical infrastructure of the cities. The second year is called 'candidature stage' and is a rather political phase, which ends with a secret ballot of the Olympic city by all IOC members but not those that have the nationality of the bid city. The seven years of preparation for the Games are important, especially if there is a lot of permanent construction planned. The economic legacy comprises all economic effects that are related to the Olympic Games after the closing ceremonies.

Olympic Games preparation triggers many direct and indirect investments and consumptions. The direct money entering a host city stems from investments in sport facilities, the organization of the Games and spending by thousands of tourists. The indirect impact stems from investments in housing, telecommunication and transportation, but also from post-Games exports and post-Olympic tourist spending. These post-Games-related expenditures last for more or less ten years, mainly sustained by post-Olympic tourism and some sport-related exports. If special tourist attractions (for example, Olympic Park such as in Munich, Montreal or Seoul) were created or sport-related events are carried out, this period might be prolonged. In the case of missing attractions (for example, Los Angeles, Atlanta) it will be shortened.

Only the so-called autonomous expenditures (new money) in a local economy have an impact. In order to compare the annual net impacts (benefits minus costs) they have to be homogenized. Figure 5.3 is a simulation of potential Olympic Games in Frankfurt 2012, Germany.

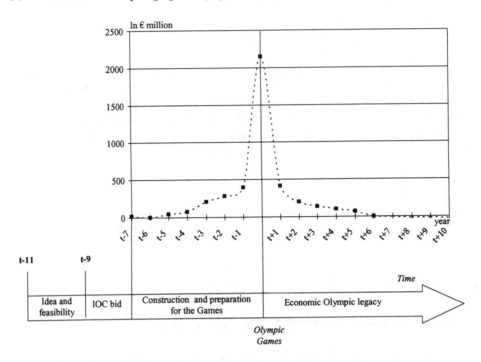

Source: Preuß and Weiss (2003, p. 213).

Figure 5.3   Discounted net benefit of Olympic Games (data from case study: Frankfurt 2012)

Figure 5.3 shows the annual impacts in a curve over the entire time under consideration. A strong single impact occurs during the Olympic year, which is also typical for other major sport events (see Rahmann and Kurscheidt, 2002, p. 185). However, the peak is not necessarily positive as politicians like to interpret. In cases where there is a strong economic situation during the Olympic year, crowding-out effects are likely to occur. If the post-Olympic phase additionally goes along with a recession, the payment for the Olympic debts will weaken the local economy. On the other hand, if the economic situation is vice versa, the staging of the Games would be an economically wise decision because the peak impact betters the regional economic situation.

The size of the annual impacts differs from city to city depending not only on the strength of the economy, but also on the capacity of tourist accommodation and existing infrastructure. However, the peak at Games time is most likely to be very strong, but single. Therefore organizers, business people and politicians should try to leverage the curve before and after its peak (Chalip, 2002).

So far we have looked at the shape of the annual economic impacts of Olympic Games. But what influences the dimension of the Olympic economic impact?

- The amount of autonomous money entering the city (primary impact) and
- the size of the multiplier (secondary impact). Its size depends on the amount of autonomous expenditures that remain in the host city/region and creates income that is being spent again and again. The marginal propensity to consume expresses the part of the income that is spent again. An outflow from the region is determined by imports and taxes.

The challenge of calculating the economic impact of Olympic Games is to regionalize the economic impact. Therefore, it is crucial to distinguish between autonomous and regional means. Olympic Game's primary impact stems from three fields: 'Consumption of the OCOG', 'Exports/Tourism' and 'Investments' (Figure 5.4).

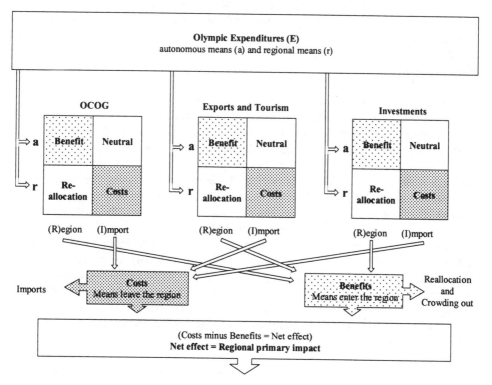

Source: Preuß and Weiss (2003, p. 25).

Figure 5.4   Model to identify the regional primary impact

To calculate the regional primary impact (P) the expenditures (E) for each category (i = 1 - x) can be calculated by the following formula:

Where:

P =	primary impact	E =	expenditures
i =	category of expenditure	R =	expenditures in the region in %
a =	autonomous means in %	I =	Imports in %
r =	regional means in %		

$$P = \sum_{i=1}^{x} E_{(i)} \cdot (a \cdot R_{(i)} - r \cdot I_{(i)}) \qquad (5.1)$$

To understand the calculation (and formula) of the regional primary economic impact you just have to follow the arrows in Figure 5.4. For example, a foreign tourist spends some money in a hotel of the host nation. In that case the tourist's expenditure (E) is autonomous (a) and therefore creates a benefit (money enters the region). It is counted as a benefit that creates the regional primary impact. The origin (autonomous or regional) and destination (Region or Import) of each finance stream determines which economic effect occurs:

- Benefits (autonomous means which stay in the region) ($a \cdot R$).
- Costs (regional means which are used for imports) ($r \cdot I$).
- Reallocations (regional means which are spent in the region) ($r \cdot R$).
- Neutral effects (autonomous means which are used for imports) ($a \cdot I$).

Once the regional primary impact is calculated, the regional multiplier has to be used to calculate the net effect of the Olympic Games. Owing to the increasingly international division of labour and the related increase in import dependency, the multipliers for a region are steadily declining nowadays (Lager, 1995).

All direct and indirect expenditures form the primary effect (Figure 5.5). Sooner or later, the Olympic Games increase production in the city to satisfy the increased demand. These expenditures are called secondary effect, which is calculated using a multiplier of the primary effect. The sum of primary and secondary effects equals the net increase of the regional income and employment (economic overall effect).

Basically, expenditures which constitute the overall effect for the economy of a host city can be divided into:

- Direct expenditures: autonomous OCOG, private and government consumption and investments in the host city such as tourist expenditures for tickets and memorabilia and stadium construction.
- Indirect expenditures: autonomous expenditures of, for example, tourists and others in the host city, transportation, food, and so on.
- Induced expenditures: effects caused by spending the direct and indirect expenditures again.

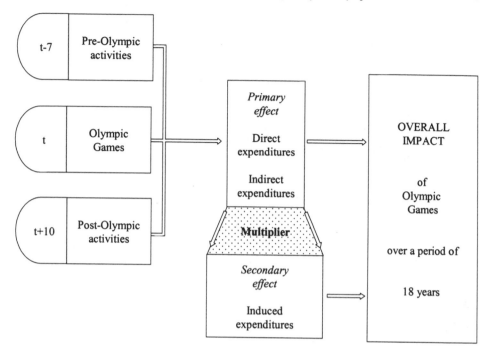

Figure 5.5 Diagram to display the multiplier effect

Before explaining and actually applying the multiplier theory to the olympic effects in a host city it should be explained that this is a simplified macroeconomic model. This model was developed for application to a national economy rather than to a region. In the simple Keynesian model, unemployment, rigid prices, interest and wages as well as a lack of government activities are assumed. Furthermore, multipliers always refer to a certain point in time and not to a period. These assumptions make it difficult to transfer the theory to the economy of host cities.

None of past Olympic Games analyses have interpreted the multiplier with its clear limitation, namely that the effect of a non-recurring expenditure weakens in the course of time and vanishes completely. This means that the income increase declines with every new period and, in the long run, the falling demand leads back to the equilibrium income that existed before the Games. Nevertheless the peak impact is strong and can change the structure of the host city.

Figure 5.6 shows that the income increase in the tth period amounts to $ct * dA$. For n against infinity, the value tends towards zero. But the Olympic Games are a special case. The increased demand lasts for about 18 years. During this period, autonomous expenditures are made so that the equilibrium income will not immediately return to the starting point. Caused by varying autonomous expenditures (dA), there will be permanently changing demand functions during the remaining time.

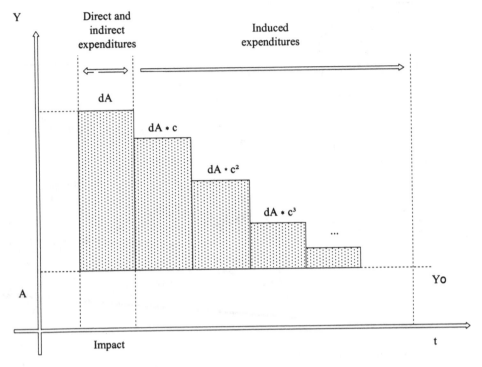

Source: modified from Peto (1989).

Figure 5.6 Multiplier impact in case of non-recurring autonomous expenditure

Long after the Games, there will be an increased demand depending on the amount of long-term investments. These are, for example, the operation and the maintenance of sports facilities or the increased visitor numbers due to up-valued attractions and the Olympic image. If the sports facilities and the changed structure of the city rise, and so does the level of attractiveness – as can be seen in the example of the Munich Olympic Park – lasting income increases can be the consequence.

The varying amount of autonomous expenditures (investments) can be illustrated using the examples of the Barcelona, Sydney and Beijing Olympics. In this simplistic consideration, imports and crowding out and any consumption expenditures are not yet considered. Figure 5.7 shows the amount of investments during the seven pre-Olympic years as percent ages. Figure 5.8 shows the effect of the investments based an estimated multiplier. In the subsequent years each investment induces further expenditures. The data refer exclusively to investments in the host cities.

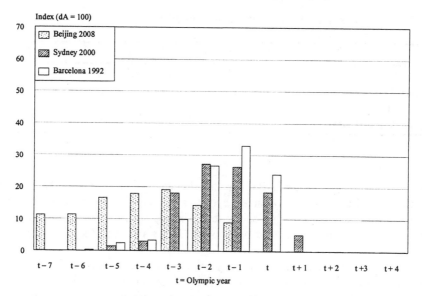

Sources: Modified based on Andersen (1999); Bidding Committee Beijing 2008 (2001); Brunet (1993).

Figure 5.7 Investments in Barcelona 1992, Sydney 2000 and Beijing 2008 by index (dA=100)

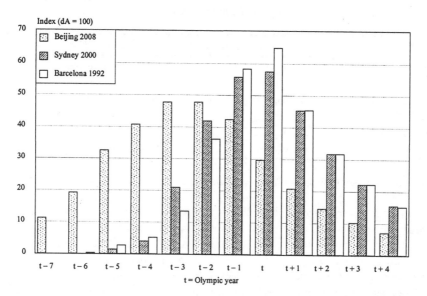

Sources: Modified based on Andersen (1999); Bidding Committee Beijing 2008 (2001); Brunet (1993).

Figure 5.8 Effects of the multiplier for investments in Barcelona 1992, Sydney 2000 and Beijing 2008 by index (dA=100)

Table 5.1   Distribution of investments (in percentages)

	t − 7	t − 6	t − 5	t − 4	t − 3	t − 2	t − 1	t	t + 1	t + 2
Seoul 1988	0	1	3	4	10	26	32	24	0	0
Barcelona 1992	1	2	5	9	13	17	22	31	0	0
Sydney 2000	0	0	2	3	18	28	26	18	5	0
Prognosis (average Olympics)	0	0	3	5	14	29	30	15	4	0

Source: Preuss and Weiss (2003).

The main difference between Beijing and Barcelona/Sydney is that the city, state authorities and the private sector invest earlier in Beijing. In Seoul 1988, the highest investments were also made earlier due to the Asian Games in 1986; in Barcelona 1992 the main investments made one year prior to the Games and in Sydney it was two years before.

For the macroeconomic benefit to a city, which results from staging the Games, the economic situation at the time the expenditures are made is critical. Expenditures during a recession or depression have a positive effect. During a phase of economic recovery or upswing the Games could cause crowding out and price increases, thus having rather negative effects on the host city.

Table 5.2   Economic situation during the main investments

Host City	Economic situation (t − 3 to t)	Macroeconomic effect
Munich 1972	need of capital	yes (end of depression)
Montreal 1976	need of capital	yes (end of depression)
Los Angeles 1984	up-swing	no (end of recession)
Seoul 1988	constant	no (boom)
Barcelona 1992	need of capital	yes (end of boom)
Atlanta 1996	need of capital	yes (end of depression)

Sources: Assenmacher (1998, pp. 6–17); International Monetary Fund (1997); Preuss (2000a, pp. 281–2).

Today, it is nearly impossible to obtain useful records of the income effects of the Olympic Games. For this chapter the data can only be based on past Olympic impact studies. However, most analyses were carried out solely a priori and mainly on behalf of Olympic bodies (Table 5.3). Therefore they are more or less inaccurate.

The existing analyses can only be checked for their methodical approach in order to detect deliberate falsifications and/or misinterpretations. Autonomous expenditures, which are to be ascertained in the following, are divided into consumption expenditures and investments.

Table 5.3   Analysis of economic impacts of Olympic Games

Olympic Games	Author	Year	Multiplier	Form of analysis
1972 Munich	Weber, C.	1972	1.5	CBA (short)
1976 Montreal	Chartrand, M.	s.t.	-	CBA (short)
	Molson, Rousseau & Co.	1975	-	Impact
1984 L.Angeles	ERA	1981	1.5	Impact
	ERA	1984	3	Impact
1988 Seoul	Kwag, D.-H.	1988	-	Economic Prospects
	Kim, J. et al.	1989	1.8	Impact
1992 Barcelona	Brunet, F.	1993	-	-
	Vegara, J.M. and Salvador, N.	1992	1.7	Impact
	Heinemann, K.	1995	2.7	Impact
1996 Atlanta	KPMG Peat Marwick	1990	1.2	Impact
	Humphreys, J. and Plummer, M.	1992	1.2	Impact
	Humphreys, J. and Plummer, M.	1996	1.2	Impact
2000 Sydney	KPMG Peat Marwick	1993	-	Impact
2000 Berlin	Senat von Berlin	1990	1.6	Impact
	Ewers, H.-J. et al.	1993	1.5	CBA
	Preuss, H.	1993	-	CBA (short)
2000 Hamburg	Gutachter- Arbeitsgemeinschaft	1988	1.5	Impact
2002 Graz	Lager, C.	1995	-	Impact
2010 Vancouver	Gray, J.	2002	-	Impact
	InterVISTAS Consulting INC.	2002	1.5-2.0	Impact
2010 Bern	Stettler, J. et al.	2002	-	Impact
2012 Houston	Airola J. and Craig S.	2000	1.26-2.46	Impact
2012 Frankfurt	Preuss, H. and Weiss, H.-J.	2003	1.35-1.6	CBA (regional)

Notes: *CBA*   *= cost–benefit analysis*
          Impact   *= economic impact study*

In the following chapters the three fields 'Tourism and exports' (Chapter 6), 'Investments' (Chapter 7) and 'OCOG' (Chapters 8 and 9) are investigated in order to describe the economic impact a city can expect from Olympic Games.

6.   Tourism and exports: the sleeping giants

6.1 OLYMPIC TOURISM

'Event tourism' is one of the current key phrases. The Olympics especially are seen as catalysts for driving tourism, but not just for the time of the Olympics itself. Both the Olympics and other major events can develop high profiles for host cities and are claimed to be good for attracting future tourists long after the event has been staged (Masterman, 2003, p. 460).

This chapter will focus on various aspects of Olympic tourism. From an economic point of view, it has the potential to be a 'giant' because it can attract huge amounts of autonomous money to a region or country. Here three aspects of Olympic tourists are important:

- The spectators in the stadium create the atmosphere that the television audience notice unconsciously and that also make the Olympics one of the sport events most highly sought after. This aspect is important to attract television audiences and high television rates which increase the revenues from selling the television rights.
- Foreign tourists create a significant part of the economic impact during the Games. Based on hotel capacity, accessibility and availability of tickets the number of tourists is different from Games to Games. The more foreign tourists visit the country, the bigger the economic impact.
- When tourists return home from the Games, stories about their experiences trigger off a multiplying effect of visitors by changing the perception of friends and relatives about the host city and country in general. That may motivate them to visit the country and increase post-Games tourism.

For the IOC and the OCOG the most important Olympic Games spectator is the television audience. There is a close relation between the revenues of television stations from selling commercials, the readiness of corporations to pay for Olympic emblems/commercials and the television rates. Their concern is related to point (1). The host city and nation is interested in points (2) and (3) because the tourists can trigger off a 'giant' economic impact. This aspect will be the centre of further discussion.

6.1.1 Awareness and Image of the Host Nation

The level of awareness of Athens will increase mostly in 2004. The high television rates for the next Games will transport the image of Athens, Attica and Greece to the world.

For Attica, the region around Athens, the arrivals decreased from 2.1 million in 1980 to 1.5 million in 1991 and rising 1.9 million in 1997 (Papanikos, 1999). A new and positive image could help to increase tourism in Attica after the Games. The positive impact of the Olympic Games on tourism is, 'often the first reason highlighted by the candidature committees for the Winter Games ... The publicity campaign for the first Winter Games in Chamonix 1924 was carried out ... to increase the number of visitors to this resort' (Chappelet, 2003, p. 56).

Ritchie and Smith (1991) investigated the positive awareness level the Winter Games had at Calgary. Most Canadian cities experienced a reasonable degree of stability in the level of awareness in Europe over the four-year period. By comparing the two major cities of the province of Alberta, Calgary and Edmonton, the Olympic effect becomes visible (Figure 6.1).

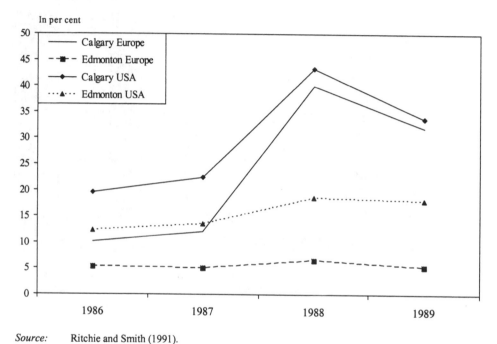

Source: Ritchie and Smith (1991).

Figure 6.1 Unaided recall of Calgary and Edmonton by European and US respondents

The impact of Olympic Winter Games can be seen in the 1988 figures where Calgary's unaided recognition level jumped to 40 per cent while Edmonton's remained at just over 6 per cent. The same impact can be observed in the USA, although growth awareness between 1986 and 1988 was not quite so dynamic.

The awareness level of a city must be distinguished from its image. While the level of awareness only reflects the percentage of people who know a certain city (quantitative), the image is a qualitative aspect that can be both positive and negative. A qualitative investigation of image has to focus on attributes that are associated with the host city. For example, Young and Rubicam evaluated the brand 'Australia' seen by Germans in January 2000 against 48 attributes. Without mentioning the Olympics, 'Australia' was tested as a brand along with others such as Sony, McDonald's, and so on. In 2002 the attributes were evaluated again.

Attributes increasing the image of Australia as a tourist destination are 'friendly', 'fun', 'trust worthy'. All these data show positive changes. However, 'good value' did only increase in USA. The increased awareness a city gains by hosting the Olympics is a very important Olympic legacy (Preuss, 2003b). The attributes related to Australia as country for investments did not increase. 'Innovative' and 'reliable' decreased as well as 'Cares about customers' in USA. Only 'high quality' did increase in both countries.

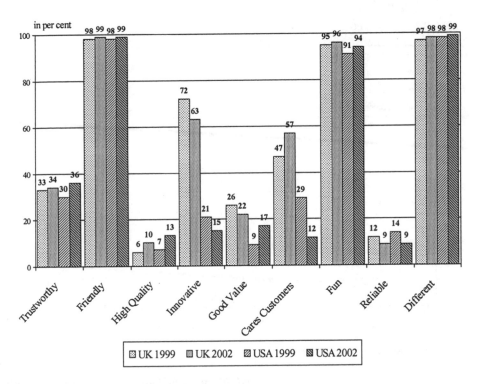

Source: Data from Young and Rubicam (correspondence, Jourdan, 2004).

Figure 6.2 Attributes of Australia seen by consumers of UK and USA

After looking at field research the theory should be considered. Figure 6.3 shows four communication channels through which a host city can influence tourists and conveys its image.

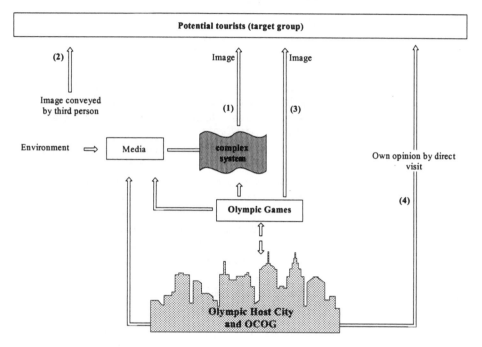

Source: Modified from Preuss (2000a, p. 84).

Figure 6.3 Ways the image of Athens 2004 affects the target groups

The transfer of a city's image differs from channel to channel. The key channel for transferring information about the host city is indirect communication (1) that is linked to media reports on the Olympics. It is incontestable that host cities receive indirect promotion from the various media for which they would have to invest large advertising budgets without the Games. For example, Sydney 2000 got a 12 times higher media coverage than the average coverage during the Olympic year (http://olympic.datops.com/ page/blanktrend.html, 6 December 2002). However, the city has limited opportunities to influence the messages conveyed through the media and risks a negative or unwanted image being created. Therefore, Sydney 2000 took action to influence the journalists in a positive way. The Australian Tourist Commission's four-year strategic programme included:

- a visiting journalist programme
- servicing 50 000 international media inquiries
- providing a specialist internet for media, bringing international broadcasters to Australia before the Games
- working with international television to provide stories, quality vision and sound resources of all parts of Australia
- cooperative arrangements and joint advertorials with Olympic sponsors

- providing media with interesting visuals of the torch relay
- providing international magazines with stories
- photography and offering a non-accredited media centre in Sydney

The ATC was supported with US$$_{.00}$ 5 million from the Australian Government to run the 'visiting journalist programme'. It is estimated that Australia obtained the equivalent of US$$_{.00}$ 1.7 billion – however this is measured – in media coverage internationally as a result of this programme (Chalip, 2003, pp. 198-200).

The second communication channel is the tourists who have contact with others (2) reporting about the host city. The third communication channel is direct advertising (3) by the host city where the city image that is conveyed to the target group must be precisely controlled. The fourth communication channel is the personal visit (4) to the host city. A visit gives an immediate impression of the city and transfers a sustained image.

Figure 6.4 shows the two strategic aims related to Olympic tourism that an Olympic host city/nation could focus on. Here Athens 2004 is used as an example. The communication channels (1) and (4) from Figure 6.3 are displayed in detail.

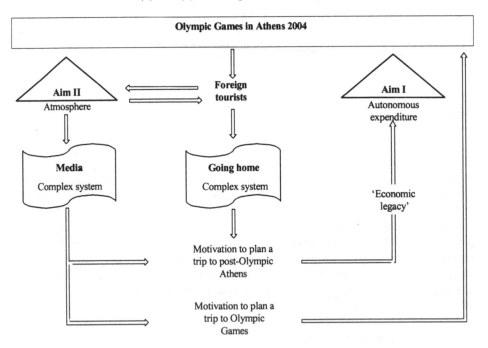

Source: Modified from Preuss and Messing (2002).

Figure 6.4 Strategic tourism aims for Athens 2004

The Olympic tourism legacy is positive not only for the past Games in Salt Lake City 2002, but also for Athens 2004. The Salt Lake Games may have motivated television audiences and Salt Lake tourists to attend the Games in Athens. Media and reports from returning tourists create a positive perception about visiting the Olympic Games. This was proven by several empirical studies of the 'Research Team Olympia' from Mainz, Germany (Table 6.1).

Table 6.1   *'Do you plan to go to the next Olympic Games in...?' (A)*
                'Would you take part in the next Youth Camp in Sydney 2000' (B)

Visit of the next Games ...	Group	Answers	Intention to visit the next Games							
			Yes		Not yet decided		No		No answer	
			abs.	%	abs.	%	abs.	%	abs.	%
Atlanta 1996	(A) German tourists	n = 579	220	38.0	185	32.0	156	26.9	18	3.1
Sydney 2000	(A) German tourists	n = 212	114	53.8	72	34.0	23	10.8	3	1.4
Sydney 2000	(B) German Youth Camp	n = 172	101	57.7	52	30.2	17	9.9	2	1.2

Source: Müller and Messing (1992; 1997a; 1997b).

6.1.2 Economic Impact of Olympic Tourism

The economic impact of the Games is very dependent on the number of foreign tourists because they bring fresh money into the city and region. The total number of tourists heavily depends on the attractiveness of the region and other conditions such as the political or economic situation (Krajasits, 1995). The literature mentions differing numbers of tourists who have visited past Olympics. The partially huge discrepancies show that it is difficult to predict tourist figures (Roaf et al., 1996). It must be assumed that most figures in pre-Olympic forecasts are overestimated. The true number of foreign visitors to the Olympic Games is probably only between 400 000 and 800 000, and the number strongly depends on the geographic location of the host country. From the 487 000 estimated guests for Sydney 2000, only 132 000 had been expected to be Olympic-specific international visitors and, finally, the Olympic month of September showed an increase of only 53 000 overseas arrivals above average (Australian Bureau of Statistics, 1999–2002).

Hosts of Olympic Games often use the event to promote their region. The 'free' promotion of the destination is a major bonus for host cities if managed correctly, as Australia demonstrated with the Sydney Olympic Games. 'The long term benefits to tourism from increased awareness and enhanced tourism image are far more significant than the short term effects from the event itself' (Carlsen and Williams, 1997). This quote was directed towards the high long-term benefit through tourism but it also covers the fact that the Olympic Games crowded out tourism through increased demand. Non-Olympic tourists and residents avoided the Olympic trouble that, in turn, led to a loss of money that would have otherwise been spent in the host city.

Table 6.2   Number of Olympic visitors with autonomous consumption expenditures

	Out of city visitors	Olympic family	Out of city visitors (total)*
Los Angeles 1984	400 000 – 608 760	28 460	770 000
Seoul 1988	less than 240 000	39 332	240 000
Barcelona 1992	250 000 – 422 666	55 000	450 000
Atlanta 1996	736 100 – 2000 000	72 543	968 000
Sydney 2000	110 000	57 000	475 000
Athens 2004	150 000**	60 000	660 000
Beijing 2008	600 000***	60 000	660 000

Notes: *   Figures estimated on foregoing columns and on additional information.
         **   Only international visitors, Olympic Family estimated
         *** According the hotel capacity (Bidding Committee Beijing 2008, 2001). Olympic Family estimated.

Sources: Bidding Committee Beijing 2008 (2001); Brunet (1993); Cox et al. (1994); Ewers et al., (1993); Humphreys, Plummer (1996); KPMG Peat Marwick (1993); Lee (1998c); Papanikos (1999); State Chamber Of Commerce, NSW (2001); Telex Dienst Tourismus (1992); TFC (1998); Vegara and Salvador(1992); Wilcox (1994).

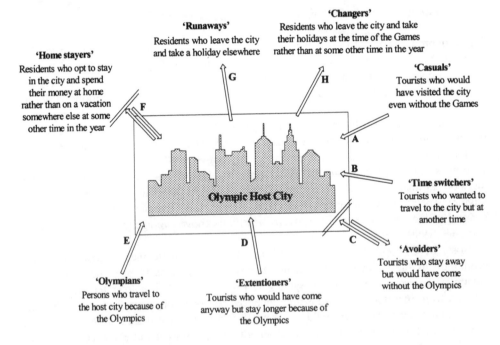

Source: Modified from Preuss (2000a).

Figure 6.5 Movements of visitors during Games time

To calculate the tourism impact we need the number of additional visitors, their length of stay and their consumption pattern. What matters is to ascertain the autonomous consumption expenditures. Therefore, the journeys into, or from, the host city must be considered.

Some movements displayed in Figure 6.5 are often overlooked and therefore lead to overestimations of Olympic-related tourism effects.

- (A) and (B) Casuals and Time switchers – reallocation of budget: often these Olympic tourists are calculated as bringing in new money. That is wrong, because they would have come and spent their money in the city anyway. But there is another effect that should be considered. Due to a limited budget this group spends their money on Olympic events rather than on everyday attractions. In Los Angeles attendance figures at popular tourist destinations were down 30–50 per cent during the Olympics (ERA, 1984). In Sydney, attractions that were not close to or directly related to the Games experienced decreased attendance numbers.
- Avoiders – crowding out of visitors: 66 per cent of Danish tourists avoided the Lillehammer region during the Olympics in 1994 (Getz, 1997). In July and August 1992 the Costa Brava region lost part of its high summer seasonal demand due to the Games in Barcelona (Figures 6.6 and 6.7). The same happened in Los Angeles 1984 to theme park hotel owners. There is a risk that 'Avoiders' who have come on a regular basis may stay away in future. Figures from the Costa Brava can serve to demonstrate how Olympics can affect the region that is surrounding the city.

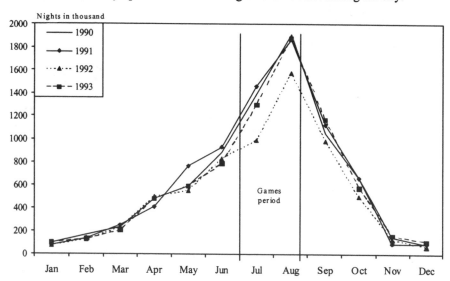

Sources: Ministerio de Economíca y Hacienda. Institutio Nacional de Estadística (1991; 1992; 1993); Ministerio de Industria (1990).

Figure 6.6 Hotel nights of hotels at Costa Brava (Girona)

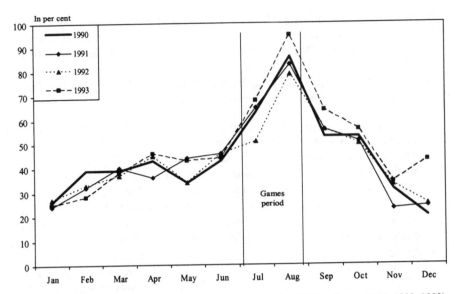

Sources: Ministerio de Economíca y Hacienda. Institutio Nacional de Estadística (1991; 1992; 1993);
Ministerio de Industria (1990).

Figure 6.7 Occupancy rates of hotels at Costa Brava (Girona)

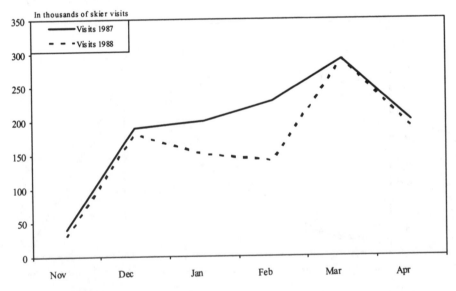

Source: GOPB (2000).

Figure 6.8 Skier visits in Calgary in 1987 and 1988

The figures show a temporary decrease of visitors in the region surrounding Barcelona. However, months and years after the Games a positive tourism effect can be noticed. The Utah Skier Survey 1999–2000 found nearly 50 per cent of non-resident skiers indicated that they would not consider skiing in Utah during 2002. When probed as to the reason for this, respondents indicated crowds (76 per cent) and higher prices (20 per cent) were the primary deterrents to Utah skiing (GOPB, 2002). Figure 6.8 seems to confirm the Calgary experience. The decrease of tourists cannot be based on low snow, since the snowfall in December, January and February has been much better than the year before.

- (D), (E) and (F) Home stayers, Olympians and Extentioners – the real Olympic tourists: these persons spend autonomous money and create a significant economic impact. Based on the bid of Frankfurt for the Games in 2012 and the hotel capacities of the Rhein-Main-Region, the economic impact of this group (without 'Home stayers') can be estimated as shown in Figure 6.9. However, these calculations show that pre-Olympic tourism is not strong in comparison to Games time and the post-Olympic years. The different scenarios demonstrate different occupancy rates and different increase in hotel construction (Preuss and Weiss, 2003).

- (G) and (H) Changers and Runaways – crowding out of citizens: in Barcelona, 16 per cent of the people interviewed in a survey six months prior to the Olympics stated that they considered spending their holidays outside the city during the Games (Brunet, 1993). In Sydney 2000 the 'Traveland survey' suggests, that only a small proportion of residents (30 per cent) have indicated no interest in the Games. Among those who do intend to leave Sydney, over 60 per cent indicated travel abroad (TFC, 1998). The risk is that 'Runaways' and 'Changers' may discover new holiday destinations and decide to return there again in the future. For Athens this might not be a problem since many citizens usually leave the city during the summer heat. The Olympics may make many of them stay in Athens (Home stayers).

Visitors to the Olympics can be divided into three groups based on consumption expenditures. The first group does not bring Games-related autonomous expenditures to the city (reallocation of funds – A, B, H). The second group brings Games-related autonomous expenditure to the city (inflow of funds – D, E, F). The third group carries out money that would have been spent in the city without the Games (outflow of funds – G, C). This raises the question whether the Olympics in their overall effect lead to additional consumption by the visitors.

$$D + E + F - G - C = ? \qquad (6.1)$$

If this equation is greater than zero there is a Games-related inflow of funds; if it is smaller than zero there is an outflow. Some of the multiplier analyses of past Olympics lack this differentiation between the various moving groups or they simplified the analyses by consideration of all consumption expenditures. The expenditures of the casuals (A) and the time switchers (B) are wrongly included and the crowded–out consumption expenditures of some residents (G) and tourists (C) are ignored. The calculations of these analyses were only correct under the assumption that group F would counterbalance all these effects. Group (C) gives good reason to consider the extent of crowding out the remaining tourists in view of the realistic assumption that regular visitors might stay away in future. Due to the fact that most tourist accommodations in the host city are sold out during the Games, the Olympic tourism effect is that the share is greater than the average occupancy rate. Each host city should carefully investigate this aspect and counteract the 'emigration' by adequate marketing measures.

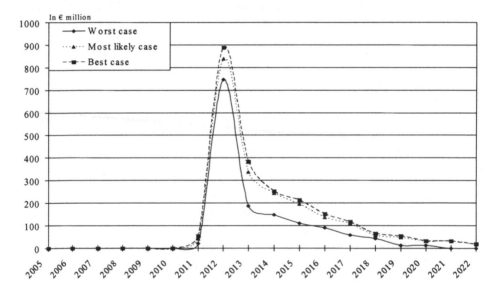

Source: Preuss and Weiss (2003).

Figure 6.9 Discounted net benefit per year

Besides tourism Olympics affect the (Meetings, Incentives, Congresses, Exhibitions) MICE tourists. During the Games there will be a crowding out in the MICE sector. The increased attractiveness and awareness of the Olympic city as a MICE destination will lead to a post-Olympic increase.

Figure 6.10 shows that during the Olympic year (t) all three host cities faced a decrease of congress participants. The first post-Olympic year (t +1) overcompensates that deficit. However, competition in the congress business remains fierce, as there had been a rapid increase in construction in rival cities in the world (Boyle, 2001, p. 5). At least the Olympic Games in accelerating development of congress facilities.

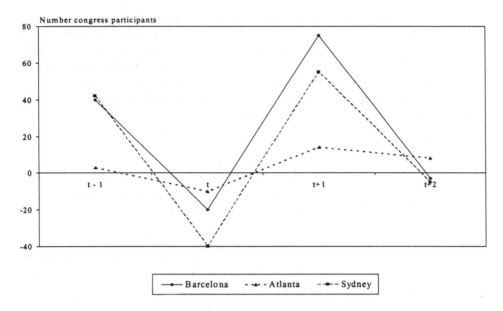

Source: Boyle (2001, p. 5); McCay and Plumb (2001, p. 10).

Figure 6.10   Development of congress participants

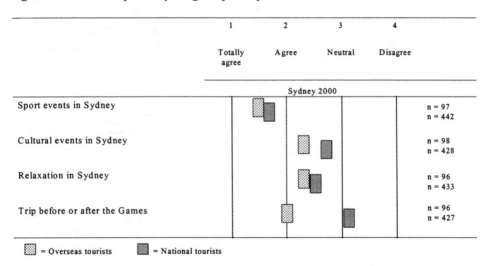

Source: Messing and Müller (2001).

Figure 6.11   Importance of vacation components during the visit of Olympic Games in Sydney 2000

Many of the Olympic tourists do not come solely because of the Olympics but, rather, combine the visit with trips in the host country. Approximately 61 per cent of the German Olympic tourists to Atlanta 1996 linked the visit to the Games to a trip to the USA (Müller and Messing, 1997a). Further research showed that tourist attractions are important for visitors but the sport events are still the main purpose of the trip.

Figure 6.11 shows that most overseas tourists to Australia judged other components of their trip as more important than national tourists.

6.1.3 Pre-Olympic Tourism

The announcement of the Olympic Games alone will not attract additional tourists to visit the city. However, the level of awareness of a future host city is increased as early as during the bid phase which could, in turn, indirectly lead to an increase in tourism (Table 6.3).

Most of the autonomous expenditures are carried out during the planning and coordination phase of the OCOG with the IOC, IFs, NOCs, media, sponsors and so on. Persons invited by the Los Angeles 1984 OCOG alone spent 29 000 visitor days with 19 200 overnight stays in Los Angeles. That lead to approximately US$$_{'00}$ 7.5 million autonomous expenditures (ERA, 1984). Similar calculations for the Atlanta 1996 Olympics revealed 18 000 visitors and 69 760 visitor days. This would correspond to approximately US$$_{'00}$ 17.8 million autonomous expenditures (Humphreys and Plummer, 1992; 1996). In Sydney the pre-Olympic training of more than 127 Teams from 39 countries brought US$$_{'00}$ 43.2 million into the state of New South Wales (PricewaterhouseCoopers, 2002, p. 55). For Athens 2004 the number of pre-Olympic visitors is estimated to be at least 25 000 persons (Papanikos, 1999). These examples show that the pre-Olympic effect is non-marginal.

Table 6.3   *Reasons for pre-Olympic visits*

Reason for visit	Persons who would not have visited the city otherwise
Cultural Olympiad	Artists, tourists
Test events	Athletes, coaches, tourists
Scientific conventions	Scientists
Meetings of sponsors	Sponsors, guests, customers
Media preparation, run-up reporting	Media representatives
Coordination meetings (OCOG)	Members of IOC, IFs, NOCs, media representatives, sponsors
Training camps	Athletes and coaches

The organizers of the Olympics are the largest group of pre-Olympic visitors. Another large group is the athletes and members, judges and guests of test events, which are, since Sydney 2000, organized in nearly each sport. Other pre-Olympic activities include, for example, events of the Cultural Olympiad and activities involving industry and media.

6.1.4 Post-Olympic Tourism – the Legacy

The Olympic tourism legacy is largely positive because the media coverage increases the desire of potential tourists to visit the country after the Games due to a change in perception (see Figure 6.2). However, there is a risk of overestimating the numbers for post-Olympic tourism. Chalip (2003, p. 197) links the quality of tourism legacy on the degree to which the Games are leveraged. To him, the effect seems to depend on what is done to capitalize on the opportunity that the Games afford to enhance tourism to the host city, region, and/or nation.

Over the years Olympic host cities and countries have run some form of tourism promotion in association with the Games, such as Barcelona 1992. However,

> Australia is the first Olympic host nation to take full advantage of the Games to vigorously pursue tourism for the benefit of the whole country. It's something we've never seen take place to this level before, and it's a model that we would like to see carried forward to future Olympic Games in Athens and beyond. (Payne, 2001)

The Australia Tourism Committee's strategy on how to use the Olympic Games as an advertisement for Australia is worth exploring. In the early 1990s, Australia was rarely on the world stage. It was a place mentioned from time to time. The Games gave Australia the chance to compete in the interest and awareness stakes on an equal footing with other famous tourist destinations. That did not happen automatically. The ATC obtained US$6.7 million from the Australian Government over the XXVIIth Olympiad (1997-2000) and created a large long-term benefit from the Sydney Olympics. 'The amount of exposure and interest the Games generated is unrivalled, and that will result in a significant increase in visitor numbers over the next 10 years' (Morse, 2001). It was estimated that the Games would attract an extra 1.7 million international visitors to Australia and generate US$$_{.00}$ 4,587 million in tourism export earnings between 1997 and 2004 (TFC, 1998, p. 13). An additional 1.8 million domestic visitors are predicted (TFC, 1998, p. 49). To increase tourism, well over 1000 individual projects were implemented in the lead-up to the Games. Some of the results are (ATC, 2001, p. 3) accelerated development of Brand Australia in ten years; media relations and publicity programmes generating US$$_{.00}$ 2.1 billion; Olympics sponsors spending US$$_{.00}$ 170 million promoting Australia; and an 11 per cent increase in visitor arrivals in 2000. Unfortunately, the terrorist attacks on 11 September 2001 strongly affected the number of tourists to Australia. Since the case without the Games is not known, most probably the decrease in visitor arrivals is still lower than it would have been without the Games.

It has to be considered that the average increase of international arrivals from 1993 to 1999 was about 7 per cent (BTR, 2001). That includes the losses due to the economic crises in Asia that led to immense decreases in arrivals from most Asian countries. Without the crises effect the average increase is 12 per cent. The most surprising fact was the low number of additional tourists in the Olympic month (September) (Preuss, 2002c). The Tourism Forecasting Council (TFC, 1998) investigated the tourism effects of the Olympics in Seoul 1988 and Tokyo 1964 compared with Australia. They estimated

75 000 additional international spectators and 36 000 additional arrivals due to the Olympic Family. The increase of only 50 000 arrivals in September 2000 (original figures) indicates that 'switch' and 'aversion' effects of other tourists occurred (see Figure 6.12).

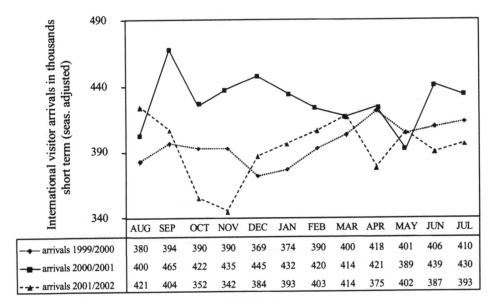

	AUG	SEP	OCT	NOV	DEC	JAN	FEB	MAR	APR	MAY	JUN	JUL
arrivals 1999/2000	380	394	390	390	369	374	390	400	418	401	406	410
arrivals 2000/2001	400	465	422	435	445	432	420	414	421	389	439	430
arrivals 2001/2002	421	404	352	342	384	393	403	414	375	402	387	393

Source: Australian Bureau of Statistics (1999–2002).

Figure 6.12   Development of tourism in Australia 1999–2002

Research conducted by the ATC indicated a significant positive shift in consumers' inclination to holiday in Australia because of the Olympics (Table 6.4).

Table 6.4   Consumers' inclination to holiday in Australia sometime during the next five years (percentages)

IND	INA	MAS	THA	CHN	SIN	TPE	HKG	JPN	KOR	USA	NZL	GBR	GER
45%	56%	41%	43 %	37%	27%	26%	19%	24%	15%	24%	17%	13%	21%

Source: Morse (2001, p. 11).

This increased interest in Australia is not only due to the coverage of the Games, but also the result of the ATC's four-year strategic programme mentioned above. The Utah 1999-2000 survey confirmed a positive effect of Olympic Games on post-event tourism. Twenty-eight per cent were likely to ski more in Utah and only 6 per cent less likely.

During the Games in 2002 only 20 per cent were more likely to ski there while 44 per cent answered less likely (GOPB, 2000).

It seems that in the case of Australia the tourism legacy was positive and has to be considered as a potential giant if the Games effect can leverage the tourism effect. Looking at the size of revenues expected from post-Olympic tourism in Australia, it is interesting to note that the tourism legacy is only mentioned along with other potential legacies. So far the main legacy effect seen in the Olympics is the reurbanization and upgrading of the host infrastructure cities. In particular the focus is put on sport facilities and not on tourism infrastructure.

From an economic point of view, it is interesting to look at the infrastructure that was built for the Games and its post-Olympic impact. Chalip (2003, p. 196) demonstrated that many sport facilities ran at a deficit or were torn down because they were so underutilized. But what about the immense need of accommodation for the Olympics? The IOC is aware of this problem. Athens 2004 and Torino 2006 especially face problems to accommodate the Olympic Family, all media representatives and the tourists. Therefore the IOC evaluation commission puts great weight on the accommodation structure when visiting the applicant cities during the bid process. Cities have to provide at least 42 000 hotel beds during Games time. That includes only a quota of 6000 for spectators (IOC, 2000c, p. 41).

Owing to the fact that hotels are private properties, the huge demand for hotel rooms in order successfully to bid for the Games forces local governments to provide public incentives for private hotel construction. Both the opportunity to get subsidiaries and high expectations in the Olympics may create an oversupply of hotel rooms after the Olympics. Table 6.5 seem to justify this concern.

Table 6.5   Hotel industry changes in host cities

	Munich 1972	LA 1984	Seoul 1988	Barcelona 1992	Atlanta 1996	Sydney 2000	Athens 2004	Beijing 2008
Games-related increase in the number of hotel rooms (%)	12.2*	5.8	41.9–48	38	9.1*	12.5*	N/A	62.5
Hotel occupancy rate during Olympic year	N/A	75	72	65	68	N/A	N/A	N/A
Relative change in occupancy rate during Olympic year compared to previous year (%)	N/A	-1	-2	-5	-3	N/A	N/A	N/A

Note: * Calculation to year preceding the Games.

Sources: Bidding Committee Beijing 2008 (2001); Brown (1997); Brunet (1993); Carswell (1996); Davidson Peterson Associates Studies (1996); ERA (1984); Kim et al. (1989); Statistisches Landesamt München (1973).

It must be questioned whether a possible gain in image and the publicity effect of the Olympic Games will suffice to increase the bed supply for the few days of the Olympics in such a way that an adequate occupancy rate of the hotels after the Olympics can be achieved. The occupancy rate of hotels in a majority of host cities fell during the Olympic year. Even an occupancy rate of nearly 100 per cent during the Olympics can hardly change the average annual figures. For example in Metro Atlanta the occupancy of hotels during and after the Games of 1996 developed as follows:

- July 14–20, 1996 = 76.5 per cent pre-Olympic week
- July 21–27, 1996 = 95.2 per cent Olympic Games (swimming etc.)
- July 28–Aug 3, 1996 = 97.4 per cent Olympic Games (track and field etc.)
- post-Olympics August 4–10, 1996 = 58.0 per cent.

Although frequently overestimated, the nominally largest revenues are registered during an Olympic year. However, in spite of the less-than-expected Olympic benefit, 1996 was a record year of profitability for Atlanta's hotel industry. Despite the fact that the occupancy rate in July was the same the year before, the revenues of the hotel industry were almost doubled (GOPB, 2000). In the long term this rate rose due to the increased attractiveness of the city, and the greater popularity. In 1997 the revenues were larger than in 1995 (GOPB, 2000).

Another example is Calgary 1988. The number of tourists dropped the year after the Olympics by 12 per cent and the next year by another 10 per cent before rising progressively for the next ten years (Ritchie, 2000). In Lillehammer 1994 the number of overnight stays rose by 38 per cent from 1993 to 1994 and fell afterwards. However, in the long run it stayed at a higher level than before (Spilling, 1997).

In general tourism developed as follows in the Olympic Cities.

Los Angeles 1984
In Los Angeles 1984, the flow of information between the tourist industry and tourism was poorly organized. It was difficult to find accommodation although the occupancy rate was at only 75 per cent. The Olympics did not trigger a considerable increase in capacity. The occupancy rate during the Games was indeed higher than in the previous year, however, the surrounding areas suffered a fall in demand. It must be kept in mind that tourism in general declined during 1984. The Olympic Games caused considerable redistributions in Los Angeles in this sector. In this way they aggravated the turnover loss of surrounding tourist facilities.

Seoul 1988
For Korea, the 1988 Olympics were a turning point for the tourist industry. Kang and Perdue (1994) estimated that the Games would generate approximately 1 million extra tourists to Korea in the years following the Olympics. Hyun (1998) obtained a more conservative estimate of 640 000 additional tourists. After the Seoul Games, numerous agencies and new airline connections opened, and in the years prior to the Games, the

tourist sector experienced considerable growth. The success of the Olympics established Korea as a safe and pleasant tourist destination, dispelling earlier fears and impressing the entire world with Korea's cultural heritage (Do, 1999).

Barcelona 1992

The Barcelona 1992 Olympics did not cause a considerable increase in tourist numbers prior to the Games. The infrastructure of the city changed to such an extent that all the prerequisites for increased tourism and new conventions were fulfilled. Barcelona was transformed through the Olympics to be a major tourist attraction today.

> The overnight stays increased from 3.8 million in 1990, to 7 million in 1997, and have steadily increased thereafter. To satisfy this demand, there has been a gradual increase in the hotel infrastructure of the city of Barcelona. The number of hotel units has grown from 118 in 1990, to 148 in 1992 and to 165 in 1997. Correspondingly, there has been an increase in the available beds from 18,569 in 1990, to 25,055 in 1992 and to 28,770 in 1997. In light of these events, the fact that many consider the Olympic Games of 1992 as being a catalyst that changed the tourism prospects of the city is justifiable and demonstrates the important impact Olympic Games can have on tourism. (Papanikos, 1999)

Atlanta 1996

The overall pre- and post-Olympic visits to Atlanta by individuals who would not have visited the city without the Games is estimated at 222 000, which equals staying 2.8 million days in Atlanta. Similar to the calculations of Los Angeles, this would correspond to US$$_{.00}$ 721.3 million autonomous expenditures (Humphreys and Plummer, 1992; 1996, Table 6.2).

Sydney 2000

Australia, as mentioned above, focused on tourism. The ATC estimated US$$_{.00}$ 4,587 million in tourism export earnings between 1997 and 2004 (TFC, 1998, p. 13). However 11 September 2001 totally changed tourism and, therefore, an increase in tourists over a long-term average cannot be proven. During the Games, however, there was partly a miscalculation. Sydney OCOG, for example, booked too many hotel rooms and some of these remained empty. The very attractive 'live sites' drained locals' trade and therefore some hotels had to close their bars (Southgate, 2001, p. 41). This phenomenon is not new to Olympics. The consumption patterns of tourists and locals change during Games time. The usual entertainment industry can partly suffer from that. The Sydney Zoo, for example, had a 300 per cent decrease in visitors during Games time.

Athens 2004

The central scenario of Papanikos (1999) estimated around 6 million induced arrivals of foreign tourists during the period 1998–2011. The maximization of tourist expenses was achieved during the year of the Games, with US$1.4 billion. For the entire 14-year period, total expenditures are estimated at US$10.6 billion with an annual average of US$758 million. During the year of the Olympic Games (2004) the additional increase in gross domestic product will reach 1.4 per cent. The Olympic Games do not only improve economic indicators, but are also beneficial to society. The Olympiad in Athens and the Cultural Olympiad are expected to add significantly to the prestige and the prosperity not only of Greece, but of the whole world.

Beijing 2008

In Beijing, which is one of the most famous tourist destinations in China, there are numerous first-rate hotels and conference facilities. By 2008, star-grade hotels in Beijing are to reach 800, up from 392 in 2000, and the total number of hotel rooms will reach 130 000, up from 80 000 in 2000.

The left side of Figure 6.13 shows how a destination can be positioned through the Olympic Games. It could be the aim for 2004 to strengthen the 'Athens' or 'Greece' brand, or at least make the tourist profile more interesting. The right side shows the hard location factors. Tourism infrastructure, such as parks, pedestrian zones, sports facilities, public transportation, tourist attractions or the airport will improve. Additionally, tourism products will be developed: for example, additional sport events or exhibitions, fairs or concerts in the new facilities and congress centres.

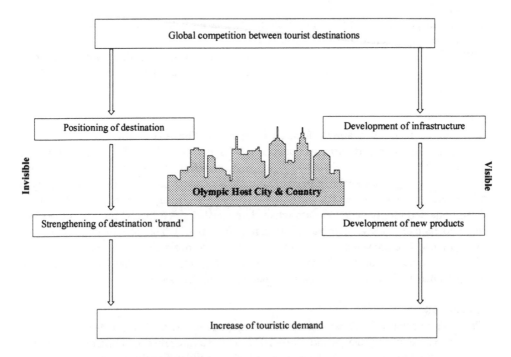

Source: Modified from Keller (2001, p. 30).

Figure 6.13   Potential 'tourism legacy' for an Olympic city/country

A new image and higher awareness, new and upgraded infrastructure and additional tourist attractions, such as those in Barcelona and Sydney (Boyle, 2001, p. 5), will increase post-Olympic tourism. However, to what extent depends on the ability to use the short Olympic impact to leverage tourism.

6.2 EXPORTS AND FOREIGN INVESTMENTS

This section discusses the business development and investment attraction of an Olympic city. Products and service exported from the Olympic region after the Games will be focused on, as well as the attraction of investments during the post-Games period.

Concerning foreign investments, until now, very little research has been done on decision-makers' perception of the Olympic city. It is not important if, and how, Olympic Games improve location factors. However, it is important how the location factors improve in the entrepreneurs' perception. Admittedly industry does not settle somewhere only as a result of hosting the Olympic Games. The Games may improve the chance that an Olympic city becomes recognized and is examined as a possible business location. The following two examples demonstrate how this can happen.

The world rediscovered the beauty and dynamism of Barcelona following the hosting of a highly successful Olympic Games. As a result, Barcelona and the entire country experienced tremendous growth in foreign investments. This resulted in a rapid rise for Barcelona with an index that doubled every year from 1986 to 1991. A total of more than 200 American and some major Japanese enterprises settled in Catalonia and its surroundings (Garcia, 1993, p. 263; Tillier, 1994, p. 33).

Following the hosting of the 1996 Olympic Games, Atlanta also became recognized as a great east coast location by many entrepreneurs. The favourable investment situation attracted foreign enterprises prior to the staging of the Olympics (Rademacher, 1996b, p. 15). It was expected that the Games would improve Atlanta's image in ways that would encourage more European, Asian and Latin American companies to locate operations in the city (Greising, 1996, p. 35; Harris, 1997 pp. 25-26; Hiskey, 1994, E7). Later, Adranovich et al. (2001, p. 125) mention 18 companies that relocated to Atlanta, and French and Disher (1997, p. 391) report that the sponsor Georgia Power alone attracted 12 enterprises to Atlanta, creating 3400 new jobs.

Harris (1997) conducted a detailed investigation of the image of Atlanta among corporate decision-makers after the 1996 Olympics. He interviewed 620 managers from 13 nations. Apart from a comparison of Atlanta to ten other American metropolises, the managers revealed that the Olympic Games generated a 17.4 per cent improvement in Atlanta's image. A mere 1.8 per cent had gained a poorer impression of Atlanta. But it is more significant that 24 per cent said: 'They now feel more favourable about the possibility of business expansion or relocation in Atlanta as a market' (Harris, 1997, p. 24). In connection with the infrastructure expansion in telecommunications, transportation, accommodation and quality of life launched by the Olympics, a host city improves its chances of being chosen as a location for industry.

Concerning exports, PricewaterhouseCoopers (2002, pp. 50-73) did some post-Games research on the Sydney 2000 Olympics. Sydney's Games planners were successful in leveraging the effect of the Olympics. Therefore Sydney 2000 will be used here as a case study. Based on the research of PricewaterhouseCoopers the post-Olympic activities were:

- The investment attraction programme called 'Investment 2000'. That attracted 45 investments, which equal US\$'$_{00}$ 391 million in inward investments.
- The 'Australian Technology Showcase'. That programme highlighted 301 innovative NSW technologies and has contributed to US\$'$_{00}$ 216.6 million in new sales, investments and exports to December 2001.
- The 'Business Club Australia' programme. That provided significant networking opportunities. It was linked to the 'Commonwealth's Trade Visitors Business' programme and attracted 16 000 visitors to events.
- The founding of the 'Olympic Commerce Centres'. These maximized the share of contracts (especially in construction) to local companies.
- By June 2001, the government had conducted seven trade missions to California, India, Singapore, Malaysia, the United Arab Emirates, New Zealand, China and Japan.
- The 'Department of State and Regional Development' has worked with NSW businesses, assisting them to win almost US\$'$_{00}$ 1,504 million in sports infrastructure and service contracts, leveraging from their experience gained from the 2000 Games.
- By June 2001 the 'Australia Sports International' programme had attracted 90 members and generated US\$'$_{00}$ 9.8 million in new exports, with a further US\$'$_{00}$ 75.2 million pending. This programme delivered an estimated 250 new export opportunities to Australian clients.

In other words, the first post-Olympic year brought the state of NSW approximately US\$'$_{00}$ 2256 million of exports and foreign investments. The main share of this money stems from exports of sport infrastructure and know-how (US\$'$_{00}$ 1504 million). However, it was lucky for Australia that the upcoming Olympics were awarded to Beijing. These Olympics continue to represent a major opportunity for Australian businesses to capitalize on its own Games experience. The greatest opportunities lie in winning business in the first two years of the development phase of future Olympic hosts. Then Australia's Olympic skills and knowledge will be highly sought after (PricewaterhouseCoopers, 2002, p. 68). Therefore the Asian Games 2006, first planned for Doha, but might be passed to Kuala Lumpur, will offer further chances. While Doha (Bahrain) was forced to construct almost all sport facilities from new, Kuala Lumpur is in the Commonwealth and there will be huge time pressure to organize the Games, but however, most of the facilities already exist from the Commonwealth Games 1998.

While exports are physical and easy to measure, the establishment of new trade relations is difficult to evaluate. The variables which determine import and export are manifold. However, as seen in Sydney, Olympic Games can simply trigger new trade missions. Although it would be wrong to trace the South Korean foreign trade surplus between 1986 and 1989 solely back to the Olympics, presumably, the Games contributed their share. Even if the Olympics did not directly affect the national income, they involved a lasting benefit by proving the effectiveness of the Korean economy (Federal Statistical Office, 1995; Kwag, 1988). It is emphasized that the Olympic Games were only one element in influencing the decision to resume economic relations between the Eastern bloc and South Korea. However, the Games served as a 'catalyst for improvement of relations between East Europe, the Soviet Union and South Korea' (Goldstar, 1988a; Kramar, 1994; NN, 1988d). Furthermore McBeth (1988d) and Kim (1990) describe the establishment of international relations and formalization of trade relations.

The extent of new trade relations depends, among other aspects, on the image of the host city or country and its products. The Olympic Games offer a special chance for the local Olympics organizers to reposition previously weak products. The Games not only specifically provide sponsors and future licensees, but also more generally all enterprises of the host country, with the opportunity to improve their own image. The Munich 1972 Olympics were a 'single huge public relations enterprise for the Federal Republic' (NN, 1972c). Seoul 1988 eased tensions in trade relations between the Eastern states and Korea. Both Korea and Spain were able to demonstrate their high level of technological development to the entire world (Goldstar, 1988a; Kim et al., 1989; Vall, 1995). For China, which has just entered the World Trade Organization (WTO), this aspect offers a great chance that not only will Chinese brands gain a better image (as was the case for the Koreans after 1988 and the Spanish after 1992) but membership expands the market. That will bring China real economic impact and not just a good image.

7. Investments and the reconstruction of a city: burdens and opportunities

Autonomous investments form the second part of the primary economic impact. Owing to the lack of money in the public sector, ever more politicians develop plans for major festivals, which can be seen as a new type of politics – the politic of mega events (Burbank et al., 2001; Häussermann, 1993). Big sports events such as the Olympics are 'festivals' for all citizens. For a short time, the host city gets worldwide recognition, welcomes international guests and offers experiences which usually can only be seen on television. But behind the fun there are often strong municipal political considerations. The staging of Olympics triggers measures outside sports, such as city development or embellishment. Quite frequently the Olympic planning overrides rigid political, functional and technical relationships, and provides tremendous financial rewards, which cities could not have experienced otherwise.

This chapter will show how the Olympic Games trigger different impacts, which affect urban development. However, there is no general rule to guide city development through Olympics. City development is a slow and continuous process. Usually less than 1 per cent of a city's physical characteristics change during a single year (Siebel, 1994, p. 8). Depending on the size of the necessary Olympic-related structure, far greater changes can temporarily occur.

7.1 URBAN RECONSTRUCTION THROUGH OLYMPIC GAMES

Every city has a different infrastructure. Once in a while changes in the environment (industrialization, immigration, wars, and so on) or 'festivals' (for example, world exhibitions, royal events, sports events) trigger large impacts on urban development. These help form the history and structure of each city in different ways. Depending on its structure a city may stage large sports events without a need for change. For example, Los Angeles was able to stage the Olympic Games in 1984 with minimal investments in its infrastructure (Essex and Chalkley, 1998, p. 192). However, Munich 1972, Barcelona 1992 and Athens 2004 had to implement major developments in order to host the Games. All multi-sports events, which are staged in one city, cause a very compact impact and develop different parts of a city simultaneously.

Depending on the size of the city and its urban history, upcoming Olympics create different developmental pressures. Table 7.1 classifies typical Games-related investments.

Table 7.1   Classification of investments in host cities

The Olympics require ...	This leads to investments in ...	... and provides the host city with ...	Financing tends to be ...
Olympic and media villages	house building industry	additional housing area	private
Sports facilities	leisure time and entertainment offers	higher quality of living (improved leisure time and sports for all facilities)	public
IBC and MPC	office buildings and/or convention centres	convention centres, schools, office and administration buildings	public
Telecommunication	construction industry	updated fibre optic cable system, power systems, Internet and mobile phone capacity	public
Transportation	public transportation, road construction, airport expansion	higher quality of living through time saving and positive ecological effects (for example, air, dust)	public
Atmosphere	renovations/improvements and creation of parks, pedestrian zones	higher quality of living through good atmosphere and recreational areas	private
Tourist industry	tourist attractions, leisure facilities and accommodation	more hotel beds and tourist attractions	private
	⇩	⇩	
	These investments lead to employment in the building sector, additional income and additional tax revenues. Post-Olympic events can be organized more easily and bring new impacts.	This leads to an interest in the city beyond the region (foreign investments and trade, selection as convention location, tourism) involving additional employment, income and tax revenues.	

It is obvious due to the scarce means available that an OCOG itself can only pay for the overlays of the sport facilities, but not for new construction. Public or private property developers have to finance all big Games-related projects, such as the construction of an Olympic village. In most cases, the village is sold after the Olympics as happened in Munich, Montreal, Seoul, Barcelona and Sydney (Brunet, 1993; Herzog, 1993; Kim et al., 1989; McBeth 1988a; Medialdea, 1993; Montreal OCOG, 1976; Reth, 1993; Woo, 1988). Depending on the population development and the housing situation of a host city, the question arises whether the new construction of a village is necessary or whether the renting of accommodation facilities (such as students' residence halls in 1984 and 1996) should be preferred. With a housing surplus caused by a decreasing population of a city, renting or temporary structures should be the choice. With a lack of housing facilities in expanding cities, such as in Seoul 1988, the building of new houses is the better alternative. Indeed, in Seoul it was possible to make a profit by selling the Olympic and the media village for US$$_{'00}$ 264 million as early as before the Games (Seoul OCOG, 1988). However, in Barcelona, even a year after the Olympics, 33 per cent of the apartments were not sold (Reth, 1993).

Therefore it is important that a city compares its existing long-term development plan with the necessary Olympic-related structural requirements before it starts to bid and exposes that weakness. The Olympic Games generate revenues, which are often enough to cover the operational costs, but only very few investments. Most investments must be covered by public or private entities. However, if the Olympics are able to expedite municipal development in a desired direction, a bid is justified.

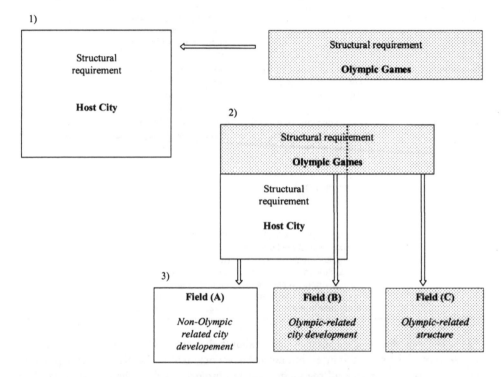

Figure 7.1 City developments and development through Olympics

Figure 7.1 shows three fields. Field (A) represents the city development that is planned regardless of the Olympics. Field (B) the structure needed for the Olympics, which is anyhow planned for the development of the city. At least the construction of Games-related facilities should fit in the economic and social development plan. Field (C) shows the necessary structure that is only needed for the Olympics and does not fit the city's long-term development plans. These can be single facilities, but also over capacity in structures such as public transportation, tourist accommodation or spectator stands at sport facilities. Investments only pay for themselves and the related follow-up costs can only be financed if the expanded capacities can be used after the Olympics (Daume, 1976, p. 155; interview, Tröger, 1998). Otherwise, they would also lack their political justification (German, 1993). It is crucial if field (C) is so expensive that fields (A) and (B) are negatively affected. In case field (C) is too large and develops a structure, which is not needed in the long term, there should be no bid for the Olympics. This scenario is relevant for developing countries and newly industrialized countries that currently would like to bid for Olympic Games.

Olympics trigger only a one-time surge of development. Huge parts of the new structure will not be used for their original purpose after the end of the Olympics and Paralympics. The Olympic structure of field (B) develops the city and is socially and economically sustainable because it is needed anyhow. The field (C) structure has to be rebuilt. Either the structure was temporary and disappears after the Games or it has to be maintained. Then the city should try to pull in other sports events in order to have follow-up impacts. By this the city risks developing a structure that does not conform to that of the long-term development plan. That means the impact of city development proceeded in the wrong direction or something was developed which was not needed. Both create unnecessary costs and unused oversized facilities.

7.2 IMPACTS OF OLYMPICS ON THE URBAN STRUCTURE

Olympics create different impacts which themselves change the urban development.

The arrows in Figure 7.2 show the impacts of Olympics on urban development. The urban functionalism of the 'Charta from Athens' (1933) demands cities serve four functions: 'Housing, Labour, Recreation and Transportation' (Siebel, 1994, p. 1). Soon it became clear that the healing of urban problems through splitting a city into functional areas changed the quality of urban space. City centres became empty and the rather rational structure of living, working and recreational areas was reached by destroying city history and urbanity as defined by variety and vitality. Having this in mind, Olympic Games have the potential to develop the urban structure in all functional areas but with another quality (Figure 7.3).

The primary structure is often built only for the Olympics. Therefore it is important to plan the post-Olympic utilization. It is interesting to see what Pierre de Coubertin thought as early as 1911: 'It would be very unfortunate, if the often exaggerated expenses incurred for the most recent Olympiads. A sizeable part of which represented the construction of permanent buildings, which were moreover unnecessary – temporary structures would fully suffice ...' (Coubertin, 1911).

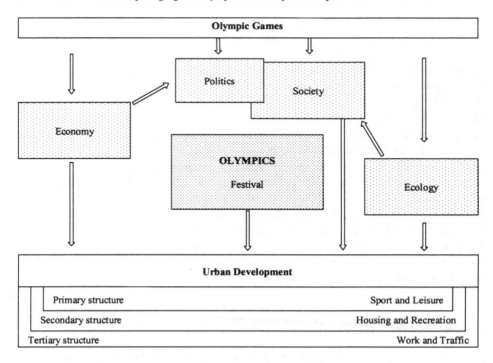

Figure 7.2   Impacts of Olympics on urban development

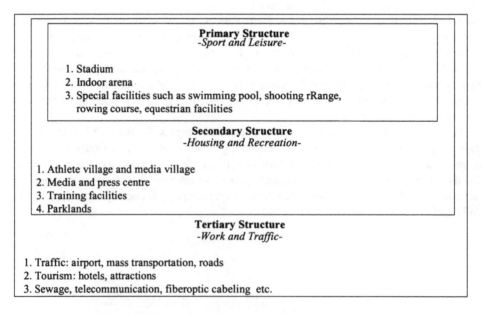

Figure 7.3   Primary, secondary and tertiary structural demands of Olympics on cities

The construction of stadiums started at the beginning of the twentieth century. That is why big cities today already have a large stadium. However, these are not sufficient any more in terms of size, atmosphere, service and hospitality facilities. Modern sport arenas are no longer only functional buildings, but create urban stages for extravaganzas. Therefore the stadium has often to be reconstructed for the Olympics, as in Athens 2004. The 1950s indoor sport arenas were built in cities (Wimmer, 1975, p. 43). Unfortunately, today many of them are in the same deplorable conditions as stadiums. Special sport facilities (for example for swimming, shooting, rowing or cycling) are often not available in cities and need to be constructed for Olympic Games. In the early 1970s, the requirements placed on sports facilities increased. The fact that many sports were shifted from outdoors into halls changed the demand for sports venues in the host city both in terms of quantity and structure. In short, evolution has progressed from a need for stadiums at the very early Games to the additional need for halls in the 1960s to the present day need for special facilities such as velodromes (details in Schmidt, 2003). For special venues, however, social and economic sustainability frequently causes problems, with the consequence that more of these facilities and/or stands will have to be built temporarily. Table 7.2 classifies the sports venues required to host Olympic Games.

Table 7.2   Classification of Olympic venues

Types of Olympic venues	Types of events	Remarks on location costs
Olympic stadium	Ceremonies, track and field, football	In most cases, the host cities already have a large stadium. Nevertheless, the Olympic stadium was often newly erected. As the centre of the Games, it should have a capacity of at least 80 000 spectators. If the city cannot provide an adequate stadium, it must build a new one or the OCOG must temporarily extend an existing one.
Olympic hall	Volleyball, handball, basketball, gymnastics	With the exception of the Deutschlandhalle of 1936, no major halls were built in Germany until 1956. Since then many sports have moved into halls which have a capacity of up to 25 000 spectators today. Without a follow-up demand for the Olympic hall, a city should carefully re-examine whether it should host the Games.
Multi-purpose hall, fair hall, convention or congress centre	Taekwondo, judo, wrestling, boxing, weightlifting, fencing, badminton, table-tennis, basketball, volleyball	Many of these sports were outdoor sports for a long time. But due to increased professionalism, they were also moved to halls. At the Olympic Games, these sports are frequently staged in multipurpose halls, trade fair halls or convention centres because the host cities do not have enough large halls. Since these sports neither require large surfaces nor large stands, renting existing sites seems a suitable solution.
Large halls	Volleyball, handball, basketball	In view of the many qualifying matches, a single Olympic hall is not sufficient for these sports. Since spectator capacities for preliminary rounds can be lower, smaller halls can be rented or staged in other cities.
Small halls	Training	Today about 100 training facilities are required for the Olympic Games. These should already exist in adequate numbers in large cities. Many halls can be rented from schools/clubs/cities.

Types of Olympic venues	Types of events	Remarks on location costs
Smaller stadia	Football, hockey, training	Host cities mostly have smaller stadia. In addition, football matches are frequently hosted in other cities of the host country. For preliminary rounds, stadium capacities can be smaller since experience has shown that for these sports the capacities were not used to the full.
Outside; green areas for temp. conversions	Equestrian, archery, beach volleyball	These facilities can be erected temporarily on free grounds at low costs.
Olympic villages	Athletes, press, youth camp	An OCOG can only rent existing facilities (universities) or new buildings which were constructed by private industry or the public sector.
Special facilities	Swimming stadium	Swimming stadia have been used since Melbourne 1956 (with the exception of Rome 1960). Apart from the Olympic hall, they are another large cost factor for a city.
	Velodrome	For a long time, the cycling track was inside the Olympic stadium before it was moved to an independent covered venue in Rome 1960 for the first time (Wimmer, 1975). In most host cities, the velodrome must still be constructed.
	Shooting	In most cases, constructed especially for the Olympics.
	Equestrian	In most cases, constructed especially for the Olympics.
	Baseball	In countries where baseball is less popular football stadiums could be changed temporarily to provide the stadium and the training grounds.
	Tennis	In most cases, constructed especially for the Olympics.
	Canoeing slalom	At first, Sydney 2000 declined this competition because there would be no follow-up demand for the venue in Australia and the costs for a temporary facility would be too high. Finally the facility got constructed with large subsidies and is after the Olympics a highly used facility (interview, Feldhoff, 2004).
	Regatta course, sailing port	Today, these courses are designed artificially. Due to numerous building measures at the shore they are often very expensive. Like the sailing competitions which can be hosted in another city of the host country, the IOC also allows the use of regatta courses in other cities. Thus, a city with a follow-up demand for the facilities can be chosen.

On the occasion of the Grenoble 1968 Olympics, Brundage said that 'the modern buildings are a blessing for those cities which host the Olympics' (Wimmer, 1975). Nowadays, however, they are often a great burden. Until Montreal 1976, the idea of architectural challenges prevailed when constructing sports venues. While this was reversed for the Los Angeles 1984 Olympics when the organizers restricted themselves to what was absolutely necessary, Seoul 1988 was in a conflict 'between budgetary or sports considerations vs. artistic considerations' (Kim, 1990). In Barcelona 1992 and Atlanta 1996 both financial as well as sports aspects were the main criteria when constructing sports facilities.

Table 7.3 Existence of sports facilities and Olympic villages in the host cities under review

	Munich 1972	Montreal 1976	L.A. 1984	Seoul 1988	Barcelona 1992	Atlanta 1996	Sydney 2000	Athens 2004	Beijing 2008
Olympic stadium	new	new	existing	existing	existing	new	new	existing	new
Olympic hall	new	new	existing	new	new	existing	new	existing	new
Multi-purpose halls; trade fair halls	new / existing	N/A	existing	new; existing	new	existing	new / existing	new	existing
Large halls	new / existing	N/A	existing	new	new / existing	new / existing	existing	new	new / existing
Small halls	existing	N/A	existing	existing	new; existing	existing	existing	existing/ temp./ new	existing
Smaller stadiums	existing	new / existing	existing	existing	existing	new / existing	new / existing	new / existing	new / existing
Outside; green areas for temp. conversions	new	N/A	existing	N/A	N/A	existing	existing	new	existing
Olympic village	new	new	existing	new	new	existing	new	new	new
Special facilities									
- *swimming*	new	new	new	new	existing	new	new	existing	new
- *velodrome*	new	new	new	new	existing	new	new	existing	new
- *shooting*	new	N/A	existing	existing	new	new	new	new	new
- *equestrian*	new	new	existing	new	existing	new	new	new	new
- *baseball*	-	N/A	existing	N/A	existing	existing	new	new	existing
- *tennis*	-	-	new	new	new	new	new	(temp.)	new
- *white water*	new	N/A	existing	N/A	new	new	new	new/ existing	new
- *regatta / canoeing*	new	new	existing	new	new	new	new	new	N/A
- *sailing*	new	N/A	existing	new	new	new	existing/ new	new	new

Sources: Preuss (2000a); Bidding Committee Beijing (2001); Athens OCOG (2002).

Table 7.3 offers a survey of the facilities which already existed and which had to be newly built in the host cities. The word 'new' means both permanent and temporary structures, the word 'existing' means all facilities, which existed before the Games even if they had to be modernized or extended.

A look at the bids of several Olympics reveals that the number of sports facilities already existing in the bid cities varied greatly (Table 7.4)

Table 7.4   Existing facilities of bid cities (percentages)

2000		2004		2008	
City 2000	Existing during bid	City 2004	Existing during bid	City 2008	Existing during bid
Sydney	*44*	*Athens*	*72*	*Beijing*	*48*
Berlin	24	Buenos Aires	80	Cairo	71.5
Brasilia	48	Cape Town	58	Havana	80.5
Istanbul	12	Istanbul	35	Istanbul	34
Manchester	60	Lille	62	Kuala Lumpur	91
Beijing	68	Rio de Janeiro	60	Osaka	43
		Rome	79	Paris	53.5
		Seville	56	Seville	71.5
		San Juan	64	Toronto	52
		Stockholm	83		
		St. Petersburg	53		

Sources: Bacia (1997); IOC (1993b; 1997e; 2000c).

It can be seen from Table 7.4 how difficult the measurement of facilities is. That becomes obvious by looking at the changes in Beijing and Istanbul. What was declared as existing for the Games in 2000 was judged differently by the 'Olympic acceptance working group' in regard to the Games in 2008.

In the course of the Olympiads, however, the number of already existing facilities has steadily risen above the number of those that need to be newly erected for the Games. It is therefore reasonable to assume that the availability of the sports facilities within the major cities of the world will continue to improve. In the future, the hosting of the Olympic Games will primarily lead to modernization and investments in special facilities. However, the challenge is to meet the requirements of the IFs concerning the size of the spectator stands (Table 7.5) and the quality of the supporting structures. Past Games showed that temporary constructions could be used in order to meet both the requirements and a sustainable size for post-Olympic demand.

State-of-the-art technology enables the construction of temporary facilities. While this is not new for spectator seating, it is for the facilities. In Fukuoka 2001 the swimming world championship were staged in an exhibition hall by utilizing a plastic pool (NN, 2001a, p. 43). Another example is the velodrome in Atlanta 1996, which was transported to Florida after the Games. However, the demand for primary structures (Figure 7.3) is an important impact for the development of cities. Modern facilities create an urban living memorial that preserves for decades symbols that are a visible memory of the Olympics for citizens and tourists. Furthermore only permanent structures create an 'Olympic legacy' for sports.

Table 7.5 Size of spectator stands during Games time by sports

	Sydney 2000	Athens 2004	Beijing 2008	IOC standard 2012
		Seating Capacity		
Archery	4500	5 500	5000	4000
Athletics	115 600	75 000	80 000	60 000
Athletics (Marathon)	(Finish) 115 600	(Finish) 45 000	(Finish) 80 000	(Finish) 60 000
Badminton	6000	5500	7500	5000
Baseball	(Court 1) 14 000 (Court 2) 4000	(Court 1) 9 000 (Court 2) 4000	(Court 1) 25 000 (Court 2) 15 000	8000
Basketball	(Finals) 20 000 10 000	(Finals) 18 000 15 000	(Finals) 20 000	(Finals) 12 000 8000
Beach Volleyball	10 000	10 000	(Court 1) 10 000 (Court 2) 7500	12 000
Boxing	(Ring 1) 10 000 (Ring 2) 7500	8 000	13 000	6000
Canoe-Kayak Slalom	12 500	5000	15 000	8000
Canoe-Kayak Flatwater	22 000 – 24 000	14 000	20 000	10 000
Cycling (Track)	6000	5000	6000	5000
Diving	17 500	6500	17 000	5000
Equestrian	(Jumping) 50 000 (Dressage) 50 000 (Cross Country) 40 000	(Jumping) 20 000 (Dressage) 8000 (Cross Country) 40 000	(Jumping) 30 000 (Dressage) 30 000 (Cross Country) 50 000	(Jumping) 12 000 (Dressage) 12 000 (Cross Country) 0
Fencing	10 000	(Final) 5000 3500	10 000	(Final) 4000 2000
Football	(Final) 115 600 42 000/37 000/ 20 000	(Final) 75 000 28 000/20 000/ 27 000/17 000	(Final) 80 000 72 000/40 000/ 60 000/35 000/ 60 000/80 000	(Final) 50 000 20 000/20 000/ 20 000/20 000
Gymnastic (rhythmic)	6000	6000	19 000	5000
Gymnastics (artistic & trampoline)	16 900	15 000	19 000	12 000
Handball	(Final) 10 000 6000	(Final) 15 000 8000	(Final) 19 000 7000	(Final) 8000 5000
Hockey	15 000	(Court 1) 12 000 (Court 2) 3000	(Court 1) 15 000 (Court 2) 5000	(Court 1) 8000 (Court 2) 5000
Judo	9000	8000	9000	6000
Modern Pentathlon	(Swimming) 17 500 (Ride/Run) 11 000 (Fencing) 6000 (Shooting) 6500	(Swimming) 2000 (Ride/Run) 5000 (Fence/Shoot) 4500	(Swimming) 6000 (Rid/Run) 40 000 (Fence/Shoot) 5000	(Swimming) 12 000 (Rid/Run) 10 000 (Fence/Shoot) 3000

	Sydney 2000	Athens 2004	Beijing 2008	IOC standard 2012
		Seating Capacity		
Rowing	27 000	14 000	20 000	10 000
Sailing	Unlimited	3000	9000	0
Shooting	7000	8000	(Final) 2500 6500	3000
Softball	8000	5000	11 000	8000
Swimming	17 500	11 000	17 000	12 000
Synchronized	17 500	5000	17 000	5000
Table Tennis	5000	6000	10 000	5000
Teakwondo	5000	8000	9000	5000
Tennis	(Center Court) 10 000 (incl. all courts) 17 400	(Centre Court) 8000 (Court 1) 4000 (Court 2) 2000	(Centre Court) 12 000 (Court 1) 5000 (Court 2) 3000	(Centre Court) 10 000 (Court 1) 5000 (Court 2) 3000
Triathlon	N/A	3000	10 000	2000
Volleyball	(Finals) 11 000 6 000	14 000	(Final) 19 000 18 000/10 000	12 000
Water Polo	3900	(Outdoor) 11 000 (Indoor) 6500	(Final) 17 000 6000	5 000
Weightlifting	3800	5000	5400	5000
Wrestling	9000 / 3800	9300	10 000	6000

Sources: Athens OCOG (Nov, 2002); Sydney OCOG (2001); Beijing Bidding Committee 2008 (2001); IOC (2004, 36–7).

The development of the secondary structure is often affected by multi-sports events. In particular it is the function 'Housing'. For Olympic Games whole neighbourhoods are constructed for the athletes and media representatives. In Sydney the Olympic village hosted 15 000 athletes in 1113 new houses and the media village accommodated 6000 media people in Lidcombe. The private sector spent approximately US$$_{,00}$ 284.3 million for the Olympic village (Olympic Co-ordination Authority, 2002, p. 17). However, there is the question of the social distribution of new housing units. In Munich 1972, the Olympic village was built for a socially weak population (Daume, 1976). In other cities, the Olympic villages were mostly sold to the middle and lower-upper social classes. In Los Angeles 1984 and Atlanta 1996, the villages were returned to their former usage as student residence halls. In general, the construction of villages results in a gentrification of this part of the city in contrast to the previous use of the area.

Additionally, the secondary structure covers the function 'recreation'. The arrangement of several sport facilities in one city is often accomplished through sports parks. These parks offer not only a diverse high-quality sport and cultural programme for prosperous spectators, but also spaces for 'sports for all', recreational and leisure areas through parkland and service infrastructure around the facilities.

The tertiary structure is the periphery important to stage large sports events. This is for example tourism structure. Tourists arrive at the airport or train station, stay in hotels, use public transportation and enjoy the city by night. To set up that structure two welcome effects can be seen, new employment and a better traffic situation. In most cities the tertiary structure necessary to stage Olympic Games is not in existence. Therefore, the Games have come to assume an increased significance in urban renewal strategies (Chalkley and Essex, 1999, p. 371).

In their enthusiasm to be chosen as host city in competition with other bid cities, many cities succumb to starting huge projects. Olympic Games politicians push to build sport facilities and also start construction programmes for secondary and tertiary structure, which sometimes are in conflict with the city's long-term development plans. One might argue that exactly this motivation has created all the huge symbols that are the visible memories of the Olympics. Certainly today many of these are tourist attractions such as the tent roof of the Munich Olympic Park or the Olympic pool in Tokyo. However, that enthusiasm also can ruin a city financially as, for example, with the realization of the idea of 'Parc Maisonneuve' in Montreal that failed after 40 years of planning, due to gigantic architecture. Also, in Barcelona, the required size of some sports facilities and the tendency towards representation exceeded in several cases the need and the consideration of neighbourhoods (Meyer-Künzel, 2001, p. 437). This aspect will be focused on in detail in the next chapter.

7.2.1 Impact of Society and Politics on Urban Development

The idea to bid for Olympic Games often stems from politicians who hope to achieve new impetus for urban development (Preuss, 2003b).

From the moment a city is chosen as a host city it suffers great time constraints. The event cannot be postponed and the entire country and world anticipates the Games. If a city did not succeed in changing its infrastructure in time to meet the demands of hosting the Olympic Games, national or even worldwide criticism would be the result and the image of the city would be severely damaged. The time constraints and the possible 'disgrace' push urban development so strongly that the period of 'normal' development is skipped. Munich is said to have experienced a development thrust of 15 years during the six years of the preparatory phase for the Olympics. In the traffic sector, projects that were to be realized in 1990 were finished a whole generation earlier (Daume, 1976; Geipel et al., 1993). In Barcelona, urgent investments would not have been carried out in such a short time at such an early stage without the Olympics. The city gained ten years and the traffic problem, for example, was solved in only five years (Cox et al., 1994).

Frequently, the external pressure solves internal urban conflicts. If there were immovable positions between planners, politicians and citizens regarding important projects, these are now weakened by compromises. Everybody fears negative effects on one's image, such as those Montreal suffered when the international press reported on the stadium, which had not been finished for the Games (Wright, 1978). The Olympics often create a new unity directed towards the outside. If the city, region or nation hosting the Games had a low level of international awareness or a certain unwanted image, there now is the desire to show the world what they are capable of. The prospect of international praise and recognition releases unexpected feats of strength. Seoul 1988 was a demonstration directed at the contender Japan, Barcelona 1992 was an expression of the striving for local autonomy in Spain (Chalkley and Essex, 1999, p. 371) and Atlanta 1996 was an expression of the suppressed Southern/Northern states problem. What was always at issue was to show not only the world but also certain other groups one's own strength.

Regarding the acceleration effect in urban development, the following can be stated: on the one hand, there is an advantage of non-bureaucratic cooperation and the uniting of all forces to achieve a single aim. On Athens 2004 Höhler (1997) states: 'The great infrastructure projects which had developed only sluggishly for years like the new subway, bypasses and the future major airport can now gain impetus from the pressing date of the Olympics.' On the other hand, however, there is the threat of irreversible planning errors due to time pressure or infringements of social principles by special regulations (Lenskyj, 2000). Additionally, there is the above mentioned danger of suppressing justified reservations for absolutely necessary projects if the mutual compromises of the representatives of interested parties merely serve the aim of promoting urban development for the Olympic Games. Olympic Games give urban planners a reason to evacuate whole suburbs or relocate the people living there. This was at least true for Atlanta 1996, Seoul 1988 and Munich 1972 (Preuss, 2000a).

As regards the social impact of Olympics on urban development, Häussermann (1993) and Burbank et al. (2001) describe the chance that Olympics can provide international prestige. Additionally, the Games can move the central highlight back to the city centre. The Olympics can create an identification and pride among the citizens of the host city. Furthermore, by providing a common area of interest, sport encourages communication and information exchange between socially differentiated groups. Contact with groups from other communities increases the social network of city residents (Cowie, 1987, p. 43). This supports the view that people keep living in the city and do not move into suburbs. This is particularly important for entrepreneurs who may intensify their effort to develop and invest in a city if they identify with it.

The commonly held perspective of many government authorities of the social benefit of mega-events is that the question of enlivening public spaces and extending usage of downtown areas after 5 p.m. are as important as breaking down barriers and turning barren spaces into bustling places. There is a chance to achieve that through siting sports facilities near the city centre.

However, potential negative impacts also have to be considered (Hall, 1989; 1994; Lenskyj, 2002; Rutheiser, 1996). All the changes in the city required to stage the Games become so important that the interests of socially weaker groups are frequently ignored. Socially deprived groups of the population are especially affected by airport expansion, road building or the decision on the location of the athletes' village. Moreover, the people who are often seriously impacted by Olympic Games are those who are least able to form community groups and protect their own interests (Hall, 1992, p. 70).

7.2.2 Impact of Ecology on Urban Development

Environmental issues emerged in relation to Olympic bids as early as 1972, when Denver had to turn down the IOC's offer to host the Olympic Winter Games in 1976 due to politicized environmental issues (Lenskyj, 2000). From then on, green groups undermined bids such as in Toronto 1996 or Rome 2004. The IOC started to warn bidding cities for the 2008 Olympics that 'environmental protection is an area where Candidature Cities often experience tough public scrutiny and opposition' as early as 1999 (IOC, 1999c). However, the ecological matter became very important. 'In 1998, four European groups organized the International Network against Olympic Games and Commercial Sports ... Their opposition was based, for the most part, on environmental concerns' (Lenskyj, 2000). Modern technology facilitated cheap and speedy international networking between groups in Nagano, Sydney, Toronto, Salt Lake and elsewhere. In this venture the Network carries on the work.

However, it was not before 1991 that the IOC amended its Olympic Charter to cover environmental issues (Lenskyj, 2000). On the occasion of the first World Conference on Sport and the Environment in Lausanne in 1995, J.A. Samaranch expressly stated that the IOC considered environmental aspects as a third column of its future work apart from sport and culture (Balderstone, 2001; Jägemann, 1997; Kidane, 1997). Soon after that meeting the IOC formed the 'Sport and Environment Commission', to advise future organisers of the Olympic Games (Samaranch interviewed in Kühnle, 1996). It is only ten years that the Olympic Movement has striven for the protection of the environment. In the early 1990s, there were two significant developments. The 1994 Lillehammer OCOG, faced with a difficult environmental issue, joined with environmental groups, bringing them into the fold, to develop alternative plans and a solid programme of environmental considerations and actions. In 1993, the Sydney Bid focused on the ecological compatibility of the Games (Atkinson, 1997; Prasad, 1999). With the 'Environmental Guidelines for the Olympic Summer Games' a document was prepared which could almost be called a philosophical basis. It considers economic criteria for sustained developments (construction of sports facilities, energy/water/waste/air concepts) as well as for the event's organization (merchandising/ ticketing/ catering/ waste management/ transportation/ noise) (Environment Committee Sydney Olympic 2000 Bid Limited, 1993). The issue of how to judge the environmental performance of the Sydney 2000 'Green Games' has caused heated debate in the green movement. The irony of locating the Olympics on a toxic waste site has fuelled scepticism around the world about the validity of the Green Games image. Greenpeace's 'Olympic Report Card' has assessed Sydney's 'Green Games' with a 'C-rating'. Good marks have been given for subjects such as solar energy in the athletes' village and the Millennium Park, energy efficiency and environmental design in the athletes' village and Olympic venues, train line expansions and airport link, treatment of 400 tons of toxic dioxin waste, elimination or reduction of PVC in the athletes' village, the Olympic water recycling system and temporary housing in the athletes' village. Other opportunities have been missed. There was extensive use of PVC in temporary venues, a lack of commitment to natural gas buses, GM Holden completely failed to provide less polluting vehicles, ice-cream wrappers did not comply with the waste strategy, all venues used ozone-depleting air conditioning and Homebush Bay remains one of the most toxic waterways in the world (Greenpeace, 2000). The greatest impact that was missed was the avoidance of ozone-destructive chemicals in Olympic venues, which would have provided a great showcase for this technology and use the 'Olympic Spotlight as an opportunity to force companies to make changes they might not otherwise have moved on' (Rich, 2000).

In conclusion, the Sydney Games did not really improve Sydney's main ongoing environmental problems such as air and water quality and a lack of biodiversity (Weirick, 1999; Lenskyj, 2000). However, the living conditions in Sydney improved through additional recreational sites. For Athens 2004 Greenpeace has been successful in putting pressure on Coca-Cola's HFC coolers. The company announced that their equipment will be HFC-free world wide in 2004. Furthermore, the Sydney Olympics 2000 Bid Limited developed environmental guidelines.

In future, all cities bidding to host the Games will need to include further-reaching environmental considerations in their plans. This raised the hurdle for bid committees (Balderstone, 2001).

The environmental protection in the Host City Contract for Beijing 2008 is already much more strictly formulated than in the Athens 2004 contract (IOC, 1997d, II para. 18; 2001e, II, para. 18). That might have been the reason why the bid committee of Beijing formulated that 'Green Games' is one of the three key themes for the Beijing 2008 Olympic Games' (Bidding Committee Beijing 2008, 2001). Beijing plans to invest US$$_{.01}$ 7037 billion in environmental projects (Xianpeng, 2003, p. 228). Today the Olympic Charter states:

> that the Olympic Games are held in conditions which demonstrate a responsible concern for environmental issues and encourages the Olympic Movement to demonstrate a responsible concern for environmental issues, takes measures to reflect such concern in its activities and educates all those connected with the Olympic Movement as to the importance of sustainable development. (IOC, 2003d, Rule 13, para. 2)

Depending on the ecological situation in the host city prior to the Olympics, there are different intangible benefits as well as tangible and intangible costs incurred by the Games. In Table 7.6, the Olympics cannot be assessed individually, but the ecological costs and benefits caused by the Olympics are outlined.

Depending on the situation in the host city, the Olympics may have an overall surplus of ecological costs or ecological benefits. When the locations of Olympic venues and Olympic parks since Munich 1972 are examined in detail, it becomes obvious that all host cities of the Olympic Games tried to choose sites which were disused or had to be decontaminated (Table 7.7). This fact is not surprising since the construction of new sports facilities requires space in the vicinity of the city centre and only land with a former industrial usage is affordable for this purpose. City planners often want to move sport facilities to the city centre in order to revive a part of that centre. Additionally, parks and sport facilities develop 'recreation' areas in the middle of a hectic city and people do not need to leave the city to relax. Often run-down districts, or places in the city ring that industrialized society has put around the city centres from the middle of the past century onwards, are spaces for new construction near the city centre.

Table 7.6   Ecological effects of Olympic Games

Benefits	Costs
OCOG	**OCOG**
• 'Green image'	• Covering individual environmental projects
City population	*City population*
• recreational value (public parks) • Quality of living in the city • Less noise due to new traffic concept • Reduced emissions due to new traffic concept • Better quality of water • Environmental education of population • Environmentally sound construction of villages and sports facilities by adhering to the environmental guidelines	• Noise through construction/operation of sports facilities • Higher emissions through construction/tourism • Socially unjust crowding out, for example park instead of nursery school or kindergarden • Sealing off of land • Possible destruction of nature/water reserves through traffic links/new sports facilities
City	*City*
• Improved 'green image' • Realization of long-planned redevelopment programmes • Benefits from Olympic environmental projects	• Investments in environmental projects

Table 7.7   Changed land utilization caused by Olympic Games

	Previous utilization of selected areas (Ecological view)	Post-Games utilization of selected areas (Benefit for the population)
Munich 1972	Disused estate, rubble, wasteland	Olympic park, traffic connection, recreational area, housing
Montreal 1976	Wasteland	Olympic park, recreational area
Seoul 1988	Contaminated site (Chamsil, Han River)	Olympic park, leisure time venues (sports facilities), water purification, recreational area
Barcelona 1992	Decaying industrial site, old railway lines, run-down port, wasteland	Housing area, port atmosphere, parks, services complex, recreational area, sport
Atlanta 1996	Contaminated site (city centre)	Office buildings, recreational area
Sydney 2000	Contaminated site, wasteland, dump site	Olympic park, residential area, recreational area, 100 000 trees and shrubs planted
Athens 2004	Airport region, military base and industrial site at coastal area	Recreational area, wetland ecosystem

Sources: Lee (1989); Environment Committee, Sydney Olympic 2000 Bid Limited (1993); Garcia (1993); Geipel et al. (1993); NN (1997g); Dunn and Mc Guirk (1999); Meyer-Künzel (2001); Pyrgiotis (2001).

The redevelopment of these areas causes high costs but the ecological benefit from the upgrading of the area may compensate for the costs in the long term. It is clear that the Olympics are used to solve urban problems and this is an essential portion of the macroeconomic benefit of Olympic Games. The time pressure to prepare for the

Olympics may, on the other hand, force existing environmental guidelines to be ignored or crowd out other, ecologically better, projects.

Olympic Games often have additional environmentally positive effects besides just cleaning dumpsites. For example, for the Rome 1960 Olympic Games a new municipal water supply system was constructed. In Tokyo the Games brought a new water supply system, three sewage disposal systems, and garbage collections took place. In Seoul the Han River was cleaned and an environmental beautification programme was started. The Olympic Games of 1988 introduced 389 new parks and 152 refurbished parks to the citizens (Chalkley and Essex, 1999, pp. 380-5). Finally, Beijing will replace the current coal consumption by clean energy and will plant thousands of trees to green the city for the Olympics in 2008 (Xu et al., 2003, p. 423). The IOC is aware of the growing importance of ecologically sound Olympic Games and the damage the Olympic Movement could suffer if environmental negative effects are communicated throughout the world. Therefore, the IOC added environmental questions to its questionnaire to 'applicant cities' from a very early stage and, later on, asked the candidate city to describe, for example, its 'environmental key-point action plan for the Games', a list of 'environmental impact assessments' and an 'environmental awareness programme' as well as to provide a description of the current ecological situation of the city (IOC, 1995a; 1999c).

The urban planners thus become aware of the ecological situation of their city and start actively to plan environmental projects when preparing to bid for the Olympics.

7.2.3 Impact of Economy on Urban Development

Autonomous investments form the second part of the primary effect. Disregarding the problems of collecting data and their origin the overall amount of investments in urban development are listed in Table 7.8.

Due to incompleteness the differences in the total amount of investments are high. However, it has to be considered that even a post-Olympic perspective does not allow to differentiate autonomous and non-autonomous investments, owing to the missing information as to what would have been invested without the Olympics.

Almost all investments are made in the short period prior to the Olympics. That results in a short but strong economic impact. Depending on the overall economic situation, it has a negative or positive effect on the regional economy. Regardless of the economic situation, it pushes the urban development of the host city.

Before dwelling on the amount of investments in host cities, these should first be differentiated by their origin and the respective interest which triggered them (Figure 7.4). Only then can it be decided whether they belong to the Games-related primary impact.

Table 7.8 Investments in the host cities from Munich 1972 to Beijing 2008

	Munich 1972	Montreal 1976	LA 1984	Seoul 1988	Barcelona 1992	Atlanta 1996	Sydney 2000	Athens 2004	Beijing 2008***
					(in million US$·oo)				
Olympic villages	89.7	207.8	8.0	N/A	2296.3	212.6 - 275.4	380.4	N/A	445.7
Sports facilities	891.2	2412.0	275.3 *	1502.1	1079.6	556.4	1279.9	N/A	1683.0
IBC and MPC	28.3	N/A	169.2	N/A	N/A	N/A	temp.	N/A	38.4
Transpor-tation	340.8	N/A	N/A	2561.1	3711.6	N/A	633.7	N/A	N/A
Accommo-dation (tourists)	N/A	N/A	N/A	N/A	1294.4	N/A	N/A	N/A	N/A
Other investments	407.5	775.0	96.0	N/A	1752.2	226.1** - 329.3	306.6	N/A	2.6
Total	1757.0	3395.6	549.5	4063.0	10134.2	1182.5 1324.4	2600.6	N/A	2169.7

Notes: * The velodrome, swimming stadium and other modernisations and expansions were paid by sponsors and are estimated to have cost US$·oo 227.2 million.

** Among others, it includes the Centennial Park for US$·oo 164.6 million (French and Disher, 1997). For the rowing facility at Lake Lanier, the government is said to have contributed US$·oo 329.3 million.

In total the subsidies have been US$·oo 609 million.

*** Conservatively estimated by Bidding Committee Beijing (2001).

Sources: Bidding Committee Beijing 2008 (2001); Brunet (1993); Burbank et al. (2001); interview, De Frantz (1997); ERA (1981; 1984); French and Disher (1997); German Bundestag (1975); Kwag (1988); Madden et al. (1997); Atlanta OCOG (1996); Montreal OCOG (1976); Olympic Co-ordination Authority (2002); Schöps (1983); Xianpeng (2003, p. 228).

Since a large share of Olympic investments is frequently made by local public authorities, the share of autonomous investments is difficult to determine. In Barcelona, for example, the share of investments made from outside the city is said to have amounted to 33 per cent of the total Olympic investments (Brunet, 1993).

Thus far, investments in a host city have not been investigated in detail. Analysts have basically concentrated on case E, namely the investments which supposedly were made in the city because of the Olympics. With reference to investments, it must also be asked whether the overall effect of the Olympic Games induces additional investments after deducting outflow of funds from inflow.

$$D + E + F - G - C = ? \qquad (7.1)$$

If this equation is greater than zero there is a Games-related inflow of funds caused by investments, if it is less than zero there is an outflow. Cases C and G refer primarily to post-Olympic investments since they depend on the impression the Olympics gave and the promotion of location factors. Sydney 2000 started a programme called 'Investment 2000' in order to attract foreign investments (PricewaterhouseCoopers, 2002). Hosting the Games usually leads to a better image and promotes the location for tourism, congresses and investments. However, due to the neutral groups A, B and H the assumed inflow will be smaller than generally expected in many studies of the Olympics. Group H, in particular, comprises a large part of the investments since it includes all public investments, which would have been made even without the Games. Investments in the long-term improvement of the city infrastructure must therefore not be called Games-related. Investments by the city are 'financed by residents within the host community who therefore have to forgo something else, and there is no extra generation of income. Thus, an expenditure on sports facilities by a local government cannot be considered an injection of new funds' (Howard and Crompton, 1995). On the other hand, public investments which do not crowd out other public investments in the city or which are not pulled forward increase the primary effect. However, this differentiation strongly depends on the size of the area under review. In national analyses, any state activity must be ignored. If the investments are differentiated in this way, the investments forming the primary effect are far less than assumed in most analyses.

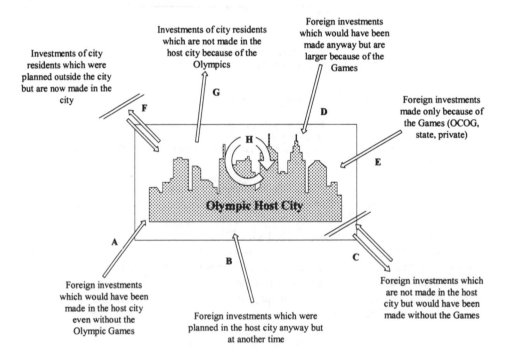

Figure 7.4 Origin of and reason for investments in a host city

The effect of urban development shown in relation to politics (see section 7.2.1) was solving problems of internal coordination and the directing of all efforts and innovative power to a single objective, namely that of successfully hosting the Olympics (Cox et al., 1994; Burbank et al., 2001). An economic related observed effect for development leaps is the mobilizing of considerable resources originating from outside the city. The Olympic Games are so big and prestigious for a country that the state and other public authorities subsidize the host city in respect of infrastructure and security. Even the US government, in a country which usually did not want to support cities to stage the Olympics, subsidized Salt Lake 2002 with US$.$_{99}$ 1.3 billion, Atlanta 1996 with US$.$_{99}$ 609 million and Los Angeles with US$.$_{99}$ 75 million (Burbank et al., 2001, p. 33)

Today, the Olympics must fit into the overall concept of urban development due to their sheer size. Only a limited number of countries are able to stage the Games at its current size. The IOC is aware of this fact and established an 'Olympic Games Study Commission' in order to 'propose solutions to help manage the inherent size, complexity and cost of staging the Olympic Games in the future; and to assess how the Games can be made more streamlined and efficient' (Olympic Games Study Commission, 2003, p. 4).

7.3 FOLLOW-UP BENEFITS AND COSTS

An often underestimated, but central topic during the bid is the sustainability of the Olympic venues. It has already been mentioned that a lack of post-Olympic demand should promote temporary structures. However, only a specific number and size of temporary structures justifies a bid for the Games in regard to urban planning and a social, ecological and economic sustainable point of view.

Today, the mistakes of oversized facilities and gigantism are well known. As early as during the bid, the IOC looks in detail at the post-Olympic utilization of the sports venues and the Olympic villages for the media and athletes. If there is only a small post-Olympic demand, the follow-up costs of the facilities lead to a permanent financial burden on the city. The profit and loss account of the Münchner Olympiapark GmbH, for example, states annual payments of more than US$30 million. These payments increase annually because maintenance measures become ever more necessary (Münchner Olympiapark GmbH, 1991; 1992; 1993; 1994a; 1994b; 1995; 1996; 1997; 1998; 1999; 2000; 2001).

The general question is to what extent follow-up costs and benefits of Olympic venues may be considered an economic effect of the Olympic Games. Many venues were built only for the Games. Only the cooperation and acceleration factors described above and the autonomous means a city received enabled their construction. Generally, a future demand, which ensures a utilization of the capacities generated, cannot be traced back to the Games. The demand instead results, for example, from the increased desire to practise sports, go to concerts or from the lack of school sports facilities and flats.

7.3.1 Allocation of Follow-Up Effects

In a case where Olympic facilities have a post-Olympic demand in the city, the investments can be called 'non-Games related'. Consequently, with regard to follow-up cost and benefit, only those effects, which were induced by the Olympics are regarded as Games related.

Figure 7.5 shows that only those follow-up effects which were incurred by the Olympic Games may be considered. The effects, which would have occurred even without the Olympics must be ignored. In view of the follow-up usage of the Munich 1972 sports facilities and the then planned Berlin 2000 Olympics it becomes obvious that the most frequent follow-up utilization is not linked to the Olympic Games (Berlin 2000 Olympia GmbH, 1992; 1993; Organisationskomitee München, 1974b).

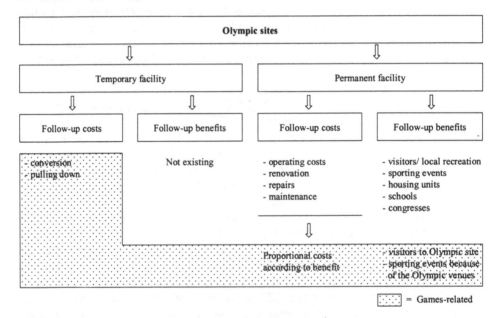

Figure 7.5   Allocation of follow-up effects of Olympic venues

Figure 7.5 reveals that only a small portion of the follow-up costs and benefits (shaded area) should rank as economic impacts of the Olympics. The Games-related follow-up benefit is limited to the visitors of the sports facilities (post-Olympic tourism) and to the events which came to the city only because of the Olympic park (image). All costs for removing overlays and temporary facilities after the Games must be considered Games-related, whereas follow-up costs of permanent facilities should only be calculated as a proportion of the amount of the Games-related follow-up benefit. It will, however, be difficult to determine this proportion, especially if it is kept in mind that not all facilities were newly constructed for the Olympics. It is also important to distinguish between new constructions and conversions, extensions or modernizations (allocation problems in terms of quantity) as well as the additional costs for accelerating the construction (allocation problems in terms of time).

7.3.2 Follow-up Usage of Olympic Facilities

All Olympic-related changes to the urban structure have macroeconomic effects. Owing to complexity, only the Olympic facilities such as villages and sport facilities are reviewed here. In general, there are four types of follow-up usage of these facilities:

1. Identical usage of the facility – these are the sports facilities which are available for school sport, sport for all (sports clubs, public swimming pools, and so on), for professional team sport, for a university sport or as training centre of a national federation.
2. Alternative usage of the facility – trade fair halls, congress and convention centres are often converted temporarily into sports facilities. Sometimes new constructions for the media centre or village hospital are used as office or school buildings after the Games (Genscher, 1971; IOC, 2001d; Lenskyj, 2000; Maennig 1992). The Olympic village is converted into apartments or houses for residents or students. Parts of the village facilities such as the canteen, team offices or administration are transformed into schools, homes for the elderly or other social buildings.
3. Mixed forms of follow-up usage – these are the 'multifunctional sports arenas'. They can be transformed according to the needs of the organizers of other mega-events. Between the events, they offer space for recreational activities. Sometimes, they even comprise hotels, convention rooms, and so on (Ernst-Motz, 1996). It is difficult to satisfy the structures needed for the Olympics and to construct an economic and socially sustainable facility for post-Olympic utilization. The IFs expect the most modern facilities for their sport at the Olympics. In addition, the IOC and IFs expect a certain minimum of spectator stands to satisfy the demand for tickets and the atmosphere spread through television (Garcia, 1993). On the other hand, the sports facility must be flexible enough to cover the costs of the facility by attracting sufficient cultural, political, religious and sports events after the Games.
4. Temporary facilities – in case a facility is not needed in future, technology enables huge temporary venues to be built. For example the velodrome and water polo pool in Atlanta, the badminton gymnasium in Athens and the beach volleyball stadiums in Sydney and Beijing are temporary buildings.

Following the classification of sports facilities, the Olympic facilities are now investigated for a possible follow-up benefit. Here, the foregoing four types of possible utilization are considered. Depending on the country, there may be variations. In 2001 approximately 3.7 million people visited the Munich Olympic Park, approximately 2 million the Montreal Olympic Park and, in 1996, approximately 5 million the Seoul Olympic Park (Münchner Olympiapark GmbH, 2001; Parc Olympique Montreal, 2001; correspondence, Sohn, 1996):

Table 7.9   Post-Olympic utilization of sports facilities required to host Olympic Games

Type of Olympic venue	Type of follow-up usage 1	2	3	4	Remarks on the follow-up benefit
Olympic stadium			X	X	If newly constructed, a big stadium is designed for national and international sports, political, religious and cultural mega-events and, primarily, for commercial utilization. The existence of a stadium may attract other events.
Olympic hall			X		Most host cities already had a large hall for sports, culture, entertainment events, conventions or trade fairs. It is questionable whether a city can fill other large halls apart from the existing one since these halls are not viable for cost reasons if they are only used for sports for all.
Multipurpose hall; fair hall; convention and congress centre		X			It is an option for host cities to use an existing fair hall or convention centre temporarily as a sports venue. The new construction/modernization of a fair hall can secure the location of the city for trade fairs or increase the importance of the trade fair. An attractive convention centre and the image of a city as an Olympic city could make the city a city of conventions.
Small halls; small stadiums	X			X	These are multipurpose halls and stadiums without large stands. During the Games, they are used for training. If the hall capacities in the host city are not sufficient, the new halls are used mainly for sports for all or college and school sport. In most cases, there should be a sufficient number available.
Outdoor; green areas	X	X		X	Outdoor venues are temporary installations on free spaces. In this sense, the spaces will have a different usage after the Games and mostly become recreational zones. In general, parks will remain parks. However, in Atlanta 1996 the Olympic park was temporary by about two thirds since the sale of real estate in the city centre is very lucrative.
Olympic villages; media villages		X			The follow-up usage of Olympic villages is limited to housing in general or for students in particular. In Barcelona 1992 the press village is said to have been used as a university building after the Games (Bidding Committee Barcelona 1984, p. 5). The types can be divided as follows: social housing schemes (1952, 1956, 1960, 1968, 1980); homes for families/students (1972, 1976); luxury housing (1988, 1992); students 19 residence halls (1984, 1996) (Muñoz, 1996, p. 49).
Special facilities					Special facilities have the disadvantage that they can be used for only a very limited number of sports. These facilities, which can only be used as training centres or for sports for all mostly incur a deficit.
• Velodrome	X			X	Velodromes can only be used as training centres or for cycling races. Therefore, most cities do not have such facilities prior to the Games. For Munich 1972 and Seoul 1988, the velodromes could be used by the public but rather by clubs and for cycling events (Münchner Olympiapark GmbH, 1996; letter, Sohn, 1996). In Montreal the velodrome was used as an exhibition hall, because it was not possible to cover the operational costs by a mere utilization for sports (Phillips, 1989; Scott, 1989). After 1989, the Montreal velodrome was converted into a museum (Ha, 1996; van de Will, 1989). Today, it is a 'biodrome'. In Atlanta, the velodrome was temporary and later moved to Florida (Atlanta OCOG, 1998).
• Swimming pools	X			X	Swimming pools are mostly opened to the public, which increases the sport and recreation offer of the city. In Munich, Montreal, Seoul and Sydney, the Olympic pool is open to the public. In Montreal, the hall was to be converted into a water adventure park in 1988, but the swimming federation had objections (NN, 1988a). In Atlanta, the pool is given of Georgia Tech University (Atlanta OCOG 1996). Since these are competition pools and not 'leisure pools' it is unlikely that entrance fees cover operation and maintenance costs. However, they can be used as training centres of the respective IF. Additional commercial events can be staged.

Assuming that a part of the benefit for the population through the new Olympic facilities can be assessed by the amount they are ready to pay (entrance fees, rents, and so on), there is the question of how the free usage of Olympic facilities (visits, walks, sports for all activities) should be assessed. Until April 1994 the entrance fee to the Seoul Olympic Park amounted to US$.$_{00}$ 0.70 while access to the Munich and Montreal Olympic Parks are free of charge. The scope of such a free usage after the Olympics can only be estimated vaguely due to the lack of empirical research.

7.4 OPPORTUNITIES FOR URBAN DEVELOPMENT THROUGH OLYMPIC GAMES

Frequently, the structural changes of an Olympic city are of major significance and have a lasting effect. Meyer-Künzel (1999) formulated four groups of city development through Olympic Games:

1. Ephemera: especially early Games staged the Olympics during world exhibitions. Games of this group have been: Paris 1900 and 1924, Antwerp 1920, Los Angeles 1932 and 1984, and Atlanta 1996.
2. Parks: St Louis 1904.
3. Sports and Fairs: London 1908 and 1948, Stockholm 1912, Amsterdam 1928, Berlin 1936, Helsinki 1952, Rome 1960, Montreal 1976, Sydney 2000 and Beijing 2008.
4. City development: Munich 1972, Barcelona 1972 and Athens 2004.

It becomes obvious that the early Games were staged in existing fair grounds and parks (1, 2), while the more recent Games create sport parks and supported urban development (3, 4) (Meyer-Künzel, 2001, p. 433). This fact makes it necessary to look at the kind of change that nowadays happens through sports events. A reason for the increasing number of cities bidding to host could be the wish to create 'New Urbanity' or to become 'global cities'.

There are five sectors of a city particularly affected by the Olympics:

- Transportation: The traffic system is changed by an expanded infrastructure and new concepts of public transportation. Despite large investments in almost all host cities, the traffic and the transportation of the Olympic Family remains a problem. In Munich 1972 the subway was expanded (Brügge, 1972; Geipel et al., 1993), in Seoul 1988 many major roads were improved, in order to show to the world their national economic creed (Goldstar, 1988a; Ricquart, 1988; Greising, 1996), in Barcelona 1992 ring roads were built which nowadays are considered the greatest post-Games benefit (Millet, 1995). In the 1970s the construction of these roads aroused fierce resistance in the Spanish population but eventually the roads were built because of the Olympics (Garcia, 1993).

- Telecommunication: a high standard in telecommunications is another important location factor to keep existing corporations or to attract new corporations. In this sector, the Olympics bring the latest technology into the city to satisfy the demand for telecommunications services during the Games. After the Games the systems remain in existence.

- Sports venue: the Olympics certainly have the strongest influence on the sports venue structure in the city. As mentioned already, the sports facilities for all sports must comply with the demands of the IFs, and an adequate number of training facilities must be available.

- Housing: in this sector, there is the question of a social distribution of newly created housing units. In Munich 1972, the Olympic village was built for socially weak groups of the population (Daume, 1976). In other cities, the Olympic villages were mostly sold to the middle and lower-upper social classes. In Los Angeles 1984 and Atlanta 1996, the villages were returned to their former use as student residence halls. In general, the construction of the villages results in a gentrification in contrast to the previous use of the area. Olympic opponents frequently use this fact as the basis for their criticism.

- Urban culture: the general embellishment of the city, an improved transportation system, additional leisure time facilities and numerous ecological projects frequently lead to a revival of the city centre by improving the 'city atmosphere'. In Atlanta 1996, for example, about US$'00 71.7 million was invested (Hiskey, 1994).

Subsequently, the contribution of the Olympics regarding the 'New Urbanity', which Siebel (1994) proclaimed is reviewed. Previously, the change in the infrastructure of a host city was primarily investigated with regard to the settlement of new enterprises/institutions (jobs) and the generation of additional autonomous demand (income). This analysis investigates the extent to which the Olympics give a city this 'New Urbanity'.

The contribution of sports events on 'New Urbanity' will be analysed by using Siebel's understanding of 'New Urbanity':

- 'Presence of history': the process of 'historization' (Vergeschichtlichung) mainly takes place in the city ring that industrialized society has put around the city centres from the middle of the twentieth century onwards. These areas encompassed slaughterhouses, railway stations, large industry plants, harbours, and so on. Urbanity neither means to pull down the locations completely nor to convert them to museums. Parts of the installations should be preserved. As mentioned already, many Olympic venues are erected exactly in these industrial belts where they often destroy old structures. In addition, it becomes socially questionable if complete settlements such as workers' housing estates must give way to new sports facilities or Olympic villages. Examples are the Munich suburbs from the Gründerzeit, which were changed by the Olympics, and the housing estates in Seoul and Atlanta, which were destroyed completely. On the one hand, Olympic Games help to upgrade industrially polluted areas and, on the other, they damage the urbanity of a city by removing old buildings.

- 'A different relation to nature': the ecological reconstruction of a city becomes necessary if the separation between living, working and leisure time/recreation, which prevails at present, is questioned. If these areas are merged, the city centre must offer a pleasant living atmosphere and the suburbs must provide conditions for employment. In this area, sports events have a particularly positive effect since most facilities are situated near the city centre and offer new housing areas or new leisure facilities after the Games. The ecological projects such as parks or green areas and the revival of the city's urban atmosphere underline this positive effect.

- 'The quality of public space': the future urban quality of cities will substantially depend on the differentiation between public and private areas. The way in which municipal policy deals with the trend to privatize public space will be critical. Examples of this trend are lockable pedestrian precincts or closed indoor centres for consumption and recreation (Burbank et al., 2001, pp. 34-42). Privatizing public space always includes social marginalization. Increasingly, cities are developed for the adult consumer with purchasing power and not for the children, elderly or poor. Thus, the city loses a major element of its urbanity, namely its openness to the entire public. On the one hand, host cities increase the quality of public space by installing pedestrian precincts or public parks. On the other, they support exactly that structure which is to the benefit of citizens with money to spend, in other words those who are prosperous. The impoverished sector of the population gain little benefit if leisure time quality is improved by attractive follow-up events or if living is improved by offering expensive housing near the city centre in a nice city atmosphere (Roaf et al., 1996).

7.5   GLOBALIZATION THROUGH OLYMPIC GAMES

Many of the host cities gain from the development within the city that is associated with the event-related impact. This changes the soft and hard location factors. It is interesting that, in this context, the host cities of big multi-sport events develop the factors that are important to becoming a global city. These factors include new bureau houses, improvements in telecommunications, gentrification of a part of the city, first-class tourism and an international airport (Sassen, 1996).

In general, the development of a network system of global cities that is based on a combined global and transnational-regional level can be noticed. In this system, global cities build important links through which the international economic relations of industry are coordinated (Sassen, 1996). Global cities are centres where economic power is concentrated. In contrast, other cities that have, in the past, been the primary locations for industry will no longer be as important (Sassen, 1996). For cities that have experienced this loss in importance due to their changing environment, sports events such as Olympic Games serve as an opportunity to gain from new structures. On the one hand, the location factors of the producing sector are ever less important and industry moves outside the cities. On the other hand, the sector of industry-related service is growing, even if it is not directly linked to the production sector. This agglomeration of industry-related services leads to a location advantage. Owing to the fact that many international corporations are dependent upon an industry-related service complex, the Olympic Games offer the opportunity to create new jobs by pulling the Games into their city. Nevertheless, global cities bear a high risk of destabilization of the employment structure which, in turn, leads to the emergence of a gap between the social classes.

With all the positive changes to the structures of a host city and with all the risks that are linked to the accelerated development due to the Olympics, the following statement is certainly true: 'In a world where economic relationships are as complex as they are today, nobody could say it was a single event that changed a city once and forever' (Rademacher, 1996a, p. 34).

Considering the fact that each sporting event has a different impact and size, and that each city has a different history, culture and structure, there is no guidance on how sporting events – of whatever size – create urban development. However, as shown before, politicians use sporting events to develop a city. Sports events can accelerate urban development by putting an emphasis on construction and unifying opposing political forces. That is positive. But there are also several risks. Irreversible planning errors due to time pressure or infringements of social or environmental principles by special regulations often occur. Furthermore there is a risk that long-term urban development plans get crowded out by simple 'festival' project plans. Another risk is that politicians sometimes use a sports event to bring their personal development plans to reality or to construct monuments of gigantic dimensions with a lack of post-event use. Therefore, the matching of urban development plans and the event-related development plan are very important.

A future global city

- is easily accessible by air, rail and road
- has international citizens and is culturally complex
- is equipped with excellent telecommunication systems
- is economically important
- is visited by first-class tourists
- has a high degree of exchange of knowledge and culture
- has mixed areas for 'living', 'working' and 'recreation'
- has no major traffic problems

Olympic Games can especially help to develop some of this structure. Already the construction of a single modern sports facility provides a new urban quality that meets this demand for a small part of the city. The preparation of a big 'festival', such as the Olympics, develops the city simultaneously at different locations and creates a larger impact.

8.   The great source of income: revenues of the OCOG

An OCOG is a corporation with a limited lifetime. It has the task of planning and organizing the Olympic Games. The OCOG objectives are to at least cover the required expenditures to host the Games with adequate revenues or, if possible, to achieve a surplus. This book will look in detail at in which areas and for what amounts must revenues be generated and expenditures made. The possibilities of an OCOG influencing these figures as well as the system-related constraints must also be analysed. It is difficult to determine expenditures since sources state figures as a balance or do not provide detailed balance sheets at all. Therefore, the investigations often only determine the quantities of resources to be provided.

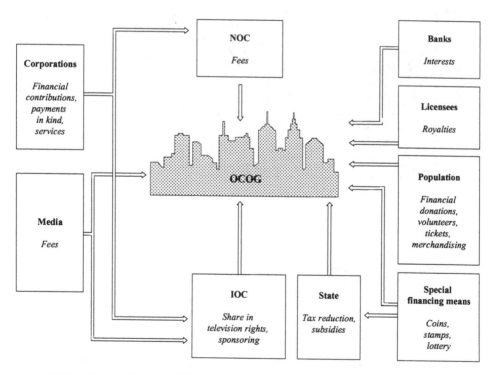

Figure 8.1 Origin and type of OCOG revenues

The OCOG is responsible for the entire organization of the Olympics and must also ensure that the competition organization complies with IF requirements. The size of today's Games increasingly calls for host cities to be able to finance the required urban structure. The investments of the city can only, if at all, pay off in the long run with a positive Olympic legacy.

All OCOG revenues discussed in the following sections are displayed in Figure 8.1. The revenues include both financial means and value in kind (VIK). Before dwelling on the individual financing sources of an OCOG, the overall revenues of the OCOGs from Munich 1972 to Beijing 2008 are listed. Figure 8.2 displays the development of the overall revenues and the share of the financing sources.

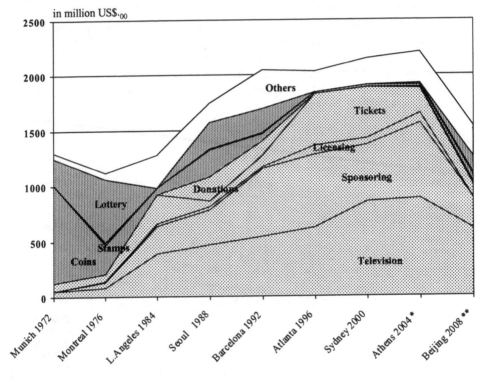

Notes: * estimated in January 2004.
          ** estimated and conservatively set by the Bidding Committee Beijing 2008 (2001).

Sources: Athens OCOG (2003b, p. 22); Bidding Committee Beijing 2008 (2001); Preuss (2000a)

Figure 8.2 Revenues of OCOGs from Munich 1972 to Beijing 2008

It is striking that between Munich 1972 and Los Angeles 1984, the OCOG revenues increased very little. It can be seen from this that the surplus of the Los Angeles 1984 Olympics, for example, was based on low expenditures and not on increased revenues as is generally assumed. None of the OCOGs achieved an excessive surplus. The large growth of the Games and the related costs for organization and infrastructure are reflected in the development of the overall OCOG revenues. The OCOGs even had to open new financing sources and/or expand existing ones in order not to run the Games at a deficit. From Los Angeles 1984 to Barcelona 1992, the financial means at an OCOG's disposal increased considerably.

Table 8.1   *Revenues of OCOGs from Munich 1972 to Beijing 2008*

	Tele-vision	Spon-soring	Licen-sing	Tickets	Dona-tions	Coins	Stamps	Lottery	Others
					(In million US$·₀₀)				
Munich 1972	48.08	0	4.93	70.32	0	883.47	3.77	244.61	48.56
Montreal 1976	84.46	48.08	6.92	67.48	0	261.27	24.43	574.52	53.29
Los Angeles 1984	386.75	248.78	24.88	258.55	0	59.64	0	0	297.22
Seoul 1988	464.84	278.86	30.22	47.99	220.49	242.80	8. 44	238.18	177.30
Barcelona 1992	543.76	611.59	16.58	102.06	132.45	62.66	8.09	217.48	348.99
Atlanta 1996	623.20	658.22	81.09	466.64	0	16.36	0	0	190.04
Sydney 2000	851.90	515.90	54.30	463.90	0	18.76	0	0	244.30
Athens 2004 *	883.47	683.55	84.50	224.18	12.25	20	20.21	0	290.82
Beijing 2008 **	604.78	281.49	N/A	119.42	17. 06	6.82	10.24	153.54	278.08

Notes: *   Estimated in January 2004, in July US$·₀₀ 400.35 for tickets estimated (IOC 2004b).
       ** Estimated and conservatively set by the Bidding Committee Beijing 2008 (2001).

Sources: *Athens OCOG (2003b, p. 22); Bidding Committee Beijing 2008 (2001); Preuss (2000a)*

Figure 8.2 shows that the revenue structure completely changed with Los Angeles 1984. Revenues of private financing sources (grey areas) outweigh public financing sources (dark grey areas). This change in the OCOG revenue structure becomes more obvious when the individual revenue types are represented as percentages of the overall revenues (Figure 8.3). The figure clearly shows the Games that correspond to the private financing model and which correspond to the public financing model. In the 1970s, the

OCOG revenues almost exclusively depended on special financing means (coins, stamps, lotteries). Consequently, the OCOG depended on the favourable attitude and financial power of the host country. In contrast to this, since Los Angeles 1984, private financing sources have increasingly come to the fore.

Figure 8.3 clearly reveals a moderately increasing but relatively high share of revenues from selling television rights and from marketing since Los Angeles 1984. Today, these key financing sources are IOC controlled. For future bidders they represent a financial security of approximately 40 per cent of their revenues as early as in the preparatory phase. Despite ever-growing organizational costs, this could help to lower the obstacle to bid for the Games (interview, Payne, 1997). All other revenues depend on the specific situation in the host city and the readiness of the state to become involved in the event.

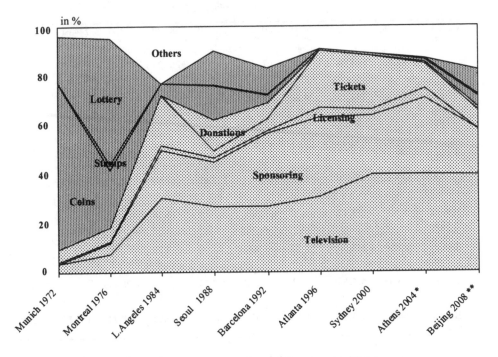

Notes: *   Estimated in January 2004.
        ** Estimated and conservatively set by the Bidding Committee Beijing 2008 (2001).

Sources: Athens OCOG (2003b, p. 22); Bidding Committee Beijing 2008 (2001); Preuss (2000a)

Figure 8.3 Revenues of OCOGs from Munich 1972 to Beijing 2008 in per cent

In the following sections, all OCOG financing sources are analysed individually. Their key factors are investigated to show the development and the potential inherent in the individual sources, with the objective of determining an increasing or decreasing importance of a specific financing instrument for the future. At first, the most important financing source of recent Games, the selling of television rights, is discussed. This is followed by Olympic marketing, which has gained in significance owing to an increased awareness level of the Games. Ticketing revenues primarily depend on the size of the sports venues and are analysed in a separate section. Finally, special financing means which were important for the Games of the 1970s – especially for publicly financed Games – as well as other revenues are discussed.

8.1 SELLING OF OLYMPIC TELEVISION RIGHTS

Since Los Angeles 1984, selling television rights has become one of the major financing sources for OCOGs and the Olympic Movement. Caused by the multiplier effect of the media, marketing has developed at a correspondingly later date into the second column of Olympic revenues. Therefore, the interdependencies between media, industry and Olympic Movement are manifold.

Television is the engine that has driven the growth of the Olympic Movement. Increases in broadcast revenue over the past two decades have provided the Olympic Movement and sport with an unprecedented financial base. Frequent critical arguments have been that the influence of television on the Olympic Movement is too strong, that the IOC enriches itself by selling television rights and that industry exploits and commercializes the Olympics. In this chapter such arguments are investigated from an economic point of view. At first, the history of Olympic television is displayed as a phase model, which considers the development of the revenues. The basic relationship between television, on the one side, and OCOG/IOC, on the other, is integrated as well. Next, the interests and interdependencies of these three institutions are reviewed in detail.

8.1.1 Development of the Relations between Television and the Olympic Movement

The history of Olympic television is divided here into six phases, which were formed based on economic considerations (details in Barney et al., 2002; Preuss, 1999; Wenn, 1993).

1896–32 First media interest
The print media have always shown an interest in the Olympic Games. Newspapers and magazines provided the first consumer advertising links to the Games, followed by radio. In 1928, for example, a Portuguese travel agency received monopolistic rights for a wireless distribution of Olympic news (Bernhard, 1928a; 1928b). The Amsterdam 1928 OCOG earned as much as US$$_{,00}$ 172 835 in photograph and film rights which were sold even before 1936 (Nederlands Olympisch Comité, 1930). The first payments go back to 1912 when the concession for photograph and film recordings was granted to ten Swedish companies in Stockholm. The OCOG earned US$$_{,00}$ 94 218 (Stockholm OCOG, 1912; Scherer, 1995).

1936–55 Proliferation

This period was characterized by the objective to achieve a broad proliferation of competition results and the development of the first live coverage in Berlin 1936. The awareness level of the Olympic Games quickly rose. Since coverage mainly focused on results and facts, and less on entertainment, television stations did not pay broadcasting fees, with the exception of London 1948. The British Broadcasting Corporation (BBC) negotiated to pay 1000 guineas (approximately US$3000) for the right to provide live and delayed coverage of the Olympics. Until 1952, no policy governing OCOG sale of television rights existed (details in Barney et al., 2002).

1956–68 Legal basis

Since 1960, television rights have been sold exclusively by OCOGs without providing any broadcasting centre for the television stations. These net revenues for the OCOGs represented only a small share of the total revenues. During this period, the IOC received only 1 to 4 per cent of the television rights revenues. Therefore, the IOC created the legal basis to include directions to OCOGs on the sale of television rights. Brundage, however, was aware of the fact that 'through television there is a wonderful opportunity to develop public interest in the Olympic Movement' (Brundage, 1959). This should pay off for the Olympic Movement in the future.

1969–80 Expanding IOC power

The IOC increased its influence on the negotiations for television rights because some OCOGs had tried to maximize their short-term profit by earning revenues to the disadvantage of the Olympic Movement. The IOC's right to approve all contracts and distribute the money at its discretion formed a recipe for conflict between the IOC and OCOG. The share of money from selling the television rights revenues steadily grew. In this period, the distribution of the rights selling revenues for the Munich 1972 Olympics was clearly regulated. Since television rights revenues now were to be divided between the IOC and the OCOG, the OCOGs pushed through a distinction between revenues from television rights and so called 'technical services' to increase their share. The IOC agreed because the costs for the technical services such as installing and organizing a television centre frequently surpassed the revenues from selling television rights. At that time television revenues already amounted to up to 10 per cent of the total OCOG revenues.

1981–2000 Growth

This period is characterized by the enormous increase in television revenues. At the same time, the interest of industry in Olympic marketing and television commercials grew considerably, putting the IOC and the OCOGs in a position to charge higher fees for television rights. These covered the increasing costs of the OCOGs for the ever more sophisticated media centres, which, above all, became independent of the television stations. During this period, the selling of the television rights covered more than 30 per cent of the overall OCOG revenues. Since the organizers mainly invested the profit in the urban infrastructure, the IOC permanently diminished the relative share of the OCOGs in the revenues from television rights. 'It is not the task of the IOC to pursue urban re-development but to support sport' (Hahn, 1996). This was confirmed by IOC member R. Pound and marketing director M. Payne who pointed to the fact that the IOC would soon stipulate in the Olympic Charter that all Olympic revenues had to be used for organizing the Olympics and not for renewing the infrastructure of the city. In absolute terms, however, the amount increased.

2001– ? Control

The IOC successfully sold the US rights for 2010 and 2012 to NBC. Despite the catastrophe the International Football Federation (FIFA) experienced with the collapse of Kirch for its football World Cup in 2002 and voices of many experts forecasting a decrease in selling television rights, the IOC increased its revenues in the American market by 32.6 per cent (IOC, 2003d) and in Europe by 40 per cent. In this period the IOC has successfully set up its own broadcasting organization (OBS), which controls the signals from the Games. The OBS co-operates with the OCOG. For Athens 2004 Athens Olympic Broadcasting (AOB) was established by the OCOG and the International Sports Broadcasting. For the first time in Olympic history 100 per cent digital technology will be used (Lewis, 2004, p. 55). For Beijing the Beijing Olympic Broadcasting (BOB) was formed. The new establishment will be in charge of producing the International Television and Radio Signals (ITVR) for the Olympic Games. Furthermore, BOB will build and operate the International Broadcasting Centre (IBC) and the necessary facilities and equipment at the other venues, and provide other relevant services of broadcasting to the rights holders. The near future will see the next era of advertising technology and Olympic coverage. Internet television could prove to be a phase of economic boom. Since Nagano 1998 the IOC has claimed sole responsibility for selling the rights. The OCOGs will receive less than 50 per cent of these revenues.

8.1.2 Evolution of Revenues from Selling Television Rights

Many sources assume an exponential increase for selling television rights. However, this assumption is not exact since the authors compare nominal values to each other. Paying television rights in US$ saves currency conversions but the development of the value of money must also be considered. After adjustment for inflation, there is only a linear increase in the total revenues. When analysed by international regions, there is sometimes even a regressive course.

Reviewing the development of the total revenues, the inflation-adjusted revenues rose slowly until Montreal 1976, and afterwards until Beijing 2008 more quickly (Figure 8.4). The kink in the curve was caused by US television stations competing for television rights, which started at the end of the 1970s (Barney et al., 2002; Berlioux, 1985). Until Los Angeles 1984, they had decisively influenced the development of total revenue by mutually outbidding each other. This was possible because American corporations were prepared to pay ever higher prices for commercials. At the end of the 1980s, the same situation developed in Europe as a result of the increasing number of private stations (interview, Moragas Spà, 1997).

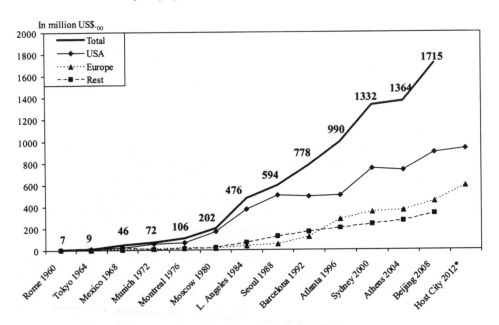

Note: * Figures inflation adjusted, inflation estimated (EBU = 746 US$·04).

Sources: IOC (2003a); Preuss (2000a); IOC (2004a); IOC (2004b).

Figure 8.4 Olympic Movement revenues from television rights from 1960–2012

The figures deviating from the linear increase since 1976 can be explained as follows: the Moscow 1980 Games earned lower revenues because the contracts were partly adapted due to the boycott. The German television, ZDF, for example, managed to dissolve 50 per cent of its material supply contracts. NBC did not pay US$·00 12.1 million (Lyberg, s.t.). The revenue decrease of Seoul 1988 was probably caused by the fear of a new boycott and the large time lag to the financially strong regions of North America and Europe (Kim, 1990). The increase rate will fall again in future, leading to a second kink. Until Beijing 2008, and for the US rights until 2012, the development can already be foreseen, since television rights have been sold already to the decisive regions. The latest NBC contract was signed in June 2003, the European Broadcasting Union (EBU) contract was signed on July 6[th] for 746US$·04 million. The agreement covers 51 countries, but for the first time excluding Italy and a wide range of media categories. However, the right package includes for the first time multi-media and mobile telephony (IOC 2004a).

In the USA, which is the most significant market for the television rights, there is a distinct regression. The leap for the 2000 Games is caused by the unbalanced distribution the IOC makes. It will transfer a total of US$·00 2.63 billion to the OCOGs for broadcasting until 2008. The IOC itself received US$·00 3.95 billion (Weissenberg, 1996). So far, the USOC has received 10 per cent of the US television contracts. This has shifted to a share of 12.75 per cent of the payments for 2004 and 2008 (Barney et al., 2002, p. 245).

Apart from selling the rights, EBU agreed as of 2000 and NBC as of 2002 to share the profits with the IOC, which could lead to higher IOC revenues (IOC, 1996b; Westerloo, 1996). According to the Atlanta OCOG (1998), it participated in the NBC commercial revenues to the amount of US$·$_{00}$ 19.7 million for the broadcasting of the Atlanta Olympics. This sharing of profits from selling commercial time, which starts at a certain limit, could bring a further increase (interview, Payne, 2004).

Since Rome 1960 the EBU has held the European rights. For 2000 to 2008 the EBU has bought them again. US$·$_{00}$ 1.3 billion of the sales revenues are paid to the OCOGs (NN, 1996g). The IOC received US$·$_{00}$ 1.53 billion (Weissenberg, 1996). For the contract 2010 to 2012 the IOC got US$·$_{04}$ 746 million which is a 40% increase (IOC 2004a).. US$·$_{00}$ 1.53 billion are estimated to be paid by EBU, which is a stronger increase than for NBC (NN, 2004, p. 31). The increase in revenues is exponential and develops in the same way as it did in the USA 12 years ago. The competition among the stations, which led to the strong increase in the revenues, started in Europe with a time lag of about ten years compared to the USA. If the curve (Figure 8.4) of the EBU revenues is displaced to the left by three Olympiads, the increase in the revenues from the sales of the television rights is almost identical. From a certain level, however, the private networks in the USA proved to be wealthier than the public networks that are united in the EBU.

Irrespective of the legal form of a network (private or public) and its way of financing (commercial revenues or broadcast fees), the curves reveal that, up to a certain level, Olympic Games have the same value for all television networks. The difference between the more quickly decreasing curve of public networks (EBU) and that of private networks (NBC) reflects the higher potential of the commercially financed stations. It should be kept in mind that public networks in free television have the advantage of a larger proliferation of the Olympics. The interest of Olympic sponsors in buying commercial time increases competition and substantially helps the networks to refinance their fees.

The revenues from the 'rest of the world' are still low. However, with the Los Angeles 1984 Olympic Games, an increase could be detected (Figure 8.5).

Asia has the biggest television audience and shows the highest growth rates. The Sydney and Beijing Olympics are unfavourable for the prime time of US and European television markets. However, it is interesting for the Asian markets which are becoming ever more important. With a potential audience of 3.2 billion people, the significance of this region is obvious. In 1996, for example, the turnover growth of the Olympic sponsor Coca-Cola in China was 40 per cent. This is a sign of economic interest and explains the interest of sponsors in the 2008 Olympic Games in Beijing.

South and Central America have only low rates of growth and in Africa there is no increase at all. In 1996 the African market was still weak. URTNA had received payments for the Barcelona Games 1992 rights from only ten member countries. Apart from the mostly public television systems, financing through sponsoring is still not possible since the market is limited and official controls on advertising are very strict (Mensah, 1996). The largest part of television rights for Africa is paid by South Africa. That explains the sudden increase in 1992 when South Africa returned to the Olympic Movement.

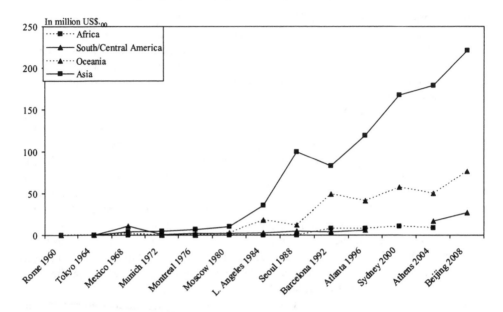

Sources: IOC (2001a, p. 10); Preuss (2000a); IOC (2004b, p. 7).

Figure 8.5   Olympic Movement revenues from television rights from 'rest of the world'

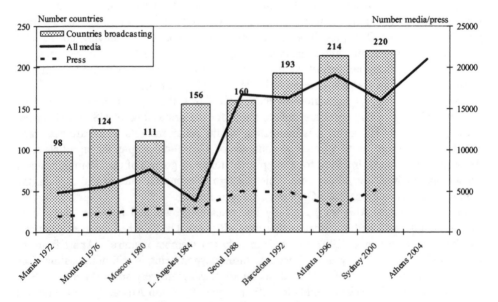

Sources: Bernardi (2001, p. 57); IOC (1997b; 1999e; 2001e, p. 223)

Figure 8.6   Development of media representatives from Munich 1972 to Athens 2004

The deviations were caused by differing levels of interest in the various Games. Organización de Television Iberoamericanas (OIT) (South America), for example, paid a large sum for covering the Mexico 1968 Games, whereas the Asian countries had a strong interest in the Korean Games in 1988. Negotiations with Oceania have always been very tough. An explanation for the temporary decrease in rights payments for Seoul could be due to a broadcast fee discount being given in exchange for material assistance to cover the sailing competitions in Busan, which Australian Channel 10 contributed (Kim, 1990).

However the interest fees for television rights and the growing interest in the Games increased the number of media and thereby supported gigantism (Figure 8.6).

8.1.3 Changes in the Legal Basis for Selling Television Rights

As an organization, which aims permanently to ensure its existence, the interests of the IOC differ from those of an OCOG. For the OCOG, its aim is to ensure short-term profit maximization since it leaves the Olympic Movement shortly after the Games. Over time, the more expensive the Olympic Games became, the more important formally legal contracts became and, thus, conflicts of interests between the IOC and the host city increased. As a result, the IOC had to have legalized power rewarded from the charter and the Host City Contract. The legal changes described below, and the IOC takeover of the negotiations, solely served the IOC's aim to control the television rights at a time when 'gentlemanly agreements' were not enough to secure million-dollar contracts. To realize its interest for this key financing source the IOC had, therefore, to assume the leadership role by installing legal ruling structures. It is noticeable that the IOC always changed rules in a period of power vacuum. In other words, the changes occurred at a time when the OCOG in question did not exist. The history of the relationship between television and the IOC is analysed in Barney et al. (2002).

In 1955, Brundage stated that television rights had a potentially high value and that the IOC had failed to reserve the rights for itself. 'We made no reservations of these rights for the Games at Rome and Squaw Valley, and perhaps we should have done so. It may be that even now it is not too late' (Brundage, 1955).

In Paris in 1955, the Executive Board discussed the distribution of possible revenues but did not find a solution. From this time on, Brundage was of the opinion that: 'The disposition of the proceeds from the sale of the television rights to the 1960 Games remains in the hands of the IOC' (Brundage, 1957a). The idea that the IOC's right to share revenues from selling television rights should be legally fixed was expressed in a document written by Mayer on 14 September 1955.

When the IOC passed the television policy in 1958, it thought that this legalization was enough and that it would participate in the revenues of the OCOGs of Squaw Valley and Rome in 1960. However, the host cities had been awarded the Games in 1955 with the confirmation that they could market all rights for themselves (Brundage, 1957b; Mayer, 1957a; 1957b). The same discrepancies arose with the Rome OCOG (Onesti, 1960).

In December 1957, Rule 49 of the Olympic Charter was drafted. It subsequently came into force in 1958. A key element of this rule was the differentiation between 'live reporting' and 'result footage'. In addition, the IOC secured for itself the power to make decisions regarding the granting of the exclusive rights for all future television broadcasts:

> The direct or what is commonly called Live Television Rights to report the Games, shall be sold by the Organising Committee, subject to the approval of the International Olympic Committee and the proceeds from this sale shall be distributed according to its instructions. ... Newsreel showing, whether cinema or television, shall be limited ... No network, television station or cinema may use more than three sections of three minutes of Olympic footage ... within twenty-four hours. (IOC, 1958, pp. 29–30)

The above quoted rule is important since it means that apart from the network that has acquired the exclusive rights, other networks may only also report from the Games in the form of footage with a time limit. Since 1996, this allowance for other networks has also required a time lag of 30 minutes (Colman, 1996, p. 8).

A general newsbreak, even if at all possible, would not be in the IOC's best interests since it would damage the popularity of the Olympics. Until 1968 the IOC received fixed sums that were negotiated with the OCOGs prior to the Games. An OCOG was the sole party in the negotiations with television stations. This is the reason why, in 1968, the IOC received only 1.5 per cent of the television revenues even though the Mexican OCOG had succeeded in signing an unexpectedly high contract with ABC (Preuss, 2000a, p. 283).

At the 1966 Rome meeting of the IOC Executive Board, the members passed a resolution that brought into being a new ratio for distributing television rights revenues (IOC, 1966a, p. 3; 1966b).

In 1971 the IOC then added a paragraph to Rule 21 of the Olympic Charter in order to emphasize the IOC's exclusive right to the revenues from selling television rights and its sole right to decide upon the form of distribution (Moragas Spà et al., 1995, p. 20). The IOC noticed that the new legal ruling that resulted from changes to the Olympic Charter was still not enough. Additionally, the Committee needed to introduce specialists. This translated into an expansion in what could be viewed as a rather small administrative unit that time. As a result of the IOC receiving, for the first time, such a large portion of the television money from the Munich Games the IOC Commission 'Television' was founded in 1973. This Commission was then given the task of regulating the future distribution of television rights sales revenues (Brundage, 1966; Landry and Yerlès, 1996, p. 72).

Negotiation of television rights

Until 1958 the IOC did not have any influence on television rights negotiations (see line 'Power' in Figure 8.7). However, after Rule 49 was put into effect for the negotiations of the television rights of Tokyo 1964, the IOC was then able to stop, due to a legal ruling, the signing of any contracts. The IOC reserved the right to intervene in order to prohibit contracts that would not have served to create a public awareness of the Games or safeguard the exclusivity of the television coverage. After the Montreal Games in 1976, the IOC decided to have a joint committee for all negotiations. Even after a short time, the IOC bowed to pressure and dissociated itself from the position adopted by the joint committee. It also refused to approve the Calgary Organizing Committee of the Olympic Games's (COJO's) agreements (Montreal OCOG, 1976, p. 79). It was, therefore, not until the preparatory phase of the Seoul Olympics that the IOC entered into a close cooperation with the OCOG. This, in turn, led to considerable conflicts of interest. In its negotiations, the Seoul OCOG acted so aggressively towards the television networks and so obstinately towards IOC decisions that the IOC restricted the OCOG's active role in television rights negotiations in 1992 (Alaszkiewicz and McPhail, 1986, pp. 211–26). Since then, the IOC has consulted with the OCOG but negotiated alone (IOC, 1995b, p. 9; Moragas Spà et al., 1995, p. 22).

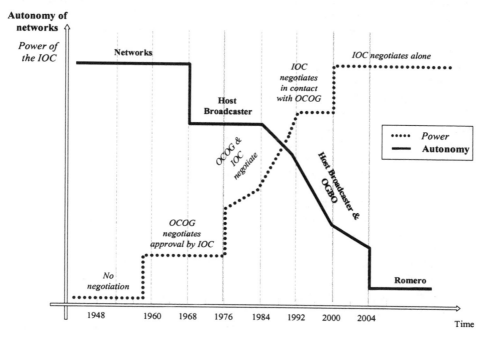

Source: Preuss (2002d).

Figure 8.7 Changes of IOC power in negotiating rights and broadcasting the Games

The position of the IOC has thus changed from that of being a partner of equal status to that of being a leading negotiator. For the Games until the 2012 Olympics, the IOC has already sold the rights for the US market and Europe. The fact that the negotiations were under way before the respective host cities were selected makes it obvious that the IOC is the exclusive leader of the negotiations.

The enormous competition and the increasing demand for sports coverage nowadays makes private television networks submit high offers. The private bidder, Murdoch, offered more than US\$'$_{00}$ 2.24 billion for the EBU rights from 2000 to 2008, that is almost 40 per cent more than the EBU eventually paid (NN, 1996p, p. 26). In view of the large influence of television on the Olympic Games, a concentration of power on the part of the IOC became necessary as a counterbalance. In view of the dimensions of today's

Olympic Games, a high number of bidders to stage the Games will only be possible if the IOC can guarantee financial security during the bidding race. In other words, it was necessary to stabilize this financing source by joining with private industry in order to secure the ongoing of the Games.

Autonomy of networks

Until Mexico 1968, television networks paying for broadcasting rights received hardly any service from the respective OCOG in return for their payment (see line 'Autonomy' in Figure 8.7). Networks were completely autonomous in designing the programmes. However, they had to cover the high production costs. As a result, poor countries could not afford coverage. This reality proved to be a problem as it directly contradicted the aim of achieving a broader proliferation of Olympic reporting. Thus, a host broadcaster was introduced and given the role of processing all pictures recorded from competition venues in the so-called International Broadcasting Centre (IBC) into an international signal that would be available to all networks paying for television rights. The host broadcaster became ever more important. This, in turn, limited the autonomy of the individual networks but increased the influence of the Olympic Movement.

With the Los Angeles 1984 Olympics, the expenditures of the host broadcaster grew to such an extent (Mount, 1985, pp. 45-51) that they mainly recorded what was of interest to their region and could be best marketed (Moragas Spà et al., 1995, p. 36). The Olympic Charter states that the international television signal shall be produced 'in an objective and universal manner so as not to concentrate on athletes from one or several countries, but rather to cover the events with the impartiality required by an international audience' (IOC, 1984, p. 103).

According to its demands, the IOC decided to transfer television recording to the sole responsibility of the OCOG, starting with Seoul 1988. The Seoul Olympics were covered with the strong support of the Korean television networks Korean Broadcasting Systems (KBS) and Mun-Hwa Broadcasting Corporations (MBC). In Barcelona 1992, however, 'Olympic Broadcasting' was founded which was independent of any television station and provided the international signal for all events to the IBC. The assumption that in Atlanta 1996 only the recordings of NBC were provided as the international signal is wrong since 'Atlanta Olympic Broadcasting' provided live images of all events in the IBC. Each station could select the events it wished to make use of. Athens 2004 will add to the service of all sports several signals showing the Acropolis and other points of interest in Greece (interview, Exarchos, 2003)

Today, the IOC has achieved great autonomy against the commercial interests of large television networks. In the near future it will produce its own international signal. The Chief Executive of the future 'Olympic Broadcasting Organization' (OBO) will be M. Romero, who has been involved in all Olympic Games since Mexico 1968. He worked as Chief Executive of Olympic Host Broadcasting in 1984, 1992, 1996, 2000 and Salt Lake 2002 (Lewis, 2004, p. 55). His company specializes in broadcasting Olympic sports and has entered a long-term joint venture with the IOC. Due to the fact that this newly founded 'Olympic Broadcasting Organization' is only 80 per cent owned by the IOC and 20 per cent is owned by a private entity, it is still a 'structural joining'. A first positive effect of introducing an independent host broadcaster is the possibility of using television experts from different networks for each sport who are familiar with recording the peculiarities of an individual sport. In Athens 2004, for example, the Athens Olympic Broadcasting (AOB) output will employ 40 different freelance production crews (Lewis, 2004, p. 56). From the financial point of view, this development will ease the burden of local networks that acted as host broadcasters at that time. On the other hand, the IOC will face higher costs because it must run all technical facilities itself. Finally, it is important to note that the IOC will have to further expand by filling positions with television experts and formulating new policies (elements of legal ruling). Soon, the IOC will have far-reaching control over the signal to be produced and sent around the world. Only some unilateral cameras will allow selected networks to keep their autonomy.

8.1.4 Revenue Distribution between IOC and OCOG

Since 1955 Brundage has said that revenues from selling television rights should be used for the Olympic Movement. From then on the IOC tried to obtain a share of the revenues. The shares of sales revenues from television rights can be divided into four phases.

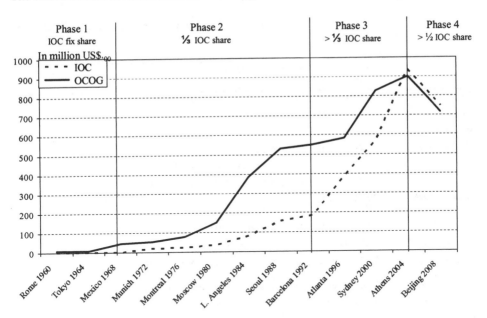

Sources: Olympic Co-ordination Authority (2002, p. 25); Preuss (2000a)

Figure 8.8 Revenue distributions between IOC and OCOG

In the first phase, which lasted until 1968, the IOC received a fixed share of the revenues, which amounted to 1 to 4 per cent of television revenues. From Munich 1972 to

Barcelona 1992 (second phase), one-third of the revenues from selling television rights was distributed to the IOC and two-thirds to the respective OCOG after deducting technical costs. During this period, the two curves divert, as the absolute increase in the IOC share of the revenues becomes smaller than that of the OCOG. A reason for this quota decision is probably due to the steadily growing OCOG costs for autonomous television broadcasts, which were backed by the IOC. In Phase three the share for the OCOG was further reduced. Since Atlanta 1996 the IOC has received 40 per cent of the television rights sales revenues. In Phase 4, from 2004 to 2008, the IOC will receive 51 per cent of revenues. From 2012 onwards, the IOC intends to guarantee an OCOG a fixed sum (interview, Payne, 2004).

> Although there will be a percentage reduction in the television rights revenue allotted to future OCOGs, the real value to the OCOGs is likely to continue to increase with rising television rights fees. The shift in the distribution of broadcast revenue is designed to serve the progress of sport in the Olympic Movement worldwide. (IOC, 2002, p. 4.14)

For example, the IOC uses the money to contribute a significant amount to Olympic Solidarity, IFs and the World Anti Doping Agency (WADA) (IOC, 2001a, p. 10).

Table 8.2   Distribution of the television rights revenues among IOC and OCOG from 1960 to 2008

City/Year	IOC share (actual)	Ratio of distribution (target)
Rome 1960	4.40 per cent	None
Tokyo 1964	3.17 per cent	Fixed
Mexico 1968	1.54 per cent	Fixed
Munich 1972	33.24 per cent	After deducting TS*, 1st million was paid to IOC, 2/3 of 2nd million to IOC and 1/3 to OCOG, 1/3 of 3rd million to IOC and 2/3 to OCOG
Montreal 1976	20.22 per cent	After deducting TS (corresponded to 50 per cent), as in 1972
Moscow 1980	17.75 per cent	After deducting TS 1/3 to IOC
Los Angeles 1984	16.83 per cent	After deducting TS 1/3 to IOC
Seoul 1988	23.14 per cent	After deducting 20 per cent or a slightly higher fixed sum, the IOC received 1/3
Barcelona 1992	23.40 per cent	After deducting 20 per cent + TS, 1/3 to IOC
Atlanta 1996	37.10 per cent	After deducting TS, 40 per cent to IOC
Sydney 2000	40.00 per cent	40 per cent to IOC
Athens 2004	51.00 per cent	51 per cent to IOC
Beijing 2008	51.00 per cent	51 per cent to IOC
Host City 2012	? per cent	A fixed sum will be promised to the host, not based on percentage

Note: * Technical services.

Source: Preuss (2000a).

It has to be considered that the share in Table 8.2 is between Olympic Movement (IOC) and OCOGs (Olympic Games and Winter Games).

8.1.5 Relations between IOC, OCOG and television

This section will examine the interests of and interdependencies between IOC, OCOG and television networks. Figure 8.9 displays the relationships of the three systems IOC, OCOG and television to their environment (spectators/population, industry).

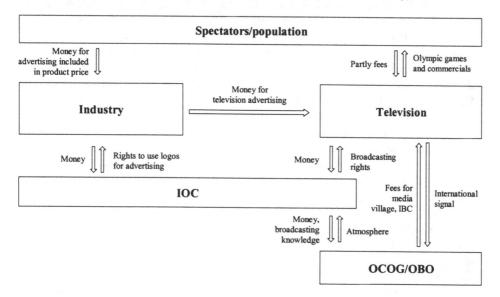

Figure 8.9 Interdependencies between IOC, OCOG, television, industry and spectators

Television receives money from industry – often from Olympic sponsors – for broadcasting their commercials. Corporations need the media (technical) and the Olympic Games (emotional) to transport their messages to consumers. The IOC is aware of these interdependencies. It must, therefore, determine the price the television networks are willing to pay for the broadcasting rights in view of the possible revenues from industry (commercials) or from the population (broadcasting fees). The higher the revenues and benefits such as image the network can achieve, the higher the price they can pay to the IOC. An OCOG, as a transitory IOC institution, organizes the Olympic Games in a way to keep or even increase the interest of the audience. Owing to the importance of keeping the interest in the Games, the IOC supports the OCOG to provide service and an attractive international signal to the rights holding networks.

8.1.5.1 Mission and vision of the IOC
In order to understand the relations between the IOC and other systems the internal relations of the IOC must be considered. To express it simply, the IOC is interested in a

permanent existence as well as financial, political and legal independence. The IOC can only enter into a dependence on industry and media because it is autonomous in its decisions regarding its existence and power. With reference to these interests, the IOC's activities are logical. In its relation to media, there are seven areas of interest.

Greatest possible public interest   A large number of spectators ensures the IOC's awareness and power with a demand for the product 'Olympic Games', thereby safeguarding its long-term existence. Thus, the IOC writes in its Charter: 'In order to ensure the fullest news coverage by the different media and the widest possible audience for the Olympic Games, all necessary steps shall be determined by the IOC Executive Board and implemented by the OCOG' (IOC, 2003d, Rule 59, para. 2).

Owing to this interest the IOC has refrained from pay TV. The IOC has often declined higher offers for broadcast on a pay-per-view basis or because a broadcaster could reach only a limited part of the population, as this is against Olympic Broadcast Policy. This fundamental IOC policy, set forth in the Olympic Charter, ensures the maximum presentation of the Olympic Games by broadcasters around the world to everyone who has access to television. Rights are only sold to broadcasters who can guarantee the broadest coverage throughout their respective countries free of charge. The Olympic Games are one of the only remaining major events in the world to maintain such a policy. Pay TV would cause a decrease in viewing rates and sponsoring revenues. The sale of the European television rights until 2008 proved that policy: 'The reason we accepted a smaller sum from the EBU than was being offered by the News Corporation is that we reach a far larger audience with the terrestrial channels, especially young people. That has always been our priority, rather than simply to accept the highest bidder' (J.A. Samaranch, in IOC, 1996b).

The European Commission 'encouraged the EU countries and the respective bodies ... to sign general agreements to offer the mass television audience as unlimited access as possible to Olympic Games broadcasts, also considering the aspect Television Without Frontiers in the internal EU market' (NN, 1997d, p. 18).

Another consequence of this interest is that developing countries have to pay only small fees or can broadcast the Games for free. For example, countries in Eastern Europe got the international signal of the 1992 Olympics free as did the African network, URTNA, for Atlanta 1996 (Hahn, 1996; Payne, 1998), Athens 2004 and Beijing 2008 (IOC, 2002).

Long-term partnerships   Confidence in the performance of television stations and Olympic experience are the basic reasons for the IOC to strive for lasting contractual partners (Hahn, 1996; Krämer, 1996). It minimizes the risk of poor broadcasting quality or bad programmes and ensures viewing rates in the long run. This explains why the IOC awards the rights only to renowned stations and not to the station submitting the highest offer. In 2001 at its 112th session the IOC decided to establish the Olympic Broadcasting Service (OBS) as a standing broadcasting organization for Olympic Games. The OBS joins the national host broadcaster from the respective OCOG and increasingly controls the production of sports coverage. The OBS and the OCOG form the so-called Olympic Broadcasting Organization (OBO).

To build long-term relations, the IOC protects its contractual partners by guaranteeing exclusive rights for a certain territory. A further protection of its partners is that, from 1996, the IOC added a 30-minute delay to the broadcasting of official press conferences for all non-Olympic television stations on broadcasting Olympic news (Colman, 1996). The 1997 awarding of rights for the Games from 2000 to 2008 brought a new dynamic to the relationship between the IOC and the television networks. However, due to the dynamic development in this sector, the IOC negotiated the TV rights only for 2010 to 2012. The interest of television stations can no longer be limited to a short-term profit maximization of an event lasting 17 days but must instead be extended to the long-term promotion of the Olympic Movement (IOC, 2002, p. 4.3):

- to ensure the financial future of the Olympic Movement and the Olympic Games
- to secure financing for the Olympic Movement and future host cities, while avoiding fluctuations in the market
- to ensure that broadcasters are experienced in providing the highest quality of Olympic programming so that a strong image of the Olympic Games is upheld
- to allow broadcast partners to develop stronger Olympic associations and to strengthen each broadcaster's identity as the Olympic broadcaster within its country or territory
- to forge stronger links between sponsors, broadcasters and the Olympic Family that will promote an agenda that supports the entire Olympic Movement with advertising and promotional programmes
- to establish partnerships that include profit-sharing arrangements and commitments to provide additional Olympic programming. This will: (a) ensure improved global coverage of the Olympic Games, (b) promote the ideals of Olympism, and (c) heighten awareness of the work of the Olympic Movement throughout the world.

Barney et al. (2002, p. 245) add another advantage of long-term partnerships: advancing the time line for negotiation of television deals provided financial security to the IOC, the Olympic Movement and prospective OCOGs. Owing to the rapid development of telecommunication technology, the negotiation of a new long-term commitment with US networks was reduced to one Olympiad (2010 and 2012). However, the contract was still made early enough so that candidate cities have financial security before they get elected.

Keeping the Olympic image   It is the special Olympic image, the ceremonies and the Olympic ideals that differentiate the Olympic Games from a mere accumulation of world championships. This mystique is embodied in the Olympic brand and includes values such as the participation of all human beings, races and nations in sport, equality of opportunities, integration of arts and sciences, internationalism and international understanding. Today, some ideals have been replaced by an atmosphere of entertainment. However, that atmosphere cannot replace the power of the Olympic ideals

(Müller, 1998). Even if the ideals seem to have partly vanished, the IOC ensures that the best athletes of the world compete, thereby attracting many spectators to the Games. One of the great threats to the Olympic Games would be the loss of the manifold sports and nations participating. The IOC is aware of the meaning of Olympic ideals and tries to counteract the threat when it selects the host cities as well as the television networks. Public television networks, such as the members of the EBU, indirectly promote the Olympic ideal by their duty to cover all disciplines and provide background reports (Hahn, 1996; NN, 1996g). American Broadcasting Companies (ABC) a contracting partner for many years and 1984 host broadcaster in Los Angeles, provided special films to support the Olympic ideal (NN, 1987). When signing the contract with NBC, the IOC insisted that from 1996 to 2002 a weekly 30-minute Olympic magazine was broadcast and that its cable stations report on fringe sports (Heim, 1996; Thurow, 1996). The recent deal with NBC shows the increased interest of the IOC in additional assets rather than just the coverage of the Games. The EBU and its members have committed a major additional programming and promotional efforts to support the Olympic brand and promotion of the Olympic ideal outside Games time which the IOC values 125 US$·04 million (IOC 2004a). The IOC's broadcast strategy includes: 'Establish long-term broadcasting rights fees contracts, which include profit sharing arrangements and commitments to provide additional Olympic programming. This will ensure improved global coverage of the Games and promote the Olympic ideal and the work of the Olympic Movement throughout the world' (IOC, www.olympic.org, 8 November, 2003).

The NBC, for example, will make a multi-hundred million dollar commitment to promote the Olympic brand leading up to and surrounding the Olympic Games (IOC, 2003). Television helps the IOC make Olympic history known to the public without incurring additional costs. In case a television network damages the Olympic brand the IOC can immediately cancel the relationship with the television network (Payne, 1998).

Avoiding competing events   To ensure high viewing rates, full stadiums and the participation of the best athletes of the world, the IOC has stated firmly in its Charter: 'The NOC, OCOG and host city shall ensure that no other important meeting or event, national or international, takes place in the host city itself, or its neighbourhood or in the other competition sites, during the Olympic Games or during the preceding or following week' (IOC, 2003d, Rule 38, para. 3).

At the IF level, care is taken not to stage international championships during the Olympic Games since this would be disadvantageous to both parties.

Latest technology   The viewing rates also depend on the quality of television broadcasts. Since 1936, when the Berlin OCOG offered the first live coverage, the Olympic Games have assumed a leading role in the technology of sports coverage. The first satellites in Tokyo 1964, colour broadcasts in Mexico 1968, multilateral cameras in Los Angeles 1984 and high definition television (HDTV) in Nagano 1998 are but a few examples of television technology development during the Olympics (IOC, 1994; Landry and Yerlès, 1996). The Olympics offer a remarkable experience for the spectators, an experience which could be even further enhanced by introducing interactive television or creating virtual realities.

<u>Financial independence</u>   Long-term existence is mainly secured by financial independence. For the relationship between financial independence and power, the following applies: First, he who has the money has the power. This refers to the distribution of funds to NOCs, IFs and OCOGs as well as towards supporting Olympic Solidarity projects. Secondly, he who has the money must pay attention not to become dependent on the person he receives the money from. The IOC is also interested in private networks, which presently have the potential to pay more for broadcasting rights than public networks. However, the rights are only sold to broadcasters that can guarantee the broadest coverage throughout their respective countries free of charge. The decision on an early sale of the rights until 2008 to the EBU, the NBC and others can be explained by the interest in long-term financial independence (IOC, 2002, p. 4.2).

<u>Securities for the host</u>   The Olympic Games are the shining light of the Olympic Movement and the IOC. They are the engines keeping the Movement going in the long run. The IOC is therefore bound to be interested in selecting a host that will stage the Olympics in a way which satisfies the local and global audience. In order to be able to select from a large number of bid cities and to make a good choice the IOC must offer the candidate cities securities. The IOC eliminated the risk factor for itself inherent in the amount of television revenues by selling the television rights early. From 2012 onwards the candidate cities get a guaranteed sum from the IOC for the television rights.

   The IOC interests are a logical consequence of its code of values and are justified by it. The IOC has, after all, assumed second place next to the United Nations Educational, Scientific, and Cultural Organization (UNESCO) as a para-state world organization. Its striving to control television in order to be linked to the population of the world, on the one hand, and to ensure a key financing source, on the other, is understandable. As a learning system, it reacts to changes in its environment and adapts its Charter accordingly. Against this background, the moral values claimed for the criticism that the IOC is turning the Olympics into 'Telelympics' and 'Commercialympics' must therefore be examined again.

8.1.5.2 Interests of the OCOGs

Once a city has been elected to be the Olympic host, the corresponding OCOG is less concerned about the question of its existence and more about the prestige that can be gained. As a transitory system, the OCOG refers to its 'have'/'have not' preference (cf. Bette, 1993). The OCOG is a non-profit organization. It exists only for a limited time. Apart from an economic impact, which is quickly dissociated from the OCOG, it leaves the image the OCOG transferred to the city by organizing the Olympics. All OCOG activities concentrate on organizing the Olympics as well as possible. Eventually, this depends on the financial means, human resources and the technology they have at their disposal or not.

The OCOGs following Nagano 1998 will have little influence on the amount of revenues generated from television. This is the result of the decision of the IOC to sell the television rights and to distribute the means prior to the formation of future OCOGs. The OCOG activities are based on the dualistic pattern of 'have'/'have not'. According to economic principles, they will be affected as a minimum principle (minimize expenditures in the case of given revenues) in their environment. Conflicts will arise if some areas (IOC and television networks) have certain expectations from the OCOG. The OCOG must fulfil its legal agreements with the IOC to produce in cooperation with OBO the international signal, provide an IBC and a media village and so on. These obligations can be met with the lowest possible costs as long as the prestige of the Olympics is not damaged. This strategy was obvious at the privately organized Atlanta Olympics. The dissatisfaction of the media with the conditions had a rather negative effect on the image of the Games. The 'having' financial resources in the sense of a surplus could be used for projects to enhance the image. The respective OCOG has reached its goal if the Olympics were successful and the IOC has been satisfied. However, an OCOG has failed if it does 'not have' means, a fact that becomes obvious in a financial deficit left to the host city and state and/or criticism of the OCOG. Criticism stems, on the one hand, from the IOC and, on the other, from the media, which transfer the images and impressions of the Olympics. Media representatives who are dissatisfied with the organization and the service they receive can negatively influence the image of the Games. In Atlanta 1996, for example, the media representatives were accommodated in different villages. 'Also, we learnt that transportation, especially for the media, can be accomplished much more efficiently if they are housed in a more concentrated area ... Our technology difficulties centred on the results reporting system and again most affected representatives of the media' (interview, Battle, 1997).

8.1.5.3 Interests of the television networks

Television networks are individual economic enterprises. Private networks aim at long-term profit maximization, public networks aim at minimizing subsidies. In contrast to the OCOG, neither aim at a short-term image maximization. The outer appearance of a television networks, its structures and processes cannot be understood without reference to the IOC, OCOG, industry, other stations and the audience. A close review of the long-term profit maximization, subsidy minimization and related circumstances explains the activities of the television networks regarding the negotiations for the television rights.

Striving for surplus   The aim of maximizing profit and minimizing subsidies must always be seen against the related circumstances of solvency and avoiding over indebtedness to ensure their lasting existence. Among all related circumstances, the economic situation and the budget of a network are decisive for even entering into television rights negotiations (Busch, 1993). The recent negotiations with the North American networks concerning the rights for 2010 and 2012 prove this fact. An important change, which was made in order not to overburden the annual rights purchasing budgets of the major networks, was to separate the Olympic Games and the Olympic Winter Games. One station alone could hardly afford both events in the same year (Kim, 1990; NN, 1992; Simson and Jennings, 1992). All networks make their decisions according to cost–benefit considerations. 'Each station has a certain budget for broadcasting rights which also covers the rights to non-Olympic events. When negotiating Olympic television rights the other events also compete with the Olympic Games, above all Formula 1 and pro boxing' (interview, Sauer, 1997).

The principle of maximization of the revenues at given costs guides the negotiations with private industry on the placing of commercials. The principle of minimization of costs at given revenues guides the negotiations with the IOC. It should be mentioned that the benefit must not always be of a monetary type. When signing the contract, costs can still be higher than revenues if the difference is balanced by intangible benefit (market control, prestige and so on).

With the exception of the costs for the television rights, the costs for the stations are mostly variable and manifold. The former host broadcasters had to pay both the television rights and the technical service to produce the international signal. The Olympic Broadcasting of today reduces the production costs of the networks by providing manifold streams and features allowing the IOC to charge higher fees for the rights. The revenues, mainly coming from television commercials with corporations and Olympic sponsors, are determined by the price at which television spots are sold. In 1996, for example, NBC sold all commercial blocks and made an estimated profit of US$100 million (Klotz, 1996). However the price of commercials depends on the viewing rates. It is understandable that the stations try to represent the interests of industry. Important factors for determining the prices for the spots are the timing of the competitions with regard to prime time, the location of the Games, the number of national champions participating, the types of sport, the number of rival mega-events and the intended target group (see Brown, 1996; Klatell and Marcus, 1988; Krause, 1993; Kühner, 1994; Moragas Spa, 1991; NN, 1987; Seifart, 1984).

Controlling the market and striving for security are two intangible interests, which do influence the decisions of television networks. Controlling the market is aimed at maximizing profit, and striving for security is aimed at safeguarding the long-term existence of the network.

Controlling the market   In the long run, controlling the market serves long-term profit maximization or subsidy minimization. All networks bidding for television rights aim to outdo their competitors and increase their viewing rates. There was a strong rivalry among the stations when negotiating the rights for the Munich 1972 Olympics. Much stronger competition occurred for the Los Angeles 1984 Olympics, which led to the initially exponential increases in television rights revenues. For the Games in 2010 and 2012 the US market had bids from NBC, Fox and ABC in a final round.

Striving for security   The stations have an interest in eradicating uncertainty factors such as a boycott or terror attacks, in order to minimize the risk of their investments. The call on the OCOGs to provide securities (Kim, 1990; Klatell and Marcus, 1988), signing external insurance policies and selling advertising rights to industry as early as possible in order to shift the risk, are measures worthy of mention here. The shifting of the risk by selling early has long-term negative effects if the Olympics do not achieve the desired promotion effect, as was the case in Sarajevo 1984 and Sydney 2000. The television rights for Athens 2004, Beijing 2008 have a clause for sharing the profits from selling commercial time.

8.1.6 Tendencies in the Development of Selling Television Rights in Different Markets

The selling of television rights has experienced a unique growth all over the world in varying degrees among the different countries or regions. The developing state of the television market of a respective country is the key factor for future revenues. The differentiation must therefore be made according to political and economic conditions and not according to the geographical affiliation to a specific continent. The critical quantities are gross national product (GNP), number of television sets and the interest of corporations in television commercials which, in turn, depends on the amount of leisure time in the population, the schedule of competitions in relation to prime time, key television markets, and so on.

Table 8.3 shows the fees of networks for 1000 viewing hours of the 2000 Sydney Olympics. Europe, North America and Australia as industrialized countries pay much more than threshold countries.

Table 8.3   Origin of television money by continents

	Total viewing hours (in millions)	US$·00 for 1000 viewing hours of the 2000 Sydney Olympics
North America	5054	123.76
Europe (including Israel)	4332	68.71
Oceania	722	64.93
Middle East	361	10.63
Asia	21 660	6.49
Africa	1444	6.20
South/Central America	5054	2.02

Source: Preuss (2000a).

Industrialized countries

In industrialized countries the market generally reacts to decisions by balancing supply and demand. There is a high competition between private stations and public networks with a strong demand for the television rights of Olympic Games. The public networks, which refinance the rights by charging the viewer fees, compete with private networks which sell advertising times. When selling the rights, the IOC is faced with a potential conflict of interests:

- Private networks: potentially higher revenues at the cost of 'disturbing' commercials and coverage of the Games in a way that the median of audience likes the programme.
- Public networks: potentially lower revenues but restricted advertising activities. Additionally, public networks have the obligation to consider cultural aspects.

Today the IOC expects of all bidders for television rights that they promote the Olympic brand and strengthen the Olympic Movement.

Threshold countries
This area includes countries with a potentially high growth, including many Asian countries such as Thailand and Korea, several countries of the broadened EU such as Poland, Hungary and the Czech Republic, and a few South American countries. Following the shift of the international economic centre to the East, the Asian market with its large share of the world population will assume a leading role in the future. The Games in Sydney 2000 and Beijing 2008 will be covered during prime time in these new markets. With a certain delay, the Asian market will develop to be the third most important market for the sale of television rights.

Developing countries
This group includes the countries which have evolved from the large number of former socialist countries not mentioned above. They are characterized by state-run television and a permanent lack of foreign exchange. If a market economy is not introduced in these countries, it becomes difficult for them to pay essential sums for Olympic television rights. In these countries, sport had a strong reputation of being a factor in stabilizing the system because it could prove the superiority of the system ideology (Holzweißig, 1981). The lack of competition decreases the power of negotiation. From 1976 to 1992, the revenues earned from television rights by the Organisation internationale de radiodiffusion et de télévision (OIRT), which encompassed the entire Eastern bloc, remained at less than 3 per cent per Olympics. In future this group of socialist countries will diminish and thus become even less important.

The group of developing countries includes many from Africa, a few from Asia and some from South America. They will need longer for a comparable development. As long as the survival of people is threatened, they will have little interest in the Olympic Games with their manifold sports that are often foreign to their own culture. Broadcasting to these regions can be considered a development aid due to the fact that the participation of these countries in the Olympic Games offers them the chance to present themselves to the international community.

A review of the future markets for selling television rights reveals two basic trends. The television market has experienced a structural change. In the 1970s the American television market changed from an oligopolistic to a polypolistic structure. The same development can be seen in Europe towards the end of the 1980s. Increasing competition made the offers of the television networks for the broadcasting rights rise. This is the explanation for the substantially stronger increase in the curve (Figure 8.4) for the total revenues from television rights from 1976 onwards. The strong increase in the payments of the EBU, which was delayed by three Olympiads compared to the development in the USA, started exactly at a time when the revenue increase from the US networks flattens out. In this way, the growth rates for the total revenues have remained constant up to now.

Since 1997, the IOC can secure the broadcasting fees for a host city before the host city is elected. The IOC has already secured a profit share in the advertising revenues of the networks from 1996 on (interview, Payne, 2004). The short-term sale of television rights revenues for each Olympiad has been changed into a long-term partnership in order to strengthen the promotion of the Olympic Movement and secure the biggest source of money for future OCOGs.

8.2 REVENUES FROM SPECIAL MARKETING MEASURES

Today, the Olympic Games are hardly conceivable without close cooperation with private industry. The IOC – and thus sport in general – gains from the financial support of corporations. In return, corporations gain from the worldwide attention which the Olympic Games receive, thereby making them an ideal platform for advertising. Marketing has developed to be the second most important column of Olympic revenues owing to the multiplying effect of television. Thus, in 2000, the share of sponsoring and merchandising amounted to 35 per cent of the total revenues of the Sydney OCOG. In Athens 2004 it is still more than 30 per cent. It is interesting to note that in many countries a huge part of the advertising revenues of the Games in Sydney originated from Olympic sponsors (Hochbrückner, 2001). This also reveals the importance of Olympic sponsors with regards to the amount paid for the television rights (IOC, 1996b). Coca-Cola paid US\$$_{'00}$ 44.8 million to the International Sport and Leisure (ISL) agency for the right to become Olympic sponsor and another US\$$_{'00}$ 67.2 million to NBC for the exclusive advertising rights (Florin and Carlin, 1995; Schweikle, 1996).

There is general discussion about the Olympic Games being too commercialized. The public considers this a very great threat to the future of the Olympics. Just over 53.4 per cent of spectators (n = 1043) interviewed in Sydney during the Games and 50.3 per cent of spectators interviewed in Salt Lake (n = 1130) thought that commercialization was a threat for future Olympic Games. It is interesting to see that 75.3 per cent of the German spectators interviewed after Barcelona 1992 and 66 per cent after Atlanta 1996 (n = 212) thought the same (Buchwalder and Messing, 2004; Messing and Müller, 1996; Müller and Messing, 1997a). However, what is understood as commercialization mostly remains unclear. Certainly, the appearance of the host city, with its advertising as big as whole buildings and the numerous street sales stands, contributes greatly to the impression of commercialization. Nevertheless, according to an SRi investigation in 1996, 92 per cent of the visitors to the Atlanta 1996 Olympics said the Olympic Games should be sponsored (IOC, 1997c). The IOC itself remarks: 'Too often, the commercial programmes run by the

City of Atlanta were confused with the legitimate IOC and ACOG [Atlanta Organizing Committee of the Olympic Games] sponsorship programmes' (IOC, 1997c). So far, neither the IOC nor the OCOG had been responsible for this development. The negative image of the street vendors in Atlanta conveyed an image of commercialization. For this high price, the city of Atlanta, which was solely responsible, earned only about US$$_{00}$ 5 million although US$$_{00}$ 66–99 million were expected (Crabb, 1996; IOC, 1997a; Waldbröl, 1996a). The IOC, therefore, decided to control the 'look of the Games' in Athens, Beijing and in the future (interview, Payne, 1997; IOC, 1997c; 2001c). Corporate design of Olympic Games was already intended for Mexico 1968, however, in Munich the concept was used very professionally. Not everybody thinks negatively of commercialization. Pound defines it as an 'association with business or commercial corporations for the mutual benefit of both parties' (Pound, 1996a) without which the Olympic Movement would not exist at its current level.

In this chapter, the essential terms of Olympic marketing will be defined. Subsequently, the relations of industry to the Olympic Movement are described in six phases according to their historical development. The IOC, the OCOG, sponsors and licensees are investigated from their respective points of view in order better to understand the individual interests in Olympic marketing. Finally, the opportunities and threats of Olympic marketing and the commercialization involved are reviewed.

8.2.1 Definition of Terms

In this book, the entire area of marketing shall be limited to sponsoring and merchandising for the purposes of closer investigation because they provide direct revenues for the OCOGs. Marketing relations concerning the finances of the IOC or the NOCs are excluded here although, in the end, their existence is necessary to stage the Games. Sponsoring is part of communication politics. Merchandising belongs to product politics since the core product is provided with an 'additional benefit' (Olympic Brand) to increase sales.

Sponsoring is a mutual business between two partners where performance and return performance are clearly defined. During an Olympiad, the sponsor pursues the aim of using the image of the event with advertising impact and transferring it to its brand. Here, sponsoring refers to the transfer of the Olympic Games image to the image of the corporation for which the corporation, in turn, pays. In this narrow definition, suppliers must be separated from sponsors because suppliers try to transfer the image of the Olympics only to the products they supply. Suppliers were in existence in a similar form in the very early days. The suppliers of royal houses, so-called purveyors to the court, used their privilege in the same way to prove the quality of their goods. In Olympic history Spalding was the first supplier. At the turn of the twentieth century this enterprise equipped US athletes with its products (NN, 1996l).

With merchandising (Böll, 1996), the corporations link their core product to the symbol of the Games or an emblem of the event, with the objective of increasing the product sales. The consumer buys the product in the first place because he or she identifies with the event and not because of the core product brand. Olympic merchandising was made possible when the symbol, the Olympic Rings, was designed by Coubertin in 1913. They were used for the first time at the 1920 Antwerp Olympics (see Coubertin, 1913; Müller and IOC, 1986) Apart from the Olympic rings, emblems for the respective Olympics and mascots have increased the marketing opportunities of an OCOG. Furthermore, a trend to have several mascots is striking: in Lillehammer 1994 (2), Nagano 1998 (4) and Sydney 2000 (3), Salt Lake (3) and Athens (2). The emblems of the respective Olympics allow the visitor to identify with the specific Olympic Games that he or she visited and not only with the Olympic Movement in general. The individual Games can be grasped rationally, while the Olympic Movement is abstract and fictitious.

First, the area of investigation on the part of the Olympic Movement is delimited by the IOC, OCOG and NOCs as recipients of goods, services and money. In return, they give the corporations appropriate 'packages' of rights and other privileges. Secondly, there are the sponsors, suppliers/providers and licensees that receive the 'packages' and provide goods, services and money in return (Figures 8.10 and 8.11).

Sponsoring and merchandising are integrated into marketing programmes at national and international levels. The names of Olympic marketing programmes may frequently change but the following five basic types can be specified for all Games.

TOP (The Olympic Programme)

This is an international IOC sponsoring programme that guarantees the corporations, as TOP sponsors, worldwide exclusive advertising rights with the Olympic symbol in their product. In return, the NOCs and the OCOGs participate in the revenues (IOC, 1996c). The TOP, created in 1985, has (IOC, 2001b):

- provided funding to all 201 NOCs, not just the key economic markets
- provided critical technology and resources to each OCOG for Games operations
- enjoyed an unprecedented renewal rate within industry
- provided a global promotional platform for the Olympic brand across 220 countries.

The TOP is run by the IOC and provides additional service and worldwide marketing platforms to those which the partners receive.

Partner

The Partners are in the national OCOG sponsoring programme that guarantees corporations advertising rights with the emblem of the event in their product or service category and a designation such as Partner of the X Olympic Games. They are subordinate to the TOP sponsors (Stupp, 1996). Since Calgary 1988, OCOGs and NOCs have cooperated to increase exclusivity and to avoid overlapping product or service categories. For Atlanta 1996, it was stipulated in the Host City Contract that the OCOG and USOC had to pursue a joint marketing programme (Atlanta OCOG, 1998). For Beijing 2008, the BOBICO (Bidding Committee) has reached an agreement with the Chinese Olympic Committee (COC) to run joint marketing. One component of the programme was that the Beijing OCOG and the COC began their implementation of the joint marketing plan from 1 January 2003. While Beijing as well as Athens and Sydney have joint marketing programmes steered by the OCOG, Atlanta 1996 founded the Atlanta Centennial Olympic Properties (ACOP) for this purpose. This action was taken as a result of the good experiences USOC had in sponsorships (interview, Payne, 2004). This first joint marketing resulted in increased revenues (Atlanta OCOG, 1994a; USOC, 1995). The partners also received the right to use the additional titles 'Partner of USOC' and 'Partner of the American Olympic Team'. An OCOG earns much more from the partner programme than from the TOP. From a financial point of view, partners are therefore more important to the OCOG than TOP sponsors. In Sydney for the first time the TOP sponsors and the major domestic sponsors (partner) were brought together as a single entity, the 'Team Millennium Olympic Partners' (TMOP). The partners had rights comparable to TOP sponsors, but for use within Australian territory only (Sydney OCOG, 2001). Also in Athens 2004 the partners have the same rights as the TOP sponsors in Greece (interview, Payne, 2004).

Sponsors

The national NOC sponsoring programme guarantees the corporations, national advertising rights with OCOG emblems and the title 'Official ...' in their individual product or service category. In the host country, they are subordinate to TOP sponsors and partners. In countries which do not host the Games, the sponsors of the NOCs are subordinate only to TOP sponsors. To protect the exclusiveness of sponsors the IOC has defined about 100 branches and has reserved 25 for itself for possible TOP sponsors. If a category remains free, the NOC can negotiate to get this category for a national sponsor for that respective Olympiad. The NOC sponsors are also protected for if the NOC has occupied a branch with a sponsor, this branch is blocked even for an interested TOP sponsorship until the next Olympiad or at least until a renegotiation (interview, Achten, 2004).

Provider, supporter and suppliers

This category is designed to provide key areas of support and products required by the OCOGs, the NOCs and the IOC. This category of relationship offers less than the TOP or the partner programme in marketing rights and opportunities. Payments are often in value in kind. This programme is a national programme which allows limited usage of the Olympic Games emblems for supplied products.

Licensees

This is an international programme, which allows the use of the Games' emblems on products or the production of Olympic mascots and so on, including the selling of these. This group is only involved in merchandising. In future Olympics such as in Beijing 2008, the IOC will support the OCOG licensees with international marketing. This will be an advantage since the IOC possesses more efficient distribution channels and the OCOG and the entire Olympic Movement will earn more revenues. However, Atlanta 1996 marketed the emblem very poorly at international level (interview, Battle, 1997). In addition, the IOC will increasingly control product quality and start programmes 'that bring the Olympic philosophy to the public, particularly youth, through OCOG products ... We are vigilant about balancing commercial value with preserving the integrity of the Olympics in the programs and products we endorse' (Payne, 1998).

Before 1992 the IOC received 3 per cent of all revenues on sponsoring and merchandising (Hill, 1992; Kim, 1990). From 1992 to 2004 the IOC got 5 per cent (Hill, 1992). The Host City Contract (HCC) for the Athens 2004 Olympics states: 'The IOC shall receive five percent (5%) of the value of the consideration of all contracts pertaining to the marketing plan and the single joint marketing programme or containing any element of commercial exploitation of the emblem, mascot or designations of the Games', (IOC, 1997d). From 2008 onward the IOC will receive 7.5 per cent from all marketing revenues (IOC, 2001e).

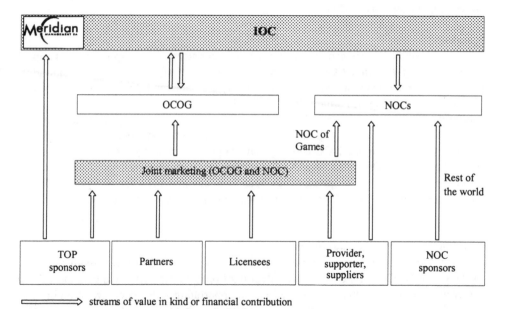

Figure 8.10   Streams of goods, services and money within OCOG supporting marketing programmes

Increasingly, sponsor fees have been paid in the form of value in kind or services, a development that has caused problems. The Atlanta 1996 OCOG, for example, received four times the number of value in kind and services than the Barcelona 1992 OCOG (Atlanta OCOG, 1998). In general, this form of 'payment' has two negative effects for an OCOG:

- It does not always need all the value in kind provided by the sponsor.
- The sponsor fixes the highest possible price, which could well be above the market price, as the value for the performance provided.

In Atlanta 1996, for example, additional allocation problems arose between USOC and OCOG because USOC mainly insisted on money. Later, it was agreed that USOC also had to accept value in kind contributions (Atlanta OCOG, 1998).

The IOC holds the exclusive rights for the Olympic Rings and allows the NOCs to use their own marketing signets, which may contain the Rings. The NOC sponsors can use that emblem in their territories. At a national level, the OCOGs hold the exclusive rights to their specific emblems and merchandise.

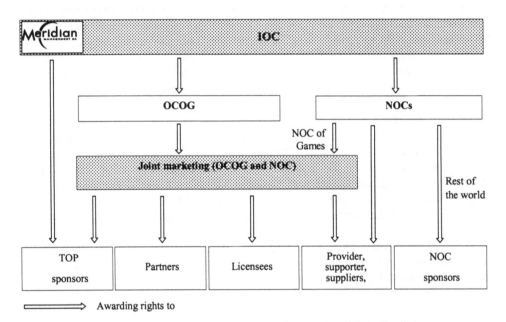

Figure 8.11   Allocation of rights to corporations within OCOG supporting programmes

In late 2002 the IOC and Beijing OCOG developed a marketing plan. During the first quarter of 2003 the IOC staged an 'Olympic Design Conference' in Beijing to assist the OCOG and design community in development of the Games identity. They started with the new 2008 Olympic Games emblem and launched a national marketing plan. In summer 2004 all national partners of Beijing will attend the Athens 2004 Games as observers, and launch Games-related programmes immediately thereafter (IOC, 2001c).

8.2.2 Development of the Relations between Corporations and the Olympic Movement

The relationship between corporations and the Olympic Movement has existed since 1896. In the beginning, the links were very loose. Today, however, the dependency of the Olympic Movement on the key sponsors cannot be overlooked. The history of the relations between industry and the Olympic Movement can be divided into the following six phases.

1896–1927 Advertising on site
In this phase, the corporations used the interest of the population in the Olympic Games for advertising purposes on site. The advertising was either directly at the sports venues (programmes/board advertising 1924, and so on) or they purchased concessions in order to receive the right to provide services during the Games or to sell products (kiosks, renting binoculars, photographic rights, and so on). These marketing activities were not organized by the OCOGs. Even at this time, suppliers hoped that the spectators would become aware of their products and link them to the positive image of the Games.

1928–47 Using the Rings
The marketing of the Olympic Rings started only a few years after Coubertin made them the official symbol of the Olympic Movement. Based on the insight that the Rings could be used to increase sales, the first forms of merchandising took shape (Harte, 1928). 'Perhaps the IX Olympic Games were staged in a more professional way than any others before. But Amsterdam certainly was not the start of the commercial development in sports. It was just that the keen eye could easily and clearly detect its symptoms there' (Meisl, 1928).

In this period, precursors of sponsoring are evident in the fact that many suppliers used the word 'Olympic' in their advertisements. In 1938, Brundage noticed the threat that was inherent in unprotected Olympic symbols:

> Obviously, if the manufacturers and dealers in the shoes, the clothing, the various kinds of equipment that the athletes use, and in the things that they eat and drink all use the name 'Olympic', the five circle symbol and the motto ... in their advertising they will soon lose their meaning. (Brundage, 1938)

In this phase, OCOGs mostly received value in kind from the corporations. The main part of the corporations' performance, however, went to the NOCs, and thus to the athletes. The IOC has relied primarily on a reactive policy in identifying violators without seeking authority to exploit an affiliation with the already globally recognized Olympic symbol (Barney et al., 2002, p. 153).

1948–75 International marketing
The subject of insignia protection was raised in IOC Sessions from time to time in the 1950s (Barney et al., 2002, p. 153). The first Olympic sponsor in its true sense might

have been the baker Helms who, in 1948, bought the rights 'to advertise without any language of limitation whatsoever' for US$10 000 from USOC (Barney, 1993; 2002; McDowell, 1950; McGovern, 1950). The OCOGs could not take advantage of this development until the first international sales programme in 11 countries was started in 1952. In the following years, marketing activities increased, although these were primarily limited to licensees. This period is also characterized by the IOC efforts to protect the Olympic Rings because 'in commercialising the Games he [the sponsor Helms, the author] is violating the whole spirit of the Games' (Brundage, 1948).

1976–84 Commercialization

The early 1980s were to go down in the history of sport as the phase when the consumer goods industry started to discover sport as a carrier of advertising messages. In 1976, sponsoring comprised 628 sponsors (Albrecht-Heider, 1996; Helyar, 1996). As approved at the 79th IOC Session in Prague in 1977, a by-law to Rule 6 of the Olympic Charter announced that the IOC should take every appropriate step possible to obtain legal protection of the Olympic symbol at national and international level (Barney et al., 2002, p. 154). But it was not until 1981 in Baden-Baden, when the Olympic admission rule was liberalized, that marketing finally entered the Olympic Movement. In 1982, the IOC founded the 'New Source of Financing Commission' to exploit all new sources (IOC, 2001c; Landry and Yerlès, 1996). Later, Ueberroth introduced the concept of exclusive but expensive sponsorship with the first commercially financed Games of Los Angeles. In 1983, Dassler (adidas) sold the concept of 'The Olympic Programme' (TOP) as a package solution to the IOC via the ISL agency, 51 per cent of which belonged to adidas (Barney et al., 2002, p. 159).

1985–96 Protecting the symbol and emblems

International sponsoring on a worldwide scale was introduced at the Seoul 1988 Olympics. Until today, TOP sponsors have had exclusive rights to the usage of the Olympic Rings on their products, in their respective product or service category, in all NOC territories for the duration of an Olympiad. Apart from TOP, the national sponsoring programmes and OCOG programmes were extended. Owing to the increasing differentiation, the significance of the individual sponsor to the Olympic Movement remained obscure to the spectator. In future, however, the exclusiveness of the sponsors shall be enhanced and the total number of corporations advertising with the Olympics shall be diminished. In 1992 the IOC launched a campaign to position ambush marketing as 'unethical' rather than clever marketing (IOC, 2001c). From 1985 to 1996, Olympic merchandising increased considerably. For the OCOGs it has developed into an important source of financing.

1997–? Strengthening the marketing

The start of this new phase is characterized by the replacement of the intermediate agency ISL by the IOC-owned agency Meridian for TOP marketing (IOC, 1996c). ISL was said to have kept 25 per cent of all revenues as a provision, which will now presumably benefit the Olympic Movement (interview, Tröger, 1998). As is the case with television rights, the IOC started to sign long-term contracts with the sponsors. The IOC has already decided that 'in light of the Atlanta experience, there is now an even greater need to exercise control and strengthen relationships at all levels' IOC (1997a). Already in Seoul 1988, discrepancies arose with regards to the locations of street vendors and their image (McBeth, 1988b). Therefore as early as in 1997, the IOC negotiated with the bidders for the 2004 Olympics on their 'look of the Games' during the Olympics. The locations in a city where and to what extent the sponsors may advertise during the Games were precisely determined (interview, Payne, 1997).

During this period the IOC started image research and analysed its 'Olympic Brand'. The 'New Sources of Financing Commission' was renamed 'Marketing Commission' in 1998. In 2000 the IOC set up the Internet working group and finally entered global marketing by launching 'Celebrate Humanity' as a worldwide marketing campaign (IOC, 2001c). This campaign will continue at least until Beijing 2008 (interview, Payne, 2004)

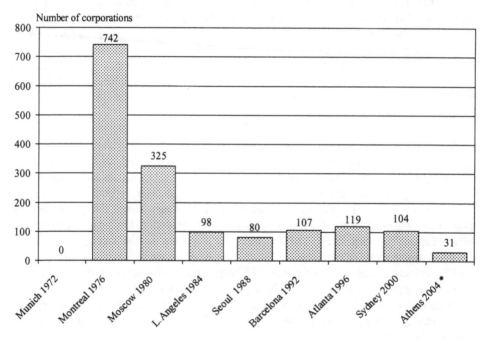

Note: * in July 2004.

Sources: Preuss (2000a); IOC (2004b).

Figure 8.12   Number of corporations advertising with Olympic Games (without licensees)

Figure 8.12 shows the development of Olympic marketing during the past 32 years. It can clearly be seen that after 1976 the number of corporations (sponsors/suppliers) who were allowed to advertise with the Olympic Games has strongly declined. The development in sponsoring was similar. In Montreal 1976 there were 628 sponsors (Helyar, 1996; Montreal OCOG, 1976). For Moscow 1980, however, their number was limited to 35, including 19 foreign corporations (Moscow OCOG, 1980).

After Seoul 1988, the number increased again, although the IOC itself remarked, 'control the number of major corporate sponsorships, with less companies giving more' and praised itself for having reduced 'the total number of sponsors relationships to under 50' (IOC, 1996c) in Atlanta 1996. However, the total number of corporations only decreased in 2004 owing to the promise to not further commercialize the Olympic Games, but also owing to the fact that Greece is a relatively small market and therefore the interest of sponsors is lower. The strengthened exclusiveness of the sponsors through their reduced number did not decrease the revenues.

During Munich 1972 there were not sponsors but, rather, many suppliers that supported the Games primarily by value in kind (interview, J. Schröder, 1997).

Figure 8.13 shows the number of sponsors and has clearly increased. The OCOG revenues from sponsoring have, however, increased. For Sydney 2000, there were as many sponsors as in Atlanta. A new increase in suppliers and licensees after a reduction until Seoul 1988 can be seen.

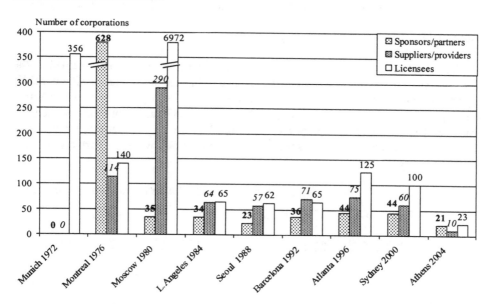

Sources: Chappelet (2001); Preuss (2000a); IOC (2004b).

Figure 8.13   Number of sponsors, suppliers and licensees at Olympic Games from Munich 1972 to Sydney 2000

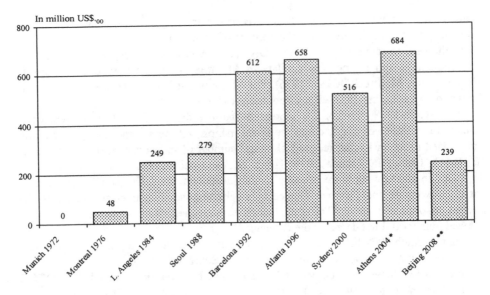

Note: * estimated in December 2003.
           ** estimated and conservatively set by the Bidding Committee Beijing 2008 (2001).

Sources: Bidding Committee Beijing 2008 (2001); Chalkias (interview, 2003); IOC (2001b); Preuss (2000a).

Figure 8.14   OCOG revenues from sponsoring

Figure 8.14 reveals the sharp increase in revenues for Los Angeles 1984 caused by the new concept of marketing. To Ueberroth, who had to finance the Olympics without public support, sponsorship was second only to selling television rights. His new marketing strategy could only be realized because the 1984 Olympic Games were staged in the USA where the OCOG found an appropriately developed advertising market to offer exclusive rights. Even today almost all TOP sponsors are from the USA, while the Partners are from the host country.

Table 8.4   Sponsors of the Olympiads from Seoul to Athens by their country of origin

	TOP I	Partner	TOP II	Partner	TOP III	Partner	TOP IV	Partner	TOP V	Partner
	85-88	1988	89-92	1992	93-96	1996	97-00	2000	01-04	2004
Number	9	15	12	9	10	10	11	13	11	11
From USA	78 %	27 %	75 %	22 %	90 %	90 %	82 %	8 %	64 %	64 %
From the host country	0 %	60 %	0 %	56 %	90 %	90 %	0 %	84 %	0 %	80 %

Sources: Hill (1996); IOC (1996a; 1996b; 1997b; 2001b); Landry and Yerlès (1996); NN (1996n); Barcelona OCOG (1992); Seoul OCOG (1988); Patterson (1994); IOC (2004b).

The high share of sponsors originating from the USA put the USOC in a powerful position to negotiate a high share of revenues made by the TOP. It took until December 1987 for the USOC to agree in principle to continue its participation in TOP. The USOC received 15 per cent of the revenues from TOP I for its participation (Barney et al., 2002, pp. 171-80). The revenues from merchandising were very high in Los Angeles 1984. An explanation could be the openness of the American market towards merchandising articles. Barcelona 1992 experienced a sharp decrease unexplainable by the author. This could be due to a different measuring method of the OCOG, to printing errors in the sources, or to a much lower interest of the Spanish people in merchandising articles (Figure 8.15).

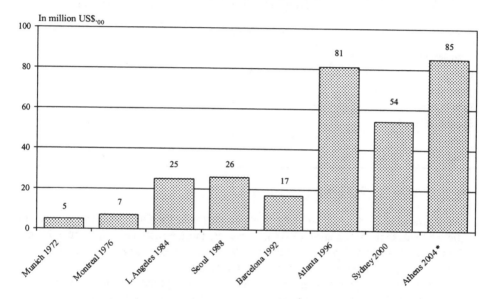

Note: * Estimated in January 2004.

Sources: Interview, Diamantidis (2003); Athens OCOG (2003b, p. 22); Olympic Co-ordination Authority (2002); Preuss (2000a).

Figure 8.15 *OCOG revenues from merchandising*

However, the general trend points to the increasing importance of merchandising. In Atlanta 1996, US$$_{,00}$ 34.7 million were earned from distributing merchandising articles and another US$$_{,00}$ 45.9 million from royalties (IOC, 1996c; Atlanta OCOG, 1996). In Sydney the royalties increased to US$$_{,00}$ 54.3 million and will probably reach US$$_{,00}$ 84.5 million in Athens (Athens OCOG, 2003b).

The fact that there were hardly any international licensees reveals the potential inherent in this financing source. However, M. Payne (interview, 2004) does not see a high potential in international merchandising in the near future. In this matter the IOC is more optimistic.

While the revenue from licensing could possibly become a third pillar of funding for the Olympic Movement, the promotional and educational benefits of using licensing to communicate the ideals of the Movement are far more significant. The IOC is now developing programmes that will set the global standard for the potential of sports licensing. (IOC, http://www.olympic.org/uk/organisation/facts/future/licensing_uk.asp, January 27 2004)

In Athens 2004 almost all licensees are from Greece. The most important licence categories are displayed in Table 8.5

Table 8.5   Athens 2004 license revenues

Product category	Forecasted retail sales	Guaranteed revenues
	(In million US$'00)	
Jewellery	64.68	4.78
Ceramic/porcelain houseware	33.81	2.52
Pins	151.41	11.36
Hats	124.34	9.31
Baby clothing	32.34	2.43
Sports clothing	180.44	13.52
Other	309.01	20.70
Total	**731.45**	**64.62**

Source: Athens OCOG (2003b, p. 83).

M. Payne considers merchandising more important to the Olympics than it is for the National Basketball Association (NBA). However, the international sale of merchandise is less successful than expected (interview, M. Payne, 2004). The figure from Sydney (Table 8.1) includes the revenues from coins and stamps.

Olympic coins, postage stamps and lotteries are special financing means. The government of the host country must approve them prior to their usage to finance the Olympic Games. Coins and stamps belong to the Olympic licensing and have a very long and important Olympic history. Therefore, they are covered in some detail here.

8.2.2.1 Olympic coins
Olympic coins form the most popular and most traditional collectible in the world. They must be distinguished strictly from commemorative medals that are minted under license, and mostly look like the Olympic medals awarded to the athletes. Olympic coins are legal tender and issued by the mint of the respective country. The first coin was issued on the occasion of the Helsinki Games in 1951. Since then all Olympic coins have been legal tender in the issuing countries. Since Tokyo 1964 they have been issued on a regular basis, which has led to a growing popularity. 'Olympic Coins, commemorating the Games, are a part of both the modern era and antiquity' (IOC, http://www.olympic.org/femkt.html, 23 May 1997).

Even in ancient times, one reason for issuing Olympic coins was to create a memento of the Olympic Games (cf. Montreal OCOG, 1976; Perelman, 1985). Today, the aim of producing the coins is to help to promote the Games and arouse interest in them (Lee, 1989; Morin, 1981). However, the most important reason today surely lies in their contribution to the financing of the Olympic Games. In Munich 1972 the issues of the commemorative coins were increased several times. Montreal 1976 and Moscow 1980 introduced international sales and today new forms of coins have been designed to increase the demand. In Sydney, for example, the first coloured commemorative coins were issued and Beijing plans to issue a 10-kilo gold coin (correspondence, Sun, 2004)

Since Munich 1972 the sale of Olympic coins has been a significant source of revenue. However, in view of the growing revenues from the sale of television rights and the Olympic Brand, their importance has declined. Similar to the Olympic stamps, which will be examined later, the success of coin programmes strongly depends on the closeness to the collector as well as on political/governmental agreements. The great potential of this source of revenue is undisputed, as was clearly noticeable in Munich 1972 and Montreal 1976 (German Bundestag, 1975; Montreal OCOG, 1976; Strauss, 1992).

In ancient times special coinages were used to commemorate the Games in Olympia, Greece. The history of modern Olympic coins can be divided into four phases.

1940–68 Start phase   For the Olympic Games in 1940, Finland planned the issue of the first Olympic coin of the modern Games. It was not until 1951, however, that the first Olympic silver coin was issued for the forthcoming Helsinki 1952 Olympics. According to Huot, the profit of the Mint of Finland was said to have amounted to US$'$_{00}$ 6.5 million. This was used to finance the Games (Huot, 1996). The financing source commemorative coins were neither used by the Melbourne/Stockholm 1956 OCOGs nor by the Rome 1960 OCOG. It was only in Tokyo 1964 and Mexico 1968 that coins were issued, although the OCOGs did not receive a direct share of the profit. In the official reports of the Games, Olympic coins are not mentioned at all (Mexico OCOG, 1969; Tokyo OCOG, 1964).

1969–80 Boom phase   In Munich 1972 the coin programme revenues made up an essential portion of the financing of the Games. It was first planned to issue 10 million pieces; however, in order to relieve the public budget, approximately 100 million pieces were minted in the end. Coin revenue developed into the most important financing source of the Games. The total revenues of US$'$_{00}$ 972.4 million were distributed as follows: the Olympia-Baugesellschaft (Olympic building association) received 73 per cent to finance Games-related investments in Munich, the OCOG received 11 per cent to organize the Games, the city of Kiel received 6 per cent to finance local investments and the federal government received 10 per cent to finance post-Olympic costs. Montreal 1976 also made great use of the Olympic coins as a financing source. The international sales of the first gold coin were expected to earn revenues of US$'$_{00}$ 610.8 million. The actual revenue, however, amounted to approximately US$'$_{00}$ 310.4 million (correspondence, Huot, 1999). Moscow 1980 expanded the coin programme with small editions and launched the first platinum coins onto the market. Even the international distribution of the coin programme comprising 45 coins was successful, especially since the sales took place before many nations decided to boycott the Games. According to the share stipulated since 1976, the German NOC, for example, received 3 per cent of the face value of the coins sold nationally, approximately DM·$_{80}$ 4 million, without sending an Olympic team to Moscow (interview, Roth, 1997). Since Montreal 1976, the NOCs receive 3 per cent of the sales/face value of coins sold in their territory (Huot, 1996; Morin, 1981; Nagano OCOG, 1997; Montreal OCOG, 1976; Sydney OCOG, 1997; Perelman, 1985).

1981–96 Regression phase   In this phase the number of coins in the programmes as well as their editions strongly decreased. For the Los Angeles 1984 Olympics, the American government allowed only three coins out of the 29 originally planned for. Since the OCOG only participated in the sales surcharges the state did not subsidize the programme (Los Angeles OCOG, 1984; Perelman, 1985). Seoul 1988 and Los Angeles 1984, could not sell all the coins minted and a part of the already small editions was melted down. Nevertheless, the Korean coin programme was a success (Kim, 1990; Lee, 1989; Park, 1991). Since Barcelona 1992 the revenues from selling Olympic coins have been low when compared to the major financing sources – sponsoring and television rights. Despite innovations such as the first European Currency Unit (ECU) coin, Barcelona 1992 could not match the Seoul 1988 revenues (data in Brunet, 1993).

1999–2008 Stabilization phase   In the US, where the government authorized the minting of 16 coins on the occasion of the Atlanta 1996 Olympics, profits were low despite extensive promotion activities. It is said that the US mint has suffered a considerable deficit with the coin programme (*USA TODAY*, http://web.usatoday.com, 27 May 1997; interview, Heine, 1997). In this phase the participation of the NOCs in the coin revenues also declined. Sydney 2000 issued a higher number of coins. However, the edition was similar to other Games of this phase. Athens 2004 plans to issue 24 coins and also a similar edition than the previous Games. Therefore the revenues from this source seem to stabilize.

Figure 8.16 shows great differences in the edition of a rather small variety of coins in first phase. During second phase the variety of coins increased with smaller editions. Probably, the aim was to increase the collectors' interest. If the quantities released are too large, an increase in the value of Olympic coins is prevented (Lee, 1989; Maennig, 1992). This phase represented the climax of coins as financing source. The third phase experienced a smaller variety with smaller editions. Compared with other financing sources, Olympic coins have lost their significance and stabilized to a certain level in fourth phase. This development must not be generalized, however, since the success of a coin programme depends on many factors which an OCOG has only limited opportunities to influence. In Athens six 500 Drachma coins were issued in 2000. The entire programme had 12 silver (800 000 in total) and six gold coins (100 000 in total). In Beijing 2008 the Olympic coin programme covers the entire Olympiad. Coins will be issued in batches each year from

2005 to 2008. It is anticipated there will be 12 different coins produced of which four will be gold (60 000 of each type) and eight are silver (200 000 of each type) (Bidding Committee Beijing 2008, 2001).

Despite the general decline in the importance of coins for the financing of the Olympic Games, an increase in the worldwide interest in Olympic coins can be noticed.

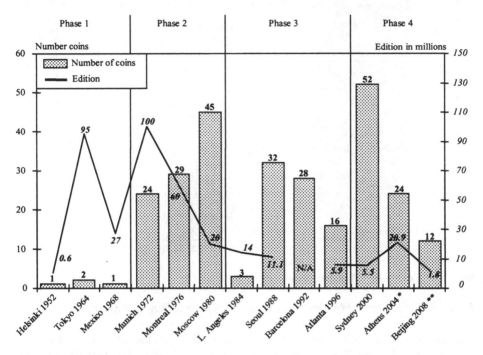

Note: * Estimated in January 2004.
           ** Planned by Bidding Committee Beijing 2008 (2001).

Sources: Bidding Committee Beijing 2008 (2001); Diamantidis (interview, 2003); IOC (2001a); Preuss (2000a).

Figure 8.16   Number of Olympic coins and editions in host countries

If Olympic coins are to be used as legal tender, agreements between the respective government and the mint institution are required due to the fact that any edition of coins, being money supply, increases the money supply, M1. Former host countries with their different laws provided various forms for using the Olympic coins to finance the Games. Each OCOG has participated in one of the following forms in the profit gained from selling coins (Figure 8.17):

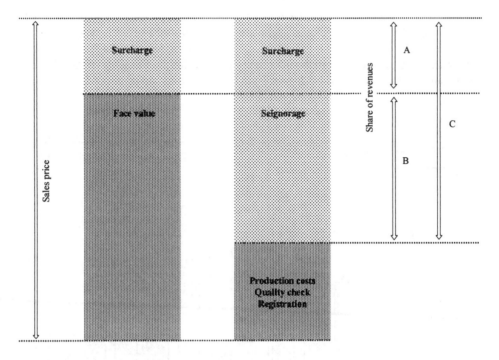

Note: *   Reduced by the respective distribution costs.

Figure 8.17   Forms of OCOG share in the profit from selling Olympic coins

A Surcharge: the OCOG receives the difference between the sale price and the face value of the coin. The state keeps the face value of the coin. From the fiscal point of view, the minting of Olympic coins is thus identical to that of usual ones. This form was selected for Montreal 1976 and Los Angeles 1984 (Montreal OCOG, 1976; Perelman, 1985). If the direct costs – due to high material cost – exceed the face value, the surplus from the surcharge is reduced accordingly. The surcharge has finally to be split between the OCOG, the retailer and the licensee. In Athens, for example, the gold coins will cost €440. The face value is paid to the government, €150 to the licensee, €50 to the OCOG of Athens and the remaining €140 to the retailer (interview, Diamantidis, 2003).

B Seignorage: this form of sharing the seignorage corresponds to a public subsidy of the Games. If the effective money supply is not expanded, the state loses the same amount as the OCOG receives as revenue. In Munich 1972 the money supply was expanded. The state did not suffer direct losses since additional Olympic coins were minted, but the money supply was increased (Federal Government, 1970). In fact, extra money was thus made for the Olympic Games. As long as the money supply increase is controlled, there is no danger of additional inflation caused by the minting of Olympic coins. Many of the coins disappear from the market because collectors keep them. Experience indicates the number of coins, which return into payment transactions. This amount is infinitely small. However, irrespective of whether the money supply is increased or not, the state renounces the seignorage. The advantage of this form is that coins can be sold at their face value. High issues do not cause problems since they are legal tender equal to any other coin. This form was applied for Munich 1972, Lillehammer 1994 and Athens 2004 for the 500 Drachma coins. In Athens the seignorage was split half between the government and the OCOG, which equals an indirect subsidy. The high edition of Munich 1972 prevented any increase in value (Lee, 1989; Maennig, 1992). If the value of a coin reaches its face value, it increasingly returns to payment transactions. This has happened in Germany due to the conversion of Deutsch marks into euros.

C Seignorage and surcharge: this form bears the greatest profit for an OCOG. But the number of coins issued and the surcharge must be weighed up. The higher the sales surcharge, the higher the profit per coin but the lower the demand and thus the sales figures. So far this form has not been used. It is only sensible if the issuer produces a limited edition in order to ensure a sufficient demand in the marketplace.

If one considers the revenues of OCOGs from selling Olympic coins, a decline in the significance of this financing source is becoming evident (Figure 8.18).

No uniform system for using this financing source has been developed for the OCOGs to date. Therefore, only individual factors which influence the OCOG revenues or which an OCOG can influence are discussed in the following.

Face value   During most Olympics, coins were sold with a surcharge since the issuing institution received the face value in most cases. However, if an OCOG receives the seignorage, the face value and the direct costs of the coins will basically determine the amount of the OCOG revenues. In the past, Olympic coins had the inflation-adjusted face values listed in Table 8.6.

The relatively low face values lead to the assumption that the material value was frequently above the face value of a coin. In this case, material value and mint costs can only be compensated for by a surcharge.

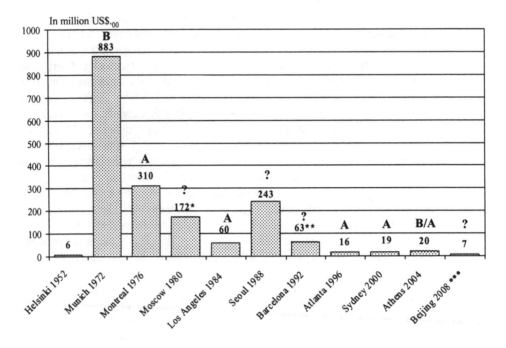

Note: *   value calculated solely by means of exchange rate.
         **   according to R. Huot, indirect OCOG revenues were higher (correspondence, 1997).
         ***   estimated and conservatively set by the Bidding Committee Beijing 2008 (2001).

Sources: Bergman (2003, p. 213); Bidding Committee Beijing 2008 (2001); Preuss (2000a).

Figure 8.18   OCOG revenue from selling Olympic coins

Table 8.6   Face values of Olympic coins from Munich 1972 to Beijing 2008

	bronze/copper	Olympic coins ... silver (Face value in US$‚00)	gold
Munich 1972	–	13.02	–
Montreal 1976	–	12.22 and 24.44	244.45
Los Angeles 1984	–	1.66	16.59
Seoul 1988	2.01 and 4.02	10.05 and 20.10	50.25 and 100.49
Barcelona 1992	–	21.59	107.96; 215.92; 863.69
Atlanta 1996	0.55	1.10	5.49
Sydney 2000	3.77	3.77	75.18
Athens 2004	–	12.25	122.50
Beijing 2008	–	8 coins	4 coins

Sources: Bidding Committee Beijing 2008 (2001); Diamantidis (interview, 2003); Preuss (2000a).

<u>Surcharge</u> If the government does not give the seignorage to the OCOG, or if there is no seignorage an OCOG only earns sales surcharge revenues. In Los Angeles 1984, the OCOG received US$·$_{00}$ 16.59 for each silver coin sold and US$·$_{00}$ 82.93 for each gold coin. It had to pay half of this to the USOC (Perelman, 1985). In Seoul 1988, the sales surcharge amounted to 280 per cent for silver coins and 1400 per cent for gold coins (Seoul OCOG, 1988). Only a high share of precious metal and/or a very small edition can lead to a collector's value above the face value. Sales prices which are out of proportion to the face value, material value or an expected value increase, worsen the chances of high revenues from coin sales from the start. In this case, collecting the coins is no longer sensible as a monetary investment.

Table 8.7 *Precious metal share and material values of Olympic coins from Munich 1972 to Athens 2004*

	Silver coin				Gold coin			
	Material share/ 1000	Fine- ness in g	Material value US$·$_{00}$*	Face value US$·$_{00}$	Material share/ 1000	Fine- ness in g	Material value US$·$_{00}$*	Face value US$·$_{00}$
Munich 1972	625	9.69	1.94 <	13.02	-	-	-	-
Montreal 1976	925	18.95	3.76 <	12.21	917	13.33	196.37 <	244.45
		37.90	7.53 <	24.44		15.55	109.78 <	244.45
L.A. 1984	900	24.50	3.24 >	1.66	900	15.04	210.98 >	16.59
Seoul 1988	925	15.55	3.36 <	10.05	925	15.55	249.05 >	50.25
		31.10	6.72 <	20.10		31.10	498.09 >	100.49
Barcelona 1992	925	24.97	4.63 <	21.59	999	3.36	46.18 <	107.96
						6.74	91.52 <	863.69
						26.97	370.66 <	
Atlanta 1996	900	24.06	4.49 >	1.10	900	7.52	104.00 >	5.49
Sydney 2000	999	31.60	7.55 >	3.77	999	9.99	176.65 >	75.18
Athens 2004	925	34.00	6.43 <	12.25	999	10.00	151.12 >	122.50

Note: * Only share of precious metals: gold (430.16 US$·$_{00}$/oz), silver (5.80 US$·$_{00}$/oz) (Federal Statistical Office, 1996)

Sources: Bidding Committee Beijing 2008 (2001); Diamantidis (interview, 2003); Preuss (2000a).

<u>Direct costs</u> Direct costs comprise material and minting production costs. The material costs heavily depend on the world market price for gold and silver. Production, quality control and registration cause additional costs.

With a high share of gold, a sales surcharge is indispensable. A material value above the face value prevents the coins from flowing back into payment transactions. There are no negative effects of a de facto increase in the money supply. However, in this case neither the government nor the OCOG receive any seignorage.

Table 8.7 shows that for the OCOGs in Seoul 1988 and Athens 2004 (only for gold coins), Los Angeles 1984, Atlanta 1996 and Sydney 2000, the respective material value of the coins exceeded that of the face value.

Distribution costs   Costs are also incurred with the distribution of coins to NOCs or, in most cases, to retailers appointed by the NOCs. In general, the costs are limited to the agreed upon share per coin sold (Nagano OCOG, 1997; Sydney OCOG, 1997). Moreover, 3 per cent of the retail price of the coins sold must be paid to the IOC as royalties (interview, Payne, 2004). These costs are only indirect distribution costs and should at least be covered by the coin sales profit. All other distribution costs are charged to retailers who are not limited to price maintenance (interview, Heine, 1997).

To summarize these factors, an OCOG should keep the following in mind when planning its coin programme. The coins should be legal tender in their respective country, otherwise they would only have the status of Olympic commemorative medals. In addition, all coins should depict Olympic topics and the name of the host country (Morin, 1981). Collectors are interested in high mint quality and limited issues that raise the value. However, the issue should be large enough to avoid speculative purchases. Thus, the Barcelona 1992 OCOG, for example, pursued the following philosophy with its coin programme:

> a model which does not include an excessive number of coins in circulation, a clear relationship between attractive design and collector's interest in a clear subject relationship to the Olympic Games, a reasonable price which does not exceed the market average, face values higher than face values with an adequate relation to the sale price, a policy of sale price control to prevent speculation, a policy of stimulus and control over the creation of a secondary market which aids the development of the primary market for the issues as they appear. (Barcelona OCOG, 1988)

The licensee should work to ensure that the coins are distributed to the largest collectors' markets in the world. It is, therefore, necessary to cooperate with competent partners who are experts in the worldwide distribution of coins and with the NOCs to make the sale of coins a success. The number of coins delivered to other countries should be linked to the demand in the respective country and, taking the whole issue into account, should be distributed accordingly. In the end, most coins will be sold in host countries, especially in those with a large collectors' market, since collecting national coins is far more popular than collecting subject-specific coins.

8.2.2.2   Olympic stamps
The first Olympic Games in Athens 1896 were decisively financed by issuing Olympic stamps. This action created the first collecting sector for sports stamps. Today, Olympic stamps are perhaps the largest sector among the sports motifs (Preuss, 2000a). The Olympic philatelic programmes are much more complex than just stamps. However, since the main participation of the OCOG is related to stamps, these will be the subjects to

study in this book. With the exception of Athens 1896 and Tokyo 1964 the revenues of the OCOGs mainly stem from the sales of Olympic stamps. However, they hardly exceeded 2 per cent of the total OCOG revenues. After Moscow 1980, the share fell below even 1 per cent. Nevertheless, this means of financing should not be dismissed as insignificant since the absolute revenues from the sales of Olympic stamps show a rising trend. In addition, Olympic stamps have reminded people of the Games, promoted the Olympics, have been collector objects which are sought after in the entire world and have offered the postal authorities opportunities to gain additional revenues for over 100 years.

Today, 'the IOC encourages, in collaboration with the NOCs of the countries concerned, the use of the Olympic symbol on postage stamps issued in liaison with the IOC by the competent national authorities' (IOC, 2003d, para. 17, By-Law 5).

Before investigating in the following the share the OCOGs received from the revenues of the postal authorities, the history of this financing source will be described in brief. By considering the aims and motives of a postal authority for issuing Olympic postage stamps, some factors, which determine the amount of the revenues an OCOG receives from the issuing of Olympic stamps, will be explained in detail.

The 100-year history of Olympic stamps shows four phases. The number of stamps, their time of issue and the way in which an OCOG shared the revenues are used as criteria (Preuss, 1999, app. 4-13). The history of the stamps is a typical example of product life cycles.

1896–1936 Test phase   In this first phase only a few stamps were issued. With the exception of Paris 1924 and Amsterdam 1928, they were issued exclusively by the postal authority of the host country. The way in which the OCOGs shared in the revenues differed strongly.

1937–60 Introduction phase   All stamps – with the exception of Helsinki 1951 – were isued only in the Olympic year, shortly before the Games. In this phase Olympic stamps were not used to finance the Olympic Games – with the exception of St Moritz 1948 (correspondence, Lippert, 2000) and Helsinki 1952. However, an enlargement of the series can be observed. Countries whose teams participated in the Olympic Games increasingly started to issue commemorative stamps. Even non-participating countries issued Olympic stamps, presumably to make money from collectors.

1961–72 Boom phase   In this phase each OCOG participated in the postal authority revenues. All publicly subsidized Olympics used this financing source. Figure 8.20 shows how countries, other than that of the host nation, also increased the issues of stamps. This phase could also be called the phase of overheating. This short period is characterized by an exponential increase in the number of countries issuing Olympic stamps. The increase in the total number of stamps is also directly linked to this development. The reason for this, on the one hand, is that the series became more extensive and, on the other hand, the periods when they could be bought were expanded. In the host country, the first stamps were issued as early as right after the previous Olympic Games.

<u>1973–2000 Consolidating phase</u>   During this phase the issue of Olympic stamps as semi-official stamps was established. With the exception of Los Angeles 1984, Atlanta 1996 in the USA and Sydney in 2000, where semi-official stamps are unknown, all OCOGs received a share of the revenues the postal authorities received. The early issue of the first stamps in Barcelona 1992, which was pulled forward to the OCOG founding phase of 1986, is striking. Nevertheless, it is clear that the number of stamps issued in the host country has declined.

Concerning Athens 2004 the Hellenic Post (ELTA) is one of the 'grand national sponsors' of the OCOG. It is planned to issue 18 million Olympic stamps (interview, Chalkias, 2003). For the 2008 Games, Beijing OCOG, in consultation and cooperation with the State Post Bureau, will ask governing institutions to issue Olympic stamps (Bidding Committee Beijing 2008, 2001).

Figure 8.19 surveys of the stamp programmes in the host country and the OCOG share of the revenues. After Rome 1960 the issuing of Olympic stamps boomed worldwide. It is obvious that host countries, which used stamps to finance the Games, issued more stamps than those countries which issued stamps for commemorative purposes only. Circles indicate the Games where the OCOGs shared in the stamp programme of their country.

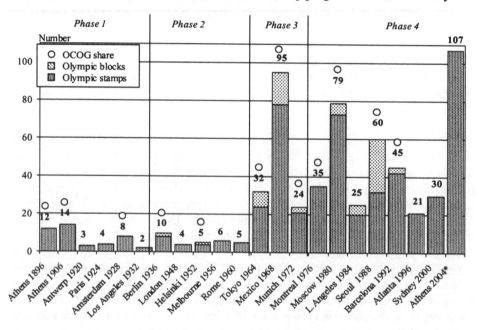

Note: * including blocks, final figure after the Games, including 16 stamps of Greek medallists

Sources: Chalcias (correspondence, 9 February, 2004); Preuss (2000a)

Figure 8.19   Number of Olympic stamps in host countries

Figure 8.19 shows that – disregarding the host country – the series have become smaller (third and fourth phase) and that there has been an absolute increase in the OCOG revenues from Olympic stamps.

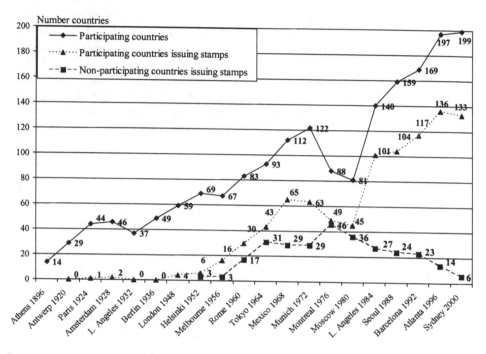

Source: Bergman (2003, p. 208).

Figure 8.20   Evolution of the Olympic stamps issues

Depending on the way an OCOG participates in the revenues from selling Olympic stamps, there are three forms:

1. Surcharges on the face value: if the sales price of a postage stamp is higher than the imprinted face value and the difference is not stated on the stamp, a surcharge is charged. Amsterdam 1928 used such a surcharge for the first time in Olympic history. The resulting revenues flowed to the Netherlands Olympic Committee, which, in turn, used the money for organizing the Olympic Games (Fioretti et al., 1984). In Mexico 1968 a block of stamps was sold at a higher price than the face value of the individual stamps contained in the block.
2. Supplementary charges on the face value: if a stamp has another value imprinted on top of the face value it is a so-called semi-official stamp or supplement stamp. This type of stamp was first used for Antwerp 1920. The supplementary charge was intended for the invalids of the First World War. However, the small number of

stamps sold (11 per cent of the amount printed) leads to the assumption that the surcharge hindered sales. On 3 March 1921, the remaining stamps were therefore marked with an imprint (all at 20c) and sold again (Comité Olympique Anvers, 1920). Semi-official stamps have only been allowed in international post traffic since 1 January 1922 (Häger, 1973). In Berlin 1936 the supplementary charges were used for a special fund to stage the Olympic Games (Binfield, 1948; Germann, 1996). Thus it was Germany that introduced the financing instrument 'semi-official stamps' for Olympic Games, which has become well established today. In 1935 the first semi-official stamps were issued on the occasion of the Olympic Winter Games of Garmisch-Partenkirchen 1936. A distinction must be made between rigid supplement rates as they were used in Tokyo 1964, Montreal 1976 and Barcelona 1992, and variable supplements, which increase with the face value of the stamp. Apart from Berlin 1936, the variable supplement rates were also applied in Helsinki 1952, Munich 1972, Moscow 1980 and Seoul 1988.

3. Sharing part of the face value: the first Olympic Games in Athens 1896 were substantially financed by sharing a part of the revenues received from selling Olympic stamps. Among the supporters of the Olympic idea was the president of the Hellenic philatelists, Sacoraphos, who suggested issuing a stamp series to finance the Games as early as on 15 June 1895 (Bura, 1960). Later, it was regulated by law that 50 per cent of the sum obtained from the sale of commemorative stamps would go towards the organization of the Olympic Games. According to the official report, 400 000 drachmas were firmly promised by law (Philemon, 1996 [1896]). This form of participation was also applied towards financing to the Greek 'Intermediate Games' of 1906 (Binfield, 1948; Bura, 1960). Afterwards, no postal authority ever again involved an OCOG in sharing a part of the face value of the Olympic stamps. This financing form must be considered a subsidy – comparable to sharing the seignorage from Olympic coins. In this case, the Greek postal authority refrained from collecting revenues and, thus, even from a part of their contribution margin, as long as the issuing of Olympic stamps did not create an additional demand from collectors.

In the past, there were countries which did not issue Olympic stamps or whose OCOGs did not share in the revenues gained from the sales price of the stamps (see Figure 8.19, bars without circles). In Paris 1900, St Louis 1904, London 1908 and Stockholm 1912 no Olympic stamps were issued. Since then, Olympic postage stamps have been issued for all Games.

In France 1924, UK 1948, Australia 1956/2000, Italy 1960 and the USA 1932/1984/1996, postage stamps with Olympic motifs were issued without the respective OCOG receiving a share of the revenues. The high number of English-speaking countries is striking. Thus in the USA, Australia and in England semi-official stamps are little known or not accepted. They are called 'semi-postals' (Häger, 1973) and are listed in special catalogues under 'semi-official.' Semi-official stamps to support the Olympic Games certainly would not be widely accepted in these countries.

The commemoration of the corresponding Olympic Games plays a major role with regards to the objectives and motives for issuing Olympic stamps. Until London 1948, Olympic stamps – with the exception of Portugal and Uruguay – were only issued by the host nation in the Olympic year. From 1948 this motive was superseded more and more by the quest for additional revenues. This is also reflected in the fact that other nations also issued stamps to commemorate their participation in the Olympics. The strong interest of philatelists in Olympic stamps has caused more and more countries to issue postage stamps with Olympic motifs (Figure 8.20). Collectors, in particular from industrialized nations, but also from Russia and China, buy these stamps or have them cancelled with special postmarks (interview, Volk, 1996). Large collector markets are the USA, Germany, France, Canada, Switzerland, Japan, the Netherlands and Singapore (Moscow OCOG 1980). In view of relatively low production and distribution costs, the postal authority of the respective country makes a profit because no utilization of the postal system takes place. In this case, the profit is determined by the revenues to the amount of the face value minus design, print, distribution costs and the running of special post offices during the Games.

Since Sydney the OCOG and post issue stamps of gold medallists of the host country. Therefore it is not clear now, how many stamps Greece will issue in 2004.

Some of the critical factors influencing the amount of the OCOG revenues (Figure 8.21) gained from a postal authority stamp programme are explained in the following.

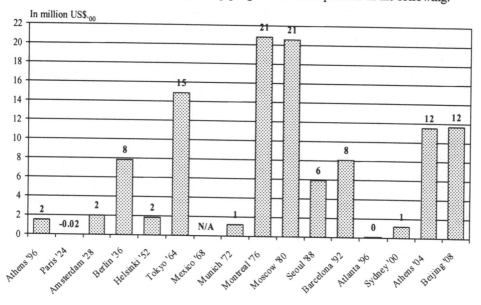

Sources: Bergman (2003, p. 212); Preuss (2000a).

Figure 8.21   Revenues from Olympic stamps

<u>Organizational form of the systems</u>   Cooperation between the postal authority, NOC and OCOG is the prerequisite for an Olympic stamp programme. 'The Olympic Symbol may be used on postage stamps issued by competent national postal authorities in collaboration with the IOC and their respective NOCs' (Stupp, 1996). The OCOG, in turn, works in close cooperation with the NOC and IOC. If all parties are state organized, the carrying out of an Olympic stamp programme should not cause any problems. But if a single system is organized as a private business, numerous coordination activities are required. Otherwise, an Olympic stamp programme could even fail, as was almost the case in Atlanta 1996 (Preuss, 2000a)

<u>Acceptance in the population</u>   The success of a stamp programme primarily depends on how it is accepted by the population and collectors. Care must be taken not to produce editions which could scare off potential buyers. The Fédération Internationale de Philatélie (FIP) commission names the following characteristics of such 'unwanted editions' (correspondence, Bergman, 1999; Häger, 1973):

- the face values or supplementary charges are too high
- the series of commemorative or special stamps are too large
- the issues are kept too small on purpose
- the formats of blocks are too large
- the topic of the edition is not related to the issuing country.

With the exception of the characteristic 'supplementary charges are too high,' most of the factors mainly concern collectors and must be considered as factors that can diminish the buying intention. Throughout the history of Olympic stamps there have been a few of these 'unwanted editions'. These most probably have prevented a possibly greater success of the financing source Olympic stamps.

<u>Number of copies</u>   Apart from the amount of the supplementary charges, OCOG revenues are also determined by the quantity issued. This is an important factor for determining the later collectors' value of the stamps, which generally influences the international demand. In Athens 1896 the first edition was so much sought after that speculative purchases were made. However, this was not in the government's interest and so a second edition of the stamps was printed (Bura, 1960). After Tokyo 1964, the number of Olympic stamps and the number of issues rose strongly. A small edition increases the value and thus the collector's interest in the stamp. Small number of copies means low revenues for the OCOGs, since they only receive a share of the sale price in the form of supplementary charges and not of the collector's value of the stamps.

<u>Time of emission</u>   With the exception of Helsinki 1952 and Melbourne 1956, Olympic stamps were only issued in the Olympic year until Tokyo 1964. In Japan stamps for the 1964 Olympics were issued as early as in 1961. This model set an example for the next decades to come. The Spanish postal authority issued the first Olympic stamps as early as

seven years prior to the Games of Barcelona 1992. Keeping in mind the maximization of revenues for an OCOG, the number of stamps in the Olympic year should be kept small, while the selling of Olympic postage stamps years before the Olympics is recommendable. Today one can also see bidding cities issuing stamps during the bid period such as Beijing and Istanbul for 2000 or Rio de Janeiro and Buenos Aires for 2004 (correspondence, Lippert, 2000).

<u>Legal conditions</u> In countries, where semi-official stamps are issued for charity purposes, an OCOG might not participate in the supplementary charges. In Germany, for example, the supplementary revenues from sports stamps flow exclusively to the 'Stiftung Deutsche Sporthilfe e.V.' (foundation to promote top-performance sport in Germany). In such a situation, the usual revenues from selling sport stamps could be calculated by statistical procedures and then possibly the OCOG could be given the extra revenues which result in the case of increased sales due to the Olympic Games (Maennig, 1992).

An OCOG should aim at producing an extensive offering (series range and quantity of issue) without discouraging collectors from buying due to the high numbers of stamps or high values. For 30 years the semi-official stamp has proved an appropriate form of revenue participation for the OCOG. Fixed supplementary charges earn the highest revenues for small values and presumably the largest profit for the OCOG. Variable supplementary charges appear to be fairer to the consumer but diminish the OCOG profit because the supplementary charges for 'everyday stamps' are relatively low. Care should be taken to avoid supplementary charges exceeding 50 per cent of the face value, otherwise they would be an 'unwanted edition'.

8.2.2.3 Olympic pins

During the past several celebrations of the Games, the selling of Olympic pins has increased and even higher royalties have been achieved than with the sale of Olympic stamps. The manufacturing of the first Olympic pin is documented for the Los Angeles 1932 Games. However, the revenues from the pin sales went to the gas companies of Los Angeles rather than to the OCOG (Trumpp, 1991). In Atlanta 1996, the first international pin trading society in Olympic history was founded (IOC, 7 Jun 1995b). In total, the ACOP produced more than 900 different pins for the 1996 Olympics. It was said that there were more than 10 000 different pins and that approximately 25 000 pins were sold on a daily basis throughout the Games (IOC, 1997a). Even in Sydney, where pins are not popular at all, a huge pin programme was set up (interview, Elphinston, 1999). In Athens 2004 it is expected that the pin business is the second biggest of the licence programmes with an estimated turnover of US$$_{.00}$ 151.4 million.

8.2.3   Relations between IOC, OCOG, Sponsors and Licensees

Based on the knowledge of the history of the four groups (IOC, OCOG, sponsors and licensees), their interests in Olympic marketing are investigated here. First, each group is reviewed separately to reduce the complex network of interdependent interests. Thus a better analysis of the frequently asserted issue of 'over-commercialization' will be possible.

8.2.3.1 Interests of the IOC

Former IOC President J.A. Samaranch and his striving for financial independence and guaranteed solvency of the IOC opened the Olympic Movement to marketing. At the beginning of the 1980s, the Olympic Movement mostly depended on the revenues from the sales of television rights. When, in 1981, Alexander called upon the IOC to open up new sources of revenue apart from those gained by selling television rights, the IOC was subsequently self-critical enough to see in New Delhi in 1983 that the Olympic Movement depended too much on television stations. Thus, J.A. Samaranch transformed the Commission for the Protection of the Olympic Symbol, which had been founded by Brundage, into the 'New Sources of Financing Commission' (Lyberg, s.t.).

Until 1996, the ISL coordinated TOP. The ISL supported, controlled and optimized the sponsoring activities among the corresponding OCOGs, NOCs and sponsors. A large part of the revenues from TOP go to the NOCs, which, in return, protect the Olympic symbol and brands in their countries. Previously, the Olympic Charter urged the OCOGs to sign contracts with every NOC. The IOC coordination, however, has enabled worldwide marketing whereby the rights could be sold more expensively than before. J.A. Samaranch signed the final contract with the ISL on 28 May 1985. Later, M. Payne said: 'The biggest achievement of TOP in the early days was getting all countries – capitalist, communist from inner Africa to outer Mongolia – to agree to a single marketing programme' (Rozin, 1996).

The IOC's interest in the field of marketing, which also affects the OCOGs, can be summarized as follows: it must increase or at least keep at a very high level the value of its symbol, the Olympic Rings. This is important since the Rings represent the entire Olympic Movement and become visible and real for people all over the world through the Olympic Games. For long-term, successful and worldwide marketing of the Olympic Rings the following four components are of special significance.

Profile of the product   The product to be marketed is the Olympic Games, which represents sports competitions for the 'youth of the world', signified by the five interlaced rings symbol created by Coubertin in 1913. The profile of the Olympic Games themselves, however, was for a long time not known. In 1997 the IOC started some market research to harmonize the marketing with the product 'Olympics'. It was not until 1999 that the IOC commissioned a global brand assessment to determine which attributes consumers associated most with the Olympic insignia. It was found that the strongest brand attributes transcended 'sports' and featured the Olympic values. In detail, the

Olympics were seen as 'a peaceful and festive forum for cultural exchange and fair play' with 'ideals of equality, tradition, honour and excellence'. The brand assessment analysis led to the creation of a 'benefit pyramid' built on a level of functional and emotional equities. It was proposed that this benefit hierarchy be translated into four strong positioning options with which Olympic partners can align their own brands: these being, 'Hope – Dreams/Inspiration – Friendship and Fair Play – Joy in Effort'. The characteristics of the Olympic Brand where analysed and it became clear what had to be left unchanged in order not to damage the Olympics brand (IOC, 2001b; Weissenberg, 1996). This profile is important in order to give the corporate partners an idea of what they could expect as service in return for their commitment and how they could and should use their rights to the symbol for advertising impact. It is also known that the 'Olympic idea ... [embodies] ... performance and fairness, two basic values which should be part of any enterprise philosophy and which offer immense opportunities for a global image transfer' (Klink, 1996, p. 17), thereby making corporations prepared to pay very high sponsoring fees. The IOC must take care to record, maintain or even enhance those elements, which determine the Olympic profile. Today, attention is paid to which products (Payne, 1996) may carry the Olympic symbol or which elements of the Olympic Movement should not be linked to advertising. This includes the torchbearer as well as the Olympic venue sites. The Olympic Charter (IOC, 2003d, Rule 61, para. 1) states: 'Commercial installations and advertising signs shall not be allowed in the stadiums, nor in other sport grounds.' 'No form of publicity or propaganda, commercial or otherwise, may appear on persons, sportswear, accessories or, more generally, on any article of clothing or equipment whatsoever worn or used by the athletes' (IOC 2003d, By-Law to Rule 61, para. 1).

Awareness of the Olympic symbol   Since the Olympic Rings have been used for worldwide marketing their level of awareness has been investigated. An in-depth analysis by SRi in 1995 carried out in nine countries revealed an average level of awareness of the Olympic Rings of 78 per cent (n = 10 357; IOC, 1996c). A closer review of the data proves a correlation between the awareness level and the prosperity of the corresponding country, which is linked to the proliferation of television units (r = 0.62). A correlation to the number of medals won (r = 0.47) can also be proven statistically but this should be reflected upon critically.

Investigations on the level of awareness of the Olympic Rings (Table 8.8) were carried out by:

- ISL 1985: USA (n = 300), Germany (n = 312), Portugal (n = 300), Singapore (n = 306)
- SRi 1995: UK, Australia, India, Japan, USA, Jamaica, Brazil, Nigeria and Germany. More than 7000 people were surveyed. The selected countries were chosen according to the criteria 'Olympic host', 'developed' and 'less developed'.

Table 8.8   *GNP/capita, number of medals and level of awareness of the Olympic Rings in the countries investigated*

Country	Year	GNP/capita of year	GNP/capita in US$'00	Number of medals (Olympic year)	n	Level of awareness in per cent
USA	1985	16 690	26 320 (1984)	174	300	87
Germany	1985	10 940	17 252 (1984)	59	312	98
Portugal	1985	1970	3107 (1984)	3	300	89
Singapore	1985	7420	11 701 (1984)	0	306	43
England	1994	18 340	21 034 (1992)	20		89
Australia	1994	18 000	20 643 (1992)	27		95
India	1994	302	346 (1992)	0		69
Japan	1994	34 830	39 946 (1992)	22		97
USA	1994	25 880	29 681 (1992)	108		81
Jamaica	1994	1540	1766 (1992)	4		52
Brazil	1994	2970	3406 (1992)	3		62
Nigeria	1994	280	321 (1992)	4		53
Germany	1994	25 580	29 337 (1992)	82		87

Sources: ISL (1985); Kaiser and Maegerlein (1984); World Bank (1987; 1996).

<u>Protecting the emblems and symbol and guaranteeing exclusiveness</u>   The revenues from sponsoring depend on the number of consumers that can potentially be reached and the guarantee of exclusiveness gained from protecting the emblems and symbol. The IOC can only achieve high revenues if it assigns rights, which are exclusive on a worldwide level. It must avoid the 'depreciation of the Rings' (Brundage, 1938). Maus (German sponsor) observed critically: The Olympic symbol of the five rings must not be marketed to an exaggerated extent. Otherwise the brand will be lost. The tendency to dilution has already taken place and is hard to control internationally, (Klink, 1996, p. 17). The IOC must take the greatest care to protect the emblems and symbol because they are a prerequisite for exclusiveness.

<u>Long-term partnerships</u>   Similar to selling television rights, a long-term partnership between international companies and the Olympic Movement enhances the sponsors' interest in using the emblems and symbol in their advertising activities in a way that it is not damaged (IOC, 1996b).

R. Pound thought 'the greater the investments [of the corporations], the greater the promotion' (Thurow, 1996, p. R14) of the Olympic Movement. M. Payne said: 'The more sport gives the industry, the greater the benefit it will receive in return' (Payne, 1989). It is understandable that the corporations must permanently integrate the Olympic Movement in order to make the rising sponsoring commitments pay off. This results in both a long-term benefit for the corporations and indirect advertising for the Olympic

Movement which is not only limited to the period of the Games (interview, Payne, 1997). Long-term partnerships allow the IOC to develop long-term strategies to foster the Olympic Movement and to support the OCOGs better by earning higher revenues (Payne, 1996) (Table 8.9). A strong Olympic Movement and the high financial support for the OCOGs give the IOC power and guarantee its permanent existence.

Table 8.9   Categories and corporations of the TOP

	TOP I 1985–88	TOP II 1989–92	TOP III 1993–96	TOP IV 1997–2000	TOP V 2001–04	TOP VI 2005–08
Number of companies	9	12	10	11	11	N/A
Office material	3M	3M	–	–	–	
Optical products	–	Bausch & Lomb	Bausch & Lomb	–	–	
Typewriters	Brother	Brother	–	–	–	
Non-alcoholic beverages	Coca-Cola	Coca-Cola	Coca-Cola	Coca-Cola	Coca-Cola	Coca-Cola
Film/imaging photographic	Kodak	Kodak	Kodak	Kodak	Kodak	Kodak
Snacks	–	Mars	–	–	–	
TV/audio/video equipment	Panasonic	Panasonic	Matsushita/ Panasonic	Matsushita/ Panasonic	Matsushita/ Panasonic	Matsushita/ Panasonic
Life insurance	–	–	John Hancock	John Hancock	John Hancock	John Hancock
Document processing	–	Ricoh	Xerox	Xerox	Xerox	–
Publications	Time/Sports Illustrated	Time/Sports Illustrated	Time/Sports Illustrated	Time/Sports Illustrated	Time/Sports Illustrated	
Express mail/ package delivery services	Federal Express	US Postal Service	UPS	UPS	–	
Credit cards	VISA	VISA	VISA	VISA	VISA	VISA
Information technology	–	–	IBM	IBM	Atos Origin	Atos Origin
Computer	–	–	–	–	–	Lenovo
Retail food service	–	–	–	McDonald's	McDonald's	McDonald's
Wireless communications equipment	–	–	–	Samsung	Samsung	Samsung
Timing, scoring and services	–	–	–	–	Swatch	Swatch
Lighting	Philips	Philips	–	–	–	
N/A	–	–	–	–	–	General Electric
In million US$'00	119.17	215.04	384.16*	523.6*	557.2*	N/A

Note: *   Value in kind is included in these figures.

Sources: Hill (1996); IOC (1996a; 1997c; 2001c; 2003b, p. 2; 2004b); Landry and Yerlès (1996); NN (1996n).

Since there is a direct link between the financing sources of television and sponsoring, the IOC interests regarding the selling of television rights shall be repeated here. If the marketing activities were expanded to advertising in the venues and on the athlete's apparel and equipment, corporations would pay less for commercial spots during the events. M. Payne said: 'The [Coca-Cola] group, has now told us it will immediately stop its Olympic sponsoring if we allow board advertising' (Weissenberg, 1996). This could result in a considerable loss of revenues from the sales of television rights, which could not be compensated for by the additional marketing of the advertising areas. An increase in the number of sponsors could also lead to a decline in the revenues from television rights if this increase gave the viewer the impression of exaggerated commercialization. Corporations are not willing to pay for spots which create negative feelings in the consumer. However, this statement must be analysed in a differentiated way because the acceptance of commercials in North America, for example, differs from that in Europe. According to ISL investigations, products of Olympic sponsors have a good image (83 per cent, n = 1218; ISL, 1985).

How much the Olympics depend already on the payments of the sponsors becomes obvious by looking at the amount of sponsors that are buying television spots during the broadcast. A study done during the Sydney 2000 Olympics shows how dominant the sponsors are in buying television commercial spots. Figure 8.22 shows the percentage of commercials recorded on the 29 and 30 September 2000 during prime time in different countries. The commercials where analysed by Hochbrückner (2001).

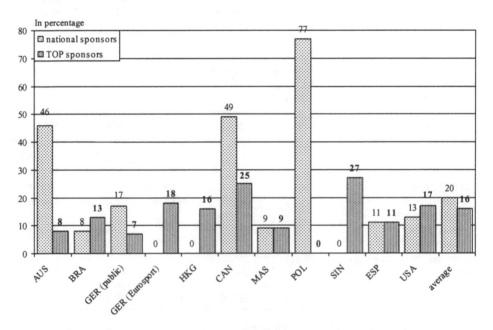

Figure 8.22   Percentage of TV commercials of sponsors during the Sydney Olympic Games

The IOC can only secure marketing revenues as a second major financing source of the Olympic Movement if it permanently maintains the high reputation of its symbol. The Olympic aura and the special atmosphere during the Olympic Games must not be underestimated. The monetary amount for the sales of television rights is considerably influenced by these Olympic values. The IOC existence is linked very closely to the Olympic image. An increase in the image and the reputation of the Olympic Brand could increase revenues.

8.2.3.2 Interests of the OCOG

Nowadays, an OCOG is not in position to influence the revenues from the sales of television rights. However, it has numerous opportunities in marketing. An OCOG runs its own sponsoring programme, and is responsible for the licensing. It can be assumed that the corporations of a host country are particularly interested in the Games and are willing to pay higher fees for sponsoring or a licence than corporations in other countries. The OCOG and the respective NOC attempt to optimize the revenues from their joint national sponsor programme. There are two objectives for sponsoring which are not easy to combine: first, to enhance the image and, secondly, to maximize profit (interview, Battle, 1997).

Enhancing the image   The image of the Olympic Games is strongly influenced by the media. Reports about the quality of the organization or unexpected incidents, for example, strongly influence the image of the Games and the city. The city will keep this image for years. Despite hundreds of sponsors, the Montreal 1976 Olympics are still thought of as deficit Games, the Los Angeles 1984 Olympics are considered profit-making Olympics because of their excellent marketing and the Seoul 1988 Games are considered to have opened the door to the world market for Korean corporations (Greising, 1996). Atlanta 1996 entered Olympic history as a 'fair' due to the exaggerated street vending that dominated the appearance of the city. However, mainly non-Americans have this impression. 'Besides, Americans are much more used to a commercialization of sports than Europeans. If each baseball club ... and each basketball team can market its emblem ... and mascot to millions, why should it be different for the Olympics?' (IOC, 1997a). The IOC also felt: 'The subsequent tented city of stalls selling food, gifts and merchandise was an ugly eyesore' (Rademacher, 1996a). Finally, Sydney 2000 is considered the perfect Games with a green touch. It must be the objective of an OCOG to earn enough money from its sponsoring programme without negatively affecting the image of the Olympics and of the host city.

Maximizing the profit   Increasingly, the Olympic Games are financed by private sources. The OCOG must maximize revenues these from private sources since the costs of the Games continue to increase while public funds decrease (Catherwood and van Kirk, 1992). The OCOGs urge the IOC to allow an increase in the number of sponsors to a higher level than the IOC would like to see. M. Payne referred to the pressure regarding negotiations with Nagano 1998 (interview, 1997) and Battle in regards to Atlanta 1996 (interview, 1997). The OCOG is particularly interested in having its own sponsoring programmes. The Atlanta 1996 OCOG received approximately US$$_{.00}$ 658.2 million from its sponsors and suppliers, whereas it received only US$$_{.00}$ 89.6 million from the IOC marketing programme (TOP) (Atlanta OCOG, 1998). Sydney's OCOG received US$$_{.00}$ 515.9 million from national sponsorship whereas it got US$$_{.00}$ 190.4 million from TOP (IOC, 2001b). Athens 2004 established a new era of exclusive sponsorships. On Greek territory 21 of the 30 sponsors receive the same rights from the OCOG as for the Greek territory. The OCOG got US$$_{.00}$ 350 million stems from national sponsorship whereas the OCOG gets US$$_{.00}$ 333.2 million from TOP (interview, Chalkias, 2003). This emphasizes the significance of the national sponsoring programme. Its success is mainly determined by the following factors:

- Guarantee of exclusiveness for sponsors: the official right to use the emblems and symbol, which is granted by the OCOG and possibly the NOC, must be protected in the territory of the host country and may only be awarded to one sponsor per product or service category. In future, it will be hardly possible to clearly demarcate the product or service categories since many corporations distribute products of different categories. The IOC or OCOG/NOC would have to award the rights not to an entire corporation but to a corporation for a certain product category. Care must also be taken to limit the number of sponsors and to clearly demarcate the individual product or service category. In Beijing 2008 the sponsors of the joint marketing programme will have priority and exclusive rights over the use of advertising areas at billboards, sky space and the public mass transportation system (Bidding Committee Beijing 2008, 2001).
- Protection against ambush marketing: ambush marketing 'is a planned effort (campaign) by an organization to associate themselves indirectly with an event in order to gain at least some of the recognition and benefits that are associated with being an official sponsor' (Shani and Sandler, 1989, 8.11). To protect the Olympic insignia, ambush marketing must actively be fought against. The Atlanta 1996 OCOG spent US$$_{.00}$ 11 million on its 'sponsor protection programme' alone (Cater, 1996; Florin and Carlin, 1995). Furthermore, the 80 000 OCOG staff was called upon to report any misuse of the insignia. In Sydney there was a 'brand protection' for merchandising which employs 100 'special agents' and during the Games with additional 50 law students (NN, 1999b). Since the NOC of the respective country registers for the rights to all emblems and the Olympic symbol, it is the only institution which can take legal steps against infringements. An OCOG can only fight ambush marketers through legal action and public relation actions. The IOC is also looking seriously at this matter (IOC, 1999a).
- Offering sponsor packages: these packages contain offers and services for sponsors which are directed towards the inside and the outside. Inside services are the so-called hospitality packages, which may include tickets, accommodation and private hospitality such as a 'sponsor house', space in the sponsor village, receptions, gifts, VIP parking and transportation for sponsors and their guests. In Sydney the

sponsors brought 6000 guests to the Games. The so-called visibility packages offer the sponsors opportunities to be recognized publicly (Catherwood and van Kirk, 1992).

In Atlanta 1996 and Salt Lake 2002 the OCOG and USOC jointly marketed the Olympics, owing to the great marketing experience of the USOC (interview, Payne, 2004). In Sydney the same exclusivity was reached by transferring all rights from the NOC to the OCOG. The OCOG paid the NOC US$'$_{00}$ 11.2 million in general as well as value in kind from each sponsor to get the exclusive rights for the entire Olympiad (interview, Elphinston, 1999). This joint marketing is also planned for Athens 2004 and Beijing 2008, and will be the model for all future Games.

The OCOG interests are similar with regards to licensing. The aim is to maximize profit without creating an impression of completely commercializing the Games. In future, OCOGs can expect higher revenues from merchandising (interview, Battle, 1997; Howard and Crompton, 1995; interview, Payne, 1997; Ruffenach, 1996b), although unlimited marketing is not possible due to the fact that the IOC no longer permits Olympic emblems and the symbol to be used on all products (Payne, 1996).

In Atlanta 1996, the OCOG operated its own merchandise sales stands for the first time. Compared to the preceding Games, it achieved higher revenues because the OCOG could not only enlarge its trade margin, but also use the most attractive point of sale. The licences were awarded as early as 1991 and the licensees promoted the sales of their products early (Ruffenach, 1996b). Apart from the one-off licence fee it is common that licensees involve the OCOG in the turnover. Athens 2004, for example, gets a fixed fee from each licensee and additional royalties if the turnover is greater than the estimated amount (interview, Diamantidis, 2003). Therefore, it is also in the OCOG's best interests that the sales of Olympic products begin as early as possible. However, the start of a merchandise programme is limited to the Olympiad. The official Beijing Olympic merchandise will start after the Athens 2004 Games.

The benefits the OCOG receives from the various sponsor programmes are financial and value in kind, such as services provided by the sponsors. Without these, today's Olympics could no longer be staged. Sheinman of Coca-Cola said that in the future, the sector payments in kind would come to the fore (NN, 1995a). This is understandable in view of the ever-rising sponsor services because the value of the products is calculated at market prices. For the corporation, however, production costs are applicable at the most. For an OCOG, this is a negative development since it must settle extensive payments. The Atlanta 1996 OCOG, for example, faced severe financial problems owing to the large amount of value in kind and services (interview, Battle, 1997).

For each OCOG the promotion of Olympic Games ultimately brings an additional benefit. This benefit is linked to sponsoring and merchandising because the sponsors, suppliers and licensees promote the Games with their products all over the world free of charge. 'Advertising and promotions help us to tell the Olympic story. And at all levels we could never afford to run. Several sponsors spent over $200 million worldwide' (Payne, 1998). The television stations, with their interest in high viewing rates, must be integrated into this network. With their reporting, for example, they increase the excitement prior to the Games. This is in the interest of the OCOG, in the form of promoting the Olympics, and of the sponsors, in the form of high viewing rates and a stronger appeal to potential customers. The OCOG has an additional benefit if it succeeds in contracting sponsors (partners) as early as possible. Since they make payments directly to the OCOG, this early influx of cash improves the OCOG's solvency.

Marketing activities also involve manifold costs for an OCOG. Apart from the administration and the acquisition of sponsors, opportunity costs are caused by giving away free tickets, VIP space and parking spaces in the sports venues as well as by other services of the sponsoring programme (gifts, arrangements, and so on). Furthermore, it can be assumed that the costs associated with campaigns to fight ambush marketing will rise further.

8.2.3.3 Interests of sponsors

Internationally uniform sponsoring activities require corporations with international budgets, internationally standardized brands and centralized decision-making processes in marketing. National or regional sponsoring activities can, on the other hand, also be pursued by smaller corporations.

Apart from granting and protecting exclusiveness, OCOGs offer packages adapted to the interests of the individual sponsor. Sponsor interests can be directed towards the inside or towards the outside. Internal interests are very significant for the Olympic Games. The situation will be explained by way of a list of concrete goals a sponsor may pursue.

Initiating business   During the sports events, the corporation has the opportunity to discuss business matters in the business launches or in the sponsor village. Business dinners and incentives with customers during the Olympics must be regarded as one of the most effective incentives.

Maintaining customer and supplier contacts   Apart from signing contracts, it is the objective of any corporation to care for its customers and suppliers. Therefore, the free tickets numerously included in the hospitality packages are distributed among customers and suppliers. Fuji, as a sponsor of the 1984 Olympics, gave its free tickets to American wholesalers, for example, and was thus able to win shares in the American market (Catherwood and van Kirk, 1992).

Internal image   Since the image of the Games is partially transferred to the sponsors, an involvement in the Olympics can be seen as a sign of power and help to create trust in current and potential shareholders, customers and suppliers (Collins, 1996). In 1995, SRi made a survey in nine countries, which proved that 74 per cent of the people interviewed linked the Olympic Rings to success and high standards. In addition, 73 per cent said the Rings represented international cooperation (IOC, 1996c). The TOP sponsor John Hancock also asked 300 US households about their opinion of sponsors. The persons answered that in their opinion Olympic sponsors are 'financially stable' and 'successful' (Cater, 1996).

Cooperating with other corporations   The rights to the Olympic emblems and symbol are always sold to a single sponsor per product or service category. Basically, therefore, competition among the sponsors does not arise. In view of continuously growing corporations which do business in several branches, it could be that the corporations become competitors. However, there is the opportunity to form a lasting cooperation, ranging from the simple exchange of information to the acquisition of new customers. Thus, the TOP III sponsors cooperated closely for one and a half years prior to Atlanta 1996 in order to exchange information and plans.

Motivating the staff   Staff motivation can be achieved through the distribution of tickets for events. Many employees also like to work in the host city during the Olympics. On the occasion of the Atlanta 1996 Olympics, John Hancock (TOP III), for example, promised his best insurance agents a trip to Atlanta and paid approximately US$$_{00}$ 1.7 million for that. However, this resulted in a strong increase in insurance sales (Cater, 1996). Sponsors of national programmes such as OBI and the Bankgesellschaft Berlin (German sponsors 1996), also tried to increase the motivation of their staff through their involvement in the Games (NN, 1996e; 1996f).

Avoiding the loss of rights   Many of the long-standing Olympic Games sponsors buy rights in order not to lose them to competitors. Kodak had a bad experience when the film rights for Los Angeles 1984 went to Fuji, giving the Japanese corporation access to the American market (Catherwood and van Kirk, 1992). Thus, Pepsi Cola would also be interested in Olympic sponsoring, if Coca-Cola abandoned sponsoring (Simson and Jennings, 1992).

Personal interests   Although it cannot be proven, the decision in favour of Olympic sponsoring has always been influenced by the personal interest of the decision-maker towards the conveniences offered by the 'hospitality packages'. Provided that the sponsoring commitment can be justified to the shareholders and that the corporation can afford the sponsoring, the motivation of the decision-maker to increase his or her personal advantage through Olympic sponsoring should not be underestimated.

All interests listed above are directed towards the inside and can be realized by acquiring rights. It can thus be understood why some of the large sponsors pursue only a little promotion. To the Olympic Movement, sponsors with interests primarily directed towards the inside should be more favourable owing to the fact that they have a lower public profile and, therefore, do not add to the impression of increasing commercialization. On the other hand, they do not serve to promote the Games and do not bring advertising revenues to the television stations.

Sponsoring is a suitable instrument of corporate communication if it is combined with promotion, sales promotion and public relations (PR) activities. Most corporations use the acquired rights for advertising purposes because these help to realize their externally oriented interests. In contrast to the internal activities, this rule of thumb applies: 'Whoever wants to profit from advertising, must invest three times the license fees in ads and spots' (Hagelüken, 1996, p. 19).

The interests directed towards the visibility can be explained as follows.

Enhancing the image   According to the SRi survey, the image associated with the Olympic Rings is representative of a first-class sports event (82 per cent), success (74 per cent), high standards (74 per cent), excellence (74 per cent) and international cooperation (73 per cent) (n = 10357; IOC, 1996c). Sponsors try to transfer this image to their corporation by including the Olympic Rings in their communication policy. Many investigations prove that the linkage of a sponsor commitment to the Olympic Games guarantees high esteem in the population (Gotta, 1996).

The image associated with being an Olympic sponsor is not automatically gained by every sponsor. An appropriate promotion effort may be required. A corporation advertising during the Olympics or a competitor pursuing ambush marketing could wrongly appear to the consumers as an Olympic sponsor. Table 8.10 shows the result of a survey to determine the extent to which the public knew Olympic sponsors (actual sponsors are printed in bold).

Table 8.10 Awareness of corporations as actual and assumed Olympic sponsors (percentages)

	Corporation	Year/activity	Before	During the Olympics	After
1.	Adidas	1992 – usual advertising	20	13	15
	Nike	1992 – usual advertising	31	39	40
	Reebok	1992 – sponsor	51	68	69
2.	American Express	1992 – ambush marketer	22	27	26
	VISA	1992 – sponsor	4	55	48
	American Express	1994 – ambush marketer	52	–	52
	VISA	1994 – sponsor	68	–	72
3.	Ford	1992 – usual advertising	14	18	21
	Chrysler	1992 – sponsor	17	15	19
4.	Wendy's	1994 – ambush marketer	18	–	68
	McDonald's	1994 – sponsor	69	–	55

Sources: DDB Needham SponsorWatch, in Emory (1996); Performance Research, Newport, RI, in Schlossberg (1996).

In view of these figures, sponsors who are interested in visibility must critically ask themselves about the basis for their commitment. These figures also raise the question of whether the respective corporation used its Olympic rights properly. Thus in Lillehammer 1994, McDonald's only promoted their super-value meals and double Big Macs, whereas Wendy's linked their general promotion to sports. American Express used the words 'Spain' or 'Norway' to a larger extent in their commercial spots (Schlossberg, 1996).

Level of awareness   Due to the public interest in the Games, the perception of Olympic sponsors is enhanced. A smart positioning of corporation names and emblems or the symbol may considerably increase the level of awareness. The number of advertising areas and the size of the territory where advertising is allowed depend on the sponsor programme. As a national sponsor for Atlanta 1996, the Georgia Power Company was only allowed to undertake marketing activities in the state of Georgia, whereas Nationsbank, as a partner 1996, used the Olympic Games to establish itself in the USA as Interstate Brand. Coca-Cola, a TOP sponsor for 1996, advertised all over the world (Emory, 1996). International sponsors use the Olympics to increase their level of awareness in new markets or to stabilize it through market presence. Kodak used the Seoul 1988 Olympics to present itself in the new market of China. After the Atlanta 1996 Olympics, Coca-Cola was able to increase sales in Eastern Europe by 41 per cent and in China by 40 per cent (Guest, 1987; NN, 1997a).

Market presence   The sponsors' striving for market presence is closely linked to their striving for awareness. When there is a high degree of awareness and/or the presence of strong competitors it is particularly important to remind the consumer of one's own presence through advertising activities.

These external intents of sponsor will exist as long as the image of the Olympics does not suffer from 'over-commercialization' and as long as they are maintained as an efficient carrier of advertising messages. Hunter (Coca-Cola, Vice-president) said: 'One of the best ways to grow our business is to associate with the events that are important to our consumers and customers around the world' (NN, 1994).

The sponsors' interest is based on the benefit they expect from the Olympic Games. This rather insecure intangible benefit contrasts with the substantial tangible sponsoring costs, which arise in the following areas:

- Acquisition of rights: in general, the revenues generated per sponsor have increased despite the increase in the total number of corporations using the Olympic emblems and symbol for advertising. This helps to explain the apparent contradiction that the IOC, despite efforts to limit the number of sponsors and to fight against commercialization, has allowed ever more sponsors. At the Atlanta Olympics, there was a tendency towards fewer sponsors, a fact which reminds one of the need to seriously reflect on the number of sponsors allowed for future Olympics.
- Advertising rights in the media: as mentioned in the section on the rights to advertise on television, sponsors frequently pay more for television spots than they

pay to acquire the rights to the Olympic emblems and symbol. Coca-Cola is said to have had an Olympic budget for the Atlanta Olympiad of approximately US$$_{,00}$ 274.4 million (Mädler and Hetzger, 1996). AT&T as a partner of the Games in 1996 is said to have spent US$$_{,00}$ 329.3 million on advertising (Cleland, 1996). Furthermore, there are additional advertising costs for other forms of media.

- <u>Producing advertising means:</u> once the rights, television times and advertising areas have been bought, the sponsors must produce the advertising media. For example, 3M and VISA spent about US$$_{,95}$ 15.7 million to acquire the rights, but invested US$$_{,00}$ 28.4 million each in 1984 (Hill, 1992). Today, this investment amounts to three times the costs for acquiring the rights.

- <u>Sales-promoting communication</u>: in comparison with traditional promotion, corporations do not often use direct marketing, PR activities and sales promotion in the sports sector (cf. Kotler and Bliemel, 1992). At the Olympic Games, however, these marketing measures are used more and more frequently. Coca-Cola, for example, used these communication channels in Atlanta 1996 when they operated the Olympic City at the costs of US$$_{,00}$ 32.5 million (NN, 1995a) and supported the torch relay. The Hellenic Olympic Committee prohibited Coca-Cola from using the torch run commercially. Thus the runners had a newly designed logo on their garments, which Coca-Cola, nevertheless, used in its commercials. In addition, large Coca-Cola parties were organized along the course in the USA (NN, 1995a; Schweikle, 1996; Ueberroth et al., 1985). In Atlanta and Sydney Coca-Cola operated a pin-trading centre. In Athens 2004 Coca-Cola and Samsung are the presenters of the torch relay around the world.

Since the benefit of sponsorship cannot be quantified and the tangible costs are high it is difficult to increase the prices charged for the rights. Higher revenues for the OCOGs, which result from increased prices, mean higher costs for the sponsors. Higher costs will only be accepted if the corporations evaluate the benefit as being higher than the costs. Therefore the IOC protects the symbol and guarantees exclusiveness. Above all it strives to keep the number of sponsors at a level where commercialization is bearable for the consumer. Therefore, sponsors with internally oriented interests should be preferred. However, sponsors with externally oriented interests who promote the Olympic Games and decisively determine the revenues of the television networks by the sponsors' commitment are equally important (IOC, 1996b). Their number must be limited though, since consumers consider them to be responsible for the advanced commercialization of the Olympic Games.

8.2.3.4 Interests of licensees

Licensees are basically national corporations that will buy licenses, which are limited to the duration of an Olympiad. It is common to promote the local industry. Therefore 60 per cent of the Los Angeles 1984 licensees were given to Californian corporations (Los Angeles OCOG 1981; 1984). In Seoul 1988, licensees frequently went to Korean corporations, which were even supported with loans, whereas foreign corporations received only about 10 per cent of the contracts (NN, 1988h; Seoul OCOG, 1988). In Sydney 2000, all licensees were from Australia. In Athens 2004 only 10 per cent of the licensees were from abroad (interview, Diamantidis, 2003).

The lack of subsequent business opportunities makes them interested in short-term profit maximization. Their sales actions could trigger an Olympic boom, as was the case in Seoul 1988. Public relations efforts of the Olympic Movement are supported (Seoul OCOG, 1988), but the commercialization of the Olympics also becomes evident. With merchandising, there are also conflicting long-term and short-term interests. The IOC strives for lasting, high-quality merchandising, while licensees aim at short-term profit. In general, merchandising can be divided into 'highlight' and 'brand' topics. With the highlight topic, they try to sell as many licensed products as possible in a short period of time. Certainly, this is the objective of licensees at Olympic Games. A brand topic corresponds more to the IOC's interests, however, lasting themes must be carefully built up on order to ensure that the merchandise products match the brand 'Olympic' (NN, 1997b).

In Atlanta 1996, the turnover of licensees was said to have amounted to US$·$_{00}$ 560 million (Atlanta OCOG, 1998). Of this, the OCOG received only US$·$_{00}$ 81.2 million (interview, Battle, 1997). This amount corresponds to the merchandising value of the National Hockey League for 1995 (Ruffenach, 1996b). In Sydney there was a turnover of US$·$_{00}$ 608.6 million, of which the OCOG received US$·$_{00}$ 54.3 million in direct revenue. That surpassed the Sydney Bid target of more than 55 per cent and shows how much this market is growing (IOC, 2001b). In Athens 2004 the revenue for the OCOG will be a minimum of US$·$_{00}$ 37 million due to the fact that licensees will have to pay a guaranteed minimum fee even if turnover is lower and the 20 per cent royalties. The OCOG 2004 also gave a licence to sales locations such as the 'Olympic superstore' or other merchandise stands at the venue sides. Besides the mentioned 20 per cent royalties the licensees have to pay an additional 14 per cent of their turnover to the Athens OCOG (interview, Diamantidis, 2003).

The costs of the licensees are limited to the fixed fee to be paid to the OCOG and royalties based on the turnover. Traditionally, the OCOG is the only Olympic institution to distribute merchandising licences (Weissenberg, 1996). Athens also has international licences such as in France, the USA or Cyprus. For Beijing the OCOG will work with the IOC to develop special products for the 2008 Olympic Games (Bidding Committee Beijing 2008, 2001).

8.2.4 Risks and Chances of Future Olympic Marketing

This section will examine the key factors that the OCOG revenues from marketing activities depend upon. Possible risks are explained, followed by reflections on the future of the financing sources of sponsoring and licensing. If the population rejects the sponsors because there are too many, a higher number of sponsors will decrease the corporations' willingness to become involved in a sponsorship. Therefore, when the number of sponsors reaches a certain level, the perceived 'over-commercialization' may lead to negative marginal revenues. This, in turn, would mean an absolute drop in the revenues of an OCOG.

Thus, the maximization of the number of sponsors does not necessarily lead to a maximizing of the revenues. The optimum number of sponsors depends on the costs, the sponsors' interests (internally/externally oriented), the size and economic power of the area the sponsor is allowed to advertise and on the attitude of the population of the respective region towards the sponsorship. The higher the acceptance of the sponsorship within the population and/or the fewer sponsors that present themselves externally, the higher the OCOG revenues can potentially be.

It has been shown that there are risks for the Olympic Movement linked to Olympic marketing. When an OCOG strives to maximize its revenues from marketing by increasing the number of sponsors, the acceptance of the Olympic sponsors and the value of the Olympic symbol to the population decreases. When the media coverage of Atlanta 1996 is examined, much has been written and said about 'over-commercialization'. The IOC and the OCOG 2004 successfully decreased the number of sponsors, in particular of those with interests directed to visibility. Additionally, a great effort must be made to fight against ambush marketing. Two other risks for Olympic sponsoring can result from a poor economic situation of the sponsoring corporations and from a possible loss of the Olympic aura.

Over-commercialization
Recent research has proven that many spectators at Olympic Games are of the opinion that the Games could not be staged in their present form without the support of industry. According to an ISL study (1985), 76.5 per cent of the people interviewed said 'sport sponsorship ... provides vital funds for organizing major sporting events'. In 1995, SRi carried out the same study and the result was 86 per cent (average of three countries) (IOC, 1996c). In a survey among 620 senior managers of 13 nations after the Atlanta Olympics only 5 per cent were of the opinion that there was 'over-commercialization' (Harris, 1997).

To the spectator, indicators for commercialization are the visibility of advertising and the number of corporations using Olympic emblems or the symbol in their advertisement. Merchandising, as well as sales stands in the vicinity of Olympic venues, also conveys the impression of commercialized Games. Therefore the IOC strengthened its policy in regard of the 'look of the Games'. One year after the negative experience from Atlanta the IOC took special care to have 'clean venues' and less commercials in the host city for 2004. However, the way in which a population perceives the commercialization differs greatly among the individual nations. For example, the American viewer is used to seeing more commercial television breaks than is the European viewer (Weissenberg, 1996).

The IOC has taken measures to fight the imminent threat of 'over-commercialization'. Advertising in Olympic venues sites and on the athlete him or herself is prohibited. An exception is the garment supplier who can use a logo of 12 sq. cm. in size. (IOC, 2003d, Rule 61, By-law 1.4). A market research study, however, revealed that 80 per cent of consumers did not know that advertising was forbidden in Olympic venues (Weissenberg

1996). Similarly, Messing (1993) was able to prove this with pupils' drawings (n = 7008) on the topic of the Olympic Games.

Not every corporation may become a sponsor. After Tokyo 1964, the tobacco industry was no longer allowed to use the Rings in advertisements (Gotta, 1996). In addition, individual corporations like Mars in Barcelona, that have too aggressive marketing tactics and refuse the IOC clean venue policy, are no longer welcome (interview, Payne, 2004). Atlanta 1996 faced another problem. Among the many street stands authorized by the municipal authorities, there were competitors of some sponsors that used the Games for an Olympic self-presentation. Nike erected a large white promotion tent directly in front of the entrance to the Centennial Olympic Park. The promotion campaigns during the Atlanta 1996 Olympics alone cost US\$$_{00}$ 39.2 million (Liwocha, 1996). M. Payne said that there will be no unlimited marketing in future (NN, 1996n). T. Bach talked of a 'controlled commercialisation' (NN, 1996j, p. 17). 'If one day the facade of the Olympic Games was at the time their content, the end would be near. Sport must not give up its very intrinsic rules and its identity, not at any advertising price, however high it may be' (Maurer, 1996). The IOC is successfully fighting against this tendency. Bid cities must enter into a binding option that, if the city is elected, gives the IOC or the OCOG the right to purchase at a predetermined price all advertising spaces close to Olympic venues (interview, Payne, 2004). Furthermore, Athens 2004 and Beijing 2008 already have advertising control written into their Host City Contracts. In Beijing during the required period the OCOG will have complete control over billboard advertising, sky space advertising and advertising on the public transport system (Bidding Committee Beijing 2008, 2001).

Ambush marketing

The ambush marketing already mentioned is particularly widespread at Olympic Games (Netzle, 1996; interview, Payne, 1997; Séguin, 2003). The prime purpose of ambush marketing is to benefit from the image of being a sponsor without paying for it. It also tries to counterbalance the Olympic commitment of market competitors. In the end, ambush marketers damage Olympic sport and themselves because they increase the apparent number of sponsors for the spectators and bear the risk of receiving a negative image when their marketing strategies become publicly known. The best example of Olympic ambush marketing is the advertising of American Express, which competed against the Olympic sponsor VISA as an ostensible sponsor for a long time. In 1986 American Express competed against the official TOP sponsor VISA. In Albertville 1992 they used commercials with the Olympic symbol. For the Barcelona 1992 and Lillehammer 1994 Olympics, the commercials also used misleading phrases. American Express spokesmen said they did not aim as much at deliberate ambush marketing as at correcting the VISA commercials. In Atlanta 1996 American Express no longer used misleading commercials (Netzle, 1996; NN, 1996c; interview, Payne, 1997; Schlossberg, 1996).

Investigations by Shani and Sandler proved that ambush marketing is only worthwhile if the ambush marketer advertises more in terms of exposure as well as in a more creative way than the sponsor (Schlossberg, 1996). Table 8.10 clearly reveals that ambush marketing can increase the popularity of the 'unfair' sponsor. This method is worthwhile financially because 34 per cent of the American consumers prefer products of Olympic sponsors, whoever they regard as being one (Schlossberg, 1996). The SRi proved, however, that corporations pursuing ambush marketing would fall in the estimation of 68 per cent of the persons interviewed. A similar investigation by Shani and Sandler revealed that only 20 per cent would react in this way (IOC, 1997c; Schlossberg, 1996). In another study by the Sri, 76 per cent answered this question in the affirmative (IOC, 1996c). Netzle (1996) backed this by saying: 'The subtle hints [of the ambush marketer, the author] frequently cause smiles and a certain liking for the advertising corporation. The general public considers ambush marketing rather a trivial offence to be tolerated.' In fact, it must be differentiated by nationality. According to an SRi investigation, 67 per cent of the Spanish people interviewed thought that corporations which did not pay for an Olympic advertising message were 'smart.' In Australia, only 17 per cent were of this opinion (IOC, 1997c).

According to R. Pound, ambush marketing is 'non-creative, non-ethical and non-professional. Corporations that feel forced to sink to this level should fire their marketing people and look for a new advertising agency' (Pound, 1996b, p. 1). Nevertheless, the IOC has no alternative but to fight ambush marketers (Florin and Carlin, 1995; NN, 1996c). NOC and OCOG activities range from warnings via PR measures to public trials that frequently have a telling effect. The NOC alone can take legal action in its country because it has protected the Olympic Rings. An OCOG can only take action if there is a misuse of the emblems or symbol it has protected. The IOC can only support the plaintiffs. Legal steps can be taken, however, if there are definite legal infringements. The situation is more difficult if ambush marketers do not use the protected words, the symbol or the other emblems (Schlossberg, 1996). The IOC and OCOG can only use PR activities, such as press conferences, press releases and the like, in order to make the public sensitive to these unfair advertising methods. Atlanta 1996 took appropriate steps, which ultimately paid off. As an example, the American population was informed about ambush marketing long before the Games started; 1000 renowned advertising and PR agencies were made aware of this problem; a corporation was charged to watch and listen to television and radio programmes in order to detect prohibited advertising; a research group was charged with the task of asking the person in the street which advertising he/she would find misleading (Atlanta OCOG, 1998). According to M. Payne, there were no infringements against the big sponsors. In Germany, approximately 50 smaller infringements against German sponsors were supposed to have taken place. The agency of the German NOC sent information letters, and all advertisers agreed to stop their advertising immediately. However, the legal position in Germany regarding advertising with Olympic symbols, which has not been completely clarified, must not be underestimated. Effective campaigns are also needed to fight against the still large amount of faked merchandising articles (interview, Achten, 2004; Windlin, 1998). The IOC had told potential ambush marketers that an advertising campaign against them would start if they engaged in ambush activities. The spots were ready and could have been broadcast at very short notice (interview, Payne, 1997). The IOC is of the opinion that the term to be used in future, 'parasite marketing', will make the consumers more sensitive to the infringements (IOC, 1997c). In order to safeguard the interests of Olympic sponsors, Beijing authorities have pledged that specific statutes and rules in line with the legislation implemented for the Sydney 2000 Games will be adopted to prevent ambush marketing during the 2008 Olympic Games (Bidding Committee Beijing 2008, 2001).

Economic situation

As long as the Olympic Games do not have either a tangible benefit for the sponsors or a clear profile, or as long as the commitment to Olympic sponsorship depends on personal preferences, the economic situation of a corporation will be the key factor in deciding whether the Olympic sponsorship programmes will be continued. The thesis put forward here is that financially weak sponsors will be the first to refrain from sponsoring in a bad economic situation.

If this idea is expanded to the economic situation of an entire economic region, such as a crisis in the American market that most of the TOP sponsors currently come from, for example, or in the market of the host country that the majority of the Olympic partners come from, this could result in a sharp decline in the revenues for an OCOG. The same is relevant for the NOC sponsors. This risk can only be reduced if the one-sided commercialization caused by growing financial dependency on the sponsors and television networks is stopped and replaced by a move towards limiting the growth of the Olympics and a return to their original values. In other words, a growth in quality is required. Emphasizing the Olympic idea can increase interest in the Olympics if people think this ideology is worthy of acceptance. The increased intrinsic value of the product Olympic Games can be marketed more securely since the one-sided dependency on private industry is balanced by the uniqueness of the event Olympic Games. There is a lack of exchangeability.

Olympic aura

For sponsors, the Olympic Games are significant primarily due to high public interest. This interest is mainly based on the previously mentioned special Olympic aura, a symbiosis of Olympic ideals which is demonstrated by the atmosphere in the Olympic venue sites during the Games as well as by the variety of sports and cultures. If this content was conveyed, but behind a 'facade of advertising' the sponsors and television networks would lose their interest in the Games. If sport is nothing but an 'empty shell' for advertising, corporations will lose interest in seeing it as a carrier of their messages. Olympic sponsoring must, therefore, be questioned as to whether the consumer regards the advertising of the sponsors as a nuisance, or if advertising causes negative feelings or even rejection.

Once it has become evident that the Olympic ideals are missing, there is the threat that the unique Olympic aura dies. If doping scandals and corruption, for example, shatter the ideals of 'fair play' and 'equality of opportunities', if the exclusion of certain sports limits the ideal 'unity of all sports', if the fast life cycles of sports do not create a 'tradition' or if the repeated awarding of the Games to only a few cultures – especially Western – negatively affects 'internationalism' and 'cultural variety', the credibility of the product Olympic Games will be severely threatened (cf. for ideals Lenk, 1972; Müller, 1998). This last point seems to be more important today than ever before. Therefore it was a wise decision of the IOC to award the Games to China since the Games had been in Western societies in 1992, 1996, 2000 and 2004. A lack of credibility would soon cause a loss of interest among the public and, consequently, among the sponsors.

The future of Olympic sponsorship depends on the ability of the Olympic Movement to maintain the Olympic aura and the exclusiveness of the sponsors (anti-ambush programmes), as well as to limit the number of Olympic sponsors and determine the way in which the rights will be used internally or externally. With its long-term orientation, the IOC must find the optimum number of sponsors. However, the decisive factor is not necessarily to limit the total number of sponsors but, rather, to balance the number of sponsors that present themselves externally, especially as the consumers notice these sponsors. In Athens 2004 the number of corporations was successfully reduced from approximately 100 in Atlanta and Sydney to 30. However, Beijing 2008 with its big market will have more sponsors (interview, Payne, 2004).

The corporations that consumers perceive as Olympic sponsors are (1) the TOP sponsors, (2) the partners of the OCOGs, (3) the national sponsors, (4) some of the suppliers/providers and (5) the licensees, however, more so in the form of their products. The only variable, which can influence the image of commercialization, is the number of regional and national sponsors. It is their number, which must be based on the public acceptance of the corporations that advertise with the Olympics (Ehm, 1996). The number of countries with their own Olympic marketing programme increased from 60 countries (in 1992) to 100 countries (in 1996) (IOC, 1997a).

Both the TOP sponsors and the IOC are interested in active advertising not only during the short period of the Olympic Games, but also over a longer period since the sponsors can only offset the ever more expensive rights during this time. Owing to the high revenues, the IOC can thus operate Olympic educational, environmental and social programmes during the entire Olympiad (Payne, 1996). Apart from sports sponsoring, corporations could also become involved in social and environmental sponsoring. In the case of sponsorship, the IOC also focuses on long-term cooperation with the sponsors. Long-term programmes that consider the interests of both parties can thus be realized (IOC, 1996c; Thurow, 1996).

In future, the importance of Olympic merchandising is likely to increase, as will probably be the case with all mega sports events. This can be seen looking at the Games in Athens which is rather a small population and will reach approximately the same revenues as Atlanta 1996 (market of 285 million) and Sydney 2000 (market of 19.4 million). Beijing 2008 (market of 1271.8 million) will even top that. However, the Games are a single event with the purposes of merchandising, whereas the largest revenues have, until now, been achieved in the USA by the National Football League (NFL) and the NBA. Spectators can identify themselves with 'sports stars' over a long time, buy their shirts and permanently support their team. The OCOG only offered emblems of the event and the Rings, which is limited to the short period before and during the Olympics. However, there are first signs of a long-term use of the symbol. Adidas, for example, offers a collection of jumpers showing historical Olympic motives. The absolute revenues of licensing are far below that of the big American sports leagues. If, however, the revenues achieved in the short period before and during the Olympic Games are compared with the revenues of the largest single American sport event, the Super Bowl, the turnover of the Olympic Games is four times higher (Ruffenach, 1996b). While the revenue from licensing could possibly become more important step by step, for the IOC the promotional and educational benefits of using licensing to communicate the ideals of the Movement are far more significant.

The worldwide interest in the Olympic Games offers considerable potential. Even if international licensing is small and basically limited to the organized collector market of stamps and coins, a large sales market can be opened up where the IOC and the corresponding OCOG operate worldwide via the Internet.

8.3   REVENUES FROM TICKET SALES

Historically, the sales of tickets have contributed to the financing of the Olympic Games since Athens 1896 (Philemon, 1996 [1986]). Not surprisingly, ticketing has declined in significance, because television rights and marketing have grown at an astonishing rate. The evolution of ticket sales as a percentage of overall OCOG revenues and the decrease of the importance of ticket sales since the 1970s is depicted in Figure 8.23.

Although ticketing as a financing source has declined in significance, it is still in third place after the revenues from marketing and the sales of television rights. In contrast to the considerable growth potential inherent in marketing and television, the potential revenues from ticket sales are limited. The number of tickets to be sold mainly depends on the venue capacities. The prices for the tickets, however, primarily depend on the prosperity and the sports enthusiasm in the respective host country. If an OCOG wants to increase revenues from this source, it must optimize ticket sales under given conditions.

This section discusses the interests of the IOC and the OCOG. Furthermore, measures to create revenues through selling tickets will be derived from looking at historical data. Additionally, the basic factors, which include the number of events, venue capacity, degree of capacity utilization and price required to calculate the possible overall revenue and the variables affecting them are explained.

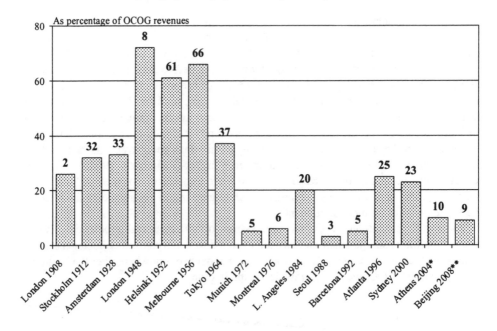

Notes: *   Estimates in December, 2003.
         **   Conservatively estimated by Bidding Committee Beijing 2008 (2001).

Source: Bidding Committee Beijing 2008 (2001); Athens OCOG (2003); Preuss (2001b).

Figure 8.23   Ticket sale revenues as percentage of overall OCOG revenues

8.3.1 Interests of IOC and OCOG in Ticket Sales

The IOC directly receives a share of the revenues from the sales of the rights for television and marketing. The ticket sales are basically the business of the OCOG. Until Athens 2004 5 per cent of the revenues from the ticket sales, must be paid to the IOC. In Beijing 2008 7.5 per cent have to be given to the IOC. The IOC interests (IOC, 1994; 1997d; 2001e) can be summarized under four headings, as follows.

Free entrance for Olympic family and media

Regarding tickets, the following stipulation applies for the Olympic family: 'The accreditation card gives ... access to the sites and events' (IOC, 2003d, Rule 66). The number of free seats the OCOG must provide in the venues has increased continuously. The development of the number of free seats for the press from 1987 to 1994 may serve as an example. The Olympic Charter (IOC, 1987, Rule 60, By-Law) said: 'For journalists (1000 maximum), photographers (150 maximum), and for radio and television commentators and operators (150 maximum)', whereas the 1994 Olympic Charter (IOC, 1994b, Rule 66, By-Law) stated: 'For journalists (at least 2200), photographers (at least

600) and radio and television commentators (in accordance with the relevant broadcasting agreements)'. Under the assumption that the seats could be sold to paying spectators, the OCOG would face opportunity costs to the amount of the lost revenues. The Host City Contract for the Games in Athens 2004 as well as that for Beijing 2008, however, states that the OCOG shall provide to the IOC, at face value cost, such tickets as may required by the IOC, for itself and for its guests (IOC, 1997d; 2001e).

Full venues and appropriate ticket prices
If these demands are met, they will contribute to a good atmosphere in the host city. The atmosphere in an Olympic venue is transferred by television, thereby polishing the image that the worldwide television audience receives of the Olympic Games. In Montreal 1976, Seoul 1988 and Barcelona 1992, many of the facilities were only partly filled because too many tickets were given to the Olympic Family and sponsors who did not use them (ERA, 1981; Maennig, 1992; Messing and Müller, 1995). Today, more care is therefore taken to keep the share of spectators paying for their tickets as large as possible (NN, 1996j). When setting the prices, OCOGs consider the readiness to pay and the prosperity of the population in order to achieve as high a degree of utilization as possible. For Beijing 2008 the IOC especially claimed: 'Ticket prices must be kept as low as reasonably possible and be established taking socio-economic factors into consideration' (IOC, 2001e). In tradition with previous Games the Beijing OCOG plans to distribute a significant number of tickets to the disadvantaged and school children to help ensure the future generations benefit from the legacy of the Games (Bidding Committee Beijing 2008, 2001).

Complying with sponsor and television station contracts
The packages sold to sponsors contain the right to use the Olympic emblems and symbol as well as a ticket quota. Apart from the number of free tickets supplied, sponsors buy additional tickets. However, the 'right to buy' can be a problem. In Calgary 1988, approximately 10 per cent of the tickets went to sponsors with the guarantee stated in contracts. In Barcelona 1992, as many as 12.6 per cent of all tickets went to sponsors. In Atlanta 1996, the sponsors received 8 per cent (Sydney 15 per cent) of the tickets, which was in absolute figures twice the number of Barcelona. In Atlanta, Coca-Cola alone received 80 000 tickets whereas only about 45 000 tickets were provided for the whole of Germany. From the financial viewpoint of an OCOG, the safe sales of as many tickets as possible to the sponsors are appreciated. Problems arise, however, if many customers of the sponsors do not use their tickets, or NOCs or their agencies cannot return tickets if they do not sell them. Then, seats remain empty. The Host City Contract for Athens 2004 and Beijing 2008 states that the OCOG must have 'a proposed method of filling empty seats on the dates of the events' (IOC, 1997d; 2001e). In Athens 2004, sponsors must collect their tickets by a specified time. All tickets not picked up will then be released for sale (Fischer, 1998). This is a conflict of interests: on the one hand, the IOC tries to maximize the revenues from Olympic marketing by submitting interesting offers to

sponsors. On the other, it knows about the significance of the 'good atmosphere', which is most likely achieved with full venues.

International sales of a ticket quota

The worldwide sales of tickets give the Olympic Games and the host city an international atmosphere. Figure 8.25 shows the national and international share. Outside the host country tickets are sold through the Internet, the NOCs or their agencies. This channel of distribution offers a good opportunity to ensure worldwide distribution. The involvement of intermediate dealers increases ticket prices by the provisions charged.

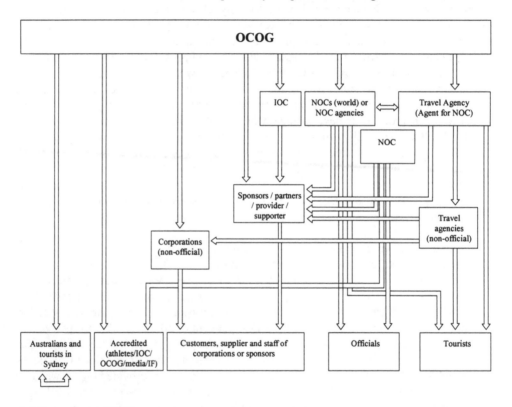

Source: Preuss (2001b).

Figure 8.24   Distribution channels of Olympic tickets (Sydney 2000)

Furthermore, wrong distribution quotas prevent an optimization of ticket sales in view of the OCOG interests mentioned earlier (Catherwood and van Kirk, 1992; Moscow OCOG, 1980; Organisationskomitee München, 1974a).

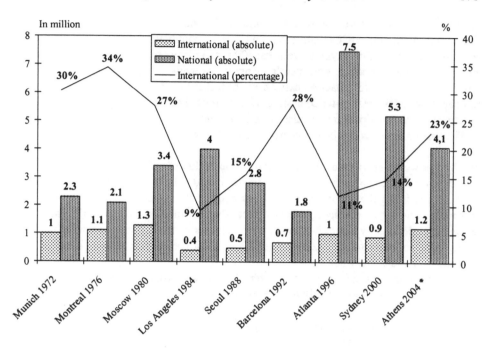

Note: *   Data from December 2003.

Sources: Montreal OCOG (1974); Preuss (2000a); IOC (2001b), Mamangakis (interview, 2003).

Figure 8.25   *National and international ticket sales from Munich 1972 to Athens 2004*

Figure 8.25 shows a low percentage of the international share for the US Olympics in 1984 and 1996. A reason for this could be due to the size of the country and the high demand from the American population for top-class sporting events. This could also explain the many tickets sold abroad for Montreal 1976 (Montreal OCOG, 1976). Despite the boycott, the Moscow OCOG 1980 was able to sell many tickets to foreign countries, thereby leading to the foreign exchange revenues they had hoped for. Seoul 1988, on the other hand, only sold a few tickets on an international scale. An explanation for this is surely the large distance to the European and American markets. For Beijing 2008 the national share will be high due to the strong demand of the Chinese market.

The number of tickets that can be sold to foreign tourists is limited by the tourist capacity of the host city. This is mainly determined by the number of hotel beds in the host city as well as the number of citizens who accommodate relatives and friends. For some countries such as Korea, Australia and China air transport capacity is also a limitation. Not all tickets sold in foreign countries are used, since many from quota sales remain unused. Tickets, which are sold nationally to inhabitants outside the Olympic region, can be considered as positively affecting tourism. In Los Angeles, for example, 70 per cent of the tickets were sold within a radius of 100 miles of the city (Roughton, 1994). The ticket quota the OCOG allocates to foreign countries can be regarded as the regulating quantity for Olympic tourism. This regulates tourism revenue, which is important to the economy as a whole. Host cities with extensive tourism capacities should, therefore, try to attract as many visitors from abroad as possible. Since interests and capacities of the respective tourism industry strongly differ among host cities, general statements on international ticket sales are impossible.

The OCOG interests can be summarized under the following two headings.

Full venues/satisfied citizens due to fair and just ticket distribution
If this was the case, only revenues could be optimized. The two interests of maximizing revenues and filling the venue can only be harmonized if the maximum revenues meet the maximum capacity of the sports venue. A conflict of interests occurs if the maximum revenues, as defined by a certain number of tickets at set prices, do not reach the capacity limit for the sports venue utilization. The OCOG must then decide which objective shall be considered more important.

Apart from the internal conflicts of interest, there are also discrepancies between the IOC and OCOG, which are briefly mentioned here:

- The free ticket quota for the Olympic Family always involves opportunity costs when there is a general demand for these seats. Many tickets allocated to sponsors and Olympic family are not used, therefore OCOGs reduce free tickets for events with a high demand. Since Barcelona, members of the Olympic Family have to show a ticket as well as their accreditation card for certain events.
- The number of media representatives exceeds the number of tickets to be provided according to the Olympic Charter. The IOC must meet its obligations towards the television networks paying for their rights, resulting in a necessity for free ticket quotas. In Atlanta 1996, this led to an obvious division between rights paying and free media representatives. Journalists of print media and radio stations, which did not pay fees, received a lower accreditation than those of television and the sponsors (interview, Kühner, 1996).
- The maximum profit for the OCOG, as a monopolist, is not necessarily limited by the capacity as defined by the sports facility utilization.

Maximize ticket sales revenues
In most cases this objective takes second place. C.H. Battle (interview, 1997) commented that it requires a lot of sensibility to achieve the highest possible profit without annoying the spectators. The conditions stated by the IOC in both the Host City Contract and the Olympic Charter, as mentioned earlier, must be met when pursuing this objective. Moreover, the IOC must approve all prices.

Now that the IOC and the OCOG interests have been explained, the capacities of sports venues are investigated since they are the key limiting factor for revenues which can be achieved in total.

8.3.2 Factors Determining Possible Ticket Sales Revenues

The continued addition of new sports, disciplines and events to the Olympic Games increases the number of tickets to be sold in the long term. The spectator capacity (C) depends on the number of events (E) and the size of the facilities (S) available in the host city. The seating capacity corresponds to the maximum number of tickets if free seats (F) are subtracted from the entire seating capacity of the facilities. The following equation can be applied:

$$C = \sum_{n=1}^{E}(S_n - F_n) \tag{8.1}$$

Figure 8.26 (light bars) shows the total number of tickets sold from Munich 1972 to Beijing 2008. Throughout the history of the Olympics, there has been a tendency to increase the number of seats, in part due to the expansion of sports and events offered as well as the prolongation of the Olympics. On the other hand, no specific trend with regard to the size of the sports facilities can be seen. The facilities that exist in cities vary in size, and host cities plan new facilities according to the expected follow-up demand. Irrespective of the size of the venues, most Olympics manage to sell at least 75 per cent of the available seats. Since Barcelona 1992 highly accredited persons no longer require tickets for most of the sports. Actual utilization rates of the sports venues of 1992, 1996 and 2000 are thus higher than stated in Figure 8.26. Free admission amounted to 13 per cent in Atlanta and 17 per cent in Sydney.

To calculate the possible revenue (R) from ticket sales in advance, the utilization rate (o) and the average ticket price (P) must be integrated into equation 8.1:

$$C = \sum_{n=1}^{E}(S_n - F_n) * o_n * P_n \tag{8.2}$$

Increasing one of the four factors (E, S, o, P) by keeping the others constant leads to an increase in revenue. These four factors will now be examined in more detail. Each OCOG should adjust the factors to the specific conditions of the host country in order to achieve the highest possible revenue.

Events (E)

The number of events is determined by (1) the number of Olympic sports, (2) the number of disciplines, and (3) the number of sessions. For all factors, the Olympics seem to have reached their limit. It is likely that new sports/disciplines added to the Olympic programme will lead to reductions in other sports or disciplines. However, care must be taken that the IOC does not exclude a small sport (few athletes and few sessions) in order to add a big one – that will support gigantism even if the number of sports keep being 28.

There could be shifts caused by planning an increase in the number of events for sports or disciplines with strong demand and a reduction in the number of those with a weaker demand. To maximize revenues, the interest of the host country's population in certain sports should be considered without threatening the diversity of sport.

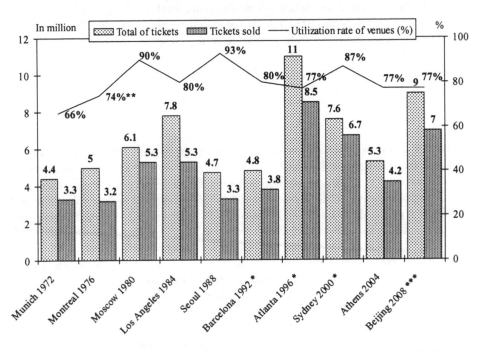

Notes: *   Free tickets are not considered in the utilization rate since they were included in accreditation.
         **   ERA (1981) stated a utilization rate of 65 per cent.
         *** Estimated by Bidding Committee Beijing 2008 (2001)

Sources: Athens OCOG (2003a, p. 135); Bidding Committee Beijing 2008 (2001); Preuss (2000a).

Figure 8.26   *Total number of tickets and share of tickets sold from Munich 1972 to
                  Beijing 2008*

Size of sports venue (S)
With reference to the size of the venues, the number of tickets to be sold depends on (1) the size of the facilities that existed before the Olympics, (2) the space required to erect temporary stands, and (3) the type of sport. Existing facilities should be used and the construction of new facilities should be guided by the sports facility requirements of the city. If there is no follow-up demand, the construction of temporary seats in existing facilities is only worthwhile if the additional revenue at least compensates for the costs of erecting and dismantling temporary stands, as was the case with Atlanta 1996 and Sydney 2000. Irrespective of this, the minimum requirements of the IOC and the IFs with regards to the size of Olympic venues must be met. However, since the size of the stands is

specific to the type of sport, this makes the venue size (S) an almost fixed quantity for the individual sport. Using large stadiums for football, baseball and track and field simply offers a larger capacity than for judo, weightlifting and swimming. Large facilities may also be split in half and be used for two sports, such as gymnastics and basketball in Atlanta 1996, in order to adapt the capacity of the stands to the average demand.

Utilization rate (*o*)
Utilization rates of the facilities are determined by (1) the facility size, (2) the closeness in time of the event to the final, (3) the attractiveness of the respective sport, and (4) the framework conditions such as access, ticket distribution and price. The OCOG has influence only on the framework conditions.

Price (*P*)
Prices of tickets are determined by many factors (see Table 8.11). The difficulties in determining the optimum price and the few points of orientation an OCOG has in determining the price are explained in the following.

When anticipating the revenues from the ticket sales, uncertainties in defining the number of events (*E*) and facility size (*S*) are relatively low. The utilization rate (*o*) and the best price (*P*), however, are hard to determine. Utilization rates of the venues ultimately depend on the buying decision of the consumer. According to Nieschlag et al. (1994) the following aspects determine any purchasing decision:

- Cost awareness: these are all the direct costs incurred by the buyer, such as getting to the event, accommodation, and so on.
- Presentation of the price information: this is the design of the external form of the price indication as well as the design of competing offers. At the Olympic Games this tends to be insignificant.
- Readiness to pay the price: this is the idea of a price the consumer has according to his or her more or less accurate estimate of a fair price and his or her upper and lower price limits. Due to the fact that Olympics for the home crowd is a 'once in a lifetime' event, the readiness to pay is quite high.
- Quality awareness: this is the 'often proven fact that consumers infer the quality level from the price level'.

When selling tickets for the Olympic Games, readiness to pay the price forms the decisive aspect.

When determining ticket prices for the Olympic Games, an OCOG is a monopolist that 'sells' a number of new products of highest quality which can be more or less substituted. In other words, an OCOG 'sells' the various sports events featuring top athletes, and spectators can select which sport to watch. Another peculiarity is the uniqueness of the event, which excludes any price change in the flow of time (Preuss, 2001b).

An OCOG searches for orientation points when determining ticket prices. It cannot use prices of competitors or prices of past Games as a basis. Classic price theory models can hardly be used since they call for the knowledge of price/sales and cost functions, a call which cannot be fulfilled in practice. The actual prices can only be determined by estimating the best price, an estimate which is based on incomplete information. Both the range of factors influencing the ticket price and the unpredictability of many factors cause problems for all OCOGs when calculating the optimal ticket price. The official Montreal 1976 report stated: 'But in 1973 it was extremely difficult, if not impossible, to justify this figure [net revenues]: even the number of seats in the stadium was not known' (OCOG (Montreal OCOG, 1976). In Los Angeles 1984 the 'LAOOC researched comparable events and prices' (Catherwood and van Kirk, 1992). In Atlanta 1996 they only used the popularity of sports and the pricing scheme of former Games as a guide (interview, Battle, 1997). Even in Sydney the OCOG noticed a miscalculation of the number of seats (NN, 2000a). The complexity in pricing is best explained by this quote from J. Bosiljevac: 'Many factors were used to arrive at the pricing – local sport costs, popularity, demand for specific sports – irrespective of price, previous Olympic prices, budget pressures. All final sessions could be greatly increased because demand always outstrips supply' (correspondence, Bosiljevac, 2000).

Irrespective of the price level of tickets for events in great demand, such as opening ceremonies, OCOGs tend to be oriented towards profit. Another way to increase revenues is to sell luxury boxes in the stadium, such as the stadium in Sydney which has 125 boxes, or sell premium tickets (Howard and Crompton, 1995; Voigt, 1999). An OCOG should fall back on information, which must be compiled for each sport.

Table 8.11 Bases on price level selection

Dimension	Attributes	Flexibility	Uncertainty
Time	Closeness to final	Fixes	No
	Time of day	Variable	No
	Day in the week (weekend)	Variable	No
	Timing of competition in schedule	Variable	No
Location	Distance of facility to Olympic centre	Fixes	No
	Distribution of seats in the facility	Variable	No
Quality	Attractiveness of sport for national audience	Fixes	Yes
	Attractiveness of sport for international audience	Fixes	Yes
	Price elasticity	Fixes	Yes
Social aspects	Prosperity of population	Fixes	Yes
	Price idea	Fixes	Yes
	Willingness of population to pay for leisure	Variable	Yes
	Willingness to watch sport with a group	Fixes	Yes
	Consideration for special target groups	Variable	No
	Opportunity of host nation to succeed in sport	Fixes	Yes
Framework	IOC or International Federation (IF) contracts	Fixes	No

Attributes may be 'fixes' in the sense that the levels of the attributes cannot be determined by the OCOG. It simply has to accept the level of the attribute when calculating the price. However, a problem is the uncertainty an OCOG has about some values of certain attributes.

Due to knowledge of the competition schedules, there is no uncertainty about the dimension 'time'. The OCOG has great flexibility, however restricted by contracts with television networks claiming a specific timetable for competition. Data can be used from past Games, and the time when most people are interested in watching sports as well as the closeness to the final have to be considered in order to differentiate prices. The dimension 'location' is fixed and known. However, data about the facilities and their capacity have to be evaluated. 'Quality' is the dimension an OCOG has to do research on. The attractiveness of sports for national and international audiences has to be figured out. It is also critical to know the price elasticity for different sports. Maximum revenues can only be reached by considering the 'social' dimension. While the prosperity level and price idea is given, the willingness to pay for events can be influenced, for example by commercials. It is important to consider that others, when deciding to buy tickets, influence spectators. The consideration for special target groups depends on the opportunity costs an OCOG has to bear when ignoring them. Finally, the constraints put up by framework conditions have to be evaluated.

Learning from past Games is limited to Games' schedules (dimension 'time') and optimal seat distribution (dimension 'location'). Knowledge about the attractiveness of sport for an international audience is obtained from the number of tickets given to international agents and, since Salt Lake 2002, to Internet sales of past Games. A falsification occurs because, since Montreal 1976, tickets are sold as packages by linking 'non-attractive' with 'attractive' tickets. Concerning the overall interest in specific sports, OCOGs could also look at venue utilization rates. Here different seat capacities and free tickets in order to fill the venues create falsifications.

When determining the price, an OCOG must consider these conditions in order to achieve a high utilization rate for the facilities. Considering the relatively even utilization of the venues, Figure 8.27 does not indicate the host country prosperity but rather an idea of the average willingness to pay on the part of Olympic spectators.

It can be seen that the average ticket prices strongly differed among all Olympics investigated. The bottom curve represents the average prices as stated publicly (Catherwood and van Kirk, 1992; IOC, 1996a; NN, 1995c; Barcelona OCOG, 1992; Montreal OCOG, 1976; The Audit Office, 1999). The discrepancy between these and the average prices calculated by the author may be due to the fact that revenues for renting luxury boxes were ignored in the press. The Atlanta OCOG 1996, for example, sold 209 boxes for the entire duration of the Olympics between US$'00 439 040 and 1.46 million per box. It distributed only 240 or 848 tickets per box (NN, 1995c). The Sydney prices might also be so high because the Sydney ticket management established a special ticket programme. One idea was to sell some tickets up to three times the face value in order to avoid a deficit. However, that ended in a scandal. Approximately 800 000 tickets were not given to the general public but held back as 'Premium Tickets' in order to sell them to clubs, agencies, and sponsors (Lenskyj, 2002, pp. 121–2).

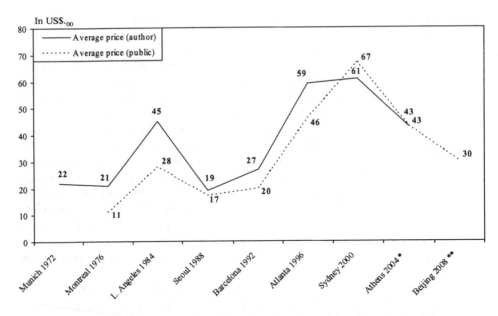

Notes: *   Average premium events US$80 and secondary events US$15, inflation rate estimated.
         **   Price announced by Bidding Committee Beijing 2008 (2001)

Sources: Preuss (2000a); IOC (2001b); Bidding Committee Beijing 2008 (2001).

Figure 8.27   Average ticket prices from Munich 1972 to Beijing 2008

The ticket prices for the Olympics in the USA (1984, 1996) strongly differ from those of other Western countries (1972, 1976, 1992, 2004) and Asia (1988, 2008). The average prices for the tickets give a clear insight into the different willingness to pay of the buyers. Future bid cities may use the data as an initial idea of prices. The average price data, however, do not reflect a clear trend. The basic factor when determining prices is the willingness to pay combined with the prosperity level of the host country population. The fact that all OCOGs sold at least 75 per cent of the tickets leads one to assume that differentiated price strategies, which would take into account high and low price strategies, appear rarely to have been applied up until now. The respective OCOG in charge tried to sell as many cheap tickets as possible (NN, 1995d; 1999c; Organisationskomitee München, 1974a).

It is shown that there is no trend for average prices. For the opening ceremonies, however, a continuous rise can be noted (Figure 8.28). The OCOGs have realized the low price elasticity referring to this unique event (cf. Catherwood and van Kirk, 1992; Kim, 1990; NN, 1987). The growing gap between the lowest and highest price is striking. This indicates a stronger price differentiation. There is a political reason for this. By offering some relatively cheap tickets, an OCOG can justify high prices because it offers tickets for almost all residents of the city. Irrespective of the price level of tickets for events in great demand, such as opening ceremonies, OCOGs tend to be oriented towards profit. In the future, it will not be possible to maintain the increase that can be seen in Figure 8.28. Prices for opening ceremonies, however, are likely to remain at a high level.

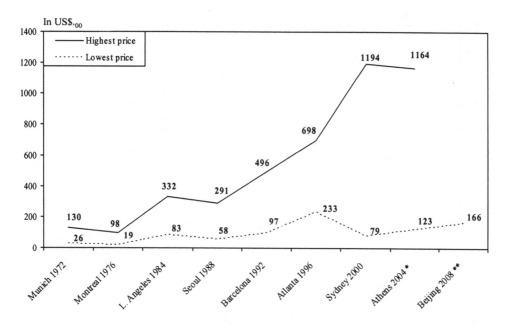

Notes: *   Average price, inflation estimated.
          **   Estimated by Bidding Committee Beijing 2008 (2001).

Sources: Bidding Committee Beijing 2008 (2001); Catherwood and van Kirk (1992); IOC (1996a); NN (1995c); Athens OCOG (2003b, p. 139); Barcelona OCOG (1992); Montreal OCOG (1976); Preuss (2000a); The Audit Office (1999).

Figure 8.28   Prices for opening ceremony tickets from Munich 1972 to Beijing 2008

Consideration of special target groups such as school classes and the poor is another way to differentiate prices (Bidding Committee Beijing 2008, 2001; Howard and Crompton, 1995; Moscow OCOG, 1980; Schöps, 1983). However, this does not greatly influence total revenues and, therefore, will not be discussed further. The IOC and the IF requirements form the framework conditions which an OCOG must meet. When the Games are awarded, the OCOG is legally obliged to fulfil these conditions, as dictated by the Host City Contract. The conditions also influence the price policy. The most critical factor in determining the ticket prices depends on the OCOG's objective – to maximize profit or to provide tickets for as many visitors as possible. Battle (interview, 1997) emphasized that for Atlanta the profit was very important but they had to learn 'to feel for the population'.

It has been shown that a comparison of ticket sales revenues of different Olympic Games is impossible due to the manifold factors which are influenced by location and country as well as by the policy pursued by the respective OCOG.

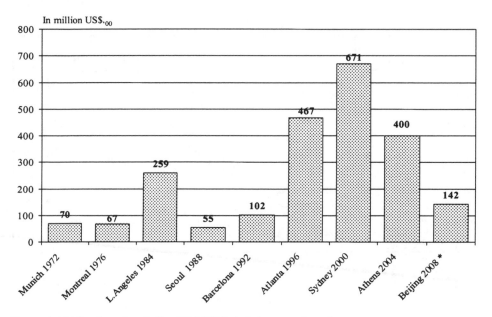

Note: * Bidding Committee Beijing 2008 (2001), inflation rate estimated.

Sources: IOC (2004b); Bidding Committee Beijing 2008 (2001); IOC (2001b); Preuss (2000a).

Figure 8.29   Total ticket sales revenues from Munich 1972 to Beijing 2008

Figure 8.29 shows the financial potential of ticketing in the US$'$_{00}$ 670.2 million achieved by Sydney 2000 which represented approximately 23 per cent of the overall revenues. The high revenues at the Los Angeles 1984, Atlanta 1996 and Sydney 2000 Olympics were owing to the large number of tickets sold at relatively high prices.

8.4 OTHER REVENUES

All other revenue sources of the OCOGs are summarized in this section owing to the fact that it is not possible to classify them in detail. Moreover, there are not sufficient data available to compare individual Olympic Games. It can be stated, however, that these sources are important since their share amounts to approximately 10 per cent of the overall OCOG revenues.

On the following pages, the sectors of donations, interest earnings, commemorative medals, rents/fees, test events, subsidies and special revenues are reviewed. The focus will centre on the basic phenomena of these sources. In addition, it must be noted that the revenues from cultural events are included in Chapter 9 since their costs generally exceed revenues.

8.4.1 Donations

Before looking at the donation sector for Olympic Games, the reader shall be reminded of the difference between patrons, donors and sponsors.

- Patronage has a long tradition and can be traced back to the Roman Maecenas. Patrons promote and support organizations or causes based on truly altruistic motives.
- A donor's motivation is rather to 'do something good and talk about it,' and at the very least they expect a donation receipt for the tax office.
- A sponsor expects a service in return for his or her payment, which is fixed by a contract (Scheibe-Jaeger, 1996; Zollinger, 1994).

For the Olympic Games, donors and patrons have always played an important role. The Athens 1896 Olympics were largely financed by donations from Greek people living abroad. Foreigners, however, were not allowed to support the Hellenic Games (Philemon, 1996 [1896]). Possibly the most important patron in Olympic history was G. Averoff, a Greek national who lived in Egypt and donated 920 000 drachmas to expand the Panathenaic stadium which will be used for archery in 2004. The budget of the London OCOG, 1908 also consisted of donations to the tune of 73 per cent of the total (calculation based on data from the British Olympic Council 1908). In the history of the Olympic Games, the significance of donations as a financing source has varied greatly. In most cases, the donations were very small and did not even receive a mention in the official reports. However, in Rome 1960 and Tokyo 1964, the names of all enterprises that made donations in kind were listed (Rome OCOG, 1960).

Revenues of Munich 1972 that were declared as donations should be questioned owing to the fact that it is at this time that the transition to sponsorship started. For the 1972 Olympics an association to promote the Games was founded (Verein zur Förderung der Olympischen Spiele 1972 in München e.V.). This grew out of a foundation to promote the Munich stadium, which was founded on 12 June 1955 to close the OCOG financing gaps. The 'promoting association ... suggested that the donating enterprises depict their donation in kind in their own publicity material for advertising impact ... It awarded the title Official Supplier of the Olympic Games (Organisationskomitee München, 1974a). The donors received 0.5 per cent of all tickets and a promoting association distributed the tickets to the enterprises in relation to their donations (Organisationskomitee München, 1974a). Due to the service the OCOG offered in return for the financial contributions of the enterprises, the term 'donation' is less suited than 'sponsoring'. In Montreal 1976 and Moscow 1980, sponsoring finally entered Olympic financing. For these Olympics, no major donations were made and Los Angeles 1984 expressly refrained from donations in order not to be in competition with the USOC (Hill, 1992).

Similar to Tokyo 1964 in Asia, donations were decisive again in Seoul 1988. Koreans living in Japan donated the largest share for the 1988 Olympics, with US$.$_{00}$ 105.3 million. The total donations in Korea contributed 11.2 per cent to the overall OCOG revenues (Seoul OCOG, 1988). If one includes the donations of Greek people living abroad for the Athens 1896 Olympics, it may be assumed that particularly people living abroad want to contribute to the international reputation of their home country. This is, after all, one of the few opportunities to demonstrate national pride when living abroad. If this conclusion is correct, the readiness of the population of a host country living abroad to donate could be a possible source of revenue, especially for countries with a strong national awareness. Athens 2004 established a special programme to keep in contact with their citizens. It is called 'Greeks abroad'.

The readiness to donate could also be increased by granting generous tax exemptions. This, however, would correspond to a public subsidy. For Barcelona 1992, the donations of enterprises for the Games earned a 35 per cent and private donations a 10 per cent tax reduction (Barcelona OCOG, 1992). Even for Games not publicly subsidized, like those of Atlanta 1996, many enterprises and cities made contributions in value in kind or financial donations – numerous cities provided their buses (Gillam, 1996b; 1996c) or donated up to millions of dollars (Blume, 1996; interview, Battle, 1997). Athens 2004 expects donations of US$.$_{00}$ 12.3 million. For the Games in Beijing the Bid book states donations of US$.$_{00}$ 11.1 million, however, a few days after winning the bid, Vice-major Liu Jingmin said that the Olympic Games will not accept private donations. The citizens should use their money to improve their living conditions (NN, 2001b).

The most significant private donation, however, is the 'donation of work' of volunteers. Volunteers have been involved in the Games since Stockholm 1912 (Chalip, 2000b; Moragas, et al., 2000). The value of labour they give nearly for free is difficult to evaluate. It is not only the work they do, but also the image of the host nation they create by being highly motivated and acting with great enthusiasm. The reader is therefore only reminded at this point of the significance and the extent of this source.

Figure 8.30 shows the large number of volunteers OCOGs have used to stage the Olympic Games. If the work was paid for, labour costs of approximately US$.$_{00}$ 100 million would be incurred. Of course, this figure strongly depends on the wage level of the host country. The calculation is based on a conservative estimate for industrialized countries where all volunteers are engaged two weeks prior to the Games and would earn about US$1300 net per month. Thus 45 000 x US$2200 (gross) = US$99 million. OCOGs are well aware of the significance of voluntary work, a fact which is reflected in the costly training and care programmes that OCOGs offer to volunteers. Athens 2004 is paying US$.$_{00}$ 41.4 million for training, coordination and nomination of the 45 000 Olympic and 15 000 Paralympic volunteers (interview, Mamangakis, 2003).

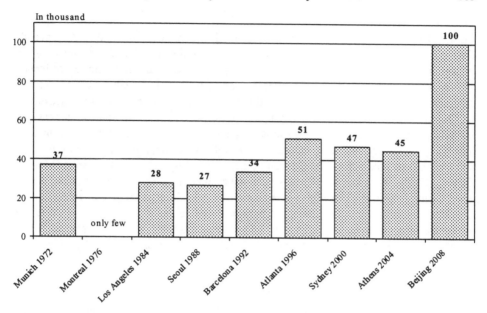

Sources: Chappelet (2001); Kidd (correspondence, 1997); Moragas et al. (2000); Athens OCOG (2003b, p. 22); Sydney OCOG (2001); Preuss (2000a); Sun (correspondence, 2004).

Figure 8.30   Number of volunteers at Olympic Games

8.4.2 Olympic Lotteries

The support of the Olympic Games by lotteries and lottery bonds has a long tradition. In the run-up to the Athens 1896 Olympics the issuing of lottery bonds was planned in view of a lack of means, but the time to carry it out was too short (Philemon, 1996 [1896]). Lottery bonds are 'bonds not earning any interest or earning low interest and instead of or in addition to low interest lottery premiums are paid. The bond amount is paid back in full. Number and amount of premiums are fixed in a lottery schedule' (Müssig et al., 1988). One can see similar obligations, for example, in Helsinki 1940 (correspondence, Lippert, 2000). The Games of the fiftieth Olympiad were financed to a large extent (51 per cent) by a lottery managed by the Swedish Central Association for the promotion of the athletics, with the assent of the Swedish Government (Lanrdy and Yerlès, 1996). Also Munich 1972 proved, at the time, that an Olympic lottery could be a significant source for financing the Olympic Games (Preuss, 1999).

Both OCOGs and NOCs have opportunities to increase revenues by increasing winning rates, using material prizes or engaging in special promotion activities. Although the Olympic lottery has proved to be an enormous financing source, it has hardly been mentioned as such in recent times. Therefore, the various forms of Olympic lotteries are displayed here.

Founding a new lottery

To finance the Munich 1972 Olympics the 'GlücksSpirale' was founded. After the Olympics, the lottery was continued in order to finance the Football World Cup 1974 and is still in existence today (German Bundestag, 1975; Organisationskomitee München, 1974a). In Montreal 1976, the Olympic Lottery Canada was founded, which was later continued as Lotto-Canada in order to diminish the deficit run in Montreal (Montreal OCOG, 1976). In the following Olympiad of Moscow 1980, the 'Sprint' lottery was established, followed by the International Olympic Sports Lottery, the first international lottery. It was carried out in the German Democratic Republic, Poland, Hungary, Bulgaria and Czechoslovakia. Prizes were, among other, trips to the Moscow Olympics (Moscow OCOG, 1980). In China the Ministry of Finance will allow an Olympic Lottery for the 2008 Olympic Games. The lottery tickets will be sold through the existing networks of China's Sports Lottery. The lottery programme will operate from 2001 to 2008 and produce a forecast revenue of US$$_{,00}$ 153.5 million. In general, it can be assumed that the expected revenues from a newly founded Olympic lottery amount to 20– 50 per cent of its turnover.

Participation in the revenues of an existing lottery

For the Korean Olympics 1988, the existing 'Housing Lottery' was renamed 'Olympic Lottery' but the Housing Fond still participated in the lottery revenues (Seoul OCOG, 1988). Apart from the new Russian lotteries mentioned, the Moscow OCOG 1980 also participated in the 'Sport-Lotto' lottery (Moscow OCOG, 1980). In Spain, the State Lottery and Betting Organization had the exclusive right to conduct lotteries. There were five additional draws from which a staggering US$$_{,00}$ 107.4 million flowed to the OCOG (Barcelona OCOG, 1992). Apart from additional draws in the national lottery, the government decided to provide 7 per cent of the revenues from the football lottery, in the five years prior to the Games, as a subsidy for the Olympics (Savoie, 1996).

A possible form of financing participation in an existing lottery could be achieved through a plan to lower the payout ratio or to have an 'Olympic surcharge' added to the price of each coupon without additional payout. The expected OCOG revenues from existing lotteries amount to approximately 10–20 per cent of the lottery turnover since the OCOG does not receive all the profit (Table 8.12).

Participation in the profits from increased turnover

This form, which has not been used thus far, was suggested for the bid candidate Berlin 2000. The OCOG would participate only in the increased turnover. The turnover of the 'GlücksSpirale' in 1972 was only achieved again in 1989 caused by the high popularity of the Olympic Games (Maennig, 1992). This form could be suitable for countries where a new lottery must not be introduced or the revenues of existing lotteries must not be used for financing the Olympics. The Games-related increased turnover could be achieved by additional promotion activities and attractive material prizes. It must be assumed, however, that this form of participation will earn an OCOG only 5–10 per cent of the lottery turnover.

Table 8.12 Figures of Olympic lotteries from Munich 1972 to Beijing 2008

	Munich 1972	Montreal 1976	Moscow 1980	Moscow 1980 (In US$‰)	Seoul 1988	Barcelona 1992	Beijing 2008
Lottery name	GlücksSpirale	Olympic Lottery	Sprint	Intern. Olympic Sports Lottery	Olympic Lottery	State Lottery and Betting Organization	Olympic Lottery
Purchasing price of lottery coupon	5.42	20.49	1.97	Varying	0.77	N/A	N/A
First drawing (years prior to Olympic year)	2	2	4	3	5	3	8
Premium (%)	25–30	45	50	Varying	45–50	N/A	N/A
Maximum prize money	1301766	2444687	16386	32774	179504	N/A	N/A
Material prizes	Tickets, trips, cars, etc.	–	Tickets, trips, cars, etc.	Tickets, trips, cars, etc.	–	–	N/A
Share of OCOG/ NOC in million	244.61	574.52	1,206.07		238.18	217.48	153.54
OCOG/NOC share of turnover in % to	46	39	30	25	25	N/A	N/A
Percentage share of financing of OCOG	19	46	49		15	11	11

Sources: Bidding Committee Beijing 2008 (2001); Preuss (2000a).

In Olympic history there were two motives for conducting Olympic lotteries. On the one hand, they were meant to finance the Games and, on the other, to enhance the popularity of the Games and their emblems and symbol. In Munich 1972, the 'GlücksSpirale' was used to more justly distribute the limited number of high demand tickets for the opening ceremony (Organisationskomitee München, 1974a). In the past lotteries proved to be extremely successful. With the exception of the Olympics in 1984, 1996, 2000 and 2004, all Games reviewed used lotteries as a source of financing. In most cases, the Olympic lottery competes with existing lotteries. This was the case why Sydney 2000 and Athens 2004 could not establish an Olympic Lottery (Parliament of the Commonwealth of Australia, 1995). In this situation, revenues for the Olympic lottery only occur by means of redistributions at the expense of the existing lotteries.

The more strongly past Games were supported by the public sector, the more important the lottery was to the overall financing. In the 1970s the share of special financing means was very high but during the last Olympiads private financing sources, such as marketing and selling television rights, contributed the largest part. In view of the ever-rising costs for the Games and the ever-tighter public funds, this development was to be expected. For the future, however, the mixed financing model seems superior to models with mainly private or public financing because it would allow the use of the high potential of special financing means to cover the costs of the Olympic Games.

8.4.3 Interest Earnings

The assumption that the main part of the expenditures to be made by an OCOG are incurred before revenues are earned from staging the Games, is actually not correct. In point of fact, the records of previous Games have proven that the expenditures in the preparatory phase of the Games were lower than the revenues being earned. The revenue surplus was invested and interest was earned. In addition, an examination of the cash flow reveals the liquidity situation and, thus, the financial development of an OCOG.

An OCOG should attempt to collect revenues as early as possible while, at the same time, postponing payments. Clever management by the OCOG of Munich 1972, for example, allowed for significant payments to be made later than planned and revenues from the coin programme to be collected early and continuously (Federal Government, 1970; 1971). In addition, the OCOG was granted inexpensive public loans. The government, the Federal State of Bavaria and the City of Munich each covered one third of the statutory OCOG expenditures until sufficient revenues were received. The subsidies were treated as a loan with an annual interest rate of 6 per cent (Federal Government, 1971). For the Los Angeles 1984 Olympics, Ueberroth credited the first payments that were made as early as six years prior to the Games. The early sales of the television rights earned 15 per cent of the overall OCOG revenues even before the Olympiad had begun (Taylor and Gratton, 1988). Ueberroth's consistent investment strategy earned an average interest rate of approximately 12 per cent in the five years before the Games (Los Angeles OCOG, 1984); indeed, his financial management skills are revealed in the fact that even the interest-free securities the NOCs had to deposit for the athletes in Los Angeles 1984 were invested.

The data in Figure 8.31 only consist of OCOG revenues and expenditures. It is assumed that the largest portion of the revenues resulted in incoming payments in the same year, while that of the expenditures resulted in outgoing payments. Deviations from this do not change the significance of these theoretical considerations. The data for Figure 8.31 have been calculated by simply reproducing revenues and expenditures of the respective OCOG. It was adjusted to inflation using the value of the respective Olympic year. This causes a slight distortion since the expenditures of the pre-Olympic years are indicated with too low a value. However, this does not influence the significance of the statement.

Clearly, it can be seen that the accumulated revenues of the Los Angeles and Seoul OCOGs were permanently above expenditures (Preuss, 2000a). Thus, means for short-term investments were always available. The low liquidity surplus of Seoul 1988 in 1986 was caused by the Asian Games. Staging this event meant that it was imperative for some sports facilities to be prepared in time for 1986 rather than for 1988. In the Olympic year both expenditures, especially for personnel costs, and revenues from tickets and so on were very high. These higher levels have been evident with all the Olympics.

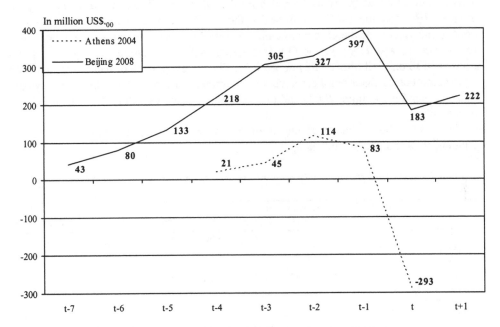

Sources: Bidding Committee Beijing 2008 (2001); Mamangakis (interview, 2003).

Figure 8.31 Cash flow in Athens 2004 and Beijing 2008

Not all Olympic Games can count on having high superfluous liquid resources. For example, compared with Los Angeles 1984, Atlanta 1996 was hardly able to build up any interest earnings. 'The highest debts the OCOG incurred were US$70 million, the largest surplus of payments was at only US$300 million for a short time' (interview, Battle, 1997). It was the first time that an OCOG had to take out a 'commercial' loan (Atlanta OCOG, 1998). Secure financing during the seven preparatory years is also in the IOC's best interests.

The bidders for the 2004 Olympics were, therefore, required to submit an estimate of their cash flow to the IOC. Most bidders anticipated a sustained surplus of incoming payments for themselves if selected as the host city (IOC, 1995a; Bidding Committee Athens 2004, 1995; Bidding Committee Rio de Janeiro 2004, 1995; Bidding Committee Roma 2004, 1995; Bidding Committee Stockholm 2004, 1995).

8.4.4 Rents and Fees for Olympic Villages

This section looks at the rents gained from the Olympic villages, youth camps, media villages, IBC and the MPC. Additionally the OCOG receives money from guests of honour and visitors of the Olympic Family. Revenues gained from awarding concessions for restaurants and so on in the Olympic sports facilities, Olympic villages and press centre and so on shall only be mentioned here. The largest portion of what is earned from this source comes from renting rooms and equipment to the NOCs within the Olympic village (interview, Arnold, 2004) and to media representatives within the IBC, MPC and media village.

Table 8.13 shows the development of this source of revenue with respect to the Olympic village and the youth camp.

Table 8.13 Revenues from the Olympic village and the youth camp in (US$·₀₀)

	Munich 1972	Montreal 1976	Moscow 1980	LA 1984	Seoul 1988	Barcelona 1992	Atlanta 1996	Sydney 2000	Athens 2004	Beijing 2008
Overall revenues (million)	17.53	6.85	N/A	N/A	27.86	95.72	N/A	N/A	N/A	N/A
Price per athlete and day in the Olympic village	37.03	36.37	31.15	58.50 186.30*	60.96	free	free	free	free	free
Price per official and day in the Olympic village	37.03	N/A	N/A	248.78	108.95	122.43	free	free	free	free
Price per young person and day in the youth camp	26.03	13.02	27.00	no camp	41.50	53.98	free	62.95	free	22.17
Revenues from the youth camp	N/A	488 937	N/A	N/A	N/A	N/A	672 000	N/A	N/A	N/A

Note: *   When arriving more than two days prior to the Games.

Sources: Bidding Committee Beijing 2008 (2001); Lee (1989); Neuhöfer (correspondence, 2004); Preuss (2000a).

It is obvious that revenues from renting the Olympic village have greatly varied. Until Moscow 1980, the fees per athlete remained at a constant level. With the Los Angeles 1984 Olympics, however, they rose sharply and then remained at that level when the Seoul OCOG 1988 chose to adopt the prices of 1984. Since Barcelona 1992, fees have not been charged for athletes to stay in the Olympic village. Moreover, for Sydney 2000, the intention was to subsidize the athletes' travel expenses to the tune of US$·₀₀ 28.1 million (Goodbody, 1993; Hubbard, 1993; IOC, 1996c). It is becoming obvious that, in the future, renting accommodations to the Olympic Family will no longer be a source of revenue even though costs in this sector continue to rise. As a result, an Olympic bid without subsidies for the athletes will now only serve to worsen the competitive position of a candidate city.

Although less factual information is available, it is still evident from that which does exist that the role the international youth camp plays as a revenue source has also yielded varying financial results. For Montreal 1976, the OCOG earned approximately US\$$_{00}$ 596 500 in fees. For the first time in Atlanta 1996, however, it was decided that the camp would be free of charge for all participants. Instead, the Atlanta OCOG opted to meet the financial demands of the programme by recruiting a sponsor rather than by charging fees to the participants. Swatch was a 'special' sponsor of the youth camp and provided US\$$_{00}$ 859 200 (interview, Arrington, 1996). In Sydney 2000 there was a mixture. On the one hand, McDonald's and Olympic Solidarity acted as sponsors of the youth camp. McDonald's took over the costs for one participant per NOC and Olympic Solidarity paid one air fare per NOC. On the other hand, the NOCs had to pay a fee of US\$$_{00}$ 63 per day for the remaining participants and the other flight expenses. Athens 2004 will not charge fees for the youth camp (IOC, 1997e). In Beijing 2008 a fee of US\$$_{00}$ 22.2 per day is planned.

8.4.5 Test Events

All OCOGs should stage test events prior to the Games. Despite the lack of obligation, the number of test events has increased and, since Sydney 2000, OCOGs will run test events in all sports but not all disciplines. One reason is the pressure from the IFs (interview, Schormann, 2004). Another is the need of the OCOG to test the venues, the infrastructure, the staff, competition management, security and technology. However, OCOGs cannot always test the final Olympic facility due to uncompleted construction work. The Olympic Charter states:

> In accordance with the formula submitted to the IOC Executive Board for approval, the OCOG, after consultation with the IFs, may organize pre-Olympic events for the purpose of testing the facilities to be used during the Olympic Games. In each sport, the pre-Olympic events must take place under the technical supervision of the relevant IF. (IOC, 2003d, Rule 55, para. 1, para. 2)

It is therefore at the discretion of the OCOG in which form it uses test events to make a profit, for example by top level international competitions. This area will generally not produce any revenues but, for example, the staging of the Asian Games in Seoul 1986 proved to be very lucky for the city. Thus, many sports facilities could be used twice for mega-events within a very short period of time. The Asian Games were awarded to Seoul only two months after it had been awarded the Olympic Games. The Koreans regarded them as a dress rehearsal (Kramar, 1994). Lee (Korean Sports Minister) said: 'We are looking to the Asian Games as a dummy run for the Olympics' (NN, 1984c). This pattern becomes very popular. Kuala Lumpur, planning to stage the Asian Games 2010 plans to bid for the Olympics in 2016, Busan hosted the Asian Games in 2002 and plans to bid for

2016 and Rio de Janeiro (Pan American Games 2006) bit unsuccessfully for 2012. Additionally, other test events, such as the dress rehearsal of the Atlanta 1996 and Sydney 2000 opening ceremony were used to invite all volunteers in order to thank them for their commitment and to motivate them for the days to come. In Sydney 2000 the OCOG also sold tickets of the dress rehearsal to cover some costs of the opening ceremony. The potential income was estimated to be US$$_{.00}$ 7.6 million (interview, Elphinston, 1999).

In Athens many test events, such as the World Cup Final in Modern Pentathlon were free for the visitors. In Sydney, visitors had to pay for the 43 test events. However, test events will hardly produce a surplus (interview, Battle, 1997), while the social impact, the learning as well as the macroeconomic impact of test events is positive. In Los Angeles 1984 US$$_{.00}$ 2.5 million was said to have been spent on pre-Olympic events. Tourist expenditures in the region amounted to approximately US$$_{.00}$ 5.5 million (ERA, 1984). Test events are very important to an OCOG in order to train and test procedures. If shortcomings are detected during a test event their removal can cost the OCOG a lot of money, but this can help to prevent even greater damage such as the loss of image. In Seoul 1988, for example, the tennis courts had to be moved because the sun was dazzling and the roof of the gym hall had to be covered to make television transmissions better (German, 1993). It is estimated, that Sydney saved up to 1000 per cent through noticing faults by testing events prior to the Games (interview, Elphinston, 1999). For OCOGs in Athens and Beijing test events are a must. Athens staged test events in all sports between November 2003 and June 2004. Competitions had the level from National School Championships to European Championships and World Cup Finals.

8.4.6 Direct Public Subsidies

Apart from the public and municipal costs, which cannot be avoided for all Olympics (in particular, administration costs), the public sector has contributed more or less to the Games, depending on the financing model. In the past some OCOGs were directly subsidized, which can be concluded from the respective balance. In the period under review, direct subsidies can be detected in the balances of the Seoul 1988 and Barcelona 1992 Olympics and especially in Athens 2004 and Beijing 2008. Even the 'private' Games of Atlanta 1996 were subsidized with at least US$$_{.00}$ 336 million since the state erected the rowing facility at Lake Lanier (interview, DeFrantz, 1997). In Seoul subsidies amounted to approximately US$$_{.00}$ 61 million (Seoul OCOG, 1988), in Barcelona to approximately US$$_{.00}$ 140 million (Brunet, 1993), in Athens 2004 US$$_{.00}$ 288 (Athens OCOG, 2003b, p. 22) in Beijing to approximately US$$_{.00}$ 55.5 million (Bidding Committee Beijing 2008, 2001). In general, the public support mainly consists of infrastructure construction.

8.4.7 Other Sources of Revenues

This part of the study will briefly mention the other sources of OCOG revenues in order primarily to highlight their innovative ideas.

The marketing of advertising spaces is only allowed outside the Olympic venues. The Olympic Charter states: 'Commercial installations and advertising signs shall not be allowed in the stadia, nor in other sport grounds' (IOC, 2003d, Rule 61, para. 1). In addition, advertising is also completely prohibited on the athletes. 'No form of publicity or propaganda, commercial or otherwise, may appear on persons, on sportswear, accessories or, more generally, on any article of clothing or equipment whatsoever worn or used by the athletes' (IOC, 2000e, By-Law to Rule 61, para. 1). Nevertheless, there are still advertising opportunities to be taken advantage of in the Olympic park, the immediate surroundings of the venues and in the unofficial programmes. However, the IOC is reducing these opportunities more and more.

The Olympics have the potential to attract the attention of the population through the use of PR means and techniques, which have thus far been unknown. In the run-up to the Seoul 1988 Olympics, posters were installed on buses and large electronic advertising boards and were a great success. This strategy earned the OCOG an additional US$$_{.00}$ 53.2 million (Seoul OCOG, 1988). In Sydney, UPS advertised in Darling Harbour by means of a laser show and covered skyscrapers totally with transparencies.

Individual Olympic venues are increasingly being financed through the direct participation of the population. For a mere US$$_{.00}$ 39.2, people were given the opportunity to become immortal by having their name placed on a pebble in Atlanta's Centennial Park. In Sydney, shares could even be purchased for the main stadium of the 2000 Olympics (NN, 1996d). However, the initial sales of the shares were not very promising (NN, 1997c).

The desire of the urban population to identify with the Olympics is also reflected in the special Olympic licence plates Atlanta and Sydney citizens could buy (Greising, 1995; NN, 1996k) as well as in the auctioning of T-shirts displaying the number of days until the opening ceremony. The auction of T-shirts was previously carried out in the preparatory phase of the Lillehammer 1994 Olympics (Strauss, 1993). In Nagano, they started 500 days before the Olympics were declared open. The first T-shirt earned US$$_{.00}$ 8232. Atlanta was said to have earned a total of US$$_{.00}$ 448 000 with this programme (IOC 1997a). In Sydney statues were auctioned 500 days before the Games, which rose in average US$$_{.00}$ 2864 (interview, Elphinston, 1999).

The liquidation of the OCOG brings in the last revenues for the organization (Busch, 1996; Kloth, 1996). Before its liquidation, the Seoul OCOG 1988 had goods amounting to US$$_{.00}$ 146.7 million of which only US$$_{.00}$ 27.2 million were property to be sold (NN, 1988i). The Atlanta OCOG 1996 auctioned items that even included boats, luxury furniture, motorbikes, sports equipment, stadium seats, and garbage cans (Atlanta OCOG, 1998). Sydney 2000 sold its assets for US$$_{.00}$ 32.6 million (AOC, 2001).

Another potential source of revenues is a contribution from an IFs. In order to stage successful Games and present the highest quality of its respective sport, some IFs started to support the OCOG. For example, the International Canoe Federation paid partly for the white water facility in Sydney and the Union International Pentathlon Moderne (UIPM) provided competition horses (interview, Schormann, 2004).

In future, the liquidation of OCOG equipment will become more important due to the fact that the proportion of value in kind provided by the sponsors will be high. Unused superfluous goods could even be sold in advance of this final liquidation effort. It would be in the best interests of the OCOG for it to establish a department that would take on the task of organizing sales of the goods as well as that of finding ways to open up adequate channels for their distribution.

In addition, the 'Transfer of Knowledge' (TOK), a sale of Olympic-specific software and databases to the IOC, has taken place with Sydney 2000 for the first time (NN, 1999a). However in future TOK is no larger financing source, because 'the OCOG shall provide to the IOC, free of charge … update guides as well as all other documents and materials … in relation to all aspects of the planning, organisation and staging of the Games' (IOC, 2001e).

One of the potential big financing sources in the future could be betting. However, the IOC is strictly against it, believing that it could result in corruption among athletes. Therefore, on ethical grounds, the IOC has banned betting (interview, Payne, 2004).

9. The flip side of the coin: expenditures of the Organizing Committee

As already described in the chapter on methodology, it is extremely difficult to compare the expenditures of the different Olympics to each other. The few publications that mention expenditures at all delimit the individual items in this category very differently. The fact that a better collection of information exists for the revenues may explain why most publications concentrate on them. Due to these factors, carrying out a similar comparative analysis to that made for the revenues is only possible to a limited extent for the OCOG expenditures. The quantity framework of the factors causing expenditures is instead used more frequently. On this basis, future bid cities could then calculate the expenditures in the individual sectors by multiplying the values with the country-specific price levels such as those for construction or labour.

There has always been a dispute over which items should and should not be included as expenditures for the Olympic Games. Due to the differing delimitations of the investments which are Games-related and non-Games-related in the sports venues and the infrastructure, each cost–benefit analysis of the Olympic Games can be influenced in a way which can produce the desired result (Preuss, 1993). In general, operational costs and overlays should therefore be distinguished from investments when preparing for the Olympic Games. Operational costs and overlays are always Games related. This distinction, however, is not always as clearly evident when looking at the investments.

Thus far, the OCOGs have financed the Olympic venues partly with their own means and then handed them over to the host city free of charge after the Games. Atlanta OCOG, for example, handed over 13 Olympic venues to the city or the state (Atlanta OCOG, 1996). The Sydney OCOG contributed US$$_{.00}$ 271.7 million to the 'Sydney Aquatic & Athletic Centres' and some other venues (Olympic Co-ordination Authority, 2002, p. 18). This strategy would correspond to a depreciation of the sports facilities in 17 days. Corporations investing in a facility to be used over a longer period of time would depreciate it over the actual life cycle in their balance. For tax reasons, however, corporations try to reduce the profit to be taxed by using the quickest possible depreciation. An OCOG and, in particular, the host city could be tempted to use a similar method when depreciating the expenditures for the sports venues. This would reduce the total surplus and thereby keep the payments to the IOC, that are both fixed in the Host City Contract and dependent on the surplus, as small as possible. In Athens 2004 and Beijing 2008 any surplus resulting from the celebration of the Games shall be divided as follows:

- 20 per cent to the Greek and Chinese NOC
- 60 per cent to the general benefit of sport in Greece and China
- 20 per cent to the IOC (IOC, 1997d; IOC, 2001e).

While tax laws clearly define the minimum allowable depreciation times, a corresponding regulation on the part of the IOC is missing. Thus, to this day, an OCOG can immediately depreciate all investments. In the eyes of the host city, an OCOG has done a successful job of managing the Games if the image of the city remains positive, the OCOG's financial statement is balanced and investments that have been made in the city are high. If, however, the OCOG stated a surplus, then a portion of it would be used to finance world sport as well as sport in the host country. A. DeFrantz lamented that, as a consequence of the investments made by the Atlanta 1996, the Olympic money remained in the city and could not be used to promote international sports (interview, De Frantz, 1997). The many differing statements regarding the surplus of the Seoul 1988 Olympics can be better understood after the above discussion. The surplus of Seoul 1988 range from US$$_{00}$ 89.5 million to US$$_{00}$ 686 million (Chang, 1989; Kim, 1990; Lee, 1989; Seoul OCOG, 1988; NN, 1989). On the one hand, the OCOG sought to have the Games be recognized as the most profitable ever staged in the history of the modern Olympics. On the other hand, the OCOG did not want to have to pay too much money to the IOC. Subsequently, they asked the IOC not to include the revenues gained from selling the Olympic village in the surplus. In the surplus of US$$_{00}$ 686 million as stated by the OCOG, more than US$$_{00}$ 389 million were said to come from selling the Olympic village (Kim et al., 1989; Kim, 1990). Officially, the OCOG made a profit of only US$$_{00}$ 192 million. It was agreed that the OCOG only had to pay US$2 million to the IOC if the profit was below US$$_{00}$ 201 million (NN, 1988i; 1989). The OCOG of Sydney, for example, was smart to give a share of US$$_{00}$ 75.2 million to the NOC in order to support sport in Australia and another US$$_{00}$ 75.2 million to the city. These payments were made before a final balance was calculated (interview, Elphinston, 1999).

It should now be obvious that all the Games-related investments in the infrastructure of the host city strongly influence the expenditures of an OCOG. This statement is made all the more telling if the depreciation is set to just the few days that make up the period of the Olympic celebration. In addition, it also becomes obvious that a different evaluation of this single position completely invalidates the statement of a surplus or a deficit of the Olympic Games. Even if the Games-related investments of an OCOG are included as expenditures, they are ignored here, since they have been dealt with in the previous section on the macroeconomic impacts of the Olympics. It is only in this way that a comparison of the remaining OCOG expenditures from Munich 1972 to Beijing 2008 is given meaning.

The IOC has also recognized these problems and, as a result of this, stipulated that the candidates for the 2004 Olympics and later were required to provide a separate list of investments from that of the remaining expenditure items. This new requirement thereby allows for a comparison of the bid cities to be made, as far as the finances are concerned. In the future, the IOC might even go as far as to forbid the OCOGs from investing any

'Olympic funds'. This restriction will be introduced in order to ensure that the OCOG properly draws on its revenues only in order to organize the Games and, in the case of a surplus, only in order to promote sport in general (interview, Payne, 1997). T. Bach made it even more clear: 'It is not the task of the IOC to pursue urban redevelopment but to promote sport' (Hahn, 1996; interview, Pound 1998). For the Games in 2004 and 2008 the Host City Contract demands that the revenues granted by the IOC to the OCOG shall not be used to provide infrastructure. It is alone the responsibility of the host city and the host country to cover all investments (IOC, 1997d; 2001e).

Now that the investments have been separated from the operational expenditures, the development of the overall operational expenditures for the OCOGs from Munich 1972 to Beijing 2008 can be seen in Figure 9.1.

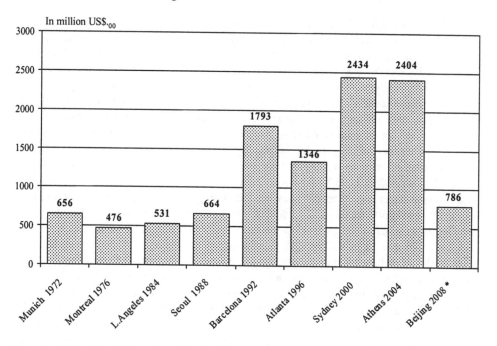

Note: * Estimated by Bidding Committee Beijing 2008.

Sources: Bidding Committee Beijing 2008 (2001); Preuss (2000a).

Figure 9.1 Overall operational expenditures of the OCOGs from Munich 1972 to Beijing 2008

In contrast to the overall expenditures for the Olympic Games, which were the basis for the financing models, only the operational expenditures of the OCOGs are compared here. It can immediately be seen that the expenditures of the Montreal 1976 OCOG were lower than those of all the other OCOGs that are looked at in this book. Since the OCOG revenues exceeded these expenditures, the often made accusation of poor financial planning on the part of the Montreal 1976 organizers must be re-examined. By the way, the IOC is of the opinion that the Montreal 1976 OCOG was responsible for the deficit of the Games (Landry and Yerlès, 1996). In addition, a re-examination must also be made regarding the praise that is just as often bestowed upon the Los Angeles 1984 OCOG for having organized the Games in an extremely profitable manner.

9.1 EXPENDITURES FOR THE LOCATION

9.1.1 Games-related and Non-Games-related Expenditures

In order to stage the Games, an OCOG requires more than just a number of sports facilities. It is also necessary for the host city to feature an adequate infrastructure for traffic, communication, an athletes' and media village, an MPC and IBC – all of which have steadily increased in number and size as a result of the corresponding increases to the number of athletes, events and sports being included at the Olympic Games and the ongoing 'medialization'. The ever more complicated requirements for Olympic venues are not a modern phenomonen, Coubertin having stated: 'As for the construction of the stadium which, in its completed state, would cost in the neighbourhood of a million, it was a permanent building to be helped by subsidies from the State and the town. Stockholm stood to gain whichever way you looked at it' (Coubertin, 1936). Later, the former IOC President Lord Killanin said after the Montreal 1976 Games: 'Who forces the cities to take on excessive costs? They use the Olympic Games to redevelop their city and to create new sports facilities ... . Mexico City, Tokyo, Munich and also Montreal used the Games as an occasion to develop their cities. Sport is not guilty for this' (Huberty and Wange, 1976 quoted in Killanin, 1983). Similarly, the former IOC Vice-president U.-J. Kim made the following remark regarding the ever rising costs for sports facilities and attempted to shift the responsibility for them to the city: 'Instead of having one facility per sport, the city could build a sports complex' (Kim, 1990). The assertion that staging the Olympic Games leads to redevelopment within a host city is entirely valid. However, it is also possible to understand the IOC's position that the funding for this redevelopment must come from the city and not from the accounts of the OCOG. The redevelopment of a city and the construction of permanent facilities should strictly be an undertaking of the public and private sector alone. Thus, an OCOG would only have to then bear the location costs – which are separated from investments in the following discussion.

Investments are 'deliberate, generally long-term capital tie-ups to gain future autonomous profit' (Sellien and Sellien, 1997). This includes all expenditures for new constructions, as well as all those that are incurred for extensions, modernisation and the redevelopment of sports venues, the installation of infrastructures, and Olympic villages. If locations are defined as 'places of industrial ... settlement' (Sellien and Sellien, 1997), then location costs include all those expenditures which are caused by the settlement at a certain place, such as those expenditures which are not investments. In the following pages, location costs include the construction of overlays and temporary installations, interest for pulled forward construction activities, maintenance costs, and rents.

Before dealing with the location costs in detail, a clear distinction shall be made between the costs for 'Games-related' and 'non-Games-related' facilities. By making use of this clear categorization for the facilities, the discussions that take place in the host cities regarding the allocation of expenditures for the 'Olympic' facilities could be quickly brought to a conclusion. Furthermore, the chance to manipulate cost-benefit analyses will be weakened (Preuss, 1993). An examination of the flow chart found in Figure 9.2 allows for the decision-making processes that are used in the planning for the sports venues of the Olympic Games to be explained and the distinction to be made between the 'Games-related' and 'non-Games-related' investments.

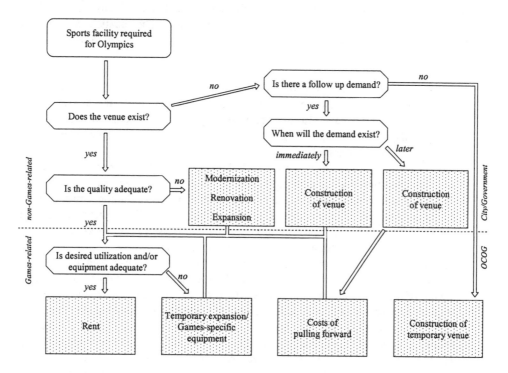

Note: * There might be costs for advance redevelopment. Due to reasons of clarity, they are not shown here.

Figure 9.2   *Flow chart to distinguish between Games-related and non-Games-related sports venues*

According to Figure 9.2, all the sports venues, which are built because there is a general need for them, even without the Games are classified as 'non-Games-related'. Thus, in these instances, the facilities that are built are not a financial burden for the OCOG. However, passing along the financial burden to the city or state is not always so straightforward for an OCOG since the costs for any facility deemed to be 'Games-related' must be especially marked and defended against the executive board of the IOC. A direct example of this is seen in the many problems that arise for potential host cities when an Olympic hall or stadium does not exist and there is no post-Olympic demand for such a facility within the city. In this situation, an OCOG would be forced to erect the facility as a temporary structure, thereby risking the possibility of quickly surpassing the financial limits of an OCOG. The costs for the temporary facilities are much cheaper than permanent structures (IOC, 2003a). They strongly depend on the climatic conditions. Cities that do not have adequate sports facilities or an appropriate follow-up demand should seriously discuss the question of whether a bid to host the Olympics should even be made at all. If only one or two sports facilities are missing and there is no follow-up demand, then these missing facilities could be erected temporarily. The related expenditures would then be allocated to the location costs. The location costs, which correspond to the Games-related expenditures listed in Figure 9.2 include the following items:

- Rents: a considerable part of the location costs consists of rents that must be paid for using existing or newly constructed facilities. In addition to the fees for sports venues, the OCOGs have also been required to pay rent for the use of Olympic and media villages, accreditation centres, offices, storage rooms, parking spaces, trade fair halls and convention centres.
- Costs of pulling forward: if there is a follow-up demand for a new sports facility that has been built earlier than planned because of the Olympic Games, the OCOG should bear all costs caused by the pulling forward. Costs of pulling forward can be based on long-term interest rates of the respective country. These costs include both the costs incurred by the provision of funding and possibly increased construction costs if there is a need for a more rapid building process.
- Additional buildings and extensions: all additional Olympic-related construction work is in the responsibility of the IOC. It is a matter of agreement between the owner of the sports facility and the OCOG as to whether the organizers will still be expected to pay a rental fee after the improvements have been carried out. This agreement was made for Los Angeles 1984. 'There will be no rental charges for facilities to which the Committee contributes significant funds for improvements' (Los Angeles OCOG, 1979). The IOC has even gone so far as to require all the bidders for the 2012 Olympics to show all additional construction as 'short-term investments'.
- Construction and removal of temporary facilities and overlays: in the instances when there is no follow-up demand for a facility or an extension, it becomes the responsibility of the OCOG to oversee both the construction of these types of structures before the Games and their subsequent removal after the Games. For the Atlanta OCOG 1996, this proved to be a significant item due to the fact that it had to remove a large number of temporary facilities and overlays (Atlanta OCOG, 1998). In Sydney the costs of overlays had been US$'00 294.3 million. That is a

significant figure and represents 16.1 per cent of the total operating expenditures (Olympic Co-ordination Authority, 2002, p. 25). In addition to the costs that are incurred from installing and dismantling any necessary overlays the OCOG might be required to pay rental fees for the real estate space that is used for these structures.

As an alternative to temporary facilities, an OCOG could offer the host city the money required for the facility. Then the city can build a permanent structure. By adopting this strategy, the host city would then be able to build facilities that were more expensive, permanent, and had no follow-up usage in the sports sector but provide it at first for the Olympic usage. In Munich 1972, for example, a new trade fair hall was built which was used for judo, fencing, weightlifting and so on during the Olympics. A new school was erected which was first used as the MPC and the former athletes' village forms a new suburb today (Genscher, 1971). A possibility could also be to make the facilities smaller after the Games as was the case with the Atlanta 1996 and Sydney 2000 Olympic stadium. Here, the OCOG would have to pay the costs for the extension and the removal of the extension while the city would have to pay for the 'basic' facility.

Today, almost all sports venues can be built temporarily on an economically safe basis. In Atlanta 1996 even the pool for water polo was built temporarily as well as the entire velodrome, which was shifted to Florida after the Games (Atlanta OCOG, 1998). In Sydney and Athens the beach volleyball stadium was temporary (Cordey, 2001) as in Athens was the badminton indoor facility. However, this certainly does not apply to the Olympic village. Even the construction of the relatively small youth camp as a temporary facility in Munich 1972 caused many problems (Organisationskomitee München, 1974a). The new construction of an entire Olympic village surpasses by far the financial capabilities of an OCOG. So far the construction of villages has been mostly financed privately, in a few cases by the public sector (social housing schemes) to be sold after the Games. The only alternative for the OCOG is to rent the villages. In addition to rents, an OCOG must cover the furnishing, temporary security facilities and other overlays (NN, 1984c). In Atlanta 1996 the furniture cost US$·00 2.2 million for the Olympic village alone (Ferguson, 1996).

9.2 EVENT EXPENDITURES

The staging of the competitions is at the centre of the organizational work that is done by an OCOG. Thus, the question of which sectors will incur costs for an OCOG and which factors could change these expenditures in the future is of primary importance.

The item 'event costs' is particularly difficult to break down since the staging of the competitions results in a variety of different expenditures. This is also reflected in the different expenditures that the OCOGs themselves have estimated for this item. For example, in the surplus balances of the Los Angeles OCOG 1984 this item is missing completely. These expenditures, which are linked to hosting the Games, have been classified into four categories for this discussion: competitions, sports equipment, victory ceremonies and test events.

Competition

This sector includes all organizational and personnel costs necessary to stage the competitions as well as the expenditures for equipment and technical installations, such as those needed for timing and displaying results. The Official Report of Munich 1972 mentions the timing installations in the Olympic stadium. The suppliers Junghans and Longines charged a flat rate of US$$_{,00}$ 0.8 million for the timing installations in all sports facilities (Organisationskomitee München, 1974a). In Montreal 1976, the installations cost as much as US$$_{,00}$ 11.2 million (Los Angeles OCOG, 1979). In Seoul 1988, a total of 170 installations for timing equipment was required, however, no costs were mentioned (Lee, 1989). Since Athens 2004 Swatch is a TOP sponsor and provides the timing as value in kind.

The costs for the organization and staffing of the competition sector vary from country to country depending upon the wage levels and the willingness of the population to work as volunteers. With the increase in the number of competitions, disciplines and sports, the Games programme has inevitably become more complex. This, in turn, has resulted in the need for a more comprehensive organization. For this reason alone, the costs of staging the competitions have risen. The technical installations required for timing and displaying results have also caused rising OCOG expenditures in the past few years, owing to the continuously evolving nature of the field of technology.

Sports Equipment

This sector includes sport-specific installations, such as pole vault facilities or volleyball net installations, as well as sports equipment. Expenditures may not necessarily increase. In Montreal 1976, US$$_{,00}$ 15.8 million was spent on sports equipment. In Los Angeles 1984, it was hoped that all sports equipment would be donated (Los Angeles OCOG, 1979). The number of suppliers that provide general, as well as sports-specific, equipment is rising. Nevertheless, each OCOG incurs expenditures for sports equipment and sports-specific installations due to the fact that it must generally procure all of these anew for each celebration of the Games. In Seoul 1988 this sports equipment alone amounted to US$$_{,00}$ 4.8 million (Kim et al., 1989). In Barcelona 1992 the costs for the equipment alone amounted to US$$_{,00}$ 31.9 million (Barcelona OCOG, 1992).

Victory Ceremonies

When preparing for the ceremonies of the Olympic Games, expenditures for victory medals (Lennartz et al., 2000), national flags/anthems (Guegold, 1996), costumes, gifts, decorations and so on, are incurred. The increase of cost can be demonstrated by looking at the cost of victory medals. The fact that the victory ceremonies are broadcast all over the world and arouse strong emotions for the viewers of the victor's nation makes the design of the ceremonies very significant. The formal appearance of the ceremony and the emotions of the winner decisively influence the image of the Olympic Games. For this reason, an OCOG must not skimp on the money it spends on organizing the victory ceremonies.

The expenditures for victory ceremonies are almost stable. Apart from the increasing prestige associated with designing more sophisticated ceremonies, expenditures only rise due to an absolute increase in both the number of sports and disciplines and the number of participating nations. These increases lead directly to both an increase in the number of victory ceremonies and the number of flags and anthems that are thus required.

Test Events

The increasing number of test events is due not only to test purposes, but also to the rising pressure that the IFs exert on the OCOGs (interview, Tröger, 1998). With an increasing number of federations by (15 per cent) and disciplines at the Olympic Games under the presidency of J.A. Samaranch (Landry and Yerlès, 1996), expenditure is also expected to rise in direct proportion to the increasing number of test events.

In Athens 2004 all IFs ran a test event prior to the Games. The modern pentathlon used the test event for its World Cup Final in order to test under real conditions. For the test 1100 persons were involved and, besides the sports, the accreditation system, security and press services were also tested (interview, Schormann, 2003).

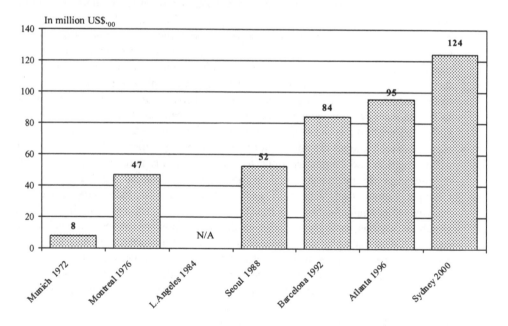

Source: Preuss (2000a).

Figure 9.3 Overview of the total event costs from Munich 1972 to Sydney 2000

If one looks at the event costs recorded in the OCOG publications, it can be assumed that expenditures for this sector clearly rose during the period investigated here (Figure 9.3). This increase is still evident despite the possible distortions that occurred due to the different calculations of this item.

Based on the statements made on the various components of the item event costs, three basic causes can be introduced to possibly explain the overall rise in these costs:

- Rising number of sports, disciplines and events: this increases the complexity of the organizational tasks, material equipment of an OCOG, staffing requirements and the demand for competition sites. Furthermore, the competition programme of the Olympic Games is prolonged and the number of test events to be held in advance of the Games also increases. However, under the IOC presidency of J. Rogge this factor will no longer increase the costs due to a proclaimed stop of expansion of the Olympic programme.
- Rising number of athletes: since the number of athletes is limited to 10 000, this factor will not result in a further expenditure increase. Until 2000, however, the number of athletes has steadily grown (Figure 4.1), thereby causing the organizational and staffing expenditures to also rise.

  In Barcelona 1992, for example, the organisational cost of the competitions alone reached a figure of US$·$_{00}$ 27.2 million (Barcelona OCOG, 1992). In addition, the competition programme would also be prolonged if the rising numbers of athletes caused bottlenecks in the stadia usage due to the number of preliminary rounds and heats. If, due to this, the sports facilities must be rented for a longer period of time then the location costs will also rise. A final direct complication of these increases to the number of athletes is seen in the related demand for more training facilities. In Barcelona 1992, for example, this increased demand alone resulted in a cost of US$·$_{00}$ 3.5 million just to ensure that training facilities were adequately supervised.
- Increasing technology: the third factor that causes rising expenditures is the increase of information and communications technology – fields that, in turn, lead to the requirements for permanent modernization of the technical installations of the Olympic competition venues. These modernizations include data processing systems, telecommunications to transfer results, and technology in the stadium, which is obvious to everyone such as display boards, telephones, acoustics and lighting. Other examples are remote-controlled carriages to return equipment of the athletes in the stadium, starting blocks with separate loudspeakers, the 'electronic eye' in tennis or the ever more technically sophisticated display boards and timing installations. In the early days, at the Berlin 1936 Olympics for example, the results were displayed by using letter boards that were joined to each other. Since Los Angeles 1984, the large technical display boards have been supplemented by large screens, which can even show replays. Nonetheless, this is progress that has translated into increased costs for an OCOG as well as expenditures for designing competition facilities that will live up to media requirements, such as providing suitable light, special backgrounds and positions for the cameras. In Munich 1972

the roof of the Olympic stadium was made translucent, in Seoul 1988 the tennis courts were moved and in Atlanta a cover was stretched over the translucent roof of the Georgia Dome, all to facilitate better television transmission (Atlanta OCOG, 1998).

It can be stated that the increase in the event costs primarily depends on the size of the Olympics and, in particular, on the scope of the competition programme. Increasingly, more complex Games require more planning efforts and, thus, incur additional staffing costs. Therefore it could be beneficial to use one facility for more sports such as modern pentathlon and baseball in Sydney 2000 or modern pentathlon and badminton in Athens 2004. Irrespective of this, however, is the fact that the more sophisticated the technology becomes, the more expenditures must be made for the required facilities.

9.3 EXPENDITURES FOR CEREMONIES AND CULTURAL EVENTS

Numerous cultural events are integrated into the Olympic Games. These events are, in fact, a kind of separate entity within the Olympic celebration. A distinction is drawn between the opening, closing and victory ceremonies of the Olympic Games and the cultural exhibitions and performances of the Olympic Arts Festival and the Cultural Olympiads. While the ceremonies serve the purpose of making the Olympics into a unit, and give the Games a festive atmosphere, the cultural events are in competition with the sports events to a certain extent.

The opening and closing ceremonies, in particular, are the most prestigious part of the Olympic Games. As such, these are investigated separately in this section. 'Indeed no other anything has ever managed to generate regularly scheduled and predictable performances which command anywhere near the same focused global attention as do the Olympic Ceremonies' (MacAloon, quoted in Goldberg, 1998). It is, therefore, understandable that there is some underlying degree of competition, which exists between the host cities to produce the best ever opening ceremonies in order to meet the growing expectations of the spectators. In the following, 'ceremonies' mean the opening and closing ceremonies, not victory ceremonies. As is the case in this study, many OCOGs count the expenditures for the victory ceremonies as event costs. The gigantic opening ceremonies of Moscow 1980 and Los Angeles 1984 are just two examples of how this competition has placed increased pressure on the OCOG of each subsequent Olympiad. The same can be said of the Cultural Olympiads and festivals. Since Melbourne 1956, they have become ever more extensive and lasted ever longer.

The next two sections will investigate the factors responsible for causing expenditures for opening and closing ceremonies as well as the costs of the Olympic Arts Festivals and Cultural Olympiads. Following this, the revenue potential of Cultural Olympiads will be investigated in order to determine the factors, which influence the amount of the potential OCOG revenues from cultural events.

9.3.1   Olympic Opening and Closing Ceremonies

Coubertin pointed out the significance of Olympic ceremonies: 'Their chief purpose is to make the Olympics something special and different from a simple series of World Championships' (Coubertin, 1967 [1910]). One such way in which Coubertin strove to achieve this vision was by incorporating the example of the athletes' oath of the ancient Games into the modern opening ceremonies in order to add a degree of dignity to the event. 'The oath can be adopted almost unchanged ... If the picture of the god was replaced for everyone by the flag of the individual's native country, the ceremony certainly would become more dignified' (Coubertin, 1967 [1910]). The Olympic Charter clearly defines the protocol part of the opening and closing ceremonies (IOC, 2003d, Rule 69, By-Law); however, the inclusion of any additional festivities is up to the OCOG to decide upon. A closer look at the Olympic Charter reveals that the binding parts of the ceremonies can be produced at a low cost. In the end, it is the organizers' effort to make their ceremonies more lavish than the previous ones that has led to high costs.

The opening and closing ceremonies consist of a protocol part and a cultural-artistic part. Although the elements of the protocol part are clearly defined in the Olympic Charter, their costs may greatly vary depending upon how these obligatory elements are realized. Due to the recurring programme elements, the costs for the protocol part can be estimated relatively precisely. A cost-increasing factor would be an increasing number of obligatory elements. In this respect, it is interesting to note that 63 per cent of the German Olympic tourists who were asked about the opening ceremony of Barcelona 1992 mentioned a protocol element as being the most impressive part of the entire opening ceremony (Messing and Müller, 1996).

The second part of the opening and closing ceremonies is the cultural-artistic part. In general, it incurs far higher costs than the protocol part of the ceremony due to the fact that the respective host nation wants to take advantage of this unique opportunity to present itself and its culture to the world. 'We consider that the maximum cultural significance of the Olympic Games is in the creation of the opening and closing ceremonies' (Moragas Spà, 1991; Riordan, 1996). It is therefore not surprising that this aspect was strongly emphasized for the first time in Moscow 1980. For the Soviet organizers, the ceremonies became a vehicle through which they could both prove the strength of their social system and show the boycotting West that the Olympic idea was in extremely good hands with socialism (Messing and Voigt, 1981). According to Birch, it was supposed to have been the most expensive opening ceremony ever held (Birch, 1998). The paradox is that the style of this opening ceremony, which was highly praised by the German Democratic Republic (GDR) press, was reminiscent of a Hollywood production of the class enemy (Messing and Voigt, 1981).

The possibility of planning the cultural-artistic part of the opening ceremonies in such a way that it reflects the culture of the host country and the fact that the opening ceremonies convey to the world press and television viewers a first impression of the Games, are the motivation for the OCOG to stage this part at a particularly high level. Since Barcelona 1992 the costs for the opening ceremony have amounted to US$25 million (interview, Birch, 1997). Since Los Angeles the duration of the cultural-artistic part has lasted about 80–90 minutes. In the past, the design of the stage and the costumes resulted in considerable costs, however, nowadays the expenditures are mainly incurred 'backstage'. Olympic opening and closing ceremonies have reached a level which even influences the construction of the Olympic stadium (Birch, 1998; Atlanta OCOG, 1998). In addition, the technology that is required to stage the ceremonies is becoming ever more sophisticated. Lighting and acoustic installations must be carefully designed in order to produce the desired effects for the audience (Birch, 1998). The opening ceremony of Los Angeles 1984 was staged in daylight. The subsequent postponement of later opening ceremonies to the evening required special, effective lighting. According to Birch, the great effort for lighting and acoustics is caused by the ever-rising demands of spectators and organizers. A decisive factor is the size of the stadium. In Barcelona 1992 there were about 68 000 spectators, in Atlanta 1996 as many as 83 000 and in Sydney 2000 some 110 000. According to Birch, the stadium floodlights which were used until 1984 are no longer adequate for the lighting demands of the opening and closing ceremonies. The bright, stable light is required for the sports competitions but not acceptable for the artistic displays of the Olympic ceremonies. Moreover, they cannot be switched on and off in short intervals. The problem is much the same in the case of the stadium loudspeakers. The first special loudspeaker system for Olympic Games was said to have been used in Los Angeles 1932. Although they are sufficient for announcing the sports results, they are not designed to stand up to the high acoustic demands of projecting live music to the audience. The loudspeaker walls used on the stage of concerts in stadiums do not fulfil the demands because they are pointed only in one direction. The stage of an opening ceremony, however, is the entire stadium area (Birch, 1998; Llinés, 1996). For a stage the size of that which is required for the Olympic Games, an oversize installation must be assembled in order to achieve all the special effects and productions of the opening and closing ceremonies. After the Games, at least a part of the equipment can remain in the stadium. Such equipment is a prerequisite for concerts and other non-sports events. All these special demands and additional costs naturally bring into question the need for such elaborate installations. The answer lies in the following consideration: 'If the spectators in the stadium are bored or cannot hear properly or cannot see properly, they will become restless – and the TV commentators will start saying that the audience does not like the ceremonies' (Birch, 1998). This again confirms the importance of atmosphere, which is a decisive element in the image of the Olympic Games.

According to data from Birch and Goldberg, the expenditures for the ceremonies of Barcelona, Atlanta and Sydney Games were broken down as displayed in Table 9.1.

Table 9.1   Expenditures for Olympic ceremonies 1992–2000

Expenditure factor	Birch		Goldberg
	in thousand US$	in %	in %
Costumes	4000	15.0	
Rehearsals	3500	13.2	
Lighting	2500–3000	9.4–11.3	58
Stage, flags, design	2500	9.4	
Acoustics	1500	5.6	
Staff and artists*	7000	26.3	11
Music	600–700	2.3–2.6	
General costs (transportation, accommodation, fees, etc.)	1000	3.8	
Research and creative meetings (choreography)	1000	3.8	
General costs (production)	1000	3.8	31
Electricity	800	3.0	
Transportation of actors to the rehearsals	300	1.1	
Catering	300	1.1	

Note: * 'My personal experience is that all the star/celebrity performers (e.g. opera singers) performed at no cost apart from their accommodation and travel expenses. We also provided their costumes/wardrobe' (interview, Birch, 1997). 'The 'star' talent was paid a very small 'honorarium' and most of the talent cost was for travel and living' (interview, Goldberg, 1997).

Sources: Birch (interview and letter, 1997, 2001); Goldberg (interview and letter, 1997).

The basic difference in the information, which Birch and Goldberg gave independently of each other, is the fact that Goldberg counted the administration staff costs as general costs (31 per cent) whereas Birch specifically included them in the category of staff costs.

Figure 9.4 shows the inflation adjusted overall expenditures for the ceremonies. The strong increase in the expenditures for the ceremonies after Los Angeles 1984 to more than double is clearly obvious.

The ceremonies create an immaterial benefit if the organizers leave a positive 'first' impression on the spectators. Furthermore it is the 'grand final' of the torch relay and the peak of the build up pre-Olympic excitement. This increases the commercial value of the ceremonies themselves and the entire Olympics because opening ceremonies have the highest viewing rates during the whole Games. The material benefit of the ceremonies is the revenues from selling the tickets. As shown, the prices for opening ceremony tickets have risen continuously with permanently sold out stadiums. A large part of the ceremony expenditures can be covered by the revenues from the tickets sales. Therefore, an OCOG must calculate opportunity costs for all free tickets such as for the Olympic Family and the media. From the financial point of view, it would be a loss if the Olympic Charter was amended in such a way that athletes should also be granted free entrance to the closing ceremony. From the ideological point of view, this would, of course, be only natural.

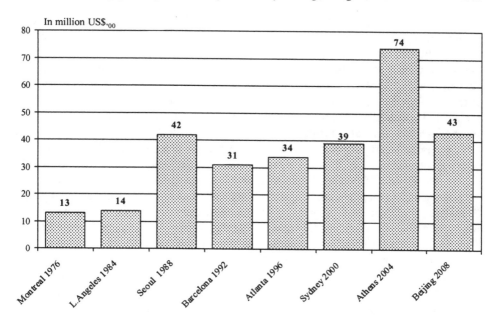

Note: * Bidding Committee Beijing 2008 (2001).

Sources: Bidding Committee Beijing 2008 (2001, p. 121); Athens OCOG (2003, p. 22); Preuss (2000a); Protopsaltis (interview, 2003).

Figure 9.4 Overall expenditures of the ceremonies of the Olympic Games from Montreal 1976 to Beijing 2008

9.3.2   Olympic Arts Festivals and Cultural Olympiads

In 1906, Coubertin called the combination of sport and art a 'marriage, which unites muscles and mind' Coubertin (1967 [1906]). This must have been the point in time when Coubertin publicly expressed his idea of introducing arts competitions as Olympic disciplines. Before 1906 no sources are known where he had expressed his attitude to Olympic arts competitions (Krüger, 1996). Nevertheless, the arts have a high status in the Coubertin family, especially music and painting (interview, Navacelle de Coubertin, 1997).

In 1891, Coubertin ascribed a special meaning to the combination of sport and the arts: 'Both a 14 kilometre race and a literary competition represent a day of victory' (Coubertin, 1891). In his opening speech for the advisory session on arts, science and sport, Coubertin stated which arts competitions should be integrated into the Olympic programme. Already Chicago had tried to bring art into the Olympic programme. Coubertin wrote in his memoirs: 'But right from the start Chicago showed an interest in this aspect of the Olympic question. The programmes I mentioned above made allowances, a trifle awkwardly but nevertheless sincerely and enthusiastically, for art and thought. From this point of view, transferring the Games to St. Louis had been a misfortune' (Coubertin, 1936). Another transfer was considered, this time to London. 'As time would then be very short, we should have to improvise a great deal and the artistic side of the Games would inevitably suffer ...' (Coubertin, 1936). They were staged for the first time in Stockholm 1912 and remained part of the programme until London 1948 (Landry, 1987; Pouret, 1976). In Helsinki 1952 arts competitions were abandoned and replaced by exhibitions. At the Melbourne 1956 Olympics the foundation stone was laid for the so-called 'festivals of culture' (Landry, 1987). Since 1992 the IOC has awarded an Olympic prize to artists without holding a competition among them (Samaranch, in an interview in Kühnle, 1996). Los Angeles hosted the first international festival in 1984 (Good, 1999). In addition to the cultural festivals which have been staged during the Games since that time, the term 'Cultural Olympiad' was introduced with the Olympiad of Barcelona 1992. This is a programme of arts and cultural events as well as exhibitions over the entire period of an Olympiad. Atlanta, Sydney and Athens were to follow Barcelona (Hanna, 1999). Beijing started its cultural Olympiad on 21 September 2003. The concept is to have an annual Olympic Festival.

It is stipulated in the Olympic Charter that an OCOG must organize a cultural programme (IOC, 2003d, Rule 44, para. 1). The cultural events must last at least as long as the Olympic village is open. The Olympic Charter, however, does not define the content. In contrast to the 1985 Olympic Charter, the 1996 Olympic Charter formulates the objectives of the Cultural Olympics more clearly while the OCOGs receive more freedom to use other means for designing the events. It is the respective OCOG that determines the extent of the cultural events. Thus, there is a tendency to prolong the Cultural Olympiads permanently beyond the required minimum duration for the events. Some bidders for 2004 intended to stage their cultural programmes over two Olympiads such as Lille, Rome and Seville from 1997 to 2004 and San Juan from 1990 to 2004 (IOC, 1997e). This also reflects a tendency towards gigantism, which, in the opinion of critical observers, is intrinsic to the Olympic Games. Above all, the programme is prolonged. The temporal expansion reveals the obvious striving for inclusion since there will be no year without Olympic activities. The quantitative offer is also impressive: 3000 performers, 19 exhibitions, 17 sculptures erected in the city and almost 200 performances show the efforts only during the time of the Games in Atlanta 1996 (Atlanta OCOG, 1996). In the 16 months of the Cultural Olympics of Moscow, 5000 performances were said to have taken place (Streltsova, 1987). Moreover, there is a contradiction if the true cultural interests of Olympic visitors are observed. Coubertin noted as early as in 1906: 'Regarding the congregation of athletes, artists and spectators it would not be wise to expect too much from it. Today everything still needs to be done since eurhythmics have been forgotten about. Today, the masses are not capable of combining different ways of enjoying the arts with each other' (Coubertin, 1967 [1906]). The Munich OCOG 1972 also wondered whether 'the visitors to Olympic Games were actually capable of absorbing artistic joys' (Harenberg, 1991). In Los Angeles 1984 even R. Fitzpatric said before he became Director of the Cultural Olympiad: 'If a culturally aware person such as myself did not know that the Olympic Games had a cultural component, how aware would other people be?' (Good, 1999). Messing and Müller detected the same phenomenon when questioning German Olympic tourists at the Games of Barcelona 1992: 'For the vast majority (n = 217), the combination of sport and arts is not a basic principle of the Olympic idea ... and, consequently, they expect sport exclusively' (Messing and Müller, 1996). Even the 'switching to the Olympic cultural program if tickets were not available for the sports events of interest does not seem a true alternative for Olympic tourists' (Messing, 1998; Messing and Müller, 1996). And, finally, in Sydney 2000 even the NOCs showed a minimum interest in purchasing cultural tickets, being less than 1 per cent. Broadcasters showed no interest at all, and the IOC purchased ten tickets in every performance after the 10 September (Sulway, Marketing Director, Olympic Arts Festival, 2000).

If the majority of spectators are either unaware of the link between sport and art at the Olympic Games, and if they even cannot envision such a linkage, then the need to educate them becomes a necessity – '59 per cent of the people interviewed must be informed about the unity of sport and arts at the Olympic Games' (Messing and Müller, 1996). Then, however, an OCOG faces a conflict of interests in relation to the financing for the cultural events. It must decide whether to approach as many spectators as possible and live up to the Olympic idea or to limit its programme to certain target groups. A cultural programme restricted to special target groups causes lower expenditures and the revenues from selling entrance tickets and from cultural sponsoring could be increased. To date, the only information that has been discovered with regards to the identification of the special Olympic target groups interested in arts is the fact that the German tourists' interest in cultural events for Barcelona 1992 depended neither on gender nor level of education. With increasing age a significant increase in visiting events and exhibitions can be seen (Messing and Müller, 1996). Already Coubertin was

astonished at the lack of interest shown for so many years in the idea of combining sports meetings and open-air choral performances. That sculptors and painters should hesitate to cross a forgotten threshold is understandable, but that the public should be so reluctant to try a combination whose individual beauties complete each other so well passes all understanding ... There is however an explanation in the distortion of taste and the growing familiarity with virtuosity which means that, nowadays, the general eurhythmic sense is weakened and that the development of virtuosity has made us grow used to the separation of sensorial impressions. The artistic education of the people needs to be taken in hand and started all over again. (Coubertin, 1936)

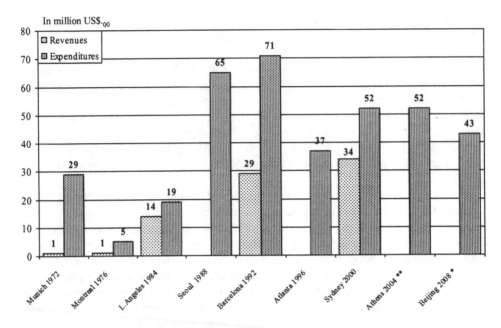

Notes: *   Estimated by Bidding Committee Beijing 2008 (2001).
          **   In case the Opening and Closing Ceremony cost US$'00 74 million.

Sources: Bidding Committee Beijing 2008 (2001); Athens OCOG (2003, p. 22); Preuss (2000a).

Figure 9.5   *Revenues from and expenditures for cultural events from Munich 1972 to Beijing 2008*

Since Munich 1972 the costs for the Cultural Olympiads have led to a deficit for each OCOG (Figure 9.5). Apart from entrance fees for some events of the Cultural Olympiad and some cultural sponsoring, it was hardly possible to make any revenues (Table 9.2).

In view of the repeatedly proven lack of interest shown by Olympic sports spectators towards the cultural events and a predictable financial deficit, the fact that the extent of the events has always been greater than that stipulated in the Olympic Charter is surprising. This supports the assumption that Cultural Olympiads are a prestigious element of the programme of the Olympic Games which, from the organizers' perspective, must be enhanced from Olympiad to Olympiad.

Since costs for cultural events are very manifold and also depend on price and wage levels of the host country, a comparison of overall costs must be regarded as very superficial. Therefore, a relationship between the costs and the programme should be made. Another factor which determines the costs of a cultural programme is its duration. If one calculates the average costs of previous Olympic arts festivals and Cultural Olympiads for a month, it can be stated that the costs decrease, as the time period encompassing all of the events gets longer. This can be indicative of the lower number of events per month or to a relatively high share of fixed costs for the entire Cultural

Olympiad. However, since 1992, Cultural Olympiads have to be distinguished from the Olympic arts festival, owing to the fact that the festival lasts only several weeks.

Table 9.2   *Budget of Olympic Art Festival Sydney 2000*

Income	In US$·00	Expenditure	In US$·00
Box office	7 308 172	Personnel	3 357 419
Government grants	1 184 648	Travel – International and domestic	1 091 555
Festival sponsorship	902 256	Administration	776 802
Other income (venue income)	1 238 001	Promotions/publications – marketing materials	2 406 640
Festival and Olympic fine art print portfolios	473 684	Programme fees/consultant fees	4 128 735
Australian Olympic Committee (IOC Opening Session Ceremony)	225 564	Sydney Paralympic Committee recoveries	-672 147
Festival project hospitality	330 827	Concerts – Olympic year 2000	3 198 870
Festival hospitality programme – Sydney Opera House	6 207 693	Opera – Olympic year 2000	255 639
		Theatre – Olympic year 2000	1 010 870
		Dance – Olympic year 2000	4 295 576
		Visual Arts – Olympic year 2000	471 690
		Outdoor Events – Olympic year 2000	1 301 804
		Film Programme – Olympic year 2000	37 594
		Staging expenditure for AOC production – Olympic year 2000	383 459
		Festival venue costs	239 542
		Festival hospitality programme - Sydney Opera House	4 703 934
		Staging cost	246 972
Total	17 870 845	*Total*	27 234 956

In Beijing there will be a Cultural Olympiad which starts in 2003, five years prior to the Olympics. Main activities will be:

- 2005: Port and Humankind – from Olympia to the Great Wall
- 2006: Environment and Humankind – from exploitation to harmony
- 2007: Culture and Humankind – from individual inspiration to common achievement.

Then, the Olympic arts festival of the year 2008 will last from July to October (Bidding Committee Beijing 2008, 2001).

9.3.3   Possible Benefits of Cultural Events and their Revenue Potential

For reasons already mentioned, this section investigates the revenues from Cultural Olympiads directly after the expenditures or costs. Before analysing possible individual revenue sources of cultural events, the superordinate (intangible) benefits the OCOG and the host city can gain from the events are listed:

- Benefit arises if the prestige is increased by the OCOG's efforts to show the public, in a way which can be compared to 'suspicious consumption' (Velben, 1981 [1899]), that they organized the 'best, largest, longest ever' Cultural Olympiad in Olympic history. Presumably, this is one of reasons for the increasingly rising costs for cultural events.
- Benefit can arise when individual elements of the Olympic idea are realized and the spectators become aware of the link between sport and the arts. This can at least superficially justify high expenditures. Moreover, bids become attractive if they offer an extensive cultural programme, thereby indicating the realization of the Olympic idea. This is an important aspect for many bids. Thus, it can be assumed that the cultural programme which Athens 2004 announced, focusing on the human being and the tradition of the Games, played a decisive role in its selection as host city (Bacia, 1997; Röder, 1997f).
- Benefit can arise by avoiding costs if, for example, the selection of the topics integrates Olympic opponents. The active discussion of problems concerning the host city can weaken the arguments of local Olympic opponents and the impact of negative press reports. In Atlanta, for example, they concentrated on 'black arts' to demonstrate anti-racism on a political level and organized the exhibition 'Olympic women' to please the women's movement in the USA. The political level becomes obvious when special emphasis was given to Catalan art and culture in Barcelona in order to win votes for the Olympic Games of 1992. This might have been the reason why the annual festivals were staged in the time before the Games and cultural events were staged at places where parts of the population still had to be won over (interview of a member of the Barcelona OCOG by N. Müller). In Sydney the first year of the Olympiad was dedicated to the Aborigines. The 'Festival of Dreaming' was the first ever held in Australia. It featured contemporary and traditional indigenous arts and it seems that it finally 'changed the nature of Indigenous discussion, in this city (Sydney)' (Strout, Executive Director, Arts Development, Australia Council, 2000).

Unrest, disturbances and negative remarks can be avoided by listening to, and even integrating, the critics and minorities. Ultimately, this improves the image of the Games and could be one reason for the lasting significance of the cultural events at Olympic Games. In the following, the revenue potentials of such events are investigated.

The organization of a Cultural Olympiad as a subsystem of the Olympic Games has its own budget which is partly OCOG financed. To avoid double counting, the revenues from third parties are only considered in the following areas.

Television rights

As long as the rights to an Olympiad are sold as one package to one exclusive television network, the network also has the exclusive right to broadcast cultural events. Additional revenues from television rights could be possible if the above mentioned differentiation model was realized. However, this would also involve all the disadvantages associated with the separate marketing of the rights of sporting and cultural events. One disadvantage could be the low viewing rates of cultural programmes, which would thereby result in lower revenue gains being obtained from selling the rights. Babcock (1996) regretted that NBC was not interested in cultural events and faulted the award for being an exclusive right. It would then be necessary to weigh whether the additional revenues from 'cultural television stations' could more than compensate for the revenue loss from the 'sports stations' that would lose a part of their exclusiveness.

Marketing

In Barcelona 1992 sponsors supported the Cultural Olympiad with US$$_{.00}$ 17.6 million (Barcelona OCOG, 1992). In Atlanta 1996 there were so-called 'signature sponsors' to support the arts events and the youth camp (Babcock, 1996). In Los Angeles 1984 the Times Mirror Company acted as official festival sponsor and singularly provided US$$_{.00}$ 8.3 million alone (Fitzpatrick, 1985). Finally in Sydney there were supporters of the cultural events, such as Fairfax, other than sponsors of the Olympic Games. In Sydney the festival sponsorship provided US$$_{.00}$ 0.9 million (interview, Brown, 1999). M. Payne (interview, 1997) thinks that culture is underrated at the Olympic Games. This is due, in one part, to the lack of profile the Cultural Olympiads have been given. Without their own profile or the interest of the Olympic visitors, he claims it is hardly possible to win over sponsors for the cultural sector.

As a result of his experience with the Cultural Olympiad of Atlanta 1996, Babcock suggests separating culture and sports sponsors, which happened in Sydney. This move could attract new sponsors who are not interested in sports, thereby bringing financial advantages to the Cultural Olympiad. However, the overall effect could also be lower revenues due to the fact that current sponsors would lose some of their exclusiveness. The loss of exclusiveness is even more likely to occur since the long-term sponsors of the Olympic Games are showing a growing interest in the cultural programmes. However, Good (1999) states that Olympic sponsors still ignore the potential increased exposure that could be gained from simultaneously associating the Olympic Games with the Olympic arts festival. Additional cultural sponsors would increase the overall number of sponsors. This, in turn, would strengthen the impression of an 'over-commercialization'. Therefore Athens OCOG 2004 decided to not have any signature sponsors.

If, however, in the future the cultural sponsors become a fixed component of Olympic sponsoring, regulations would have to be made concerning the allocation, between culture and sport, of exclusive rights for individual product categories. The increasing interest of the current sponsors in cultural sponsoring should not, however, be underestimated. If cultural aspects were increasingly incorporated into the OCOGs' package offers for sponsors and designed in a more attractive way, current sponsors could be charged higher fees. An increase in the total number of sponsors would thus be avoided. Similar considerations are to be made for merchandising as a subdivision of marketing during Cultural Olympiads.

Tickets
Thus far, the sale of tickets has been the major source of revenues for cultural events. The possibility of increasing revenues through raising the ticket prices depends on the elasticity of demand. In general, this is not known to the OCOG and, therefore, it is difficult to determine the most suitable prices.

Hospitality programme
A special Olympic arts hospitality programme, which adds value to the hospitality given through sports provides huge opportunities for additional income. Business partners and their families are not always particularly interested in sports but may be in the culture.

Others
Donors and patrons, who are frequently found in the cultural sector (Zollinger, 1994) are a further potential financing source for the Cultural Olympiad. Additionally, the cultural activities open opportunities for government grants owing to the fact that they are not the same as sport activities.

Even if the Olympic tourists' interest in cultural events is not very high in absolute terms, Figure 9.5 shows an increase in the revenues. This increase is caused by the rising number of tourists interested in the Cultural Olympiad, an enlarged cultural programme, a rising interest of sponsors in the arts and a prolonged period for staging the events. Atlanta was the second host city to stage a programme lasting several years (starting in January 1993) (Atlanta OCOG, 1994). In Mexico 1968, the programme lasted 12 months, in Munich 1972 ten months, in Montreal 1976 one month, in Moscow 1980 16 months and in Los Angeles 1984 ten months (Landry, 1987; Streltsova, 1987). In Atlanta 1996, the closeness of cultural event sites to the sports venues and good ticket distribution surely contributed to the higher revenue gain from the cultural events. Twenty-five of the 32 sites where cultural events were staged were situated in the 'Olympic circle' (three miles from downtown Atlanta). In Sydney 70 per cent of the programme was located in the Opera House (Babcock, 1996). In Beijing the first cultural festival started in 2003, five years before the Games.

Finally, Figure 9.6 lists the determining factors for revenues from cultural events. The list does not claim to be complete and concentrates only on the relationships between the key determining factors in order to highlight the complex system of interdependencies. The thick arrows are used to indicate the direct and most powerful factors, which influence possible revenues from the cultural events.

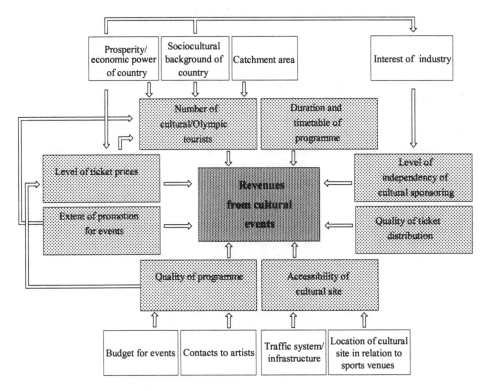

Figure 9.6   Factors, which determine revenues from cultural events

The determining factors shown in Figure 9.6 vary in their influence on the financing sources mentioned above. A substantial factor is the number of Olympic tourists; since they pay for the tickets, they provide a prime revenue source from the cultural events. With their interest in culture, it is these tourists that form the basis for sponsoring. In the long run, most of the factors shown in Figure 9.6 aim to attract as many visitors as possible to the cultural events.

It has become obvious that the cultural events compete to a certain extent with the sports events. However, there is no true competition because Olympic tourists clearly place a priority on attending the sports events (Messing, 1998). Ultimately, this reality shows how difficult it is to convey Coubertin's idea of eurhythmics through the Olympic Games. He said: 'For me ... civilisation had strayed from the right path and the "revival of eurhythmics" alone would set it back in the right direction again: eurhythmics, a lost art, about which people talk a great deal without really knowing what it was like in the olden days!' (Coubertin, 1936).

9.4   COSTS OF TECHNOLOGY

Without using up-to-date technology, it would be impossible to organize the Olympic Games of today. Modern technology is used in communications in order to transmit data, live pictures and sound signals, phone calls and in the information management system used by the Olympics organizers and media commentators. In addition, it is also used in security, results collection and transmission, accreditation, logistics and the medical service sectors of the Games. For these reasons, it can be argued that the Olympic Games in their present form could not be staged without technology; or, conversely, it can be argued that only the technological development of modern times has facilitated their gigantic growth (Bernadas and Benasat, 1995).

Technology ensures the quality of the Olympics by providing an adequate level of services for spectators, media representatives, sponsors and one's own organization. As long as it functions properly, it remains almost invisible to the spectator. However, the overall success of an OCOG strongly depends on technology. A failure of the technology is revealed by organizational deficiencies and is therefore always regarded as an OCOG shortcoming. At the same time, the failure negatively affects the image of the producer of the respective technical system. During the Atlanta 1996 Olympics there were accounts of shortcomings in the information system. It was designed to provide the competition results on the Internet within the shortest time possible for all media representatives and the public, but the system frequently failed. This was one of the reasons why IBM retired from Olympic sponsoring (Borchers, 1998; interview, Elphinston, 1999).

In the following analysis, the interdependencies between technology and organization area are structured. Several problems of data collection occurred. First, information on the 'technology' used is scarce; second, OCOGs delimit the item 'technology' very differently because technology is important in almost any sector of organization. It can thus be included in any expenditure item. A short chronological introduction, which highlights the example of information technology at the Olympics is followed by a classification of the technological installations, systems and devices used at the Games. Data processing systems are then featured as an example and subsequently investigated with regard to their costs and determining factors.

In Squaw Valley 1960 computers were used for the first time in Olympic history. In Mexico 1968 it was reported that the 'information system is functioning below average' (Lembke, in NN, 1972c), while the Golym system used in Munich 1972 virtually triggered a technological revolution at the Olympic Games (Organisationskomitee München, 1974a). Siemens provided the entire hardware and software for Munich (NN, 1972a). In Montreal 1976 IBM developed new software. Los Angeles 1984 planned to adopt the Montreal 1976 software (Los Angeles OCOG, 1979), whereas for Moscow 1980 they only provided the hardware. For Los Angeles 1984, IBM further developed the software used in Montreal 1976. Negotiations with IBM for the Seoul 1988 Olympics started early (Ricquart, 1988). Finally, however, it was decided that only the IBM hardware would be used. The software would be programmed by the Koreans themselves because they recognized an opportunity to show the world their state-of-the-art technological expertise. The Korean enterprise, Goldstar, developed the largest portion of the software and the Wide Information Network Service (WINS) (Goldstar, 1988a; Kim et al., 1989). As a TOP sponsor, IBM was then, once again, in charge of the information technology for Barcelona 1992 and Atlanta 1996. In Sydney, IBM started to develop the technology basically from the scratch, owing to the fact of the Atlanta disaster (interview, Elphinston, 1999). Thus, IBM is strengthening its links to the Olympic Games not only in the sponsoring sector but also in the field of technological cooperation (IOC, 1998b). For Athens 2004 and Beijing 2008 Schlumberger provides the main information software and follows IBM as TOP sponsor in the category 'Information Technology/System Integration'.

However, the sector information technology is only a small part of the technology used at the Olympics. The survey in Table 9.3 more specifically classifies the various types of technology.

Table 9.3   Types of technological installations at Olympic Games

Type	Installations
I Individual devices without special installation	Walkie-talkies; pagers; mobile telephones Television units; radios Copiers; printers Personal computers
II Individual devices with special installation	Safety installations; access systems Cable television Convention rooms; video conferences Accreditation photography (Imaging and photolab) Acoustics; lighting; video boards (sports facilities) Telephone system; in-house phones
III Integrated networks of devices systems(hardware/software)	Timing installations; boards; results system Computer network; display screens Data processing centre Information system (Olympic Family and public) Television technology for the production of the international signal administration system Communications network, landline and wireless communication Internet (pre Games and Games internet site)

Sources: Modified according to Bernadas and Benasat (1995).

Table 9.3 again emphasises the problem that costs for technology cannot be included in a single expenditure item since there are manifold links to the sectors of administration, media, transportation, security, competition management, look of the Games and so on. Furthermore, in the technological sector, sponsors have always provided a large share of value in kind. The value in kind provided for the 'technology' in Barcelona 1992 amounted to 60 per cent of the overall services in this sector (Bernadas and Benasat, 1995). The main reason was that the most important corporations of information technology were among the TOP sponsors. They tried to fulfil their obligations by providing value in kind (Kodak, Xerox, Brother, Philips, 3M, Matsushita Electric

[Panasonic], Ricoh and IBM). The value with which this share entered the final balances of the OCOGs could not be found in the publications and can hardly be assessed today. Therefore, the position of costs for the technology of the Games under review cannot be compared, although all OCOGs expressly state the position. According to available information from the respective Official Reports, Munich spent US$$_{.00}$ 81 million, Montreal US$$_{.00}$ 39 million, Los Angeles US$$_{.00}$ 30 million, Seoul US$$_{.00}$ 62 million, Barcelona US$$_{.00}$ 267 million and Atlanta US$$_{.00}$ 245 million on the technology. Sydney's OCOG spent US$$_{.00}$ 305.7 and already Athens has spent US$$_{.00}$ 409.2 million on technology (Athens OCOG, 2003b, p. 22; Olympic Co-ordination Authority, 2002, p. 25). Even if it is difficult to compare this position, it is no surprise that the technology has become the main cost factor in the balances of an OCOG.

The two core technological areas at the Olympic Games are telecommunications and electronic data processing (EDP). Since the communications systems (satellite structure, fibre optic and mobile transmission) depend on the infrastructure within the host city/country, the Olympic EDP systems are looked at in Figure 9.7 because their configuration and realization pose a great challenge to any OCOG.

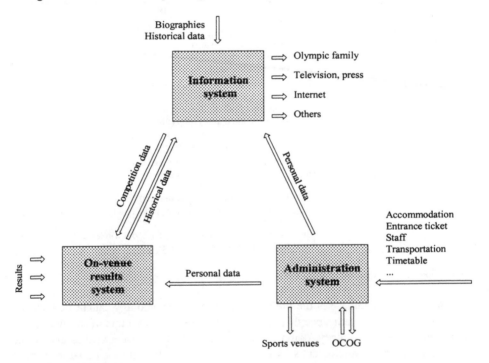

Source: Preuss (2000a).

Figure 9.7 Data processing systems at Olympic Games

Figure 9.7 displays the relationship between the three systems used in Atlanta 1996. For Barcelona 1992 these functions were even spread out amongst four systems (results system, information retrieval system, Games management system, commentator information system; Vall, 1995). In the cases of Munich, Montreal and Barcelona, for which similar data are only available for the results system because the costs were recorded as separate items, an increase in the costs of the EDP systems can be seen. From Munich 1972 to Barcelona 1992 the costs tripled from US$$_{\cdot 00}$ 21.6 million to US$$_{\cdot 95}$ 62.2 million.

Although the collection of these data did not reveal delimitation and allocation problems, the results must not simply be compared with each other. For some Games, IBM simply had to adjust the old system to the new requirements. Compared with other suppliers who had to develop new systems, this was surely cheaper to do. In 1972, 1976, 1980, 1988 and 2000, entirely new systems were implemented, while in 1984, 1992 and 1996 existing systems were upgraded. Thus, the Atlanta 1996 OCOG took over large portions of the Barcelona 1992 software, such as accreditation and ticket programmes. With effect from Sydney 2000 the 'Transfer of Knowledge' was established. The IOC provides databases to the OCOG, which in return has to update the data and return it to the IOC after the Games.

Without making any claim to be complete, the basic factors, which determine the costs for Olympic EDP systems are listed in the following:

- Becoming antiquated: compared with the rapidly changing rate of innovations made to information and communication technology, an Olympiad translates into a long period of time. Each OCOG wants to use the latest technological innovations in order to be viewed as being superior to the previous Games and to show the world it is a technologically state-of-the-art organization. This is the reason why the EDP systems of previous Games have always received comprehensive updates and sometimes have been designed anew.
- Time: the Olympic Games take place at a fixed point in time, which cannot be postponed for any reason. This means that the EDP systems must be ready to use precisely at this point in time. High costs can be incurred if time that was lost due to delays in early phases must be compensated for by increased work effort in later phases.
- Duration: the short duration of the Olympic Games does not allow for error analyses or a correction of errors (Bernadas and Benasat, 1995). Therefore, extensive test runs are necessary in advance. For the key functions, emergency procedures must be pre-programmed in order to avoid disturbing or even stopping the Games in case of an unexpected event. In Barcelona 1992 the test period started 24 months prior to the Games. In Atlanta 1996 this advance period was 18 months long (Atlanta OCOG, 1994b; Vall, 1995). This situation causes increased costs due to the fact that the systems must be provided for earlier within the planning timeframe of an Olympic Games.

- Complexity: the high complexity of the systems in combination with the data flood caused by both the ever growing size of the Games and the ever more extensive provision of information increases the demands placed on the system software (Bernadas and Benasat, 1995). Capacities and numbers of computers must continuously rise as a result.
- Experience: costs can be lowered if the enterprise supplying the hardware and software has experience with mega-events. For example, Goldstar as a newcomer to the Olympic Games and a corporate competitor against IBM for the Seoul 1988 Olympics, had to reduce their price to a level whereby they would no longer achieve a profit (Ricquart, 1988). The 'Transfer of Knowledge' of the IOC will lower the costs for Athens 2004 and Beijing 2008.
- Maintenance/operation: the OCOG staff for the technological sector numbered approximately 5500 persons in Barcelona 1992 and Atlanta 1996 respectively. Parts of this total number were volunteers (Barcelona 2600 and Atlanta 2000) and another part was provided by the sponsors (Bernadas and Benasat, 1995; Atlanta OCOG, 1996). At each of the two Olympics approximately 35 experts were required for data processing alone (Maennig, 1992). Although the OCOG does not necessarily incur labour costs, both types of workforces cause additional costs as well as opportunity costs. For volunteers, the additional costs are incurred, for example, through training schemes and activities to permanently maintain their motivation. For personnel provided by the sponsors, their value reduces the sponsors' financial contribution to the amount of the hypothetical procurement market costs.

For future bidders, it will be particularly difficult to estimate these costs since technology is subject to rapid changes. On the one hand, Maennig's prognosis that costs for computers and storage media could be calculated at current market prices seems sensible. However, this prognosis is only possible because of an increasingly better cost-effectiveness probably compensating for the increased demands on computers which would, in turn, lead to stable prices. Furthermore, Maennig anticipates an increase in the real labour costs in the application development, training and operating sectors, while, at the same time, improved tools will reduce the work time by the same amount (Maennig, 1992). On the other hand, it has been shown that the costs for just the results system alone greatly increased in the past. To avoid a further increase of costs the IOC has considered taking provision of information technology. Similar to their marketing run by Meridian, the IOC is developing plans to control this area (interview, Elphinston, 1999).

In conclusion, I would like to note that the technological image of the Olympic Games can have a special meaning for the industry of the host country. In other words, the country can acquire the image of being technologically advanced. For example, of Barcelona 1992 it was reported: 'The technology employed in this Spanish-made computer is the most modern in the world' (Vall, 1995). The enterprise, which provided and developed the hardware and software, had the opportunity to gain prestige at an international level (Greising, 1995; Ricquart, 1988). In Beijing 2008 one of the mottos is

'Hi-Tech Olympics' which indicates that China likes to position its image towards technology through the Olympic Games. The 2008 Olympics presents Beijing with the opportunity to showcase China's rapidly advancing technology sector. However, both parties – host country and corporation – also run the risk of suffering from a negative image if there are obvious shortcomings in the system. Finally, the Olympic Games can also push forward the development of the infrastructure for information and communications technology in the host city, an aspect which was already considered under the section on macroeconomic implications. Looking at Beijing, in 2007 it is planned to have in place (Bidding Committee Beijing 2008, 2001):

- fibre network to cover all Olympic sites
- 40 000 lines to manage all voice, data, Internet transmissions and broadband transmissions inside the Olympic precinct
- network that can cover 500 000 calls in the Olympic precinct with transportable cells
- radio network with a capacity to manage 15 000 handsets in up to 1000 talk groups
- digital television network capable of HDTV transmission for all Olympic Family venues, and the bandwidth of international transmission in order to provide overseas broadcasting
- additional optical submarine cables and earth stations.

9.5 COSTS OF SECURITY

The size and international character of the Olympic Games, the concomitant media attention and the audience of dignitaries combine to necessitate unique security arrangements. Since the Olympic Games have been abused in order to focus the attention of the world public on extraneous political issues (by means of attacks), security measures have consequently been increased. Crime in the host cities themselves also leads to the need for a special consideration to be given to the security of participants and visitors alike. Thus, the image of Los Angeles 1984 was not particularly positive: 'Los Angeles is the "last west" – weirdoes, guns, random violence' (Wilcox, 1994). In Seoul 1988 the authorities were afraid of an invasion by North Korea and in Barcelona 1992 they were afraid of ETA bomb attacks. And Atlanta, after all, was known as the city with the highest crime rate in the USA. Learning from those experiences, Sydney finally claimed to stage the safest Olympics. However, since 11 September 2001 the world focuses on the new dimension of terrorist threats. Therefore security has become an even more important issue. 28.2 per cent of the Athenians fear one month before the Games that a terrorist act may happen (MRB, 2004).

Security forms an important part of the image of the Games. This was revealed in the assaults of Munich 1972 and Atlanta 1996 which, although very different incidents, resulted in worldwide media attention and damaged the image of both the Games and, indirectly, the respective host city (Berndt, 1997). A survey of 620 senior managers from

13 nations after the Atlanta 1996 Olympics showed 'that the bombing, in retrospect, was not viewed as a major negative for the Games, albeit it certainly grabbed attention' (Harris, 1997).

This section deals with questions such as which groups are generally dangerous to the Games and how OCOGs are involved in providing security from a staffing perspective. The share of the costs that an OCOG has to cover will also be discussed. And a short digression reviews the options an OCOG has with respect to taking out insurance policies in order to cover corresponding risks.

A good security concept excels through its invisibility. IOC president J. Rogge has called for organizers to take all necessary security measures without injuring the festive atmosphere of the Olympics by being invisible as long as security can be provided (speech [see correspondence], Rogge, 2003). The aim is to keep threats away from the Games before they begin or to at least have precautions, which go unnoticed by the Olympic Family or visitors during the Games. The invisible precautions as well as the great secrecy of the costs and degree of governmental support, however, make it difficult to calculate the actual costs for security at the Olympic Games.

Besides commercial security as well as personnel and physical security, the emphasis here is on Olympic-specific security. The uniqueness and the size of the Games make it difficult to develop an Olympic security concept. Unlike other recurring sports events, it is not possible to use a long-tested concept. Nevertheless, the knowledge gained at previous Olympics can be used by the group of experts of each OCOG who gather together and evaluate previous security concepts. Sydney OCOG 2000 sent a total of 104 observers to Atlanta (NN, 1996a). Athens 2004 has employed independent security consultants with vast experience from the Olympic Games of Sydney and Salt Lake. Additionally, Athens 2004 works with an Olympic Advisory Group, a seven-nation task force with extensive experience in the security planning of Olympic Games (Athens OCOG, 2003b, p. 26). Another difficulty arises from the fact that the variation in the risk for all Games is 'not only from city to city, but also depends on geopolitical, general or local circumstances at the time of the Games' (IOC, 1993a). These difficulties explain the IOC's interest in the experience a bidder has gained though staging other large sports events. Therefore the IOC asks all bidders: 'Detail the experience of your city/region and country in the area of security with regard to the organisation of major international events' (IOC, 1995a). Beijing gained experience at the 11th Asian Games 1990 with a security force of 30 000 personnel and at the 1st East Asian Games with 16 000 persons. However the Olympic Games are planned to coordinate more than 80 000 security personnel (Bidding Committee Beijing 2008, 2001).

There has always been a strong link between top-performance sport and crime. For the purpose of this specific discussion crime can be defined by the different groups who pose this threat. First, there are the political, religious and nationalist groups that, for mainly ideological reasons, are using the Games to reach media attention, such as Al Qaeda today or Black September in Munich 1972. Second, there is the group of radical fans on the one hand and thirdly the Olympic opponents on the other who can seriously disturb the course of the Games with unrest and attacks.

The fourth group are local criminals whose number is likely to increase during the Games including other criminals from the country and from abroad. Criminal actions of all four groups are based on different motives, which must be considered in the security concept. The motive of Olympic opponents is the disappointment about the fact that the Games will be hosted in their city. A first phase of Olympic opponent protest is the bid phase of the city. In Stockholm's bid for 2004, for example, bombs were put in Olympic venue sites in order to demonstrate to the IOC that the Games were not wanted (Altenbockum, 1997). If a city is elected nevertheless, the opponents often try to exert a political influence on the preparation of the Olympics (interview, Tröger, 1998). The radical fans, however, are motivated to cause riots by the sports events themselves. For this type of fan, the sports event simply serves as a vehicle through which they can release bottled up aggression. Terrorists use the Games to attract worldwide attention. As the attack at Munich 1972 proved, they will not even refrain from hostage-taking and murder if it will draw the attention of the world to their cause. Today this is the most serious threat. For the criminal element in a city it is the actual or presumed prosperity of the tourists which motivates these individuals to commit burglary, fraud or robbery.

In view of the complexity of their motives and the diversified dangers that can be created by the above-mentioned groups, an OCOG cannot look after the security of all parties involved by itself. For Los Angeles 1984 the following security areas were transferred to the responsibility of the city and the government: security of athletes against terrorist attacks in public and during excursions outside the Olympic village, traffic checks, letter bomb checks, check of athletes' luggage, security for press and VIPs, open sea security and checks of suspect individuals (Los Angeles OCOG, 1979). State support in the form of the police, military, coastguard, the fire brigade, and special forces is indispensable. In Athens the Greek police, coastguard, fire corps, special forces, private security and volunteers will be deployed for security duties. Additionally the air force will provide three AWACS aircraft and a considerable number of fighter jets, while missile batteries will be on standby (NN, 2003, pp. 1–2). In Beijing a similar security department is planned: Beijing police, other police, civil emergency and fire, private security, volunteer groups, military liaison and others. The armed forces will be ready to assist in any security operation as well as the Chinese members of ICPO-Interpol (Bidding Committee Beijing 2008, 2001). It is important to note that for all the Games under review, the government was involved in the security concepts. As early as during the bid phase, the IOC demands a guarantee that the corresponding corporations will support the security concept (IOC, 1995a). Deliberate counter-agitation to weaken the effect of the measures of the disturbing group can be part of such a concept. An active discussion of the Olympic opponents' arguments and the consideration of their interests could reduce the risk of disturbances. Globalization may have decreased the danger of nationally organized terrorism and 'the incidence of international tourism has been tending downwards since the late 1980s' (Thompson, 1999). However, since 11 September 2001 there is a risk of attacks by fanatic terrorist groups. Since the IOC is supposed to be prosperous there is the danger that athletes or IOC members might be taken hostage for blackmail purposes. Additionally, individual assassins remain a threat due to the fact that they 'cannot be stopped because there is no logic to be applied' (Hemmerling, Sydney OCOG, Chief Executive, in NN, 1996a). Thompson shows that 'classic' terrorism (Munich 1972) will occur less in the future but 'religious' and 'amateurs' terrorism such as in Atlanta 1996 may increase (Thompson, 1999). Experienced security forces could be employed in the sports facilities to face radical and aggressive fans. General crime would have to be fought by the police. Thus far, however, very dubious methods have sometimes been used to address this potential problem. In Atlanta 1996, for example, the homeless and people previously convicted of similar offences were said to have been taken into custody or expelled from the area (Gladitz and Günther, 1995) during the Olympic Games.

In order to face the security risks mentioned above, the use of different security forces is imperative. These forces are partly provided and paid for by the city or the government (public) and partly by the OCOG (private). All security forces incur personnel and material costs. Personnel costs make up the largest part of security costs. In general, wages for persons procured by the public sector (police, military and so on) are not charged to an OCOG since the people are paid from public accounts and represent fixed costs for the government. In Los Angeles 1984 the OCOG was said to have paid a flat rate to the city for publicly provided services. However, in this situation, transportation costs, catering, and extra wages could still be charged to the OCOG as costs to be directly allocated. An OCOG will incur the full costs. According to Catherwood and Kirk (1992), a member of a security force costs about US$1000 for 24 hours in the USA. If an OCOG decides to commission private security enterprises (NN, 1996i), to lower such costs frequent use is made of volunteers as security staff, assigning them the title of stewards. Athens 2004 is planning to give 5000 volunteers a special security training (Athens OCOG, May 2002a). Figure 9.8 shows the number of security staff.

When the security concept for Munich 1972 was developed, terrorist attacks at the Olympic Games were unknown (Wetter, 1972). The assault on the Israeli athletes presumably led to a strong increase in the precautions for Montreal 1976 (Messing and Voigt, 1981). The military force of Montreal was a part of the international security network put in place in order to avoid an incident like that of Munich 1972 (Wright, 1978). Although this was not reflected in the number of the security personnel officially recorded, it is included in Figure 9.8. In Los Angeles, security was said to have been the largest item in budgeting for the Games. 'It's my greatest concern ... and our largest budget item. We'll do whatever it takes, regardless of cost' (Los Angeles OCOG, 1979; Ueberroth et al., 1985). Student unrest and the fear that North Korea could invade South Korea during the Games explain the extremely high number of security forces used during the Seoul 1988 Olympics. In addition to the 50 000 security forces personnel, a standby of 60 000 soldiers was also alerted (Lee, 1989; McBeth, 1988c; NN, 1984d). Even the US army was on call stationed in South Korea (Hill, 1996). In Barcelona 1992 the number of security forces was below that of Seoul 1988, but nevertheless it was still at a clearly higher level than those of the Games staged in the 1970s. W. Payne, President of the Atlanta OCOG, called the 1996 Olympics the 'safest Games of the world' even though the security forces were no larger than those used in Seoul or Barcelona. The

Sydney OCOG 2000 learnt a lesson from the Atlanta assault: 'This bomb attack gave crime at these locations which are not directly linked to sport a new dimension. We must adapt to this new situation' (Hemmerling in NN, 1996m). Anyhow, McKinnon said a safe environment would be provided: 'We will provide safety through meticulous planning, sound intelligence gathering, and an extraordinary network of cooperative arrangements between law enforcement and other agencies' (The Audit Office, 1999). After 2001, the security of Olympic Games has reached a new dimension.

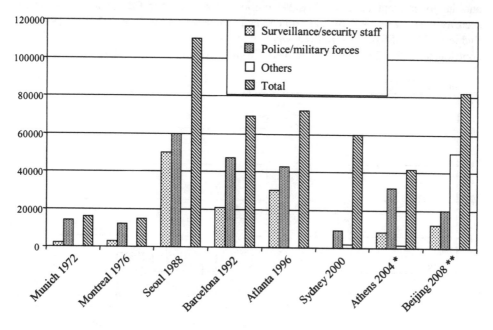

Notes: *   Estimated in 2003.
          **   Bidding Committee Beijing 2008, estimated before 11 September 2001.

Sources: Bidding Committee Beijing 2008 (2001); Athens OCOG (2003b, p. 40); Preuss (2000a); Zils (2001).

Figure 9.8 Number of security staff from Munich 1972 to Beijing 2008

The number of security forces strongly differs among the various Games. Their strength mainly depends on the geopolitical location of the respective host city. Nevertheless, after the Seoul 1988 Games a new level was reached in the security sector – this measured by the numbers attributed to the security forces working at Games time. It is unlikely that the number of security forces at the Olympic Games in the near future will fall below 50 000. This is not a striking observation though since the growing public interest in the Olympic Games only serves to motivate the criminal groups listed above. To close, the OCOG's contribution to the costs to maintain the security of the Olympic Family and visitors are considered. Because of the numerous factors influencing staff costs, which can strongly vary from host city to host city and include the wage rate per hour, number of volunteers, shift penalties, overtime and so on, and comparative costs are difficult to examine. For the privately financed Games of Los Angeles 1984 and Atlanta 1996, the OCOGs were said to have covered the costs for the security forces provided by the public sector. On the other hand, there were reports saying that the government incurred costs of US$.$_{00}$ 112 million for the security of the Los Angeles 1984 Olympics (Lee, 1989). For Atlanta 1996, the Defence Department contributed US$.$_{00}$ 51.5 million and the government another US$$_{00}$ 241 million for soldiers and FBI agents. 'Most of the security costs were paid by state and federal agencies' (French and Disher, 1997). In Sydney 2000 US$.$_{00}$ 85.2 million were paid from government funds and the OCOG contributed US$.$_{00}$ 29.7 million (Olympic Co-ordination Authority, 2002, p. 20).

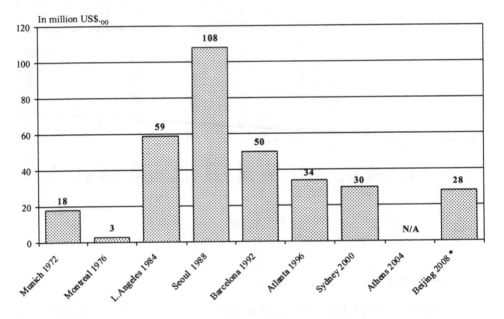

Note: *   Bidding Committee Beijing 2008, (2001) – before 11 September, 2001.

Sources: Bidding Committee Beijing 2008 (2001); Kearney (2001); Preuss (2000a).

Figure 9.9   OCOG costs for security from Munich 1972 to Beijing 2008

The above mentioned examples again prove the difficulties that can arise when attempting to compare the costs of different Olympics. The dollar figures for just the actual costs of the security sector alone make it clear that the Olympic Games can hardly be adequately staged without governmental support. Generally, OCOG costs for security will always be but a small portion of the actual costs. In Montreal 1976 the costs for security were said to have amounted to US$.$_{00}$ 244.6 million without the OCOG share

(Wright, 1978). The Salt Lake Winter Games in 2002 faced a special problem after the terrorist attack on 11 September, 2001. Therefore cost of security increased to US$'00 295.1 million (NN, 2001). The Greek Government has committed US$'00 576 million for capital investments in security (Athens OCOG, 2002a, p. 124). The total security costs amounted US$'00 1,386 million (Angolepoulos-Daskalaki, 2004). Beijing OCOG will probably also spend more money than the US$'00 28 million which is only 3.1 per cent of the estimated Games budget. However, that figure does not include the government costs for police, army and other public authorities (Bidding Committee Beijing 2008, 2001).

Apart from the personnel costs, which are mainly dependent on the wage level in the host country, there are also costs for materials, accommodations and catering which are incurred. Barcelona 1992 spent US$'00 13.4 million on security electronics alone. In Sydney US$'00 18.8 million was spent for equipment which will be used as well after the Games (NSW, 2001, p. 23).

Digression: Insurance Policies

The Host City Contract states: 'The OCOG shall secure and maintain, at its expense, adequate insurance coverage in respect of all risks associated with the organization and staging of the Games' (IOC, 1997d). The insurance must cover both the risks for the organizer and the participants. Risks to the organizer may potentially be either legal (compensation claims) or financial (lack of revenues) in nature. The participant risk refers to dangers to the persons involved (Himmelseher, 1981).

The Olympic insurance programmes were based on three main policies, which were unique to the Olympic Games risks (television broadcasting rights, legal liability, Olympic Family). Insurance policies are signed for Olympic Games under the following categories: games cancellation, general liability, legal costs, worker's compensation, consequential loss, transportation and luggage and sport venues (interview, Greib, 1996; Atlanta OCOG, 1998). For a few of the Olympics these risks have not been covered individually. Entire insurance packages cover several risks and could involve more than a hundred insurance companies at the same time. Based on the legal system of the host country, other insurance packages have to be negotiated and compiled for each Olympiad (interview, Greib, 1997). This gives an idea of the tasks an OCOG has to cope with, just in the security sector alone.

The most expensive insurance for Olympics is for Games cancellation. The more economic interests that lie behind the Games and the more sponsors and television networks that expect a service in return for their contribution, the more serious the possible cancellation of the Games would be. Already reductions or even shifts in the Olympic programme can result in high compensation claims. For example, claims can be made if a television broadcast was not possible on the planned day or the subsequent day, if the Games last less than 16 days, if an entire discipline is cancelled and so forth (Maennig, 1992).

Compared to the relatively short time span of the event, the costs for taking out insurance policies for the Olympic Games are very high. This, however, is due to the fact that the insurance companies do not have a chance to spread the risk collectively or over time (Himmelseher, 1981). The insurance costs for Montreal 1976 thus amounted to approximately US$·$_{00}$ 2 million (Montreal OCOG, 1976). After the negative experience the insurance companies had with the boycott of the Moscow 1980 Olympics – when NBC lost about US$·$_{00}$ 50 million through the boycott, although the insurance company was said to have covered the largest part of the damage (Hill, 1992; Kim, 1990) – Los Angeles 1984 faced problems in finding any insurance company. It was only possible at a very late date for the OCOG to enlist Transamerica as their insurance company. This deal freed the OCOG from paying the insurance fees in return for Transamerica being given the right to appear as a sponsor for the 1984 Olympics (Ueberroth et al., 1985). In Barcelona 1992 the insurance fees were said to have amounted to US$·$_{00}$ 9.1 million (Barcelona OCOG, 1992). Atlanta 1996 was said to have taken out the most expensive insurance so far in Olympic history. This was necessary because the banks would not have otherwise given the privately run OCOG loans without the high sums of lent money being insured (Atlanta OCOG, 1998).

Although it is recognized that the following list is not complete, there are several reasons for the increase in insurance costs for the Olympic Games:

- Accumulated danger: if a large number of persons meet in a certain place at a certain time, the probability that damage will be caused rises (for example by panicking or during arrivals and departures at the airport).
- Crime: events which interest the media have a special attraction for both terrorist groups and individual criminals (bomb attacks, assaults and so on). With the growing public interest in the Games, the risk of such criminal acts also rises. In Atlanta 1996, for example, several bombs were said to have been found (interview, Wilson, 1996). In Barcelona 1992 the insurers charged an additional 'terrorism surcharge' for this reason. After 2001 there is a high threat of terrorism for sport events.
- Gigantism: the growth of the Olympic Family caused increased costs for all insurance policies related to persons such as personal injury, transportation and so on in Seoul US$·$_{00}$ 26 128 would have been paid for each athlete and official in case of invalidity or death during the Games (NN, 1988b). In addition, the expansions of the Olympic programme result in more venues thereby increasing the fees paid out to insure the venues and their operation.
- Contractual obligation: the number of both the contracts made with sponsors, television networks and other partners as well as the contribution of the sponsors to the OCOG and the IOC have steadily increased. With these increases, the compensation risk factor associated with breaking or infringing upon the contracts has also risen. Higher fees must therefore be paid for cancellation insurance policies, which are taken out to protect against the possibility that external conditions might infringe on the contracts.

Insurance policies related to the Olympic Games have become an important economic factor. They are not only taken out by the OCOG but also by NOCs, IFs, athletes and the IOC. The IOC takes out an insurance policy against either the cancellation of the Games or contract breaches resulting from the fact that Games had to be awarded to another city at short notice (IOC, 1983, annex 6). The IOC is also mentioned as the co-insurer for all OCOG insurance policies (IOC, 1997d). The more the IOC takes over the strategy of financing the Games through the sale of television rights and international sponsoring, the greater the liability risks will be. It should also be noted that sponsors and television networks alike also take out insurance policies for the Olympic Games.

9.6   COSTS OF ADMINISTRATION

Wages are the main cost of administration of an OCOG. For Games from 2012 onwards there is a special position called "workforce" which covers all wages. Than administration will be reduced to all costs incurred for the effective management and co-ordination of all operational activities.

For the period under review there are, however, also costs for travel, renting the OCOG building, office furniture, finance, risk management, legal service, equipment and the like. In Atlanta 1996, for example, the personnel costs made up 70 per cent, travel 12 per cent, material 5 per cent, rents 3 per cent and other items 10 per cent (Atlanta OCOG, 1994a). The following examination concentrates on the gradually expanding permanent staff members that are required throughout the life cycle of an OCOG. Numbers of staff are a key factor for determining the amount of administration costs. The numbers of employees of a few OCOGs (without contract workers) are compared with each other in Figure 9.10. In Munich, as in Mexico, the curve kept low for a long time. In general before the Games, the curves rise very slowly. The slower the rise in the early preparatory phase of the Games, the lower the labour costs for the OCOG. During the Games, the curves reach their climax. After the Games, the curves quickly drop since the OCOGs dissolve within a very short period of time. The plateau, which has formed during the Games in Barcelona, Atlanta and Sydney is striking. It points to the emergence of a situation where increasingly more work needs to be done for increasingly longer time spans before the start of the Games. Concerning the high number of staff for Athens 2004, there are certain facts that explain the curve. First, the delay in planning forces more work to be done in a short time. Second, the Paralympics are for the first time in history being organized by the same OCOG. Third, a high level of bureaucracy forces an increase in staff for filing and reporting. Finally, the Greek mindset is such that the average number of secretaries is higher than in Sydney or Atlanta (interview, Mamangakis, 2003).

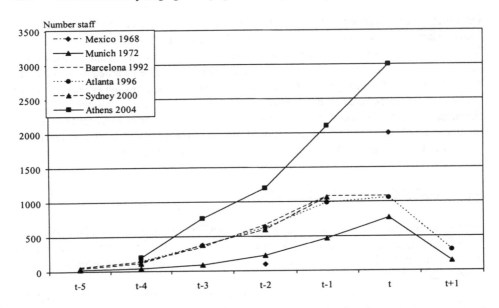

Number staff

- − ·◆− · Mexico 1968
- ─▲── Munich 1972
- ───── Barcelona 1992
- ·····●···· Atlanta 1996
- ──▲── Sydney 2000
- ──■── Athens 2004

Sources: Mexico OCOG (1969); interview, Papapetropoulos (2003); Preuss (2000a).

Figure 9.10   Staff numbers of certain OCOGs from Mexico 1968 to Athens 2004

An OCOG has a very short life cycle and can therefore offer jobs for only a limited period of time. Motivating the employees of an OCOG via payment of special wages or by offering other incentives is therefore especially important in order to attract committed and experienced staff. The senior managers of an OCOG are likely see a special challenge in organizing the Olympic Games as such (Boggs, 1996). After the Games, they will surely find a new job if they do not simply return to their previous professions.

Individuals from middle management, such as department heads, will only work for an OCOG if they do not have to give up an existing job or if their individual benefit from working for the OCOG is higher than that of their previous employment. Thus far, this employee category has not been especially well paid. In Munich 1972 they used the government pay scale in which the annual earnings for department heads amounted to approximately US$'00 50 000 per annum. The privately organized and financed Olympics of Los Angeles 1984 paid their department heads approximately US$'00 63 218 per annum (Atlanta OCOG, 1994a; Organisationskomitee München, 1974a). In Sydney directors got up to US$'00 112 800 per annum. The OCOGs basically adjust the salaries of this group to the salaries of senior officers in the public services, thereby corresponding to the general wage level of the host country.

The lower-level employees make their decisions in favour of working for the OCOG by considering the advantages of other offers in the job market. Secretaries in Munich, for example, earned US$'00 14 063 per annum, while Los Angeles paid US$'00 31 609 per annum for this position. The promise of the Korean OCOG to give all employees a job after the Games should be mentioned here. Of course, this considerably lowers the reluctance of an individual to give up an interesting job in exchange for the short-term challenge of taking part in organizing the Olympics. This, however, enabled the OCOG to recruit people with the required experience and knowledge (Kim, 1990; Lee, 1989). Working for the OCOG has a special attraction because it can lead to good opportunities to obtain an interesting job after the Games (speech [see correspondence], Rogge, 2003).

These explanations make it clear that the personnel costs of an OCOG can be anticipated relatively precisely. It can be assumed that the number of OCOG employees will further increase with the growth of the Games. The expanding contingent of employees will be in proportion to the curves highlighted above in the OCOG life cycle. The salaries for senior-level employees, in particular, should be attractive enough to make them give up their previous jobs and come to work for the OCOG. This is important since qualified and experienced managers are necessary to ensure the smooth staging of the Games. The wages for the lower-level employees can be adjusted to the national wage level – taking into consideration the existing workforce supply. In general, an adequate number of qualified staff should be available. In developing countries the recruitment of sufficiently qualified staff can become a real problem. A fluctuation of the lower level employees does not represent a problem for the organization of the Games.

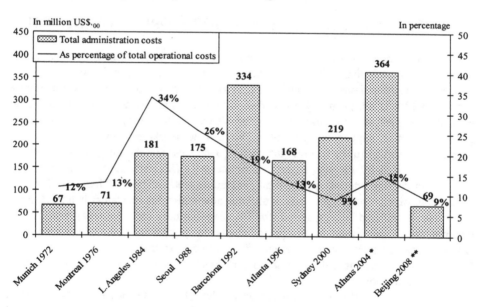

Notes: *   Estimated by OCOG Athens 2004.
          **   Bidding Committee Beijing 2008 (2001).

Sources: Preuss (2000a); Bidding Committee Beijing (2001); Athens OCOG (2003b, p. 22).

Figure 9.11   Administration costs of OCOGs from Munich 1972 to Beijing 2008

Finally, the total administration costs will be reviewed. These, however, are subject to different delimitations as mentioned above. The different delimitation is obvious in the fact that the Atlanta OCOG 1996 supposedly spent US$·$_{00}$ 346 million on wages while the administration costs were stated at only US$·$_{00}$ 168 million. For Barcelona 1992, in contrast, personnel costs were recorded at US$·$_{00}$ 236 million. Here it seems that wages were included in the US$·$_{00}$ 334 million for administration (NN, 1997e; Barcelona OCOG, 1992).

Figure 9.11 reveals the trend towards a fluctuation in the absolute administration costs. At the same time, the actual share of these costs that are related to the overall operational costs diminishes. On average, the administration costs range from between 10 per cent and 30 per cent of the overall OCOG operational costs. The fact that personnel costs are the largest part of the administration costs makes it understandable why greater efficiency was called for when employing new staff. C.H. Battle complained that for Atlanta 1996 the OCOG had too many staff members (interview, Battle 1997). Sydney 2000 tried to keep the staff members low. After all, the difference in the costs of Barcelona 1992 can only be explained by different delimitations because of the fact that the number of staff members was approximately the same for Atlanta 1996 and Sydney 2000.

9.7   COSTS OF PUBLIC RELATIONS AND CORPORATE DESIGN

For some time now the final balance sheets of the OCOGs have used the term public relations. Public relations (PR) is a parameter of communication politics as well as sales promotion and advertising (Marr and Picot, 1991). In contrast to the other two marketing instruments, PR is not primarily oriented to a market but is instead, in its true sense, an instrument to present a corporation and interpret its general policy with the objective of gaining as much support as possible. The link to marketing and communications objectives exists due to the fact that the level of awareness and the image of an enterprise that are improved by PR also serve to promote sales (Meffert, 1998). The distinction between these three terms in the final balance sheets is poor. Therefore Olympic advertising, which also includes product-related advertising for spectators in attendance at sports events, is used as a synonym for PR. Expenditures for advertising and PR are incurred by an OCOG when it attempts to increase the popularity of the Olympics and the Olympic ideals as such in order to attract visitors to the Games, increase viewing rates of Olympic programmes or make corporations interested in the idea of using the Olympic emblems and symbol.

In relation to PR efforts, the impact which the Olympic Games have on the world population is of paramount importance. This is mainly determined by the appearance of the Games, as represented by their visual presentation, being part of the corporate identity. The corporate identity comprises corporate behaviour, corporate communication and corporate design. It also relates to the overall design of visual communications which make the Olympic Games immediately recognizable. This factor is important for the marketing of the Olympics since sponsoring and merchandising are not possible without a uniform 'look of the Games'. One large cost factor of the Olympic Games corporate design is tied to the provision of uniforms for up to 70 000 persons who are engaged by the OCOG.

9.7.1 Public Relations

A large portion of PR expenditures for hosting the Olympics is spent during the bidding phase. The PR work involved in positively presenting the city, especially towards IOC members and guarantee givers, is one of the key components in the expenditures made by a bid candidate. The costs to bid for the 2000 Olympic Games were said to have amounted to approximately US\$$_{'00}$ 46.2 million for Berlin, US\$$_{'00}$ 18.6 million for Sydney, US\$$_{'00}$ 11.6 million for Beijing and US\$$_{'00}$ 10.2 million for Manchester (NN, 1993).

When the Olympics are awarded to a city seven years in advance of their being staged, the PR objectives change. As the work shifts from winning a bid to staging the Games, their PR emphasis is redirected towards focusing on an effort to promote the Olympics on an international scale. In the initial announcement phase, PR work primarily makes use of the printed medium. In Athens 1896, they used, for example, Olympic stamps to help announce the Games. Vignettes were later placed on letters in order to achieve this same strategy. The use of posters for international advertising also has a long tradition. Today, Olympic PR work uses all communication channels, including print, television, radio and the Internet. An OCOG owes a great portion of its Olympic advertising, which mainly aims at attracting the interest of people from around the world to the Olympics, to sponsors and television networks. In one respect, the sponsors' interest in appearing publicly, the television networks' interest in high view rates, the OCOG's interest in announcing the Games worldwide, and the cities' and host nations' interest in attracting tourists and foreign investment are similarly focused in their intent. There is, however, one major difference in what each of these four parties are trying to achieve through their PR efforts. While the media, sponsors and host city focus their Olympic PR work on specific target groups, the OCOG and IOC use their PR activities to focus on conveying the Olympic ideals. For this purpose the IOC has already produced its own television commercials to promote the Olympic Idea; the campaign started with the Sydney Olympics and is called 'Celebrate Humanity' and will be continued in Athens 2004 (interview, Payne, 2004). To an increasing extent, Olympic sponsors use the Olympic ideals in an effective way for their own PR work. However, by this they do promote the Olympic idea throughout the world. Individual TOP sponsors have already produced PR spots, which apart from a short appearance of the company name at the end of the spot solely promote the Olympic Movement. Through this, a dynamic new cooperation between the sponsors, IOC and OCOG is developing. Today, the Olympics are mainly announced through sponsor advertising and television station broadcasting. Therefore, recruiting a certain number of sponsors with interests directed towards the outside world is desirable for the IOC and the OCOG alike.

Taking into account the previously mentioned difficulties encountered when making a comparison, Figure 9.12 shows the share of PR expenditures, which are a part of the respective OCOG's operational costs. The share in the operational costs was, however, only calculated for the Games after Munich 1972. For the Olympics prior to Munich, expenditures in percentages were related to overall OCOG costs. However, the OCOGs of this period did not invest a lot of money in PR. The Games prior to Munich 1972 have also been included since the variations in the percentages were relatively high until Barcelona 1992. In this form, PR expenditures can only be compared owing to the fact that they have been expressed as percentages of the overall costs of the respective OCOG. Thus, differences in purchasing power and inflation cannot affect these values. The analysis, therefore, is reduced to only being able to consider the importance of PR within the overall OCOG costs. There is no analysis of absolute figures, hence the need for the inclusion of Figure 9.13 in order to show the absolute PR expenditures for the Olympics since Munich 1972.

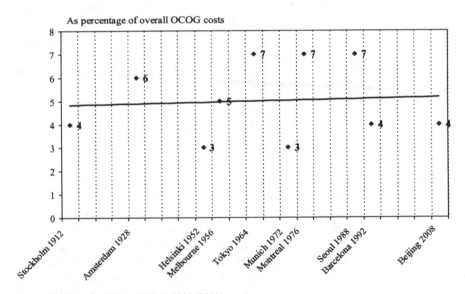

Note: * Bidding Committee Beijjng 2008 (2001).

Sources: Bidding Committee Beijing 2008 (2001); Preuss (2000a).

Figure 9.12   PR costs of selected Games as percentage of the corresponding OCOG budget

During the period under review (1912–2008) the percentages of PR costs as a percentage of the OCOG's overall costs, slightly increased. As a consequence, the expenditures for PR measures must have risen even more strongly in absolute terms since the overall expenditures rose from Olympiad to Olympiad. This assumption is confirmed by the figures from Munich 1972 to Beijing 2008. It can, however, also be assumed that the reason for the strong increase in PR expenditure percentages is surely not because the OCOGs had determined the percentage as a part of their planning, as is the case for many enterprises when they are planning their PR expenditures. Rather, it can be assumed that the increasingly larger regions where the Olympics are promoted through an increasing number of NOCs and the ever greater number of people that are reached all over the world are the true reasons for the strong rise in PR expenditures. In addition, it must be remembered that the increase was also caused by different delimitations of the items.

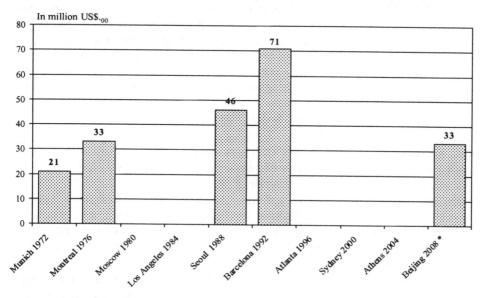

Note: *Bidding Committee Beijing 2008 (2001).

Sources: Bidding Committee Beijing 2008 (2001).

Figure 9.13   (Absolute) PR costs for the Games from Munich 1972 to Beijing 2008

9.7.2 Corporate Design

'Money is a powerful factor in the organization of the modern Olympics and effects the character of the design' (Newman, R., 1999). Due to the fact, that design is linked with marketing, the design process is very important for the Olympic Movement. Corporate design activities can be divided into three sectors – product design, graphic design and architectural design (Newman, R., 1999; Schneider, 1991).

Product design refers to the visual design of the products of the Olympic Games, which, in its narrowest sense, are the sporting competitions. In the broader sense, it also includes merchandise, which naturally corresponds to the design of the Games. Graphic design refers to the design of the Olympic emblems, as it relates to colours and typography. Architectural design deals with the design of buildings but also the overlays. Due to the short-term usage at the Olympic Games, architectural design applies less to sports venues and Olympic villages than to the smaller ticket-selling and information stands.

The Berlin Games of 1936 were a good example of how Olympic Games were politically exploited from a design perspective. However, Mexico 1968 were the first Games with a uniform appearance. Munich 1972 succeeded in implementing a corporate design at the Olympic Games (Aicher, 1996; Pabst, 1986). This is still true even if Coubertin tried to use decorations and so on to make the Games a complete work of art (Krüger, 1996; Müller and IOC, 1986). A logo, colours to promote 'freshness and ease' (Harenberg, 1991), the printing of programmes and forms as well as the clothing for security forces, volunteers and judges completed the uniform appearance of the Munich Games. Nonetheless, it was the OCOG of Barcelona 1992 which first introduced the costs for the corporate design of the Games as a separate item in the final balance sheets. For Barcelona, they amounted to US$$_{.00}$ million, while in Atlanta 1996 this cost increased to US$$_{.00}$ 57.3 million. The visual identity is nowadays called 'look of the Games' and is very important to give value to the brand. Not only the Olympic venues appear in a corporate design. The whole host city becomes decorated during the Games. Therefore the OCOG of Athens covered costs of US$$_{.00}$ 11 million. Additionally, the city of Athens is responsible for the bridges, highways, airport, buildings and ports, and is spending US$$_{.00}$ 12.2 million (interview, Mamangakis, 2003).

The uniform clothing for OCOG staff and volunteers is one of the major points of the corporate design. Thus far, OCOGs have not incurred expenditures in this sector since suppliers have provided the clothing. Generally, the employees can keep their clothes at the end of the Games. This should, therefore, be regarded, as a 'value consumption' amounting to a procurement price and as such should be recorded as a cost. The fact that an OCOG would have expenditures amounting to the procurement prices for clothing if there was no sponsor willing to provide the items is also an argument for declaring them as costs. This expenditure item should be balanced by sponsor contributions of an equal amount on the revenue side.

A basic factor influencing the costs of uniform clothing is the number of persons to be clothed. However, specific sponsors help the OCOG to cover the costs. In Montreal uniforms cost a mere US$$_{.00}$ 2.2 million since there were only a few volunteers (Montreal OCOG, 1976). On the other hand, the clothing of the Los Angeles staff was said to have cost US$$_{.00}$ 83 million while that of the Barcelona staff cost US$$_{.00}$ 31.6 million (ERA, 1984; Barcelona OCOG, 1992; Schöps, 1983). In Sydney the uniforms cost only US$$_{.00}$ 13.2 million, due to the fact that Bonds and Nike covered a big part (interview, Elphinston, 1999; Magnay, 1999; The Audit Office, 1999).

It is important, for two reasons, that the OCOG staff be uniformly clothed for the Olympic Games. On the one hand, it serves as an incentive (Preuss and Kebernik, 2000) for volunteers and increases the identification of the staff with the Games, thereby creating the necessary feeling of responsibility. On the other hand, it contributes to the corporate design of the Games. In future, therefore, this element of design should continue to be regarded as an important component.

9.8 COSTS OF THE INTERNATIONAL BROADCASTING CENTRE

As already shown, the media is the key instrument both for its ability to increase the level of awareness of the Olympics as well as for being able to attract and keep industry interested in the Games. However, the OCOG's relationship with the media, which is restricted here to television stations, incurs costs. Owing to the above mentioned transfer of broadcasting autonomy from television stations to OCOGs, the OCOGs work to have an IBC installed at the intersection of the Olympic Games and the television stations. Of course, this directly affects the OCOG's costs since the IBC represents the major portion of the costs for Olympic television broadcasting. Figure 9.14 compares the overall IBC costs and the OCOG share of these.

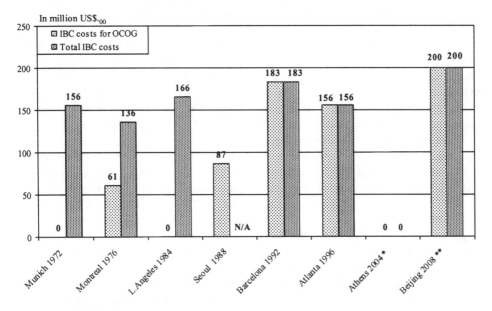

Note: *   Costs (US$'$_{00}$ 105 million) of the IBC covered by Greek government.
     ** Conservatively estimated by Bidding Committee Beijing 2008 (2001).

Sources: Bidding Committee Beijing 2008 (2001); Lewis (2004, p. 55); Preuss (2000a).

Figure 9.14   *Overall IBC costs and IBC costs for the OCOGs from Munich 1972 to Beijing 2008*

The transfer of responsibility for television broadcasts from the autonomous host broadcaster to the Olympic broadcasting of the OCOG is clearly reflected in the overall costs. Since Barcelona 1992 the OCOGs had to cover all costs of the IBC. Before Barcelona 1992 the television station broadcasting the Games for the host country was also under contract to serve as the host broadcaster. This designated host was required to produce the international signal for all the other stations (Moragas Spà et al., 1995). In the case of Seoul 1988, there was already a television centre, which was linked to the OCOG. It, however, was under the leadership of the host broadcaster, the Korean Broadcasting Commission (KBC). The Korean OCOG was therefore said to have only participated in the operational costs of the IBC. In Los Angeles 1984 ABC bought the rights and thus had to cover all the costs of the television centre such as US$·$_{00}$ 116 million for the building alone and US$·$_{00}$ 22 million for cameras (Seifart, 1984). In Montreal 1976 the OCOG covered 50 per cent of the estimated costs for the television centre (Montreal OCOG, 1976), an action, which had not been common in the period before 1976. However, in Athens 2004 and Beijing 2008 the IOC and OCOG will take over all broadcasting costs. The Olympic Broadcasting Organization will produce all pictures and provide them to all those networks holding rights.

In the final analysis, these considerations must be taken into account in combination with the opportunity costs of the OCOG. The Munich 1972 OCOG, for example, incurred opportunity costs as a result of the fact that the Arbeitsgemeinschaft der öffentlich-rechtlichen Rundfunkanstalten der Bundesrepublik Deutschland (ARD) and the Zweite Deutsche Fernsehen (ZDF) did not have to pay for television rights. Moreover, Euro-vision paid only a very small sum based on the argument that they had already 'paid millions through ARD and ZDF, via the German Olympic Radio and TV Centre – Deutsches Olympia Hörfunk- und Fernsehzentrum DOZ' (NN, 1972c). Due to that fact the television lottery also paid 'reduced' fees to the OCOG (Moragas Spà et al., 1995).

If one considers the overall costs for an IBC, as represented by the darker columns in Figure 9.14 the above mentioned thesis that costs for television and revenues from selling television rights are diverging is confirmed. An OCOG has increasingly earned more from selling television rights than it has incurred in costs for television broadcasts. In turn, the transfer of the broadcasting autonomy to the OCOGs has also translated into a tremendous financial benefit for the Olympic Movement. It must not, however, be forgotten that this relationship with the television stations has become a major cost item for any OCOG since Barcelona. Owing to this fact, the media representatives have become the biggest accredited group of the Olympics. In Athens 2004, 21 000 media representatives are expected. Finally, it should be mentioned that costs for media – apart from IBC costs – also consist of costs for the main press centre (MPC) and other media installations, which were not considered here. For example, Munich 1972 was said to have spent US$$_{00}$ 27 million on the press and Seoul US$·$_{00}$ 7.3 million on the operation of the MPC. However, the sizes of the MPC/IBC varied strongly in the past (Gratton, 1999).

Table 9.4   Sizes of IBC and MPC

	Seoul 1988	Barcelona 1992	Atlanta 1996	Sydney 2000	Athens 2004	Beijing 2008
MPC sq	35 000	51 134	27 900	40 000	52 000	83 500
IBC sq	N/A	45 000	46 500	70 000	100 000	58 400

Sources: Bidding Committee Beijing 2008 (2001, pp. 101–103); Lewis (2004, p. 55); Athens OCOG (2003b, p. 74); Sydney OCOG (2001); Preuss (2000a).

9.9 COSTS OF THE OLYMPIC FAMILY

Caring for the Olympic Family forms a core element to be considered when organizing the Games. The athletes and the IOC members comprise the main groups of individuals to be taken care of within this 'family'. The Olympic Family also includes all accredited persons, such as IF and NOC members, team officials, judges and umpires, sponsors and observers of future Olympics (see detailed list in IOC, 2001e). Questions with regards to the areas in which the above defined Olympic Family creates costs for an OCOG as well as the extent of these costs will now be investigated. The following sections are structured according to the obligations an OCOG has towards the Olympic Family, as stated in the Olympic Charter of 2000.

9.9.1 Transportation Costs

Rules 41, 42, 43 and 57 of the Olympic Charter describe transportation for the Olympic Family: 'The OCOG shall bear all expenses for board and lodging of competitors, team officials and other team personnel in the Olympic Village ... as well as their local transportation expenses' (IOC, 2003d, Rule 42, By-Law 2). In addition, the Host City Contract from Athens and Beijing mentions the detailed regulations regarding transportation.

The three key factors for determining transportation demands are the size of the Family, the duration of their stay and the location of the Olympic village or hotels in relation to the sports venues and other points of interest. The most decisive cost factor for an OCOG is dependent upon the vehicles that will be used, since the majority of the drivers are volunteers and therefore do not create labour costs. Sponsors often provide the necessary cars but buses and other vehicles must be leased. The Atlanta OCOG leased buses from 60 metropolises across the USA. Merely bringing the buses to Atlanta cost the OCOG US$·$_{00}$ 17.6 million (Gillam, 1996b; 1996c; NN, 1995e). The following accounting should therefore be applied with regards to the cost rate for the vehicles: if the entire amount sponsored is recorded as OCOG revenue – which generally is the case – the value consumption of sponsor provided cars must also be assessed along with the leasing costs for buses and other vehicles. Thus, an OCOG incurs costs for the fleet of vehicles in the form of procurement costs, leasing and operational costs as well as for the value consumption of all vehicles which are provided for free.

The number of vehicles required depends on the factors mentioned above and therefore varies from host city to host city. This makes it difficult to use the transportation costs of the previous Games to estimate the costs for future OCOGs. This is the reason why the transportation costs for Seoul 1988 recorded at US$·$_{00}$ 40.2 million (Lee, 1989), cannot simply be compared to the US$·$_{00}$ 110 million of Atlanta 1996. In the case of Atlanta, it should be noted that this amount also included the free transportation of spectators to sports events, which was said to have amounted to US$·$_{00}$ 16.8 million alone (Ruffenach, 1996a). However, in Sydney the Olympic Road and Transport Authority (ORTA) took over the responsibility of transportation. More than 4.6 million passengers travelled to Sydney Olympic Park on public transport during the Games – 3 527 500 on trains and 1 134 750 on 13 regional bus routes (NSW, 2001). The OCOG paid US$·₀₀ 37.7 million to provide free transportation for the spectators while the government of NSW gave a provision of US$·₀₀ 96.2 million to ORTA (Black 1999; interview, Elphinston, 1999; NSW, 2001). Despite the differing infrastructure of the host cities and the differing situation of the Olympic facilities in relation to each other (Table 9.5) the size of the fleet to transport the Olympic Family has remained relatively stable.

Table 9.5   Number of vehicles at Olympic Games

	Seoul 1988	Barcelona 1992	Atlanta 1996	Sydney 2000	Athens 2004
Buses	N /A	N /A	N /A	2200	1284–1550
Cars	N /A	N /A	N /A	2000	2900–3350
Total	2800	3000	3000	4200	4184–4900

Sources: Athens OCOG, (2003b, p. 62); Preuss (2000a).

In Beijing 2008 the transportation principles are the same as they have been at previous Games. The Olympic Family will be transported with dedicated cars, mini-buses, a car pool or a car rental service. The spectators will be advised to use public transport. Therefore, 16 spectator bus routes will created for the Games. Spectators living within a reasonable distance of competition sites will be advised to use bicycles (Bidding Committee Beijing 2008, 2001).

9.9.2   Costs for Accommodation and Lodging

Accommodation and lodging for the Olympic Family is described in Rules 41, 42 and 57 of the Olympic Charter: 'The tasks of the Coordination Commission include the following: ... To suggest to the OCOG ... arrangements for accommodation ... in the Olympic Village' (IOC, 2003d, Rule 41, Be-Law 4.1); 'The OCOG shall bear all expenses for board and lodging of competitors, team officials and other team personnel in the Olympic Village, (IOC, 2003d, Rule 42, By-Law 2); 'The OCOG must provide facilities separate from the Olympic Village for the accommodation of all technical officials appointed by the IFs (IOC, 2003d, Rule 57, para. 9).

The 2003 Olympic Charter clearly stipulates that the accommodation of athletes and officials in the Olympic village must be free of charge. Although this specific stipulation was not part of the Olympic Charter rules at the time Barcelona was elected as host city in 1986, the NOCs did not have to pay fees to the OCOG for accommodating their athletes. Whereas the Olympic Charter of 1987 stated: 'competitors ... can be housed ... and fed at a reasonable price' (IOC, 1987a, Rule 36), the 1995 Olympic Charter already stated: 'The OCOG shall bear all expenses for board and lodging of competitors' (IOC, 1995c, Rule 42, By-Law 1). Today, IOC employees and judges must also be accommodated free of charge. Additionally Athens 2004 must provide IOC employees with a total of 100 beds free of charge (IOC, 1995a; 1997d, App.). On the other hand, boarding is not free for

IOC members, NOC and IF officials, guests and others. However, the prices for accommodations for these groups are at least fixed in the Host City Contract: 'The room rate for the Olympic Family ... shall be as stated in the bid documentation' (IOC, 2001e). It is at this point that a distinction must be made between the IOC's demand for fixed prices for the accommodation of the Olympic Family and the general price controls that are introduced in the host city. When submitting the bid, prices for the accommodation of the Olympic Family must be fixed and secured by a guarantee. The fact that the IOC pays for the accommodation of both its members and the additional commission members explains its interest in fixing hotel prices in the Host City Contract. In contrast to this, the aim of a general price control is to avoid exaggerated prices for visitors during the Olympic year. The Host City Contract stated that Beijing, COC and Beijing Organising Committee of Olympic Games (BOCOG) should ensure that reasonable prices are charged to non-accredited persons attending the Games (IOC, 2001e).

From the legal perspective, it must be questioned whether the hotel association is allowed to guarantee a price control for accommodation and whether this interferes with the free competition of private industry which exists in many countries. Since the IOC demands a guarantee of a price control, a contract is only affected between the city or hotel association and the IOC. If private enterprises do not adhere to controlled prices – which would be legally correct in many countries – the question would arise of who has to pay for the difference. It would have to be checked whether price fixing actually represented a price cartel, which, at least in Europe, is forbidden. International Olympic Committee member W. Tröger's reply to this remark was that the IOC set strict rules in order to make the city negotiate with the chambers and large hotels. If the agreements then made are not adhered to, it is very difficult for the IOC to take legal action (interview, Tröger 1998). On this R. Pound said that the IOC simply wanted to avoid the situation where the host city and the Olympic Movement gain a bad reputation. In the long run, however, the IOC has no legal basis for enforcing the demands (interview, Pound, 1998). During the bidding phase, the hotel association of a host city should also give a guarantee for accommodations which states that prices for accommodations will be adjusted, at the most, to the inflation rate of the time period encompassing the Games. However, even if the hotels keep their price guarantee, the problem is that travel agencies buy large hotel contingencies and increase prices. These increases cannot be controlled by the IOC.

Table 9.6 displays the figures for the Olympic Family members who are to be accommodated (basic quantity of costs) and other key data, which are used to determine the accommodation costs of the Olympics in near future.

The OCOG costs for accommodating that part of the Olympic Family which must be housed free of charge arise from the rents that are paid out by the OCOG for the related facilities. Other location costs the OCOG must meet are, for example, for furnishing and Games-specific installations in the housing facilities such as medical care and security. Athens 2004 estimated the costs for just the furnishing alone at US$'$_{00}$ 36.8 million (Bidding Committee Athens 2004, 1995). In Atlanta 1996 15 000 beds, tents and pavilions, among other items, had to be provided in the Olympic village (Ferguson,

1996). Through the above discussion it quickly becomes evident just how difficult it is to calculate in detail the costs for accommodating the Olympic Family.

However, the key factors for determining an OCOG's accommodation costs can be illustrated in a simple formula. In order for this to be done, the amount of the rent prices (*p*) for villages and hotels as well as the number (*x*) and the average duration of the stay (*t*) for the people to be accommodated must be known. The OCOG must only cover the costs for certain groups (*v*) (Table 9.6, lines 1–5).

$$C_{(v)} = \sum_{n=1}^{5} (x_n * p_n * t_n) \tag{9.1}$$

It could not be determined whether the OCOG had to cover the difference if the hotel prices were above those fixed in the Host City Contract. The reduction of these costs during previous Games through the participation of the NOCs in the accommodation costs of their delegations also varied a lot and therefore cannot be generalized here. Nevertheless, equation 9.1 shows the interrelations of the factors, which determine the costs for accommodating the Olympic Family.

Table 9.6   Factors to determine accommodation costs for the Olympic Family

v		Accommodation OCOG must provide x	Accommodation type	Costs per person p	Covering of costs	Average rent duration t
1	Athletes; officials	16 000	Village	Rent of village/x	OCOG	20
2	IOC employees	150	Olympic Family hotel	Rent/day/person	OCOG	33
3	Judges	2100	Hotel	Rent/day/person	OCOG	20
4	Volunteers (specialist)	app. 1000	Private/residence hall	Rent for residence hall/x	OCOG	22
5	Youth camp	app. 1000	Village/residence hall	Rent for residence hall/x	OCOG	20
6	IOC, NOC members and guests	1800	Olympic Family hotel	Rent/day/person*	IOC/NOC/IF	20
7	NOC guests	1800	Hotel	Rent/day/person*	IOC/NOC/IF	
8	IF members and guests	800	Hotel	Rent/day/person*	IOC/NOC/IF	20
9	Sponsors and guests	7000 (up to 35 000)	Hotel/luxury liner	Rent/day/person*	Sponsors	20
10	Press/Media	21 000	Village/hotel	Rent/day/person	Press/Media	22
		app. 43 000				

Note: *   Prices to be fixed in the Host City Contract.

Sources: IOC (2001e); Athens OCOG (May 2002a); Preuss (2000a).

By using calculations similar to equation 9.1, the costs for catering can also be determined. In addition to the accommodated Olympic Family members, security staff and volunteers must also be included in the catering demands. This increases the number of persons (x) by approximately 70 000. It is also reduced by all persons that are accommodated in hotels since their catering costs should be included in the accommodation price. The price (p) per meal strongly varies from country to country and among the different groups that require catered meals. The total number of meals is determined by the duration of stay (t) or the working period of the respective person.

In Munich 1972, 27 000 persons per day were catered for (Munich OCOG, 1974a). In Seoul 1988 the number of staff (excluding security forces) and athletes that required catering for increased to as many as 63 000 persons (Preuss, 2000a). In Athens 2004 it is estimated that 226 000 people will use the food service per day.

9.9.3 Costs for Medical Care

Medical care of the Olympic Family is described in Rule 48 of the Olympic Charter: 'The Medical Code shall also include provisions relating to the medical care of the athletes' (IOC, 2003d, Rule 48, para. 1). In its truest sense, Rule 48 regulates the prohibition of doping at the Olympic Games. The costs of drug testing are high. The first Olympic doping tests were conducted in Grenoble and Mexico City 1986 (Clasing, 1992). In Munich 1972 the OCOG carried out 2000 tests (Schänzer, 2000). In Sydney 2000 the government spent US$$_{00}$ 4.9 million on testing and research (Kearney, 2001). Also in Beijing 2008 the OCOG 'at its expense, shall put into place and carry out doping controls' (Bidding Committee Beijing 2008, 2001). This investigation, however, shall concentrate on the costs for the medical care of the Olympic Family and spectators rather than on those for doping tests.

Medical care at the Olympic Games needs to be divided into two sectors – care for spectators and care for the Olympic Family. The medical care for spectators is primarily performed by voluntary medical staff and incurs costs for the OCOG. Additionally there are designated hospitals for visitors. Professional doctors care for the Olympic Family and the degree of care as stated, for example, by the ratio of doctors per 100 persons is much higher than that for spectators. The area in which medical care is provided is not limited just to the competition sites but also extends to the accommodation sites, IBC, MPC and training facilities. The OCOG only provides first-aid (medical service). In Atlanta 1996, for example, 121 first aid stations were set up (Atlanta OCOG, 1996). It is the responsibility of the injured or ill person to pay for all further medical care that is needed (interview, Tröger, 1998). Medical service has to be provided free of charge to the accredited competitors, team officials and representatives of the IOC, the IFs and the NOCs. The Medical Department of Beijing OCOG will be responsible for the provision and coordination of the health-care service for the Olympic Family. It has selected ten hospitals, on the basis of proximity to competition venues, medical expertise, equipment and emergency service. The Beijing Municipal Health Bureau will select from among the

160 000 medical workers in Beijing the best qualified personnel to serve the Olympic Family (Bidding Committee Beijing 2008, 2001).

Wages again represent the largest portion of the OCOG's costs in the medical sector (Maennig, 1992). In the following analysis, the staff required for medical care will be determined primarily based on the factors in Table 9.7.

Table 9.7, although not considered to be complete, still shows the diversity of factors that determine the number of medical staff an OCOG requires. The factor number of voluntary doctors/assistants changes the ratio of professional doctors/assistants to voluntary doctors and assistants. This, in turn, greatly affects the wages to be paid by an OCOG. In Atlanta 1996, 4100 volunteers and 30 professionals carried out the entire medical service. Only one Olympic polyclinic with 400 professionals was set up (Atlanta OCOG, 1996). In Seoul 1988 a total of only 1546 medical staff was used (Lee, 1989).

In addition, many of the factors listed in Table 9.7 depend on the respective country. It is therefore difficult to determine quantities.

Table 9.7   Classification of factors for determining the staff required in the medical sector

Category	Determining factor
Basic conditions	Climatic situation Crime rate/risk of potential terrorist attacks Traffic system
Potential patients	Number of Olympic Family members Number of spectators/tourists

Venue sites	Number of...
	   sports and training facilities
	   accommodation centres (villages/IOC hotel/youth camp/and so on)
	   sites of cultural events
	   other sites (IBC/MPC/and so on)

Medical measures to be carried out	Quality of care (first aid/rehabilitation/and so on) Number of drug tests
Prosperity of NOCs	Number of team doctors

The second cost factor in the sector of medical care is related to material and rents. These costs are mainly independent of the number of medical staff since the equipment of the medical facilities, provision of ambulances and so on are relatively fixed costs.

During the bid phase, the IOC makes sure that the bid cities can provide an adequate number of hospitals or beds for the period of the Games. Today, the IOC even asks about the investment plans of the bid city with regards to the health-care system for the next ten years (IOC, 1993b; 1997e). This indirectly encourages a bid city to check its health-care system. The argument of Olympic opponents that the Olympic Games are nothing but a prestigious object bringing no improvement to the poorer population must therefore be qualified. Future bid cities must have an adequate health-care system if they want to have a good chance of being selected as the host for the Olympic Games. A bid can therefore increase the pressure to improve a health-care system if it does not correspond to the IOC requirements. However, this also translates into a further obstacle to be overcome by bidders from cities of developing or threshold countries since the bid alone does not attract financial means to the city.

It can be stated that costs for the medical sector are affected by many factors, which are heavily dependent on national characteristics. This grows due to the increase in the size of the Olympic Family as well as in doping control. However, the number of tests is determined by the IFs or the IOC rather than by the OCOG. The costs for taking the samples and their transportation to the laboratory, however, must be covered by the OCOG (interview, Tröger, 1998). The Athens 2004 doping control programme will be responsible for delivering a maximum of 3500 tests at the time of the Olympic Games and Test Events (Athens OCOG, 2003b, p. 66). These costs, thus far not mentioned in detail, lead one to assume that costs for this sector will rise in the long run. In Seoul 1988 the medical service cost US$$_{\cdot00}$ 6.2 million and in Barcelona 1992 they were as much as US$$_{\cdot00}$ 14.9 million. In Atlanta this cost was said to have amounted to only a mere US$$_{\cdot00}$ 3.7 million (Brunet, 1993; Lee, 1989; Atlanta OCOG, 1998).

9.9.4   Costs for Accreditation and Protocol

Admission and protocol for the Olympic Family are described in Rules 49, 50, 64, 65 and 66 of the Olympic Charter. The yardstick for the total amount of the costs for accreditation and protocol is measured by the fact that not only are Olympic Family members accredited but also the entire OCOG and security staff, suppliers, media and people acting in the cultural and supporting programmes. During the course of the Olympic Games this means there is the need for more than one accreditation centre. In fact, several centres are required in order to handle the large number of individuals that are processed during the rush experienced in the few days before the Games are opened. In Athens 2004 more than 200 000 persons were accredited (Athens OCOG, 2002a, pp. 19 –20). A large portion of this total number is accredited long before the Games start.

To show the complexity of work the accreditation procedure of Athens 2004 will be used as an example (Athens OCOG, 2003b, p. 55):

- distribution of accreditation forms/access to electronic system
- return of complete forms and photos
- security background check
- production of accreditation passes
- arrival at the accreditation centre for validation of passes

In Seoul 1988 the accreditation of 133 132 persons cost US$$_{\cdot00}$ 4.5 million, in Barcelona 1992, 89 723 persons cost US$$_{\cdot00}$ 15.3 million and in Atlanta 1996, 130 587 persons cost US$$_{\cdot00}$ 2.7 million (Brunet, 1993; Lee, 1989; Atlanta OCOG, 1998; Atlanta OCOG, s.t.). These figures show that the costs for components such as the accreditation system and centres are largely independent of the number of persons to be accredited. The low costs for Atlanta can only be explained by a large share of sponsor services – a share whose value is not included in the accreditation item or by a different delimitation of the item.

Thus far, travel expenses for Olympic Family members have not been a significant cost item for the OCOGs. Since Seoul 1988 the OCOG only has to cover travel expenses for judges and IOC Medical Commission members. The Australian airline, Quantas, announced during the bid phase of Sydney that up to 20 000 members of the Olympic Family could get free flights – they wanted to provide AUS$·93 100 million. However, the official sponsor of the Olympics was the airline Ansett. Sydney 2000 contributed US$·00 14.3 million to the athletes' travel expenses. In the bid phase Manchester also planned to support the Olympic Family, primarily athletes of Third World countries (Gold and Harris, 1993; Harris, 1993; Miller, 1993). In the bid phase for Nagano 1998 there was a promise to cover travel and accommodation expenses for all athletes and officials. However, the decision had hardly been made when such generous offers ceased. IOC member W. Tröger confirmed that, at first, all travel expenses for the athletes were to be covered but in the end they paid only US$1000 per person (Schneppen, 1998; interview, Tröger, 1998). In addition to the travel expenses there are other costs that the OCOGs must absorb. In fact, further cost increases are incurred by the OCOGs owing to their obligation to accommodate the athletes and officials in the Olympic village, provide medical care for the Olympic Family, and accommodate the participants of the youth camp (IOC, 1997c). All of this evidence shows that Olympic bidders tend to try to increase their chances of being selected as Olympic city by offering free services for the Olympic Family.

10. Jobs, jobs, jobs: great opportunities or flash in the pan?

The overall economic effect the Olympic Games have on a host city can be expressed not only by the increased income but also by the employment generated by the Olympics. It must be kept in mind that the employment effect must not be added on to the income effect described earlier. Rather, the employment effect is another measure to express the additional economic activity.

What is at issue here is the extent to which hosting the Olympic Games generates employment and how long it is sustained. One of the repeatedly mentioned arguments of Olympic opponents is that the Games only create short-term employment with a low benefit to the population (New Unity Movement, 1997; NN, 1996h). In this section, the benefit of employment through the Olympics is first reviewed from the macroeconomic viewpoint. Using a simplified formula, an attempt is made to quantify the Games-related employment effect. This is followed by an investigation of employment duration and the sectors where employment is created.

From the business-economic viewpoint, the employment of personnel incurs costs for the employer. From the macroeconomic viewpoint, the employment situation must be differentiated between full employment and underemployment. With full employment, all workers are employed because the Olympics create opportunity costs for the amount of their previous wages because they are absent from their former employment and therefore are no longer producing benefit-earning goods. The demand for workers through the Olympic Games leads to a crowding out in other sectors.

This consideration may be interesting with reference to Olympics in developing countries. In some sectors (for example, that of qualified staff), there might be full employment. The Games could cause other sectors to lose personnel incurring costs in the way described above. Lee, however, is of the opinion that 90 per cent of all the work necessary to prepare the Games could be done by untrained personnel (Lee, 1989). But this raises the question of how to define 'untrained'. KPMG Peat Marwick investigated the labour market for Sydney 2000 and discovered that bottlenecks might develop in some professions (for example, physiotherapist) even in industrialized countries (KPMG Peat Marwick, 1993). If such a sector experiences an economic boom, higher labour costs could be the consequence. The concentration of building projects in the Kiel area (Munich 1972) led to bottlenecks in the Schleswig-Holstein labour market, which caused high labour costs. Attempts to evade this by placing orders in other regions of Germany or in Scandinavia failed. The time pressure and the deadline for the completion of the Olympic facilities in Kiel eventually influenced prices in the building industry. In addition, there was a general material price increase in the steel sector (German Bundestag, 1975; Weber, 1994).

In most countries, however, unemployment prevails, which means there is underemployment. According to Braun, all new Games-related jobs are directly or indirectly filled by unemployed people. He assumes that at the end of each job rotation chain an unemployed person will be employed (Braun, 1984). A possible reduction of jobs shall be ignored here. Since unemployed persons are free production factors, they do not cause opportunity costs. Their employment does not lead to benefit losses anywhere else through lower goods production. The employment of unemployed persons even increases the gross national product through the additionally produced goods and, thus, has a positive effect (Braun, 1984; Schlumberger, 1987). The argument that the employing of an unemployed person incurs a benefit because it saves unemployment relief is countered by the fact that the payment of unemployment relief is a mere financial state transfer affecting the welfare criterion not in an allocative but in a distributive manner (Plath, 1973). Underemployment is assumed for the purposes of this study.

With underemployment, the employment effects of the Olympic Games in a city might rashly be judged as being positive if at the end of all job rotations an unemployed person becomes employed. To be precise, the individual advantages and disadvantages of all persons affected by the Olympics income effect must be considered. It must be determined whether somebody already employed before the Games or somebody without work receives the additional income. The positive aspect of additional income must be contrasted with the 'sufferings from work' as a negative aspect. A net prosperity effect is only created if the income or other positive effects exceed the 'suffering from work'. This will be true for persons already employed because they had their jobs before the Olympics and would not have abandoned their old jobs if they had not improved their net prosperity by their new employment. The increased benefit must not always be of a monetary type (Preuss and Kebernik, 2000). Success can also be of great satisfaction with the new job as can higher intrinsic motivation. For unemployed people, this must be viewed differently. Apart from 'suffering from work', they face costs for possible training, must abandon recreational activities, stop work done in the black economy or move location (loss of familiar social environment) (Braun, 1984; Gladitz and Günther, 1995; Hanusch, 1992). Weighing up all these costs, an unemployed person will only face costs to the amount that individual is prepared to pay for a unit of the abandoned good. The following example explains the correlation: unemployed persons are not short of good 'leisure time' whereas their income is rather low. Therefore, it can be assumed that for unemployed people the costs of giving up leisure time are almost zero. In most cases, the benefit, in particular the reduced emotional stress caused by lasting unemployment, will exceed the costs involved in taking up an occupation, especially in times of high unemployment rates. The exact amount of the advantage/disadvantage balance cannot be determined because each person evaluates the advantages/disadvantages of their own individual unemployment differently.

It has become clear that, for the individual, employment through the Olympics may not be a purely positive experience. People will only accept jobs if they can enhance their personal level of benefit. Ultimately, the question remains how far the person can enhance the benefit level in the case of short-term employment. Irrespective of the duration of a job, it has been clearly shown that additional work will finally lead to the employment of an unemployed person or save an employee from becoming unemployed. In addition, those finding a job will improve their prosperity level. This consideration, however, is only true if compared with the 'case without Olympics' because other projects might create more jobs. Here again, a decision is taken according to the Pareto optimum. A socially just distribution of jobs is ignored. Furthermore, a high unemployment rate could lead to an exploitation of workers by neither granting them regulated working conditions nor adequate wages. In Atlanta 1996, unskilled workers are said to have received as little as US$'00 4.83 per hour (Gladitz and Günther, 1995).

10.1 EMPLOYMENT THROUGH THE OLYMPIC GAMES

This section attempts to quantify the amount of work created through the Olympic Games. The unit person-years is used to counterbalance the differences in job duration and number of weekly working hours per employee. To estimate the employment effects related to the Olympic Games, the income resulting from the primary effect is first divided into 'profit' and 'wages and salaries'. Then, it is related to the average income of employed persons. An estimate divided into industrial sectors is not possible because an input/output table, which is necessary to calculate the advance payment interrelation for the regions investigated, is not available.

It is extremely difficult to compare the employment effects of the Games from Munich 1972 onwards due to the fact that the unification of country-specific data leads to several distortions and thus reduces the preciseness of the results. This investigation relies on the original units since the unit of the result (person-years) is not only identical in all countries but does not require inflation adjustment. Secondly, a falsification through differing multiplier values can be excluded because the employment growth caused by the primary effect was calculated exclusively. A comparison with the data on employment growth in other sources shows how differently the employment effect has been estimated or calculated (Maennig, 1997).

It is important to note that the calculations are susceptible to errors. Table 10.1 shows, nevertheless, that the Olympic Games lead to considerable employment effects which would have to be rated even higher if the induced effects and the 'profit', which becomes income-effective in the long run were also included. Then the wage ratio would always have to be rated at 1.0. The induced jobs cannot be calculated because the employment multipliers of the Olympic regions are not known. Therefore I will refrain from calculating the total effect. It is natural that most jobs were created or maintained in the host cities with the strongest economic impact. Even if wage ratio and average wage were not specifically included as units, which influence employment, the basic statement that the Olympics lead to a considerable employment growth in the host city remains valid.

It is difficult to prove these positive effects by statistical data since employment in a city also depends on factors such as the current economic situation and the realisation of other projects. If, however, exclusive consideration of the Olympic Games is disregarded at this point and the Olympic Winter Games which are hosted in much smaller cities are examined, the effects can be proven much more easily because the economic impact to the host city is comparatively larger. For the Lillehammer 1994 Winter Olympics, for example, there are statistical data, which clearly prove the employment effect. The result could not have been falsified by other large projects, which did not exist at the time, or general changes in the economy.

Table 10.1   Jobs through Olympic Games from Munich 1972 to Atlanta 1996

	Primary effect*/ million/ nat. currency/ prices Olympic year (A)	Wage ratio in host country in Olympic year in percent (B)	Average annual wage in host country in Olympic year (C)	Person-years through primary effect (A * B/C)	Jobs (40 years) (A * B/C/40)
Munich 1972	1691	54	39 361	23 199	580
Montreal 1976	1328	57	19 960	37 924	948
Los Angeles 1984	952	60	19 948	28 634	715
Seoul 1988	1 891 875	41	4 053 848	191 341	4784
Barcelona 1992	845 575	46	1 383 166	281 213	7030
Atlanta 1996	2917	60**	20 000**	87 510	2188

Notes: *   Conservative calculation of primary effect.
       **   Estimated by using the data from Los Angeles.

Source: Own calculations; www.cedar.barnard.columbia.edu; Olympic Co-ordination Authority (2002, p. 12).

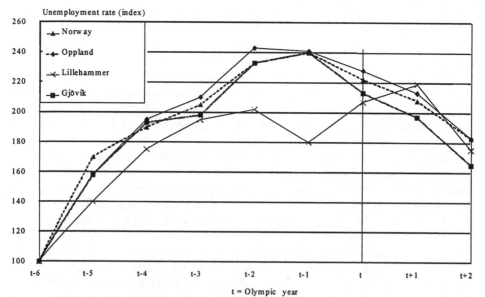

Source: Spilling (1997) based on data in Statistics Norway.

Figure 10.1   Unemployment rate change in Lillehammer 1994 by index

Figure 10.1 shows a temporary unemployment decrease. In the case of Lillehammer (see also Rønningen, 1995) a deviation from the national labour market situation can only be detected two years before the Games. In the long run, employment statistics cannot prove the extent of the positive effect, of new jobs being created by the Games, since the 'case without the Games' is not known. Undoubtedly, the Olympic Games induce additional work. This additional work may:

1. lead to new jobs
2. secure existing jobs
3. increase the stress for employees in existing jobs
4. crowd other work out.

The difficulty of a clear interpretation is apparent upon closer examination. In Case 1, for example, the dismissal of workers in another sector can keep the unemployment rate at the same level as before the Olympics. Case 2 would lead to a higher unemployment rate without the Games. Cases 3 and 4 would not have any effects on the labour market. This correlation is illustrated in the flow chart in Figure 10.2.

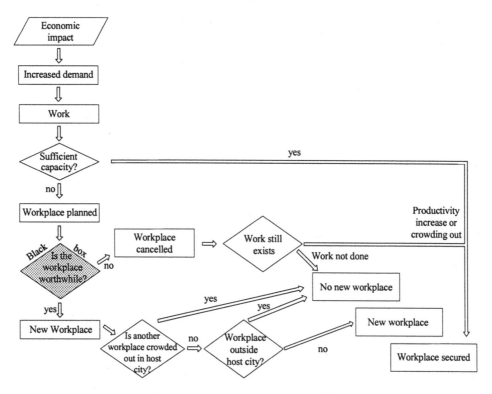

Figure 10.2   Effects of Games-related work on the jobs in a host city

Here, the case in which the work induced by the Olympic Games leads to new jobs in the host city is shown. As in the foregoing section, import (jobs outside the host city), crowding out and redistribution of jobs in the host city decisively influences employment. The core is the 'black box', which is influenced by factors such as the economic situation, future prospects of a business or the readiness of an employer to take risks.

In the following section, the clear employment effect of the Olympic Games is further differentiated according to the duration of the newly created jobs and according to the sectors where additional employment is generated.

10.2   DURATION OF JOBS AND SECTORS OF EMPLOYMENT

The jobs required to host and organize the Olympics are temporary from the start. Their duration directly depends on the schedule for preparing and staging the Olympics. Their number is linked to the varying amount of work in the schedule. Thus, the bid phase (first phase) induces additional work (Rigaud, 1997), which is increased during the preparatory phase (second phase). It is during the Olympics themselves that most of the work must be done, while shortly after the Games the work effort drops sharply (third phase). During these first three phases the jobs are directly linked to the organization of the Olympics. In addition, there is a fourth phase creating jobs, which are induced by the Games-related economic impact. Indirect employment, which is created during phases 1–3 regardless of the OCOG, is not considered. These are jobs such as those in the building industry and constructing agencies. Hence, there are four basic phases altogether with a job distribution as displayed in Figure 10.3.

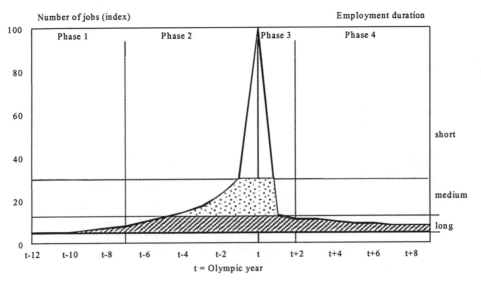

Figure 10.3   Distribution of Games-related work

The average employment duration at the OCOG may be approximately four years. For staff during the Olympic Games, employment might amount to only a few days (NN, s.t.c; s.t.d; Saltzman, 1996). In Los Angeles 1984, for example, 16 250 persons worked only 30 days for the OCOG (ERA, 1984). Seoul 1988 was similar: 300 persons worked 90 days, 700 persons 60 days, 12 100 persons 30 days, 3350 persons 20 days and 33 550 persons 10 days (Brunet, 1993; Lee, 1989; Organisationskomitee München, 1974a).

In sectors, which expand through the Olympic Games such as the building sector and the tourism and leisure industry, lasting jobs are created. Strictly speaking, the jobs are no longer related to the Olympic Games once they are over. If capacities in the sectors mentioned above remained high after the Olympics, the same influences which caused the capacity not to fall after the Games would have led to their expansion regardless of the celebration. In other words, lasting Games-related jobs are simply jobs which have been pulled forward by the Games, or which are directly linked to the Olympic legacy.

For a host city, it is, nevertheless, of special interest to see how the number of jobs will develop in fourth phase. Four cases, which strongly depend on the size of the economic impact, are differentiated here. On the one hand, there is the marked drop in the number of jobs directly after the Olympics because the OCOG reduces its work and completely vanishes after two years. Then all work contracts with the OCOG must be cancelled. After the Games, the OCOG must, for example, write the Official Report, remove the temporary facilities, update the 'Transfer of Knowledge' database, sell its assets and, finally, dissolve itself. On the other hand, the long-term development of the job supply caused by the Games-related economic impact with its income and employment effects must be considered (Figure 10.4).

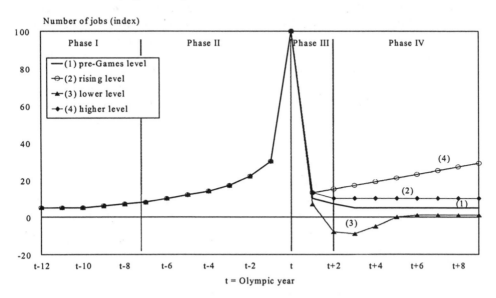

Figure 10.4   Influence of Olympic Games on the long-term job supply

Depending on the way the Olympic facilities have been financed, the building sector, in particular, may even fall below the pre-Olympic level in the post-Olympic period. This is the case if the investments were pulled forward (no effect on the budget) and thereby led to less investment in the subsequent years. Depending on the economic situation, this effect is either enhanced or weakened by the private investment activity.

The following long-term employment effects are possible which will cause the number of jobs to:

(1)   return to the level of before the Games. It is also possible in this scenario that there might have been a further drop without the Olympics. This situation is typical for the tourist industry characterized by periodically recurring events (Getz, 1997). However, this situation is also probable for Olympic Games without large investments in tourism infrastructure or without updating the location factors to attract foreign investments. This had been the case in Los Angeles 1984. Neither lasting jobs related to the new infrastructure nor follow-up investments (maintenance and so on) are induced.

(2)   rise permanently because the reurbanization and improvement of location factors in the city lead to further investment. Planners of Olympics, and analysts most frequently and most preferably, predict this scenario (Getz, 1997). It cannot be definitely stated, however, whether such an effect can be traced back to the Olympic Games.

(3)   remain at a lower level than before the Olympics. This can be caused, for example, by a negative image of the Games or by crowding out during the Olympics and the related demand migration. For example, Olympic tourists who pay higher prices crowd out regular guests who do not return to their former accommodation after the Games (French and Disher, 1997; Atlanta OCOG, 1996). Of course, the level can also fall owing to factors which are independent of the Games.

(4)   remain at a higher level than before the Games. This case is very probable owing to the lasting jobs which are created primarily in the leisure industry and in the tourist sector as a result of the changed image and the improved tourist infrastructure.

Finally, the sectors of additional employment are investigated. Irrespective of the host location, the majority of jobs are generated at short notice during the Games. They are created in the service, trade and security sectors. In sectors in which investments are made, such as in the leisure industry, tourism, transportation and telecommunications, lasting jobs are created. For the Innsbruck 1976 Winter Games, Kirchner stated 'that in almost all communities of the Olympic region, a partly considerable increase in the number of persons employed in the hotel and catering sector and in trade/traffic/services occurred ... A lasting employment effect took place... in the building sector ... which, however ... primarily affected the pre-Olympic period' (Kirchner, 1980).

Table 10.2   Job distribution through Olympic Games by sectors in percent

Sector	Average duration of jobs	Atlanta 1996 Overall effect in percentage	L.A 1984 Primary effect in percentage	Frankfurt 2012 Overall effect in percentage
Service (OCOG)	Short-term	35	35	N/A
Tourism/conventions	Long-/medium-term	18	41	26.0
Trade	Short-term	11	3	1.4
Administration	Medium-/short-term	10	0	N/A
Building sector	Medium-term	4	8	36.0
Security	Short-term	3	0	N/A
Transportation/airport	Long-term	3	0	9.4
Organization (OCOG)	Medium-/short-term	1	0	N/A
Sports venues/leisure time	Long-term	1	0	N/A
Telecommunications	Long-term	1	0	N/A
Others		13	13	27.2

Sources: Based on data by ERA (1984); Humphreys and Plummer (1996); Preuß and Weiss (2003).

The figures in Table 10.2 show the effects of the Olympics on the job market in Atlanta 1996, Los Angeles 1984 and those estimated for the bid city Frankfurt 2012. However, these results only show a tendency. Therefore, there are clear differences in the sectors and between the cities. Another example is Korea, where 35 per cent of employment was distributed to the production sector, 33 per cent to the building sector and 20 per cent to the services sector (Kwag, 1988). The Frankfurt 2012 data stem from a cost–benefit analysis (CBA) using the input-output model in order to calculate the overall effect of potential Games. The latter differences, in particular, are not surprising since the structural conditions and the investments differ strongly from host city to host city.

Investigations tend to neglect the social distribution of jobs. For Barcelona, it was ascertained that in 1989, at the climax of urban restructuring measures, the unemployment rate in the middle stratification of society was only half of that in working-class areas of the city (19.9 per cent). Employment is said to have particularly increased for the age groups between 20 and 40 years of age and for persons with academic or technical qualifications, which contrasts the statement of Lee that the organization of Olympic Games can be based on unskilled workers. Nevertheless, also in Barcelona, unskilled workers benefited from the building sector expansion, although this sector especially employed many employees from other regions or even from overseas (Garcia, 1993).

When summarizing the employment effects of the Olympic Games it becomes obvious that unemployment rates, as for example in Lillehammer and Barcelona, quickly rose to the levels of other comparable cities of the host country after the Olympic Games (NN, s.t.c). It should be kept in mind, that even short-term employment is beneficial. Employed persons would not change their job for a short-term or insecure Games-related job if it did not increase their personal benefit.

Regarding long-term jobs, there is also the opinion that they must not be included in the jobs induced by the Olympic Games. The Olympics only caused an employment relationship which resulted in a long-term job because of a demand, which continued after the Games. It is certainly true that tourism at a higher level after the Games has not just been caused by the Olympics and the newly erected Olympic sports facilities. In Sydney it is said that Australia expected between 1997 and 2004 approximately 150 000 jobs due to increased tourism (TFC, 1998). Concerning sport facilities, for example, the 'Sydney Olympic Park Authority', employ 160 persons (Hofmann, 2001). These factors on their own will attract only a few individuals to visit a host city. Similarly, the greater occupancy of the sports halls which were erected or expanded because of the Games, must be traced back to the demand for leisure time opportunities. However, it was the Olympic Games which gave the impact to change the entire infrastructure of the city and to favour sectors where lasting jobs could be secured or some new jobs were created.

11. The Olympic aftermath: price increases and economic legacy

The fear of host city residents that the Olympic Games may lead to price increases and result in a higher cost of living is well known and well promoted by Olympic opponents. An example, which proves this fear, is a survey of the Innsbruck population on the occasion of bidding for the 2002 Olympic Winter Games: 47 per cent of the respondents (n = 300) thought 'everything would become more expensive' because of the Games (Gantner, 1993). Other examples are the opponents of the Berlin Olympics 2000 bid. There is the great threat that prices will explode in the following years as a result of the effects of the Olympics and incoming capital which will affect rents, real estate prices, hotels, restaurants and the cost of living (interview, Demba, 1993; NN, s.t.c). Finally, opponents of the Cape Town 2004 bid feared: 'Greed for bigger profits will cause the price of materials, skilled labour, consultants' fees, quotations, etc. to rise ... Big supermarket chains ... will increase food prices sky-high. After the Olympics these prices will remain high' (New Unity Movement, 1997; Plessis, 1997).

This chapter will analyse if hosting the Olympics really led to an increased price level in the host cities after 1972. Therefore, the price level must be analysed using various price indices before and after the Olympics. The price indices for the cost of living and, by way of example, for building prices and for rents are used in detail.

In a functioning market economy, prices steadily change as supply changes. The coordination features of the market mechanism are its capacity to almost balance supply and demand in individual marketplaces by adapting to the changed situation. As depicted above, most Olympic Games have only led to a temporary increase in the demand which resulted in higher prices, but not necessarily in price-level changes. There is no doubt that prior to and during the Olympics the individual prices of goods and services for which there is a particularly strong demand will change. It must be investigated whether the prices decrease again after the Games and to what extent the increased prices affect the cost of living for the broad population.

The overall price level depends on the overall demand in relation to the production potential rated at current prices. If the overall demand rises because of the Olympics and exceeds the supply, price increases in the respective production factor are the consequence if perfect competition and high employment rates are assumed. However, the individual benefit is not determined by the market price but, rather, by the benefit offered by the good. Price increases, however, do not change the benefit of a good. As long as the same number of goods is produced and emit the same aggregated benefit then the goods do not have a negative impact on the economy. The simple fact is that a part of the goods is consumed because the Olympic Games are staged and, in turn, results in a short supply of the goods offered on the marketplace therefore making their prices rise. That assumes the goods were not available from stock. In other words, the staging of the Olympic Games increases the overall demand. Apart from Olympic visitors, the goods are only beneficial to those of the citizens of the host city who can still afford the remaining goods. This can be considered a socially unjust reallocation and is referred to as crowding out in the following sections. Theoretically, the price increases can be traced back to three reasons:

1. Owing to the Olympics, demand exceeds supply (price crowding out).
2. Owing to the Olympics, speculation started. In Munich 1972, for example, the rents for apartments in the Olympic village increased by 130 per cent immediately after the Games (NN, 1972a).
3. There is general inflation.

To the citizens of a host city, the reason for price increases is not obvious. Games-related speculations will primarily be limited to real estate (McCay and Plumb, 2001) acquisitions, which are not focused on in this book. Therefore, it must only be distinguished whether a higher price is due to a Games-related increase in demand or to general inflation.

Most of the analyses available ignored price-level changes, which could hardly be included anyway since almost all were a priori analyses. The following was predicted for the Sydney 2000 Olympics:

> The inflation impacts are greater for NSW because the Olympics induced increase in output in this state will, relative to Australia, represent a greater increase over the normal level of economic activity. The greatest price effect will occur during the year of the Olympics, with potentially over one percentage point being added to the NSW inflation rate, and over half a percent being added to the Australian inflation rate. (KPMG Peat Marwick, 1993)

The data used in this chapter are based on the statistical yearbooks of the host countries. This excludes the possibility that data which were falsified for bid reasons might be used. Although it cannot be determined whether the Olympic Games changed the prices in one way or another, it can be clearly assessed in retrospect whether the host city population suffered from negative impacts caused by price level changes.

In the following, the extent of the price-level changes that occurred in a host city is analysed without linking them to the Olympics. If possible, the host city will be compared with other major cities of the host country, or at least to the host region or country itself, in order to prove deviations from the normal price development in the host country. The question as to whether the Olympic Games may have led to price increases is only sensible if prices in the host city actually did increase more than in other comparable cities or regions.

The price development from Munich 1972 to Atlanta 1996 is displayed in Preuss (2000a). Here the brief results are given (see also Table 11.1).

11.1   PRICE CHANGES FOR THE CITIZENS

The price index for the cost of living refers to statistically proven data on private household purchases. The 'basket of goods and services' on which the calculation of the cost of living price index is based contains only a few goods, which experience a stronger demand due to the Olympic Games. Therefore, this index is only partially suitable to evaluate directly the Games-related price changes caused by the Olympics. Nevertheless, this index will be investigated explicitly since it reflects the cost of living in the host city and is indirectly affected by income increases. It is the only way of evaluating the argument that the Olympics cause the prices in host cities to rise.

Table 11.1   Price-level changes due to Olympic Games

Host city	Development of CPI	Development of rent
Munich 1972	Price increase since 1967	Price increase since 1969
Montreal 1976	No price increase compared to other cities and Canada	Price increase since 1971
Los Angeles 1984	No price increase compared to other cities and USA	No price increase compared to other cities and USA
Seoul 1988	No price increase compared to other cities and South Korea	No price increase compared to other cities and South Korea
Barcelona 1992	Price increase since 1991	Price increase in the 1980s
Atlanta 1996	No price increase compared to other cities and USA	N/A

Source: Preuss (1998b, p. 210).

Munich 1972

With regard to the price index development in Munich, it is striking that the index is not only permanently above that of Germany and Berlin but also rose more strongly than in Germany and Berlin between 1967 and 1974 (Federal Statistical Office, 1996; Statistisches Landesamt Berlin, 1996; Statistisches Landesamt München, 1969; 1970; 1971; 1972; 1973; 1974; 1975; 1976). A first explanation is the fact that at the beginning of the 1960s Munich had been a rather unimportant city at the foothills of the Alps. Afterwards, it developed into one of Germany's major cities. As early as in 1971, Munich was the most expensive city in the Federal Republic of Germany (Nahr, 1972; NN, 1972b). The stronger price-level increase can, therefore, also be due to the general growth of the city. Nonetheless, the Olympic Games certainly contributed to this development. The percentage price changes compared to the previous year are, however, more revealing. It becomes clear that the prices in Munich rose more strongly than the national average or that of Berlin only between 1968 and 1973, thereby backing up the assumption that this development was caused by the Olympic Games.

Montreal 1976

It could have been assumed that the immense investments in Montreal 1976 would have led to price increases in the city. However, the statistical data reveal another situation (Minister of Industry, Trade and Commerce, 1976–77, 1980–81, 1985).

Neither price index nor changes compared to the previous year in percentages show a Games-related increase in the cost of living for the population of Montreal. Compared to the figures of other Canadian cities, a Games-related price increase can even be excluded. Furthermore, during the Olympic year, Montreal even had the lowest price increase of all the cities compared.

Los Angeles 1984

The situation is similar for Los Angeles 1984 (Census, 1981; 1983; 1985; 1987; 1989; 1990). It was to be expected that Los Angeles did not experience deviating price changes. In view of the size of the city and the relatively low Games-related investments the Games-related demand was not large enough to cause permanent short supply leading to price increases.

Seoul 1988

The Games in Seoul 1988 also do not show any relevant deviations in the cost of living when compared to other major Korean cities (Federal Statistical Office, 1985; 1987; 1992; 1995; NN, 1988e). Unfortunately, data could only be ascertained until the Olympic year. However, a stronger increase in the cost of living after the Olympics is not to be expected if it was no higher than in other Korean cities even in the Olympic year. The increase in the cost of living during the Olympic year was said to have been caused by an increased solvency due to the surplus in the balance of payments (Kwag, 1988; NN, 1988c). As with Los Angeles 1984, the annual price increase steadily decreases in the period prior to the Games. Therefore, there must have been other influences on the cost of living, which were stronger than the Games-related demand increase. The residents of a host city do not have this background knowledge but rather simply notice a permanent increase in the cost of living. This fact explains the outcome of a survey in 1991, in which only 11.1 per cent of the residents of the Seoul suburb, Chamsil, did not blame the Olympics for the post-Olympic price increase. Prime Minister Rha, however, mentioned that the role of the Olympic Games for the Korean economy would be overrated (Jeong, 1997; NN, 1988d).

Barcelona 1992

In Barcelona 1992, there were massive Games-related investments, which led to a well-publicized increase in jobs and income. The resulting additional demand in the relatively small host city could have led to short supply and, consequently, to price increases.

Owing to the income effects, the cost of living sector could also have been affected. For Barcelona 1992, an increase in the cost of living could therefore have been expected with the highest degree of probability since Munich 1972.

In fact, though, the data show that the price index in Barcelona compared with Catalonia and Spain was not only constantly higher, but also mostly rose more sharply (Brunet, 1993; Ministerio de Economía y Hacienda, 1988, 1992, 1996;). Unfortunately, no data for comparable Spanish cities are available. Following the observations made in the past it can be assumed that the curve for the entire country does not deviate greatly from that of big cities. It can be shown that the years 1991 and 1992 were decisive, when the price changes compared with the previous year were clearly above national average. During this period, the cost of living in Barcelona rose more than in the surrounding areas.

Atlanta 1996

As in Los Angeles, it can be assumed that there was no Games-related increase in the cost of living due to the Atlanta Games 1996. The data show an even lower price index curve for Atlanta than in many other US cities (Census, 1992; 1996). For the changes compared with the previous year, there is a sharp turn in 1993, which is relatively stronger than in other cities in the comparison. This turn may, but not necessarily, have been caused by the Olympics since it is 1993 and therefore a little bit early.

Sydney 2000

In Sydney the cost of living exploded during the Olympic year. However, the same can be seen in other metropolises throughout Australian (Figure 11.1). Therefore, it was probably not the Olympic impact that increased the prices. However, the Australian economy is not so strong and therefore the Olympic impact could have affected the whole country for a short period. Finally, during the years after the Olympics the price increase returned all over Australia to its previous level (Figure 11.2). These facts clearly prove that, basically, the Olympic Games do not lead to a lasting increase in the cost of living. However, relatively small host cities which invest a lot may suffer slight price index increases due to greater demand through new infrastructure.

11.2   OTHER PRICE CHANGES AFFECTING THE CITIZENS

First, the goods with a generally higher probability of Games-related price increases must be determined. For this, a distinction is made between trade goods and non-trade goods. Trade goods are not a problem to import and, theoretically, their supply is unlimited. There are only small price increases to be expected when the local capacities are exploited. Trade goods include many products affecting the cost of living price index.

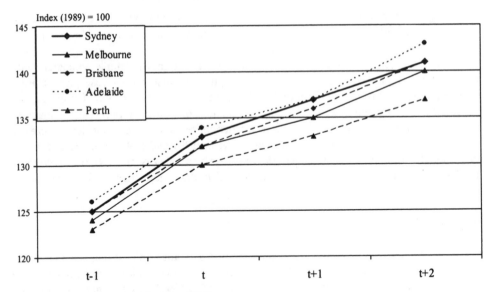

Source: Australian Bureau of Statistics (2004).

Figure 11.1   Price index for cost of living from 1999 to 2002 in Australian cities

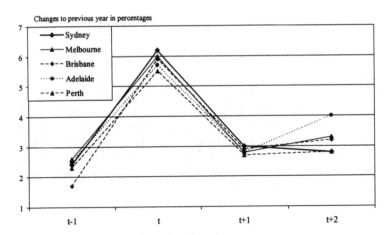

Source: Australian Bureau of Statistics (2004).

Figure 11.2   Price changes for cost of living in Australian cities compared with previous year

Non-trade goods can only be produced in the host city and their supply is limited. They include transportation services, accommodation, real estate and opportunities for recreational and leisure activities. The costs for transportation, accommodation and leisure activities are included in the price index for the cost of living.

A rising building price index in the pre-Olympic period has a considerable impact on the costs of the Games. Investments in Olympic venues do not depend on prices because the Games cannot be postponed. Here, price does not regulate demand. The prices charged must be paid and the costs for the Olympics rise. In Munich, there was a building price increase totalling 49 per cent between 1968 and 1972, which resulted in increased costs for Games-related investments. 'If the preliminary final costs of the individual building objects are compared to the final costs as of 30th September 1974, it becomes obvious that the cost increases are within the index figures with the exception of only a few objects' (Weber, 1994).

According to Brunet (1993), the costs in the building sector rose by as much as 52 per cent in Catalonia and by 62 per cent in the City of Barcelona between 1985 and 1990 for the Barcelona 1992 Olympics. However, all budget changes for these Olympics are said to have been caused by inflation. Frequently, these price increases for investments are attributed to miscalculations of the bid committee or the planners. Some of the price deviations, however, must be traced back to unexpected inflation. Therefore, a bid committee should include inflation in its forecasts by means of adequate discounting.

In general, for most of the host cities investigated 'the quantum of construction associated with the Olympics ... is relatively small in proportion to total construction activity, particularly over the relevant period for construction activity' (KPMG Peat Marwick, 1993). The possibility that the Olympics may lead to a rise in the building price index cannot be denied. Its extent always depends on the economic situation and other projects, which affect the same sector at the same time.

Another point of criticism of the Olympic Games is the alleged rent increases in the host city. First, a link will be established between the development of the rents and the Olympics: only under the assumption that a city used the funds of social housing schemes to erect the Olympic village and that less apartments were created than would have been possible through alternative housing projects costing the same amount of money, could rent increases be the consequence under the condition that an already existing lack of apartments would be aggravated. Consequently, a basic prerequisite for rent increases is that demand for housing exceeds supply. Olympics can indirectly create a lack of housing facilities if the increased attractiveness of the city causes people to move to a host city.

The rent price indices of Munich and Montreal compared with the respective national indices will be reviewed initially. Since 1969, rents in Munich have increased more sharply than the national average. As mentioned for the cost of living, this could have been induced by the increasing significance of Munich as a metropolis. In Montreal, however, rents fell below the national average. Price changes can be assessed most precisely by comparing them to other major cities of the respective host country.

In Seoul, there was a great lack of housing in the period before the Games and the city population grew quickly. Additionally, the selling of all apartments in the Olympic village prior to the Games reflects a strong demand for housing facilities. The assumption that funds of social housing schemes were misused for constructing the Olympic village could be true in this case. Among all host cities of the last 25 years, Seoul was the one where rent price increases were most likely to be expected.

The data analysis shows, however, that there was no striking deviation of the rents in Seoul compared with other Korean cities (Federal Statistical Office, 1985; 1987; 1992; 1995; NN, 1988c). Nevertheless, they claimed in Korea prior to the Games that speculations with rents in the pre-Olympic period were very popular and that an improvement was expected for the post-Olympic period (NN, 1988d). For this reason, speculations or price decreases must refer to individual cases. Considering the fact that the Korean economy is concentrated in the capital of Seoul and that 25 per cent of the Korean population live in the greater Seoul area, an even higher index curve could have been justified. The data show, on the other hand, a continuous decline in the level of rent increases in the pre-Olympic years (Lee, 1988c). Irrespective of the rents, 82 per cent of the persons interviewed in a survey in Seoul thought that the Games raised the costs for apartments in the long run (Jeong, 1997).

Due to a decreased number of subsidized apartments, Barcelona was said to have suffered a considerable rent increase in the 1980s, which Maennig (1997) did not attribute to the Olympics.

However, a study made for Sydney 2000 stated: 'The experience of previous host cities for the Games indicates that the Olympic Games have usually contributed significantly to the worsening of housing affordability and access for low-income people' (Cox et al., 1994). It should not be forgotten that host cities varied greatly in terms of pre-existing social and economic structures, such as housing markets, tenure profiles and so on.

11.3   INFLUENCE OF THE IOC ON PRICE LEVELS

The highest – albeit short-term – price changes are to be expected in the case of goods in demand directly as a result of the Olympic Games. This includes prices for accommodation in the host city as well as prices for tickets and merchandise articles. In these sectors, the IOC tries to prevent exaggerated prices having a negative impact on the Olympics as a whole. If tourists/spectators are dissatisfied or even stay away, it directly affects the attractiveness of the host city and, consequently, that of the Olympics, which the media deliver to the entire world. As early as in Munich 1972, the OCOG agreed upon fixed prices with major hotels without being asked to do so by the IOC (interview, Pound, 1998; interview, Tröger, 1998).

The OCOG has the decision on ticket prices, while the IOC has a final approval (interview, Tröger, 1998). However, as shown before, the OCOG strives for an optimum between profit and 'social justice' regarding the ticket prices. Nowadays, the IOC tries to influence all other prices in the host city, especially the hotel prices, as early as during the bid phase by demanding general price guarantees from the competent authorities: 'Provide a statement from the competent authorities concerning general price control before and during the Olympic Games, with particular reference to the hotel rates and related service and for anyone attending the Games, including non-accredited spectators' (IOC, 1995a).

In the case of Beijing 2008 the Host City Contract (IOC, 2001e, III, para. 30) states: 'the highest prices charged for hotel rooms, conference rooms and related service for accredited persons attending the Games, shall not exceed the lowest average convention price thereof for the previous four years adjusted only for such inflation'. The Central and Beijing Municipal Governments have pledged that consumer prices and hotel rates in and around Beijing will be effectively managed to ensure that prices are fair and reasonable during the Games period. A guarantee to achieve this level of price control has been jointly signed by the Chairman of the State Development and Planning Commission of China and the Director of the price bureau (Bidding Committee Beijing 2008, 2001).

Hotel price guarantees are extremely difficult to enforce by legal action if they are not adhered to later. The IOC simply wants to avoid a negative image for the city and thus the Olympic Movement (interview, Pound, 1998; interview, Tröger, 1998;). However, there is quite a lot speculation in a host city, due to the fact that accommodation is nearly 100 per cent booked up during the Games. However, if the hotel sector in a host city agrees not to increase prices over the inflation rate, there are travel agencies and so on that book large hotel contingencies in order to sell them at very high prices during Games time.

The considerable economic impact from hosting the Olympic Games certainly leads to price increases in some sectors owing to the increased demand and speculation. It was observed in Sydney and in Athens that there is a shortage of accommodation at the lower end of the price range. During the Games one can expect possible property speculation as well as escalation of rents for private rental accommodation, including caravan parks, backpackers' hostels, motels or bed and breakfast, to name a few (Cox et al., 1994). The IOC increasingly controls particularly price-sensitive sectors by demanding, for example, a general price control. For the cost of living and rent sectors, it was proven that the Olympic Games generally do not lead to price level increases. Consequently, there are no economic or social disadvantages that the citizens of host cities must suffer from.

For the host country the conclusion can be drawn that generally it will not experience Games-related price changes at a national level.

11.4   THE ECONOMIC LEGACY OF OLYMPIC GAMES

The Olympic Games are in many ways the largest peacetime event in the world. Such an event, watched by most of humankind has to be financed. It is not the intention of this book to create the illusion that cities only bid for Olympic Games to gain economic benefits and for economic legacy. It is because finances from this gigantic event must be secured and be well planned.

For Olympic cities, the investments necessary to stage the Olympic Games are higher than their financial surplus driven from the staging of the Games. From an economic and urban development perspective it only makes sense to bid for Olympic Games if the long-term city development plans are in line with those of the needed Olympic structure.

However, today, Olympic Games have reached such a magnitude that the infrastructures required for staging the Games are built larger than the post-Olympic demand requires. IOC President J. Rogge has recognized this fact and recently began activities to reduce the size of the Games.

If such is the case, one must question whether these costs incurred by an Olympic city are the 'economic legacy' of the Games. I suggest that the answer to this question is 'no' because this is a one-dimensional perspective. This last part of the book will provide an overview of the complex 'economic legacies' including negative economic legacy for cities hosting the Games. However, there is little research into economic legacies. In particular there is little written about:

- the effects of accelerated city development which results in location advantages in an ever more global world
- the increased advertising and marketing value of the Olympic emblems and symbol, which increase potential revenues for an OCOG
- the economic motivation for cities to bid for Olympic Games
- the improvement of location-factors that attract foreign investments.

While the first point has been mentioned earlier, the following section will examine the increased advertising and marketing value of the Olympic symbol, the economic motivation for cities to bid and the improvement of location factors to attract foreign investments.

11.4.1   Overview of Economic Legacies

The economic legacy includes all economic effects that are left following the Games that would otherwise not have occurred without the Games. The transitory benefits have to be distinguished from the permanent benefits. The most famous transitory benefit is the 'economic impact' that occurs from investments in infrastructure and tourist expenditure during the Olympic Games. This transitory economic impact was mentioned before and will not be considered in this chapter.

The economic legacy, other than the fear of potential deficits, and the economic impact have not been well covered in Olympic literature. Even Cashman (1999b, pp. 183–94), who gave a very detailed overview of Olympic legacies, did not exclusively touch economic legacy. Before going into details, Figure 11.3 illustrates the economic legacy of Olympic Games from a superordinated level without claiming to be complete.

The direct effects of the Games are the financial surplus, the structural improvements and possibly a new image.

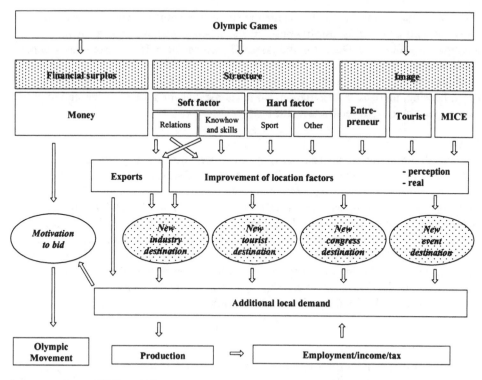

Source: Preuss (2003a, p. 244)

Figure 11.3   Overview of the economic legacies of Olympic Games

Financial surplus of the OCOG

The surplus of the OCOG has to be distinguished from the other two effects discussed below. The share of the surplus is fixed in the Host City Contract. In Athens 2004 and Beijing 2008 any surplus resulting from the celebration of the Games will be divided between the NOC (20 per cent), the IOC (20 per cent) and for the general benefit of sport in the host country (60 per cent) (IOC, 1997d, para. 42; 2001e, para. 43).

Structure

The structure can be divided into soft and hard factors. Soft factors are gained expertise and new economic and trade relations. For example, Seoul established trade relations with the eastern block through the 1988 Olympics (Kim et al., 1989; Kramar, 1994; McBeth, 1988d). Another example is Sydney 2000 where one year after the Games the New South Wales Government had conducted seven trade missions to California, India, Singapore, Malaysia, the United Arabic Emirates, New Zealand, China and Japan. Since the Games the 'Department of State and Regional Development' has worked with NSW business assisting them to gain almost US$·₀₀ 1.53 billion (PricewaterhouseCoopers, 2002, p. 66).

This huge figure was reached by marketing the newly gained expertise, particularly in sport concepts and facility construction. This knowledge was exported to Beijing for the Olympics in 2008 and Doha for the Asian Games in 2006 (PricewaterhouseCoopers, 2002, pp. 68–70).

However, depending on the size of the city, hard factors such as infrastructure for sport, housing, tourism, transportation and telecommunication are built through Olympic Games preparation (Meyer-Künzel, 2001).

Image
The overall perception of the host city is the third direct effect of Olympic Games. Ritchie and Smith (1991) have measured the image effects of Olympic Games for the first time. The new image comes from potential entrepreneurs, tourists and MICE-tourists (Meetings, Incentives, Congresses, and Exhibitions) (Chalip, 2000a). The fourth group, 'world population' comprises all three groups. It is explicitly named here because the Olympic Games create memories and associations for all people in the world. In that way the Olympic symbol gets 'loaded' every two years with new emotions and images. This 'loading' increases the interest of sponsors and television networks to pay greater sums for the rights to the Games. Both are very important for the OCOG to finance the Games and decrease the risk of ending with a financial deficit.

Structural changes and image improvement give the Olympic city a new appearance. These lead to location advantages and create 'new destinations' (circles in Figure 11.3). However, they are not directly recognizable as economic legacies and are difficult to measure. The new attractiveness as a destination for tourists, MICE, event organizers and industry ultimately create additional income, jobs and taxes in the Olympic city. The lower part of Figure 11.3 shows the Keynesian model of consumption and income circle that is not visibly linked to the Olympic Games. Thus, this effect is often not recognized by Olympic opponents.

Here it should be clearly mentioned that the direct effects of the Olympic Games could also leave a negative economic legacy. The OCOG could wind up with a financial deficit that could have long-term negative consequences for a city. The Games of Montreal were such a case. Because of a 'written guarantee that the federal government would not be called upon to absorb the deficit nor to assume interim financing for organization' (Montreal OCOG, 1976) the OCOG and Montreal alone had to completely finance the Games.

In addition, the infrastructure can create a negative economic legacy. For example, sports facilities especially built for the Olympics may cause long-term costs for maintenance and renovation that might not be covered through post-Games revenues generated by the facilities. For example, the velodromes in both Munich and Montreal are no longer used for their original purposes due to a lack of demand for such facilities (Cashman, 1999b, p. 186). The Olympic Stadium in Sydney created a deficit of US$·₀₀

2.2 million in half a year. In addition, the general infrastructure can also create costs for the city in a case where the demand is lower than the supply.

Third, Olympic Games can damage the image of a city. Although this has never happened in Olympic history, it is realistic to believe that such could be the case in some areas. Problems in transportation and information technology have led the media to report negatively about the city of Atlanta. Internally one can also notice a negative economic legacy. Olympic-related development left a legacy of ill will in Atlanta neighbourhoods, such as Summerhill, that bore the brunt of lost housing and dislocation (Newman, H.K. 1999; Rutheiser, 1996). In general it is also obvious that the lack of security and bad media reports can spoil a city as a budding tourist destination.

11.4.2   The Importance of Organizationally 'Successful' Games and a 'Financial Surplus' for the Future of the Olympic Games

This section will examine two aspects that are not visibly linked to Olympic legacy and, as such, are often overlooked. One is the psychological effect of a financial surplus of an OCOG in order to motivate as many cities as possible to bid for the Games. The second is the increase in the value of the Olympic symbol resulting from operationally 'successful' Games. That increases the interest of sponsors and television networks to buy the rights of upcoming Games. Both economic legacies do not overtly benefit the Olympic city that created the legacy, but rather they benefit the Olympic Movement in general and the next Games. The legacy of Atlanta 1996 and Sydney 2000, for example, motivated the sponsors to spend even more money for the Games in Athens 2004 and Beijing 2008.

11.4.2.1   The importance of a 'financial surplus'

It may be surprising that Figure 11.3 includes 'Financial surplus' when it was said at the beginning that all transitory benefits were excluded from this chapter. Despite the fact that the financial surplus decreases after a few years to finally totally disappear, it can be shown that it is a very important legacy that secures the continuation of the Olympic Games.

The strong financial liabilities confronting the public after the Olympic Games of Munich 1972 and Montreal 1976 did not stem from high operational costs but, rather, from high investments in sport and traffic infrastructure. After the financial experience of Montreal, cities were reluctant to bid for the 1984 Games because the costs were no longer considered bearable. At the election of the host city for 1984 on 1 July 1978, there were no candidates except for Los Angeles, which had failed in its bid for the Games of 1976 and 1980. The deficit of Montreal's Games encouraged the citizens of Los Angeles to vote against public financial support of the Olympics (IOC, 1978b). A network of positive conditions (Figure 11.4) enabled Los Angeles to finish 1984 with a profit.

The removal of the word 'amateur' from the Olympic Charter during Lord Killanin's IOC presidency was followed by opening the Games to professional athletes in almost every sport in 1981. That contributed greatly to the dramatic increase in sponsorship and television revenues for the Olympic Movement. The development of a worldwide Olympic sponsorship programme combined with the pressure to finance the Los Angeles Games without public dollars, triggered the true beginning of commercialization.

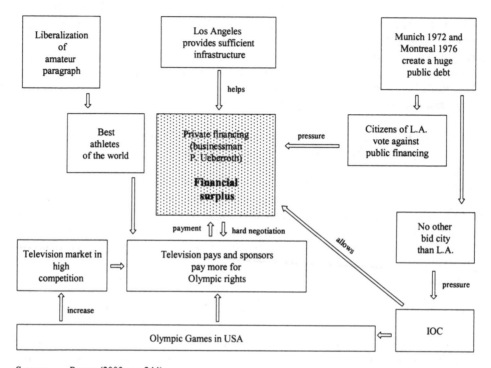

Source: Preuss (2003a, p. 244).

Figure 11.4   Condition that created the 'financial surplus' from Los Angeles 1984

The fact that the Games were staged in the USA strengthened Ueberroth's negotiating position with sponsors and television networks. Both were in highly competitive situations and knew the value of exclusive sponsorship/television rights. The absence of other bidders and the lack of public financial support enabled, and indeed forced, the OCOG to impose conditions that the IOC would not otherwise have agreed (Hill, 1992, p. 159; Reich, 1986, p. 24; Ueberroth et al., 1985, p. 53). After long negotiations, stipulations in the Olympic Charter were eventually declared void, thereby allowing the OCOG and USOC to decline a number of financial obligations associated with the Games, and furthermore, exclude the City of Los Angeles from all financial responsibilities (IOC, 1978b; 1979b). These Games were without an organizational link to the city and the first to be financed from purely private sources. Even general funds were paid by a special ticket and hotel tax (Adranovich et al., 2001, p. 119). Luckily the infrastructure of the city enabled it to avoid huge investments in transportation and sport facilities. This allowed the OCOG to end with an official surplus (Taylor and Gratton,

1988, p. 34). The Games of Los Angeles marked the transition from Games that relied overwhelmingly on public money to Games that were now increasingly dependent on private financing.

The prospect of high revenues from both sponsorship and television rights attracted the interest of many cities to host the Olympics. This fundamental change secured the financial independence of the Olympic Movement and contributed to the end of the political and financial crises of the 1970s and 1980s described in detail by Hoberman (1986).

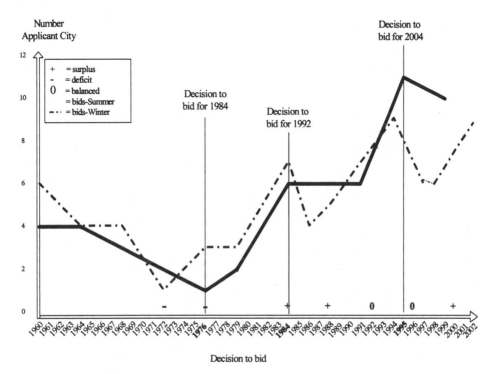

Sources: German Bundestag (1975, p. 5); IOC (1997e); Kim (1990, p. 285); Montreal OCOG (1976, p. 58); Reich (1986, p. 87); Scherer (1995, p. 375); Schollmeier (2001, p. 27).

Figure 11.5   Number of applicant cities two years before the election

Plus and minus in Figure 11.5 indicate how the respective OCOGs officially ended financially. The signs show the final balance, resulting in an increase in the number of cities that bid after 1984. The financial surplus was not the only reason for an increase in applicant cities. A further rise in the number of bids was evident after 1992. This was owing to the fact that the Games of Seoul 1988 and Barcelona 1992 demonstrated that a city could significantly improve its infrastructure by hosting the Games. Sydney 2000 improved its image, which is the third benefit from hosting the Games. The hypothesis can, therefore, be put forward that the prospect of a financial surplus is one key criterion that motivates a city to bid for the Olympic Games.

The transitory benefit of a few million US dollars appears, in the long-term, a vulnerable economic legacy for the Olympic Movement. Many bid cities bring another advantage that the IOC can select the city that is best for the Olympic Movement. Additionally, the increased competition between cities to win the Games forces them to accept the Olympic Charter and to offer benefits for sport and the athletes such as free accommodation or air transportation (Preuss, 2002e).

11.4.2.2   The importance of organizing 'successful' Games

In this section, empirical research is used to demonstrate, how decision-makers of large companies perceived the Olympic Winter Games of Salt Lake 2002. This group of decision-makers is of special interest, because it contains potential sponsors for the next Games.

Executive board members of the 500 largest German companies were contacted to take part in this study. The study was conducted in two waves, before and after the Olympic Winter Games of Salt Lake 2002. The instrument used for collecting the data was a questionnaire. The return rate for the companies interviewed prior to the Games was n = 87 (17.4 per cent). These 87, plus five further respondents, were questioned again three months after the Games. The return rate for the post-study was n = 37 (40.2 per cent). Sixteen persons and 31 companies participated in both examinations. In total 107 different entrepreneurs from 92 businesses were interviewed. The statistical analysis from the first wave showed no significant differences in comparison to the total (500 businesses). The variables used for this 'turnover' and 'employees' ('goodness of fit': turnover: $Chi^2 = 0.186$; df = 4; p > 0,05/employees: $Chi^2 = 0.97$; df = 3; p > 0,05), indicate that the returned questionnaires represent an good sample. The general attitude towards sponsoring and Olympic Games is shown in Table 11.2.

Table 11.2   General opinion of German decision-makers about Olympic Games

	1 Agree	2 Disagree	N	Mean	Standard deviation
The Olympic Games could not be staged without sponsors.	▨		100	1.1	0.31
The Olympic Games are 'over commercialized'.	▨		96	1.28	0.45

The majority of the board members believed that Olympic Games could not be organized without sponsors. This was found to be true if the size of the Olympic Games was to be kept the same in the future. In fact, local and international sponsorship programmes generated approximately 34 per cent of total revenue of Sydney 2000 (IOC, 2001a, pp. 26–7). A majority of decision-makers interviewed also agreed that the Olympic Games were too commercialized. However, it was interesting to note that 14 per cent of them would like to support possible Olympics in Germany 2012 and another 40 per cent were undecided. German business people were therefore critical of the development of the Games, but recognized the commercial value of being associated with the Games.

When examining the post-Games interviews, the attitudes shown in Table 11.3 emerged about the Olympic Games and Salt Lake.

Table 11.3   Opinion of decision-makers after Salt Lake 2002

	1 Totally agree	2 Agree	3 Neutral	4 Disagree	5 Totally disagree	
Olympic Games						
The Olympic Games could not be staged without sponsors.	▨					n=37 x̄=1.5 s=0.65
The Olympic Games leave an economic legacy.			▨			n=37 x̄=2.6 s=0.72
As sponsor of the Olympic Games, one can expect a positive image-effect.		▨				n=37 x̄=2.2 s=0.84
The Olympic Games are 'over commercialized'.			▨			n=37 x̄=2.4 s=0.92
Salt Lake 2002						
After the Games in Salt Lake City the Mormons have become more simpatico to me.			▨			n=37 x̄=3.1 s=0.72
The Games in Salt Lake City showed me to not take Utah in consideration if we should settle in the USA.				▨		n=37 x̄=3.5 s=0.99
After the Games, Salt Lake City appears to me more interesting as a business location.				▨		n=36 x̄=3.1 s=0.62

The results suggest that the general attitude towards the Olympic Games is good. This perception was built up over several Olympic Games. In that way, the impressions of Salt Lake and of other Games were believed to be economic legacies that benefit future hosts, for example, when companies decide to begin sponsorship. For Salt Lake itself no positive economic legacy was created from a German decision-maker's point of view. The Mormons did not become more simpatico and Salt Lake did not improve as a business location.

For the direct question as to whether 'Olympic Games leave an economic legacy' a slightly positive answer was given. Indirectly this question was checked by asking for the perception of the Salt Lake location factors before and after the Games 2002. No significant difference by mean value comparison (T-test) could be found. The entrepreneurs therefore seem to have an established view of Salt Lake as a business location that did not change through the Olympic Games. However, this study was limited to Germany and, as such, the results are not meant to be valid on an international scale.

11.4.3   The Attraction of Foreign Investments

Another, previously mentioned, significant economic legacy is the attraction of new investments. Therefore it just should briefly be mentioned here.

Olympic Games cause an increased benefit to small businesses such as hotels, restaurants, bars or retail. For example, the Sydney Games provided a vast array of opportunities for small and regional business. Together, these initiatives contributed to NSW business over US$$_{,00}$ 767 million in contracts for the Games (PricewaterhouseCoopers, 2002, p. 53). From experience the number of small businesses also increased as a consequence of post-Olympic tourism and gentrification. This change is similar to the 'consumption-based economic development' described by Adranovich et al. (2001, pp. 115–16). They examined it for American cities in connection with Olympic Games. This development includes the upgrading of convention centres, sports facilities, museums, shopping malls, entertainment and gambling complexes alongside new office towers and redeveloped waterfronts.

Politicians and private industry in Sydney undertook extensive efforts to attract foreign investments to Australia. To secure new investment in the state, the NSW Government participated in 'investment 2000' which targeted potential investors through information and coordinated visits. Leading up to the Games, several projects were conducted. For example, 269 companies participated on a 'Business Visitor's Program'. Survey data indicate that 90 per cent of these participants are likely to invest in Australia (PricewaterhouseCoopers, 2002, p. 57). In the period following the Games a bundle of activities was developed. The promotion of Australia as a sophisticated, competitive and attractive business location was one such activity. This resulted in having over 3000 major organizations receive information aimed at maintaining interest in NSW (PricewaterhouseCoopers, 2002, p. 71). The NSW Government has successfully leveraged its Games-related initiatives attracting 19 new investments that brought US$$_{,00}$ 85.7 million to the state and created 1219 jobs (PricewaterhouseCoopers, 2002, p. 71).

12. Reflections: the Olympics today and the challenge for future hosts

The OCOG is linked directly to the Olympic Movement for not more than seven years. The Olympic Games themselves – the climax in the link between the host city and the OCOG to the Olympic Movement – amount to less than 1 per cent of the OCOG life cycle. Today's OCOGs mainly dwell on preparing the Olympics and raising the necessary means. This, however, is not the only reason why the Olympic Games are no longer merely of sporting interest but also of economic interest. The flows of revenues and costs in the billions, which the OCOG handles during that short period of time, simply must have an impact on the income and employment situation of the host city, its region and the host country.

In absolute terms the OCOGs have been able to continuously increase their revenues from marketing and selling television rights during the previous Olympic Games. In relative terms, however, these financing sources have remained almost stable since Los Angeles 1984 despite the general opinion that the sales of television rights and sponsoring are playing an increasingly dominant role.

When investments are eliminated from the final balance sheets of the OCOGs and operational expenditures are set against OCOG revenues, it can be stated that all the OCOGs under review in this book succeeded in making a financial profit. Indeed, the organizer of the Los Angeles 1984 Olympics, Ueberroth, 'had calculated that each organiser of the Olympic Games who was not forced to erect costly facilities could achieve a surplus' (Koar, 1993).

Although not completely recalculated, the balances of the respective Games shown in Figure 12.1 demonstrate that an OCOG can host the Olympics using only the means received because of the fact that the Games were awarded to the city. According to the decision model explained above for differentiating between Games-related and non-Games-related costs for facilities used during the Olympics, an OCOG should only have to cover the costs for temporary facilities, overlay and rent. In case the expected 'surplus', which during the period under review amounted to approximately US$$_{00}$ 300 million on average, does not suffice to cover these costs, another investigation must be carried out to determine whether a city is at all suited to be the Olympic host. From a purely business-economic point of view, this 'surplus' should be enough to allow for the staging of the Games in many large cities.

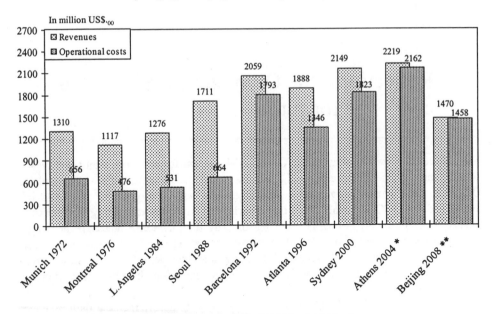

Notes: * Estimated December 2003.
              ** Conservatively estimated by Bidding Committee Beijing 2008 (2001).

Sources: Bidding Committee Beijing 2008 (2001); Athens OCOG (2003b); Olympic Co-ordination Authority
(2002); Preuss (2000a).

Figure 12.1   *Revenues and operational costs of the OCOGs from Munich 1972 to
                Beijing 2008*

Nonetheless, this fact does not seem to have been recognized for a long time, by either
the decision-makers or the general public of potential bid cities. The IOC also failed to
recognize this fact, especially when the numbers of bid cities drastically dropped in the
1970s. The media, and even official reports of OCOGs and the IOC, published different
final balances for the Olympics. Figure 12.2 also reveals the degree to which the inclusion
of investments in the final balances of the OCOGs, in turn, influenced the final result. The
calculated surplus or deficit for the Olympic Games, however, is one of the key criteria
when deciding whether to bid for the Games. At the end of the 1970s, it seemed as if the
Olympics could financially ruin a city. However, this attitude radically changed when Los
Angeles 1984 officially declared a surplus.

Finally, the IOC's growing control over the OCOG revenue sources is discussed. What
is at issue has more to do with the objectives the IOC pursues in its quest to legitimately
gain control rather than the actual issue of legitimization itself. The objectives are
grouped into the basic functional conditions of action systems according to Parsons
(1976).

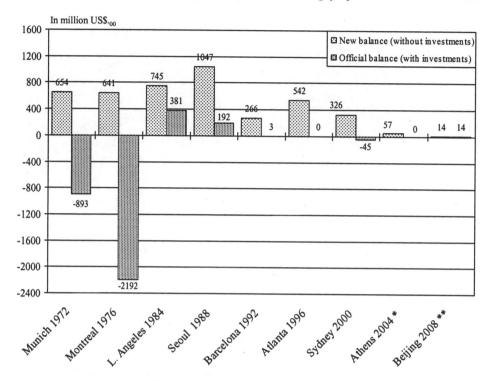

Sources: Bidding Committee Beijing 2008 (2001, p. 73); Athens OCOG (2003b, p 22); Olympic Co-ordination Authority (2002, p. 25); Preuss (2000a).

Figure 12.2   Surplus and deficit of the Olympic Games according to official reports and own calculations

With regards to the topic of pattern maintenance, the control of the financing sources brings power and financial security, thus ensuring the existence of the IOC. The stability of the institutionalized patterns of the NOCs and IFs is maintained through financial and political support, which, in turn, ensures the structure of the entire system of the Olympic Movement. In addition, the IOC offers future bid cities approximately 50 per cent of their required budget for staging the Games, thus reducing the obstacles for submitting a bid – at least from a financial point of view. This IOC strategy also ensures the existence of the Olympic Movement due to the fact that 'subsequent operations' Bette (1993), in the form of Olympic Games, take place and a lack of bid cities will never again endanger the staging of the Games.

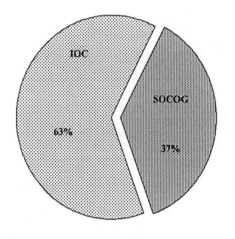

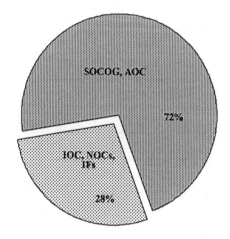

Source: IOC (2001b).   *Source:* IOC (2001b).

Figure 12.3   *Revenue generation 1997–2000,*   *Figure 12.4*   *Revenue distribution*
                 Sydney and the Olympic   *1997–2000, related to*
                 Movement   *Sydney*

In contrast to maintaining the pattern, the topic of goal attainment is mainly linked to specific situations. The IOC tries to reduce the discrepancies between the requirements of the NOCs, OCOG and IFs and the conditions of the quickly changing economy. However, this situation is very complex and contains numerous conflicts between the respective individual goals of the IOC, OCOG, NOCs and IFs. The IOC decides on both the priority and the focus of the objectives. In this way, the IOC can react flexibly to a changing environment such as those created by private television networks or unwanted sponsors. The IOC's objectives are mainly oriented towards fostering its relationship with the OCOG, NOCs and IFs. It does not necessarily involve a link to the values of society but, rather, to the motivation to make contributions, which are essential to ensuring the continued existence of the Olympic Movement. This explains the IOC's decisions – decisions that, although they may be regarded by the public as 'over-commercialization' and abuses of power, are decisions that need to be made in order to ensure the successful staging of the Games. Nonetheless, the IOC must develop a certain sensitivity to the perceptions of the population since it is only through universal acceptance of the Olympic idea that the Games become special and the existence of the Olympic Movement is secured.

Concerning Athens 2004 and Beijing 2008 the IOC has extended its control over financing and further developed the Olympic corporate identity, the so-called 'look of the Games'. The content design of the Olympics will remain the responsibility of the respective OCOG in order to 'give the Games their true colour' (interview, Payne 1997). In view of the differing interest of the IOC and the OCOGs with regard to the utilization of the various financing sources, the IOC's efforts to more closely control and secure the financing of the Games is understandable and necessary. It is only in this way that the IOC can make use of the potential resources gained from the marketing of the Games even though, at the same time, the public is objecting to this usage as a form of 'over-commercialization'.

The following list once again outlines the IOC's growing influence over the financing sources of the OCOGs:

- The IOC carries out all negotiations with television networks.
- The IOC set the fundamental principle that all television agreements be based on free-to-air broadcasting with viewing for all.
- The IOC carries out all negotiations with TOP sponsors.
- The IOC decides on the product categories in order to secure exclusivity for all sponsors.
- The IOC checks all television networks both for advertising that could be detrimental to the Games' image and advertising of ambush marketers.
- The IOC and OCOG/NOC punish every infringement of ambush marketing.
- The IOC checks television spots of sponsors for their 'Olympic' content.
- The IOC makes a careful selection of sponsors in order to ensure no advertising with products, such as tobacco or alcohol, which could harm the Games' image.
- The IOC ensures the non-occurrence of forbidden street vending excesses by including the host city in the Olympic planning.
- The IOC will not allow a staging of the Games without involvement of the city.
- The IOC checks the appearance of the city during the bid phase and books all possible advertising areas next to venue sites in a bid city well in advance of the Games.

The discussion of the expenditures of an OCOG has shown that they are strongly dependent upon the national conditions of the host city. The repeated difficulties encountered when attempting to compare the OCOG expenditures of different Olympic Games are mainly caused by the fact that a standardized accounting system is missing. Differences in the allocation of expenditure items, in valuations and in the temporal delimitation make it almost impossible to this day to carry out a complete and exact comparative analysis of expenditures. By producing uniform 'principles for the accounting of Olympic Games', the IOC could remove many of the prejudices that are based on misinterpretations. At the same time, the adoption of these accounting principles would provide the bid cities with a uniform planning instrument. Last but not least, it could turn the IOC's selection of a host city for the Games into a much easier process.

The economic aspects of the Olympic Games analysed here are very complex and the differentiation derived from macroeconomic and business-economic implications make them even more comprehensive, thereby not allowing a single conclusion. It would be wrong to arrive at a single end result or to identify a specific trend from the investigations. Despite the varying conditions under which the investigated Olympics were hosted, general principles and trends can be recognized through the numerous chronological analyses. As a conclusion, the essential results of this multidimensional problem area are stated in 23 abstracts, which are grouped into three categories:

- In the first category, investigation results are reviewed in regards to both the integration of an OCOG as a decision-maker within the system of the Olympic Movement and its relationship to the IOC. An OCOG's legitimization ultimately depends on this relationship.
- The second category deals with the impacts that the activities of the OCOG have on the economy as a whole. These impacts – in the form of environmental changes – are not specifically directed towards being the goals of the OCOG but must be taken into account in order to successfully stage the Games.
- In the third category, results are discussed regarding an OCOGs primary goal, namely to ensure that the Olympics are regarded as being successful, at least from a financial point of view.

12.1   THE OCOG AND THE IOC AS DECISION-MAKERS OF THE OLYMPIC MOVEMENT

The investigation of this book was limited to the OCOG and host city within the system of the Olympic Movement. Therefore, the relationship between the IOC and the OCOG is of special importance. As decision-makers, they both have the task to permanently secure the existence of the Olympic Movement. Special problems arise from the fact that an OCOG is a temporary organization with partly differing goals than the IOC.

Power

According to Swiss law, the IOC as guardian of the Olympic Idea, can be called a para-state organization. Compared with the OCOGs and the host cities, which enter the Olympic Movement as temporary systems only, the IOC has great power. This power is based on the right to award the Olympic Games. It is an action by the IOC, which, in turn, may bring structural enhancements to a city, increase its popularity, support a positive image, bring employment opportunities and increase income. The IOC's exertion of power, which can be called a traditional power according to Weber, is solely based on the power of reward (Preuss, 2002d). The IOC can only keep its current position in the Olympic Movement as long as the benefit of the Olympics is obvious to bid cities. Nonetheless, the IOC is not able to push through its will against the bid city's opposition since cities have the choice not to bid. The relationship to the OCOG drastically changes at the moment when the Host City Contract is signed, which obliges the host city to adhere to all Olympic Charter rules. From then on, the IOC has the power to apply sanctions against the OCOG. The IOC could damage the image of the city and the organizers by not publicly praising the Games, by holding back financial funds or it could even withdraw the Games from a city and the OCOG as a last resort.

Since the IOC itself suffers from every sanction, its power is mainly based on the fact that it has 'amplifiers', the primary of which is the provision of approximately 50 per cent of the funds necessary to finance the Games. Each successful Games also increases the power of the IOC. Therefore the rules of bidding have been strengthened each Olympiad.

Product 'Olympic Games'

The IOC derives its powerful position solely from the product 'Olympic Games', which can be characterized by four major aspects. First, it attracts the attention of the majority of the world's population. Secondly, as a consequence of this attention, it also garners the interest of the economy, which has given the Olympic Movement financial security and the IOC its power of reward. Thirdly, the pressure and wish to stage the perfect Games opens opportunities for accelerated city development and overcoming previous political obstacles. Fourthly, Olympic Games embody both a universal and country-specific culturally interpreted Olympic Idea. Thus, the Games carry a global ideology.

These aspects affect the IOC as a political, economic and sociocultural system. As a political system, the IOC assumes the position of a 'world government of sports' due to global interest in the Games. As an economic system, which trades in idealistic goods, the economy's demand in the Games makes the IOC a business enterprise. This business strives to gain profit in order to maintain its institutionalized structures. As a sociocultural system, the IOC tries to integrate the ideals of the Olympic Idea into the lifestyles of those individuals interested in the Olympics (civil religion).

The central focus of these considerations is the interest of the population in the product 'Olympic Games'. This product, which can be viewed as being in competition with certain other products, such as the football World Cup or other major events, maintains its position in the international sports marketplace by delimiting itself from its competitors. The facts that the best athletes of the world participate in the Olympics and that they are staged only every four years are decisive factors. Furthermore this work has repeatedly mentioned the significance of the Olympic aura, nourished by the Olympic Ideals, which creates a globally valid ideology. This unique ideology is the basis for the power, the financial resources and the lasting existence of the IOC.

Franchising

Based on the assumption that the Olympic Games – including the proliferation of Olympic ideals – are the product which the Olympic Movement is 'selling', the relationship between the IOC and an OCOG can be compared to a franchise system. As with franchising, the relationship is a vertical cooperation between legally independent businesses (IOC and OCOG/NOC/host city), which are regulated by a contract (Host City Contract). Thus, the OCOG, as franchisee, is controlled by (at least according to the rules of the Olympic Charter) and does business according to the instructions given by the IOC, as franchiser. The franchisee pays the franchiser a remuneration to receive the right to 'distribute' certain goods and services and use the trademarks. In other words, the OCOG pays the IOC a share of the Games surplus and all marketing revenues and finances a major part of the Games in order to receive the right to stage the Games and make use of the Olympic Rings. The franchiser (IOC) is particularly interested in maintaining a uniform image and 'look of the Games'.

However, the IOC must be considered a special franchiser owing to its having a maximum of four franchisees (hosts of future Games) under contract at the same time. It is also important to note that it is the franchisees that keep the Olympic idea alive by staging the Games. The fact that over a period of two years, there is only one single OCOG implies that the IOC greatly depends on this particular Organizing Committee. That explains the IOC's increased interest in the visible and financial success of the franchisee (OCOG, host city), since a good production of the Olympics can lead to an increase in their value, creates additional marketing opportunities and secures a certain number of new cities bidding for the Games.

'Look of the Games'

The 'look of the Games' is crucial to construct a uniform image of each celebration. For one part, the IOC strives to present a uniform structure in subsequent Olympics. For the other part, it longs to see a harmonious appearance of the individual Games within their respective cultural environment. It is the objective of the IOC to maintain a clear corporate identity. It is only in this way that the product Olympic Games receives a profile. The rapid growth of the Games in the last decades has led to a considerable increase in organizational complexity, which can, for example, be seen in the increasing costs of the OCOGs. In order to protect the Games from becoming over-commercialized, enlarged by too many accredited persons and made too complex by additional venues and, therefore, no longer financially feasible for the host cities, the quantitative boom (Samaranch era) must be followed by a period of quality enhancements. First steps have been taken by the 'Olympic Games Study Commission' which proposed solutions to help manage the inherent size, complexity and cost of staging the Olympic Games in future. The concentration on how to finance Olympics can be understandably seen in the Bid books of candidate cities. However, this must be followed by a turn towards sports, people, nature and culture in order to strengthen the Olympic Movement. The first step in this direction is already evident in the IOC voting for the 'Green Games' of Sydney 2000, the 'Games of Culture' of Athens 2004 and the 'People's Olympics' of Beijing 2008. The reduction of the Olympic programme must be handled carefully. There is a great risk that economic indicators call for an exclusion of certain sports, such as the modern pentathlon. However, this particular sport has certain values which feed the Olympic ideals and aura. For example, Coubertin created the sport to honour the perfect athlete (body, will and mind, Olympic Charter, Fundamental Principle). Additionally, the sport has a direct link to the ancient Games and therefore has a great tradition. Furthermore, pentathlon medals are often won by athletes not necessarily from nations that usually win medals, which feeds the idea of universal Games.

Olympic Atmosphere

The striving for a harmonious 'look of the Games' of all Olympics is linked to the striving for a permanent renewal of the Olympic atmosphere. It is an essential factor in determining the success of Olympic Games and thus, at the same time, the number and the profitability of the financing sources. The unique character of the Olympic Games must be maintained in order to attract public interest in the long run. As Coubertin once said, the Olympic Games must not become merely a sequence of world championships. If the elements which make the Olympic Games such a unique event could be precisely determined then the profile of the product 'Olympic Games' could be refined and slowly adapted to the permanently changing needs of society without blurring the profile by introducing quickly changing trends such as new sports. In other words, the tradition of the Olympic Games is important, the tradition of the ancient Games for its mystique, the tradition of Coubertin's age for its ideals and the tradition of the past Games for its current atmosphere. In this respect, each OCOG benefits from the success of the preceding Games. More specifically, this benefit is derived from the fact that the Olympic atmosphere, which is so critical for sponsors, television networks and licensees as well as for the paying spectators and host city, was created during the past Games. The new OCOG enters the negotiations to finance its Games with this Olympic legacy. Therefore, an 'egoistic' OCOG would not have to care about the Olympic atmosphere since its financing was determined prior to the start of the Olympics and the investments related to the city infrastructure had already been carried out. Fortunately, there is still the image of the Olympic Games that the city and thus the OCOG are interested in, and which, in turn, creates an incentive to promote the Olympic atmosphere of the Games. This fact links all OCOGs in an essential Olympic legacy. The IOC's interest in promoting the Olympic atmosphere that will ensure the lasting existence of the Games forces them to impose conditions on, and control, the OCOGs. The utilization of this form of power by the IOC can be viewed as having a positive impact on the Olympic Movement.

Profit

The lasting existence of the Olympic Movement is also secured by the desire of many cities to host the Olympic Games. In the long run, a profit at previous Olympics is critical for the bidding process. The larger the surplus of a host city is, the greater the number of cities that will bid for the next Olympics. The greater the number of bids submitted, the better the range of candidate choices for the IOC. The better the range of candidate choices and the greater the competition among the cities, the easier it is to lead the Olympic Movement in a direction that ensures its future in the best possible way.

At previous Olympics, the official 'surplus' was calculated by also subtracting investments from the OCOG revenues. This corresponded to a complete depreciation of newly constructed facilities during the short duration of the Olympics. Economically, this cannot be justified. If only the operational costs and the depreciation or the rents of the newly constructed facilities were balanced with the revenues, all Olympics investigated here would have a positive balance. However, the surplus gained cannot simply be used to finance new infrastructure. The money has to be spent to benefit both national and international sport.

12.2   MACROECONOMIC IMPLICATIONS OF OLYMPIC GAMES

The IOC and the OCOG, as the centres of action and decision-making processes, are confronted with an environment where decisions are influenced by given facts and where, in turn, Olympic decisions affect the Olympic city or region itself. These changes are not a direct objective of the Olympic Movement. However, the IOC and the OCOG can best achieve their goals if they increase the benefit of all those that are affected by the staging of the Games. A wanted increased benefit leads to the question of whether Olympic Games will be a success, which is a key prerequisite for ensuring the longevity of the Olympic Movement. This question then leads to a cascading series of questions regarding the suitability of a city as Olympic host, the overall economic impact expected from the Games and the burdens and benefits that the citizens of a host city will experience.

Suitability of a City

Whether a city is suitable as a host city depends primarily on the amount of investment required for the Olympics and on the extent to which these investments are in line with the long-term city development plans. The argument that Olympic Games are a good project of urban development has to be qualified. Depending on the size of the city and its urban history, upcoming Olympics create different developmental pressures. Therefore, it is important that a city compares its existing long-term development plans with the necessary Olympic-related structural requirements before it starts to bid and exposes that weakness. Despite the fact that the Olympics generate revenues which are enough to cover the operational costs, most investments must be covered by public or private entities.

This means that the bid candidates will become limited to those cities which already have an adequate infrastructure to stage the Games. It is said that today there are only 20 countries able to stage Olympic Games.

> It would be very unfortunate, if the often exaggerated expenses incurred for the most recent Olympiads, a sizeable part of which represented the construction of permanent buildings, which were moreover unnecessary – temporary structures would fully suffice, and the only consequence is to then encourage use of these permanent buildings by increasing the number of occasions to draw in the crowds – it would be very unfortunate if these expenses were to deter (small) countries from putting themselves forward to host the Olympic Games in the future. (Coubertin, 1911)

The OCOGs only have a limited budget to finance all pull-forward costs and necessary temporary structures in a city. The principle of 'Olympic funds are not allowed to be used for permanent construction of infrastructure' decreases the chances that the Games can successfully be staged in threshold or developing countries.

Games at All Continents

'If the Games are to survive they must be hosted in developing countries. This can only be realized if they become less expensive than they are today' (Schöps, 1983). Ueberroth made this statement in view of the Los Angeles 1984 Olympics, where no large investments were carried out. By adopting this viewpoint, he did not consider the required infrastructure, which either exists or must be provided in order to stage the Olympics. In doing so, Ueberroth overlooked the fact that cities in developed countries, with their suitably established infrastructures, therefore have an advantage when it comes to hosting Olympic Games. Projects in cities of threshold or developing countries concentrate less on leisure and recreational structures and more on hospitals, schools and other investments that will meet the basic needs of the population.

From a financial viewpoint, the monetary securities that the IOC could give host cities even before they submit their bid puts threshold and developing countries in a position where they probably could organize the Olympic Games. The operational costs for organizing the Games are met mainly by international revenues. National financing sources, such as national sponsoring, ticket sales or merchandising, could lead to lower revenues. This, in turn, would be counterbalanced by lower costs for labour, service and material. For the potential host cities in developing countries, financing the Games is less difficult than overcoming an infrastructure which frequently does not live up to the Olympic demands. The sustainability of the Olympic-required structure in these countries is not given.

In developing countries, the economic impact created by the Games is smaller than in industrialized countries. Primarily the high import quota weakens the overall impact. That means, if the Games neither support an urgently needed city development nor the economic impact to be expected then only a positive image and promotion effect might occur. However, there is a risk of suffering from negative promotion if, for example, a high crime rate or organizational problems during the Games devalues the city's image. This can deter foreign investors from settling in the city or tourists from visiting.

In the future, an increasingly efficient form of Olympic Games may offer new chances for threshold and developing countries. Mobile teams of 'Olympic experts', ongoing globalization and lower transportation costs, could address the issue of finding an adequate number of skilled individuals required to organize the Games. Temporary and mobile installations could replace the expensive construction of permanent venues that are not required beyond the celebration of the Games. The remaining investments in Games-related facilities can be integrated into urban development plans; for example, using the Olympic villages for social housing schemes or converting hotels and other venues into colleges, market halls or office buildings. Hosting Olympic Games in threshold or developing countries may not seem to be the best way to develop a region. However, it could ultimately prove to be a successful way. Despite globalization of the Olympic Movement, there is a growing gap between areas that belong to the technologically developed world and those that are part of the marginalized and fenced-off world of poverty and underdevelopment. Even the increasingly closer interrelations of the world do not always imply its globalization. Regional centres with the structural capability to stage the Olympic Games still develop distinctly. However, it will only be when cities in these regional centres develop more or less on all continents that rotating the staging of the Olympic Games over all continents will become a reality.

Minimized Profit

The suitability of a city to host the Games is one reason to bid. The prospect of a possible profit is another. To show a profit after hosting the Olympic Games serves to satisfy the IOC as well as give the OCOG the positive image of having successfully staged the Games. The true objective of the city – and of the closely linked OCOG – should be to finish the Games without profit or loss. This is similar to a corporation's goal to minimize the pre-tax profit in order to pay as little tax as possible. The Host City Contract demands the share of a profit between the IOC, the host country and the city. In the case of the OCOG, it should minimize its surplus before sharing it with other designated parties. A balance without surplus means that all funds were invested in the city and thus remain in the city. Consequently, the OCOG interests correspond to those of the host city but not to those of the IOC.

Objectives of Bidding

Each bid is backed by economic goals, such as increasing the international awareness for the city, creating a positive image, maximizing short-term profit, promoting the municipal economy or improving the urban infrastructure. Depending on these goals, the Games can be either particularly 'cheap' for the city or 'expensive' due to comprehensive investments.

If the main objectives are to create a positive image, increase awareness and achieve a short-term profit, they can be obtained through low costs while, at the same time, avoiding any investment into the infrastructure of the city. If the aim is to promote the economy of the city and bring about extensive infrastructure improvements it can only be achieved by investing in future-oriented sectors of the city. Through this, the indirect aim is to foster economic relations and to bring new corporations to the city in order to permanently increase employment opportunities and income levels. A further indebtedness of the city is difficult to avoid since the Games funds flowing autonomously into the city cannot meet the extensive investments required.

Accelerated Development

The objective to improve the infrastructure of a city has developed into a major motive to bid for the Olympic Games. Thus, the Games have turned into an instrument to concentrate all the power of a city on a single goal. This means that objectives set out in urban development concepts could be achieved within an extremely short period, which would otherwise have been difficult to reach without the Games.

It is a fact that a city must change its structure upon being appointed host city. Depending on the development level and size of the city, investments of differing extents are triggered which probably would still have been realized at some time, even without the Games. These investments should therefore not be regarded as Games-related. However, since the OCOG uses the new venues it must cover an adequate portion of the associated site costs such as rent and temporary structures.

Single Economic Impact

Disregarding the unique chance to carry out accelerated city development, the true macroeconomic benefit caused by the Olympic Games is not the single impact of increased demand launched by the infrastructure improvements in the host city.

Figures 12.5 and 12.6 use data of a case study of the Olympic bid from 'Frankfurt Rhein Main 2012' in order to demonstrate the economic impact of Olympic Games in an industrialized country.

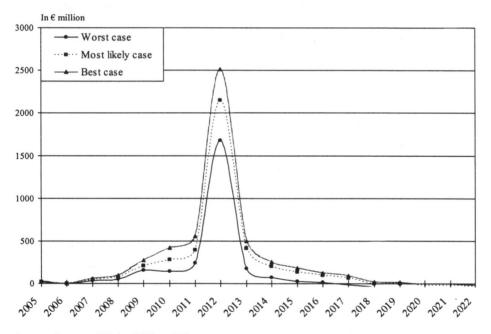

Source: Preuss and Weiss (2003, p. 213).

Figure 12.5   Discounted net benefit of Olympic Games in Frankfurt 2012

In the pre-Olympic years, as well as in the Olympic year 2012, the investments and consumption of the OCOG and the tourists trigger off a huge single economic impact. Conversely, post-Olympic tourism and potential exports are difficult to forecast. However, the city should plan to leverage the post-Olympic impacts by establishing programmes as early as years before the Games take place. In practice this significance is often overlooked owing to the immense time pressure to stage the Games. The annual net result at the post-Games phase is negative, because the debts that were needed to build the Olympic infrastructure have to be paid back.

Figure 12.5 shows the discounted net benefit for the defined Olympic period. Each curve represents one scenario. As long as the curves are in the positive part, the Olympic Games induce annually a positive economic impact. It is interesting to see the ambivalent run of the curves. On the one hand, the multiplier effects and the investments based on debts create a macroeconomic benefit. On the other hand, debts have to be paid back after the Games. That can easily over-compensate the positive post-Games effects.

Olympic Games have extremely different discounted net benefits during the period under investigation. A very strong single impact can be seen during the Olympic year. But that can also be seen at other major sports events such as the football World Cup (Rahmann et al., 1998, p. 150). Owing to dependence on a single impact, the economic situation during the Olympic year is critical for the economic success. If there is an economic boom, crowding out effects are likely to occur. If the post-Olympic phase takes place at the same time as a recession, the payment of the debts will worsen the economic situation. However, in a case where the economic situation was vice versa, the decision to stage the Games would be an economically good decision.

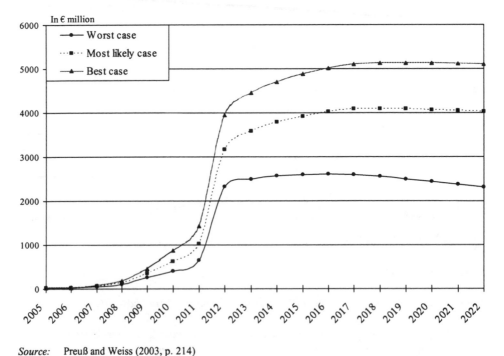

Source: Preuß and Weiss (2003, p. 214)

Figure 12.6   Net present value of Olympic Games in Frankfurt 2012

Figure 12.6 adds the annual net effects and shows the net present value of the Olympic Games at each year. A single value shows all costs and benefits added up to the particular year. Some of the curves decrease a few years after the Games, which indicate negative net values. As long as the curves are not crossing the abscissa the positive effect of the Games is not compensated. In other words, the payment of debts and maintenance costs do not over-compensate the expenditures of tourists, exports and investments of previous years.

Looking at the net present value in general (Figure 12.7), four cases of the economic impact of Olympic Games can be drawn:

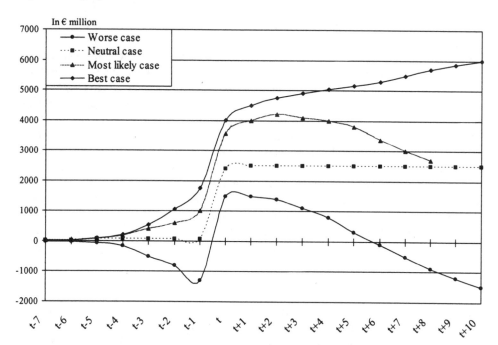

Figure 12.7   General Olympic scenarios of the net present value

- The 'worst case' for a city is to stage the Games and finance all necessary infrastructures by itself, as the case in Montreal 1976. The only positive part is the tourism impact during the Games year. The year immediately after, the costs of the infrastructure which cannot be used create additional negative impacts. Therefore the single Olympic boost loses its power after a few years and the total Olympic effect turns negative after five years.
- The 'neutral case', such as Los Angeles 1984, illustrates a case when no real investments have to be made. The Olympics are a success with many foreign visitors and after the Games there is no structure that costs or creates additional impacts.

- The 'most likely case' describes Games that need new infrastructure which is partly financed by autonomous means as well as by credits. This was the case in Munich, Barcelona, Sydney and Athens. After the Games the impact can be leveraged, but a few years later the payments of debts create annual negative balances. However, that will not compensate the overall positive impact.

- The 'best case' is, if most new infrastructure is financed by autonomous means or private investments. The Games are a success and the new structure is a structure that was needed for the development of the city. It constantly can be used to create additional positive impacts.

Overestimation of the Economic Impact

Within a very short period this single impact will lose its impetus if no additional demand is induced. It is of decisive importance whether a city manages to use the single impact to change its structure in a way that will provide a basis for further impacts to trigger a self-sustaining process. This could be the case, for example, through permanent tourism, industrial settlements, regular follow-up events or new trade relations. The improved image that the host city could gain, independent of the sustainability of the economic impact, represents the second major benefit for the national economy. The aura spread by the Olympic image can considerably promote the further development of a host city.

The economic benefit of the Games, which is frequently emphasized during the preparatory phase, is often overestimated in both publications and economic analyses produced by or for the OCOG. One example of this is seen in the overestimation of the consumption expenditures, which are not made by the OCOG. Another is when the multipliers tend to be too high and the number of tourists is estimated too optimistically.

Dilemma of Bidding

Each bidding committee is forced increasingly to cover more services in order to fulfil the promises made during the bid competition. The high competition of bid cities forces them to follow all requirements the IOC sets. For the cities bidding for 2012 it is, for example, the proper national protection of the Olympic insignias and the free transportation and accommodation of the athletes. Despite the fact, that this strengthens the Olympic Movement, it forces the bid cities into the so-called 'prisoner's dilemma'. That means the cities offer ever more to the Olympic Movement and increase their costs without gaining an advanced position due to the fact that all bid cities offer the same.

Another dilemma is the free-rider mentality. The image and governmental support that a city can already gain through a simple bid motivates many cities to bid – even without a real winning perspective. In order to reduce the free-riding attitude, the IOC claims a non-refundable fee from each bidder and has forbidden any international promotion of the city during the applicant stage. However, that increases the 'sunk costs'. Additionally, this increases the already high 'hold up costs'. The required infrastructure to stage successful

Games has to be so advanced that only a few cities currently can stage the Games. This is particularly a dilemma for the IOC.

The third dilemma is the so-called 'rat race'. That means, ever more cities build up a modern sports infrastructure, but the number of potential world-class events is limited. In general the economic sustainability of Olympic facilities through major sports events is limited.

Right Moments to Stage the Games

The extent of the benefit to the overall economy depends on the economic situation of the city when the Games-related investments are realized. Therefore, a priori analyses simply cannot quantify the true benefit of the autonomous expenditures. A phase of increased investment activity and increased consumption expenditure in line with an economic upswing or boom may weaken the positive economic effect if, for example, it results in crowding-out effects or increased import activities. Whereas, if the same increases in investment activity and consumption expenditure are in line with a recession, it is regionally weakened and the positive macroeconomic effects are strengthened. The problem is that at the time of the bid, when investments are decided upon, the future economic situation cannot be anticipated. Therefore, the proposal put forward by certain individuals to use the Olympic Games as a means to promote the city's economy is not valid.

Local Industry

Independent of the economic situation of the city, the Games have a positive impact on local industry. Even increased globalization, and therefore greater supply from outside the region, does not stop the fact that local industry will experience a huge Olympic-related demand. When there is an economic boom, prices for goods and services rise. When there is a recession, the companies receive additional orders. While sponsors are paying money to the OCOG and IOC for mainly intangible benefits, which furthermore are uncertain, the industry immediately gains from a tangible benefit through additional demand in construction, goods and service. Those having a true interest in staging the Games in a certain city are not the sponsors, which have a global market anyway, but rather local and regional industry.

Arguments of Olympic Opponents

The groups that might potentially suffer from disadvantages as a result of the Games are reflected in the five major arguments of the Olympic opponents. These are: (1) that the city might risk running up too many debts; (2) that the money could be used for more sensible projects instead of setting up the Olympic structure; (3) that the Olympics are always to the benefit of the prosperous citizens and to the disadvantage of the poor; (4)

that the Olympic Games bring only a few short-term job opportunities; and (5) that the Games may cause a rise in the cost of living which will not decline after the Games.

The outcome of this investigation reveals that a serious over-indebtedness of an Olympic host is only to be feared if extensive investments in the infrastructure of the city are necessary. The operational costs of an OCOG are mainly covered by autonomous revenues. The reproach of Olympic opponents that funds could be used for more 'sensible' projects than for the Games is not correct since the largest part of the funds would not come into the host city without the Games. Many of the required Olympic Games projects which will result in changes to the structure of a city are beneficial to all inhabitants, not only to the prosperous. For example, the Games could bring about improvements in the health system, the Olympic village could be converted into a social housing area, and the improvements in public transportation or infrastructure could lead to the settlement of new industries, independence of private vehicles and to new employment. Nonetheless the gentrification of the city has a negative impact on the weaker social classes. Additionally, the movement to become a global city also results in an ongoing polarization of rich and poor people. The OCOG itself can only create short-term employment opportunities. However, it is often forgotten that the impact generated by the Games also induces long-term employment. Price changes are only to be expected in sectors with an extremely high demand. The sectors directly affect only a minority of the citizens. The cost of living does not increase in an Olympic city more than in other major cities of the host country and is based on inflation and not on the Olympics.

The Olympic Games cause a considerable flow of funds into a city. It is difficult to allocate the funds in a way that, at the same time, solves major urban problems and prepares for the Games. The citizens of the host city must realize that the Olympic Games are not a panacea to all their problems.

Tourism

The crowding-out effects Olympic Games have on tourism of a host city and the surrounding regions are an important result of this investigation. The greater the number of tourists that come to the host city, the higher the autonomous expenditures and the greater the impact for the overall economic situation – at first, a positive effect. However, the amount of accommodation is the limiting quantity for Olympic tourism. Research revealed that during the Olympic Games the hotels in the host cities are almost all completely booked. At the same time, the pre-Games investments in this sector do not always consider the follow-up demand – thereby leading to an overabundance of beds after the Games. Furthermore, there is the risk of losing the regular host city visitors who avoid the city because of the Games. For neighbouring tourist destinations the research shows that there is a decline in visitor numbers during the Games because tourists even avoid the surroundings due to an unjustified fear of exaggerated prices and overcrowding. During the Games, citizens and tourists alike are primarily interested in sports. This fact explains the change in their consumption patterns which negatively affect the regular entertainment and leisure industry. However, the positive image effect and increased post-Olympic tourism usually over-compensates these negative effects.

12.3   ECONOMIC IMPLICATIONS OF THE OCOG

The OCOG, as a key decision-maker, when preparing and staging the Games stands between the partly contradictory goals of the IOC and the host city. Its objectives are to gain prestige and obtain a surplus, or at least to avoid a financial deficit. This is achieved if the organization's handling of the sporting events and finances are judged by the IOC, the media, and the public to be excellent.

Financing the Games

Not all OCOGs have the same financing sources at their disposal. The state's willingness to contribute to the Games, the size of the market, the readiness to donate or become a volunteer, the size of the market for merchandise, the number of national philatelists or numismatists and so on greatly differ from host country to host country.

Since Los Angeles 1984, private sources have been given an important role in financing the Games. Hence, the public financing model has become less feasible. The private financing model has also become less feasible due to lack of municipal support for Atlanta 1996. The model of the future will instead be the mixed financing model. Owing to the fact that the costs of the Games are continuously increasing it will become necessary to use all financing sources available. Signs warning against an exploitation of individual sources must be observed carefully. For example, pay-per-view television would be as harmful to the Olympic Movement as an increase in the number of sponsors or mere profit orientation when deciding on ticket prices. In addition, it would be harmful to finance the Games by introducing a lottery in competition with existing lotteries or to allow betting. However, the IOC is well aware of these threats and therefore has reduced the number of sponsors, forbidden betting and established the principle to sell television rights only to networks that broadcast free to air.

Television and Sponsorship

The detailed investigation of the individual financing sources has revealed unexpected developments. So far, analyses have mainly concentrated on revenues from selling television rights and presented the conclusion that the Games depended on the television networks. It was barely noticed that the IOC increasingly controls the television networks as mentioned earlier. As long as the IOC fulfils its commitment to provide the international signal of all events – including those less telegenic – it can control commercialization in the field of television despite the significance of high viewing rates.

The dependency of the financing source 'television' on 'sponsoring' has become obvious through the great number of commercials sold to the Olympic sponsors. The television networks are 'intermediate dealers' and broadcast the sporting events because the revenues from selling commercials exceed the additional costs for the broadcasting rights. This is true as long as the television financed through advertising prevails and the Games are not broadcast in pay television.

Among all Olympic sponsors, the national sponsors (partners) became more important to the OCOG than TOP sponsors. The number of sponsors leading to a balance between commercialization and secured financing cannot be determined because public acceptance of advertising the size of the market and the commitment of the individual sponsors vary greatly. What is at issue is not to limit the total number of sponsors but rather the number of ever-present corporations, which the consumer realizes. The 'commercialization', which the consumer evaluates as a negative effect can be mainly traced back to both the advertising that uses the Olympic symbol, to merchandising and street vending. However, sponsoring and merchandising become important sources with the introduction of a uniform 'look of the Games', event emblems and mascots. The sponsors take over a great job by announcing the Olympic Games and thereby create a worldwide excitement a few weeks before the Games start.

Globalization

The rapid development of technology and logistics, in combination with increasing globalization undoubtedly affect the Olympic Games. This growth has led to changes in both the revenue and the cost components of the Games where there is evidence of the move towards achieving increased efficiency via a more professionalized approach. The Games of ancient times were staged at the same place every four years. In contrast, the Games of the first 100 years of modern times have been mainly staged in industrialized and Western countries where they have always had to be organized anew with each celebration. In the future, there will be a mixture of both the ancient and modern.

The foundation for just such a 'wandering circus' has already begun to be defined and laid down by the changing criterion, available resources and actions of those parties with links to the Games. For example, owing to the fact that the post-Games costs for Olympic venues have become a key criterion in the bids for Olympic Games, temporary sports facilities have become ever more important for the Games. From the technical standpoint, it is possible to remove many of these venues and erect them again at another place. The IOC contributes to this more flexible approach by passing on databases (Transfer of Knowledge) from OCOG to OCOG. Even the big sponsors accompany the Olympics, since to them it does not matter where they advertise because their market is the entire world. Finally the same television networks continue to buy the television rights and establish a long-term relationship. Furthermore, the sponsors advertising based on global ideologies can be seen all over the world because of worldwide broadcasting and expanded media exposure. Already today, even camera teams accompany the Olympics because the IOC has decided to select highly experienced and 'sport specific' teams to cover the competitions rather than to rely solely on the skills of the host broadcaster. While the Olympics Games have clearly benefited from the increased efficiency that comes from utilizing existing resources and experienced workers, the gain is not achieved without detriment. Foremost among such detrimental effects is the very clear risk that the unique 'cultural-national' flair of the Games could suffer. It is important to recognize and remember that in the global world the local aspect of the celebrations is of special significance. In general, it is better to use the term 'local' to refer to locations, such as cities and regions, rather than nations. For example, the emphasis on Catalonia at the Barcelona 1992 Olympics and the Southern States at the Atlanta 1996 Games could not be ignored. At the same time, when international relations are expanded, the same process serves to create an equally strong desire to also highlight the regional political autonomy and local cultural identity. This is an obvious move to orient the 'cultural colour' of the Olympic Games more towards local regions and traditions and less towards the national. This will further increase when national sovereignty erodes. It is a move that will guarantee the Olympic Games their different characters in the future. In addition, this means that under the assumption of increasing globalization, a single state is too small (regarding the financing sources) and at the same time it is too large (regarding a uniform national flair).

Culture

Apart from sport, culture forms the second column of the Olympic Idea. Coubertin's eurhythmic idea forms a close link between culture and sport. In reality, however, there is not much to be noticed. When the cultural events are evaluated with respect to efficiency aspects, it becomes evident that they have developed largely into an object of prestige for the respective OCOG. However, they also have a political function. For example, they offer the opportunity to embellish the city with the permanent exhibition of cultural objects, attract the interest of groups not interested in sport or the Olympic Games, integrate fringe groups or Olympic opponents by addressing their interests or areas of living, and discuss topics which would cause international criticism if they were ignored.

Over-commercialization

Increasing expenditures for cultural events could not eliminate the accusation of 'over-commercialization' of the Games. There is a public perception that it is the IOC itself that fuels 'over-commercialization'. In point of fact, the IOC is the superordinate system that regulates commercialization. The IOC, too, is not only aware of the threat posed by 'over-commercializing' the Games but is also effectively fighting against it. The measures the IOC has taken to control the sources of Olympic Games financing reflect its efforts to fight 'over-commercialization'. For example, these include measures to influence the appearance of the host cities during the Games, limit the number of sponsors, better integrate the city in the organization, and avoid pay-per-view and pay television. Potentially, the IOC can take even stronger measures such as specifying further conditions the television networks or sponsors must follow. Such a demand, however, would ignore the fact that private business has contributed a great deal towards a sustained development of sports in general throughout the past 20 years – albeit that it is mainly financial need, which has opened the doors for private business into high-performance sports. When the 'over-commercialization' of the Games is criticized, it is because people fail to understand the complex interrelations and, in particular, do not take into account the economic background.

In the 1970s, citizens complained about the strain placed on their city by the Games, which were mainly financed by public funds. In the 1990s, opponents of commercialization believed that the Games dependend too much on private corporations. There is no alternative between the use of public or private financing sources except to reduce the size and complexity of the Olympic Games. The consequence of such an action is that large groups of athletes are already beginning to complain that only a few can participate in the Games. Without a doubt, it can be stated that the IOC has reacted towards the problems of publicly financed Games by taking the path leading to commercialization. To avoid 'over-commercializing', the IOC can only choose to limit the growth of the Games, strengthen the qualitative growth, control the private financing sources and return again to using public financing sources.

12.4 GENERAL DEMANDS RESULTING FROM THE INVESTIGATION

Macroeconomic and business-economic implications of Olympic Games have consequently not been analysed thus far since all former investigations had an ideographic viewpoint. The Beijing 2008 Games will definitely give new nuances to the considerations on the economic impact of Olympic Games. The analyses of future Games should be based on the results of this investigation. Among other advantages, it could help to detect an imminent 'over-commercializing' thereby giving ample warning time. Those critically observing the Olympic system from the outside will be able to detect doubtful developments earlier and more clearly than 'insiders'.

For two decades, commercialization has penetrated the Olympic Movement. Although it ensured the existence of Olympic Games, the importance of private financing sources must not get out of control. This calls for a continued analysis of the effects the Olympic Games have on the host city and the society of the world with the aim of determining trends and so avoiding wrong decisions. Data of future Games can be easily calculated and integrated into the existing periodical analyses using the US gross domestic product (GDP) deflator and the PPP of the host country.

The strongly varying balance sheets, in particular the cost positions, which individual OCOGs use, are extremely striking. The Olympic Games have led to a homogenization of sports and the rules governing them. The accounting of the OCOGs, however, are not affected at all by this process of harmonization. The balances reflect country-specific differences depending on the host country. The IOC should strive for identical balances to allow, for example, for an internal economic comparison of the Games. That could further increase the value of the 'Transfer of Knowledge'. Until now it appears that the OCOGs have intended to protect their Olympic financial records against examination by third parties through producing individual accounting systems.

The comparison of the outcome of different Olympic Games gives future bid cities and OCOGs valuable information. The difficulties, which had to be overcome for this investigation, lead to the demand to develop and implement 'principles for a unified accounting of Olympic Games'. Such a unified balance would tremendously facilitate documentation (information for future bid cities) and control (profit analysis for IOC and Olympic Movement). This not only involves unique positions for the final balance sheet but also principles to evaluate goods and services. A unified accounting system could facilitate investigations of the present type and may lead to further insights, with the objective of hosting economically successful and efficiently organized Olympic Games.

References

Adranovich, G., M.J. Burbank and Ch.H., Heying, (2001), 'Olympic cities: lessons learned form mega-event politics', *Journal of Urban Affairs*, **2** (23), 113–131.

Aicher, O. (1996), 'Olympia und Kunst', in N. Müller and M. Messing (eds), *Auf der Suche nach der Olympischen Idee. Facetten der Forschung von Athen bis Atlanta*, Kassel, pp. 17–23.

Alaszkiewicz, R.K. and T.L. McPhail (1986), 'Olympic television rights', *International Review for Sociology of Sport*, **21** (Februaryruary/March), 211–226.

Albrecht-Heider (1996), 'Atlanta wird zur Welt von Coca Cola', *Frankfurter Rundschau*, **54** (10 July), 15.

Altenbockum, J. (1997), 'Bombenexplosion in Göteborgs Ullevi-Stadion Stockholm sieht Olympiabewerbung in Gefahr', *Frankfurter Allgemeine Zeitung*, **49** (26 August), 26.

Andersen, A. (1999), Economic Impact Study of the Sydney 2000 Olympic Games, Centre for Regional Economic Research, University of Tasmania.

Angelopoulos-Daskalaki (2004), 'Die Welt hat Griechenland unterstützt, Inteview von Jörg Winterfeld', *Die Welt*, (2 August), 22.

Arnold, V. (1988), 'Nutzen-Kosten-Analyse II. Anwendung', in W. Albers, K.E. Born, E. Dürr and A. Zottmann (eds), *Handwörterbuch der Wirtschaftswissenschaft*, vol. 5, Stuttgart and others, pp. 382–99.

Assenmacher, W. (1998), *Konjunkturtheorie*, vol. 8, München.

Athens OCOG (2002a), *Athens 2002. Info Kid* (May), Athens.

Athens OCOG (2002b), 'Report to the IOC Radio and Television Commission. Annual meeting', November, Lausanne, unpublished typescript.Organizing

Athens OCOG (2003a), *Official Magazine of the OCOG Athens 2004*, March.

Athens OCOG (2003b), 'Liability, underwriters, information', Athens, typescript.

Atkinson, S. (1997), 'Sydney 2000: physical impacts and environment', in L. DaCosta (ed.), *Environment and Sport. An International Overview*, Porto, pp. 275–81.

Atlanta OCOG (1994a), '1991–1997 financial forecast update', unpublished data, Atlanta.

Atlanta OCOG (1994b), *1994 Olympic Games Press Guide*, (September) Atlanta.

Atlanta OCOG (1996), *1996 Olympic Games Press Guide, ACOG*, Atlanta.

Atlanta OCOG (1998), *Official Report of the XXVI Olympic Games*, Atlanta.

Atlanta OCOG (s.t.), *News Release. Centennial Olympic Games at a Glance*, Atlanta.

Australian Bureau of Statistics (1999–2002), 'Overseas arrivals and departures', 3401.0, monthly report.

Australian Bureau of Statistics, www.abs.gov.au, examined September 2001–January 2004.

Australian Olympic Committee (AOC) (2001), Budget Statement 2001–02, Sydney, AOC.

Australian Tourist Commission (ATC) (2001), 'Olympic Games tourism strategy. Overview – March 2001', Sydney.

Baade R.A. and Matheson, V. (2002), 'Bidding for the Olympics: fool's gold?' in C.P. Barros, M. Ibrahímo and S. Szymanski, S. (eds), *Transatlantic Sport. The Comparative Economics of North American and European Sports*, Chelterham, UK and Northampton, MA, USA: Edvard Elgar, pp. 127–51.

Babcock, J.N. (1996), 'Towards a synergistic link between Olympic Games and the Cultural Olympiad', in N. Müller and M. Messing (eds), *Auf der Suche nach der Olympischen Idee. Facetten der Forschung von Athen bis Atlanta*, Kassel, pp. 271–85.

Bacia, H. (1997), 'Die Athener versprechen die Rückkehr zum olympischen Ideal', *Frankfurter Allgemeine Zeitung*, **49** (8 September), 34.

Balderstone, S. (2001), 'Agenda 21 and IOC requirements', in IOC (ed.), *Olympic Games and Architecture. The Future for Host Cities*, Lausanne, pp. 61–6.

Barcelona OCOG (1988), *Second Official Report of the Barcelona '92, Organising Committee (COOB '92) to the 93rd Session of the IOC in Calgary*, Calgary (11 February).

Barcelona OCOG (1992), *Official Report of the Organising Committee of the Games of Barcelona 1992*, Barcelona.

Barney, R.K. (1993), 'Golden egg or fools' Gold?', in IOC/IOA (eds), *Report of the Thirty-Second Session in 1992*, Lausanne, 123–33.

Barney, R.K. (2002), 'An Olympic dilemma. Protection of Olympic Symbols', Journal of Olympic History, **10** (3), 7–29.

Barney, R.K., S.R. Wenn and S.G. Martyn (2002), *Selling the Five Rings. The International Olympic Committee and the Rise of Olympic Commercialism*, Salt Lake City.

Battle, C.H. (1998), 'Reflections on the Centennial Olympic Games in Atlanta', in IOC/IOA (eds), *Report of the Thirty-Seventh Session in 1997*, Lausanne, pp. 161–66.

Bergman, M. (2003), 'Olympic collectibles, a major contributor to the Olympic Games', in M. Moragas Spà, M.C. Kennett and N. Puig (eds), *The Legacy of Olympic Games (1984–2000)*, Lausanne, pp. 207–14.

Berlin 2000 Olympia GmbH (1992), Antworten zum Fragespiegel des NOK für Deutschland, Berlin.

Berlin 2000 Olympia GmbH (1993), Berlin 2000, Kandidat für die Olympischen Spiele 2000, Berlin.

Berlioux, M. (1985), 'The Olympic Games and the escalation of the audio-visual', in IOC (ed.), *International Olympic Academy, Report of the Twenty-Second Session in 1982*, Lausanne, pp. 199–215.

Bernadas, F.P. and J.L. Benasat (1995), 'Barcelona '92: Strategies of Technology', in M. Moragas Spá and M. Botella (eds), *The Keys to Success*, Barcelona, pp. 238–53.

Bernard, A.B. and M.R. Busse (2000), 'Who wins the Olympic Games: economic development and medals totals', working paper 7998, National Bureau of Economic Research, Cambridge.

Bernardi, V. (2001), '*The impact of European Union (EU) legislation on Olympic Broadcasting and the IOC Broadcasting Strategy*', unpublished Master thesis, Lausanne MEMOS.

Berndt, M. (1997), 'Das Attentat im Centennial Park der Olympischen Spiele 1996 in Atlanta: Ein analytischer Vergleich der Berichterstattung in ausgewählten US-amerikanischen und deutschen Tageszeitungen', unpublished Staatsexamensarbeit, Johannes Gutenberg-University, Mainz.

Bernhard, E. (1928a), Olympische Rundfunk Berichterstattung D.D.R., **6** (2), 69–70.

Bernhard, E. (1928b), Olympische Rundfunk Berichterstattung D.D.R., **6** (20), 1302.

Bette, K.-H. (1993), 'Neuere Systemtheorie', in K.-H. Bette, G. Hoffmann, C. Kruse, E. Meinberg and J. Thiele (eds), *Zwischen Verstehen und Beschreiben*, Cologne, pp. 115–58.

Bidding Committee Athens 2004 (1995), *Bidbook*, vol. 3, Athens.

Bidding Committee Barcelona 1992 (1984), *Bidbook*, Barcelona.

Bidding Committee Beijing 2008 (2001), *Bidbook*, Beijing

Bidding Committee Rio de Janeiro 2004 (1995), *Bidbook*, vol 3, Rio de Janeiro.

Bidding Committee Roma 2004 (1995), *Bidbook*, vol. 3, Rome.

Bidding Committee Stockholm 2004 (1995), *Bidbook*, vol. 3, Stockholm.

Binfield, R.D. (1948), *The Story of the Olympic Games*, Oxford.

Birch, R. (1998), 'The planning and organization of Olympic Ceremonies', in IOC/IOA (eds), *Report of the Thirty-Seventh Session in 1997*, Lausanne, pp. 120–26.

Black, J. (1999), 'Transport, staging the Olympics. The event and its impact', in R. Cashman and A. Hughes (eds), *Staging the Olympics. The Event and Its Impact*, Sydney, pp. 93–105.

Blume, E.R. (1996), 'Olympic power', *Electric Perspectives*, **21** (3), 56–69.

Boggs, K. (1996), 'IEs behind the scenes at the Olympics', *Industrial Engineering* (July), 31–3.

Böll, K. (1996), 'Merchandising. Die neue Dimension der Verflechtung zwischen Medien und Industrie' in the series by Ronneberger, F.; Rühl, M. and Stuiber, H.-W. (eds.) *Kommunikationswissenschaftliche Studien*, vol 17, Munich.

Borchers, D. (1998), 'Die Hürde Desaster wird dem Multi zu gefährlich', *Süddeutsche Zeitung*, **50** (18 August), V2/7.

Boyle, J. (2001), 'Events set a personal best after Games', *Australian Financial Review*, (5 May), 5.

Braun, H.-G. (1984), 'Die Bewertung von Projekten – zur Logik von Cost-Benefit-Analysen', in H. Majer (ed.), *Qualitatives Wachstum – Einführung in Konzeptionen der Lebensqualität*, Frankfurt/M., pp. 90–98.

Brill, S. (1996), 'Die Finanzierung der Olympischen Spiele in Amsterdam 1928 im Widerstreit der öffentlichen Meinung', in N. Müller and M. Messing (ed.), *Auf der*

Suche nach der Olympischen Idee. Facetten der Forschung von Athen bis Atlanta, Kassel, pp. 157–70.

Brown, G. (1997), 'Anticipating the impact of the Sydney 2000 Olympic Games', in Department of Tourism Studies (ed.), *The Impact of Mega Events. Papers of the Talk at the Top Conference* (7–8 July), typescript.

Brown, R. (1996), 'NBC nails Olympics gold', *Broadcasting & Cable*, **126** (30), 4.

Brügge, P. (1972), 'Wir sind da so hineingeschlittert', *Der Spiegel*, **26** (31), 28–38.

Brundage, A. (1938), Letter to William May Garland, (19 October), Brundage Collection, Box 225.

Brundage, A. (1948), Letter to John Jewett Garland (18 December), Brundage Collection, Box 225.

Brundage, A. (1955), Letter to the Executive Committee (Aug 3), Brundage Collection, Box 114.

Brundage, A. (1957a), Letter to Bartholemy (7 August), Brundage Collection. Box 165.

Brundage, A. (1957b), Letter to the OCOG of Squaw Valley (7 August), Brundage Collection, Box 165.

Brundage, A. (1959), Letter by Brundage to Garroni (15 January), Brundage Collection, Box 168.

Brundage, A. (1966), Letter by Brundage to Onesti (25 January), Brundage Collection, Box 101.

Brunet, F. (1993), *Economy of the 1992 Barcelona Olympic Games*, Lausanne.

Buchwalder, M. and M. Messing (2004), *Olympic Future – empirical investigations during the Olympic Games in Sydney 2000 and Salt Lake 2002. From the spectators' perspective – what threatens future Olympic Games*, unpublished paper.

Bura, F. (1960), *Die Olympischen Spiele auf den Briefmarken der Welt*, Cologne.

Burbank, M.J., G.D. Andranovich, and Ch.H. Heying (2001), *Olympic Dreams. The Impact of Mega-Events on Local Politics*, Boulder, CO and London.

Bureau of Tourism Research (BTR) (2001), Tourism datacard, Barcelona.

Busch, S. (1993), 'Schmerzgrenze erreicht: Vabanquespiel um US-TV-Rechte für Atlanta', in AGSPORT agency (26 July).

Busch, S. (1996), 'Atlanta-Bericht mit Rekord-Zahlen und ohne finanzielle Bilanz', *AGSFA agency* (11 November).

Carlsen, J. and P. Williams (1997), 'Events tourism and destination image in Western Australia', in Department of Tourism Studies (ed.), *The Impact of Mega Events*, papers of the Talk at the Top conference, 7–8 July, typescript.

Carswell, A. (1996), 'Atlanta is hot', *Mortgage Banking*, **56** (4), 22–7.

Cashman, R. (1999b), 'Legacy', in R. Cashman and A. Hughes (eds), *Staging the Olympics. The Event and Its Impact*, Sydney, pp. 183–94.

Cater, D.M. (1996), *Keeping Score. An Inside Look at Sports Marketing*, Grants Pass, OR.

Catherwood, D.W. and R.L. van Kirk (1992), *The Complete Guide to Special Event Management*, New York.

Census (1981), *Statistical Abstract of the United States 1981*, Washington, DC.

Census (1983), *Statistical Abstract of the United States 1982-1983*, Washington, DC.
Census (1985), *Statistical Abstract of the United States 1985*, Washington, DC.
Census (1987), *Statistical Abstract of the United States 1987*, Washington, DC.
Census (1989), *Statistical Abstract of the United States 1989*, Washington, DC.
Census (1990), *Statistical Abstract of the United States 1990*, Washington, DC.
Census (1992), *Statistical Abstract of the United States 1992*, Washington, DC.
Census (1996), *Statistical Abstract of the United States 1996*, Washington, DC.
Chalip, L. (2000a), 'Levering the Sydney Olympics for tourism', paper in www.blues.uab.es/olympic.studies/papers/chalip00-3.html, page visited 28 November 2001.
Chalip, L. (2000b), 'Volunteers and the organisation of the Olympic Games: economic and formative aspects', in M. Moragas, A.B. Moreno and N. Puig (eds), *Volunteers, Global Society and the Olympic Movement*, Lausanne, pp. 205–14.
Chalip, L. (2002), 'Using the Olympics to optimize tourism benefits', paper in http://www.blues.uab.es/olympic.studies/pdf/FL7_eng.pdf, visited 28 January 2004.
Chalip, L (2003), 'Tourism and the Olympic Games', in M. Moragas, C. Kennett and N. Puig (eds), *The Legacy of Olympic Games (1984–2000)*, Lausanne, pp. 195–204.
Chalkley, B. and S. Essex (1999), 'Urban development through hosting international events: a history of the Olympic Games', *Planning Perspectives*, 14, pp. 369–94.
Chang, J.-H. (1989), *The 1988 Seoul Olympics. A Retrospective*, Washington, DC.
Chappelet, J.-L. (2001), 'Management of the Olympic Games: the lessons of Sydney', in *European Journal for Sport Management*, Special Issue, 8, 128–36.
Chappelet, J.-L. (2003), 'The legacy of the Olympic Winter Games', in M. Moragas, C. Kennett and N. Puig (eds), *The Legacy of Olympic Games (1984–2000)*, Lausanne, pp. 54–66.
Clasing, D. (1992), *Doping – verbotene Arzeneimittel im Sport*, Stuttgart.
Cleland, K. (1996), 'AT&T sets up Olympic marketing dream team', *Advertising Age*, **67** (1 January), 1, 3, 20.
Collins, G. (1996), 'Coke's hometown olympics', *New York Times* (28 March), 1.
Colman, P. (1996), 'New Olympic event: fighting over news embargoes', *Broadcasting & Cable*, **126** (30), 8.
Comité Olympique Anvers (1920), VII Olympiade Anvers 1920, Rapport Officiel. Anvers.
Commission of Inquiry (s.t.), 'Report of the commission of inquiry into the cost of the 21st Olympiad', Montreal.
Cordey, D. (2001), 'Sydney Olympic temporary uses', *Olympic Games and Architecture. The Future for Host Cities*, Lausanne, pp. 43–53.
Coubertin, P. de (1891), 'Un concours littéraire entre athletes', *Les Sports Athlétiques*, no. 70, 2.
Coubertin, P. de (1911), *Olympic Review*, **6** (April), 59–62.
Coubertin, P. de (1913), 'L'emblème et le drapeau de 1914', *Revue Olympique*, **8**, 119–120.
Coubertin, P. de (1936), *Olympische Erinnerungen*, Berlin.

Coubertin, P. de (1967 [1906]), 'Eröffnungsrede der Beratungssitzung von Kunst, Wissenschaft und Sport. Discours d'ouverture de la conférence consultative des arts, lettres et sports', in P. de Coubertin (ed.), *Der Olympische Gedanke. Reden und Aufsätze*, Carl-Diem-Institut, Schorndorf, 17-19.

Coubertin, P. de (1967 [1910]), 'Ein modernes Olympia', in P. de Coubertin (ed.), *Der Olympische Gedanke. Reden und Aufsätze*, Schorndorf: Carl-Diem-Institut, pp. 24–45.

Cox, G., M. Darcy and M. Bounds (1994), *The Olympics and Housing. A Study of Six International Events and Analysis of Potential Impacts of the Sydney 2000 Olympics*, Housing and Urban Studies Research Group, University of Western Sydney: Macarthur:

Crabb, C. (1996), 'Steed. Olympic vending program a disappointment', *Atlanta Business Chronicle* (7–13July), 10A.

DaCosta, L. (2002), *Olympic Studies. Current Interlectual Crossroads*. Rio de Janeiro.

Daume, W. (1976), 'Organising the Games', in M. Killanin and J. Rodda (eds), *The Olympic Games. 80 Years of People, Events and Records*, London, pp. 153–56.

Davidson Peterson Associates Studies (1996), *The Economic Impact of Expenditures by Tourists on Georgia*, York, ME.

Denis, M., E. Dischereit, D.-Y. Song and R. Werning (1988), *Kein Land für friedliche Spiele*, Reinbeck.

Do, Y.-P. (1999), 'The economic Impact of the Seoul Olympic Games', paper presented at the 7th International Postgraduate Seminar on Olympic Studies, IOA

dpa (2004), 'Eine Milliarde Euro für die Sicherheit', *Frankfurter Allgemeine Zeitung*, **55** (Mar 22), 29.

Dunn, K.M. and P.M. McGuirk (1999), 'Hallmark events', in R. Cashman and A. Hughes (eds), *Staging the Olympics. The Event and Its Impact*, Sydney, pp. 18–34.

Economics Research Associates (ERA) (1981), *Report on Costs, Revenues, and Economic Activity which will be Generated by Conduct of the 1984 Summer Olympic Games in the City of Los Angeles*, Los Angeles, typescript.

Economics Research Associates (ERA) (1984), *Community Economic Impact of the 1984 Olympic Games in Los Angeles*, Los Angeles, typescript.

Ehm, P. (1996), 'Schlagzeilen und Einschaltquoten', *Süddeutsche Zeitung*, **48** (15 June), 136, 60.

Emory, T. (1996), 'The bottom line', *The Wall Street Journal*, (19 July), R14.

Environment Committee Sydney Olympic 2000 Bid Limited (1993), *Environmental Guidelines for the Summer Olympic Games*, Sydney (September).

Ernst-Motz, A. (1996), 'Nicht nur adäquat', *Wirtschaftswoche*, **29** (12), 64–6.

Essex, S.J. and B.S. Chalkley, (1998) 'Olympic Games: a catalyst of urban change', *Leisure Studies*, **17** (3), 187–201.

Ewers, H.-J. et al. (1993), *Volkswirtschaftliche Kosten und Nutzen Olympischer Spiele im Jahr 2000 in Berlin*, IfS-GIB Gesellschaft für Innovationsforschung und Beratung mbH, Bonn (May), typescript.

Federal Government (1970), *Federal Budget*, Bonn.

Federal Government (1971), *Federal Budget*, Bonn.

Federal Statistical Office (1985), *Länderbericht Republik Korea 1985*, Wiesbaden.
Federal Statistical Office (1987), *Länderbericht Republik Korea 1987*, Wiesbaden.
Federal Statistical Office (1992), *Länderbericht Republik Korea 1992*, Wiesbaden.
Federal Statistical Office (1995), *Länderbericht Republik Korea 1995*, Wiesbaden.
Federal Statistical Office (1996), *Statistisches Jahrbuch für die Bundesrepublik Deutschland*, Wiesbaden.
Ferguson, G. (1996), 'A city within a city', *Industrial Engineering* (July), 26–30.
Fioretti, G.S., M. José and V. Soler (1984), *Post, Philately and Olympism*, IOC (ed.), Barcelona.
Fischer, H. (1998), 'Zäsur bei olympischen Schwimmwettkämpfen: Halbfinals sollen für mehr Spannung sorgen', *Frankfurter Allgemeine Zeitung*, **50** (29 April), 42.
Fitzpatrick, R.J. (1985), 'Rewarding risk: the success of the Olympic Arts Festival', *Olympic Message – Sources of Financing Sports* (3), 53–68.
Florin, K. and D. Carlin (1995), 'Ambush protection for Olympic sponsors', *Advertising Age*, **66** (44), 22–4.
French, S.P. and M.E. Disher (1997), 'Atlanta and the Olympics. A One-Year retrospective', *Journal of the American Planning Association*, **63** (3), 379–92.
Gantner, M. (1993), 'Ausgewählte ökonomische Aspekte von Olympischen Winterspielen in Innsbruck im Jahre 2002', Wissenschaftliche Stellungnahme von der Abteilung Theorie und Praxis der Budgetgestaltung, Institute for Financial Sciences at the University of Innsbruck, Innsbruck, typescript.
Garcia, S. (1993), 'Barcelona und die Olympischen Spiele', in H. Häussermann and W. Siebel (eds), *Festivalisierung der Stadtpolitik. Stadtentwicklung durch große Projekte, Leviatha. Zeitschrift für Sozialwissenschaft*, vol. 13, Opladen, pp. 251–77.
Geipel, R., I. Helbrecht and J. Pohl (1993), 'Die Münchener Olympischen Spiele von 1972 als Instrument der Stadtentwicklungspolitik', in Häussermann, H. and W. Siebel (eds), *Festivalisierung der Stadtpolitik. Stadtentwicklung durch große Projekte, in Leviatha. Zeitschrift für Sozialwissenschaft*, vol. 13, Opladen, pp. 278–304.
Genscher, H.-D. (1971), *5. Bericht der Bundesregierung an den Bundestag über die Vorbereitung und Gesamtfinanzierung der Olympischen Spiele 1972*, Drucksache VI/1968, German Bundestag, Bonn (13 March).
German Bundestag (1975), *Reporting of the Federal Government Regarding the Overall Financing of the Olympic Games 1972*, Drucksache 7/3066, Bonn (9 January).
German, D. (1993), '*World's fairs and the Olympics: the planning process*', unpublished master's thesis at the Clemson University, Department of City and Regional Planning, Clemson, SC.
Germann, D. (1996), 'Athen 1896 - vor 100 Jahren Geburtsstunde der Sport-Philatelie', Internationale Motivgruppen Olympiaden und Sport, Arbeitsgemeinschaft im Bund Deutscher Philatelisten e.V. (ed.), *Festschrift 30 Jahre*, Schifferstadt, pp. 24–7.
Getz, D. (1997), 'The impacts of mega events on tourism: strategies for destination', in Department of Tourism Studies (ed.), The Impact of Mega Events, papers of the Talk at the Top Conference (7–8 July), typescript.

Gillam, C. (1996b), 'Many cities are proud of their bus contributions', *Atlanta Business Chronicle* (31 May – 6 June), 12A.

Gillam, C. (1996c), 'Federal funds help ACOG, MARTA cover $15 million bus program', *Atlanta Business Chronicle* (31 May – 6 June), 12A.

Gladitz, R. and W. Günther (1995), Das Spiel mit den Spielen. Ein Themenabend: Atlanta und die Olympiade, broadcast by the TV station Arte (18 January 1996, 23:05 hrs).

Gold, M. and S. Harris (1993), 'Brits in $11m Games offer', *The Daily Telegraph Mirror* (21 June).

Goldberg, D.J. (1998), 'Olympic Ceremonies and Rites: Themes and objectives of the Ceremonies', IOC/IOA (eds), *Report of the Thirty-Seventh Session in 1997*, Lausanne.

Goldstar (1988a), 'Olympics', *Far Eastern Economic Review*, 141 (36), add-in.

Good, D. (1999), 'The Cultural Olympiad', in R. Cashman and A. Hughes (eds), *Staging the Olympics. The Event and Its Impact*, Sydney, pp. 159–69.

Goodbody, I. (1993), 'Britain's bid sets out vision of future', *The Times* (16 February).

GOPB (Governor's Office of Planning and Budgeting) (2000), *2002 Olympic Winter Games. Economic, Demographic and Fiscal Impacts*, Salt Lake City.

Gotta, F. (1996), 'Olympische Spiele brechen alle Werberekorde', *Die Welt* 160 (11 July), 28.

Gratton, G. (1999), 'The media', in R. Cashman and A. Hughes (eds), *Staging the Olympics. The Event and Its Impact*, Sydney, pp. 148–56.

Greenpeace (2000), 'Greenpeace Olympics report card', available at www.greenpeace.org.au, visited 15 August 2000.

Greising, D. (1995), 'Let the hype begin', *Business Week* (27 February), 114–18.

Greising, D. (1996), 'Atlanta's big leap', *Business Week* (29 July), 34–7.

Guegold, W.K. (1996), *100 Years of Olympic Music: The Music and Musicians of the Modern Olympic Games 1896–1996*, Mantua, OH.

Guest, J. M. (1987), 'Global teammates: Olympics and marketing', in R. Jackson and T.L. McPhail (eds), *The Olympic Movement and the Mass Media. Past, Present and Future*, International Conference Proceedings, Calgary, 9/3–9/5.

Guttman, L. (1979), *Sport für Körperbehinderte*, Munich.

Ha, T-T. (1996), 'Montreal memories of Games not all rosy', *Globe Mail Metro Edition* (18 July), A1–A4.

Hagelüken, A. (1996), 'Bier und Benzin für Atlanta. Was sich Firmen vom Olympia-Sponsoring versprechen', *Süddeutsche Zeitung*, **48** (13 July) (160), 19.

Häger, U. (1973), *Großes Lexikon der Philatelie*, Gütersloh.

Hahn, J. (1996), 'Das Fernsehen wird nicht kontrolliert', *Frankfurter Allgemeine Zeitung*, **48** (1 February), 26.

Hall, C.M. (1989), 'The politics of hallmark events', in G. Syme, B. Shaw, M. Fenton and W. Mueller (eds), *The Planning and Evaluation of Hallmark Events*, Brookfield, VT, 219–41.

Hall, C.M. (1992), *Hallmark Tourist Events. Impacts, Management & Planning*, London.

Hall, C.M. (1994), *Tourism and Politics*, New York.

Hanna, M. (1999), *Reconciliation in Olympism. Indegineous Culture in the Sydney Olympiad*, Sydney.

Hanusch, H. (1992), *Kosten-Nutzen-Analyse*, Munich.

Harenberg, B. (1991), *München 1972: Bilder und Daten zu den Olympischen Spielen*, Darmstadt.

Harris, L. (1997), 'A Survey of TOP corporate decision-makers in the U.S., Europe, Asia, and Latin America', prepared for the Atlanta Chamber of Commerce, typescript.

Harris, S. (1993), 'Shock deal in Games bid war', *The Daily Telegraph Mirror* (21 June).

Harte, E. (1928), 'Die Olympischen Spiele 1928 in Amsterdem', *Die Olympischen Spiele in Amsterdam 1928. Die Leibesübungen*, Berlin (5 November, (21), 521–36.

Häussermann, H. (1993), 'Die Politik der Festivalisierung und Festivalisierung der Politik', in H. Häussermann and W. Siebel (eds), *Festivalisierung der Stadtpolitik. Stadtentwicklung durch große Projekte*, Leviathan. Zeitschrift für Sozialwissenschaft. Special vol. 13, Opladen, pp. 7–31.

Heim, C. (1996), 'Olympia im six-pack', *Sports live* (3), 26–7.

Heinemann, K. (1995), *Einführung in die Sportökonomie*, Kiel.

Helyar, J. (1996), 'Turning point', *The Wall Street Journal* (19 July), R16.

Herzog, W. (1993), 'Für Barcelona haben sich die Spiele gelohnt', *Stuttgarter Tageszeitung* (22 September).

Hill, C.R. (1992*)*, *Olympic Politics*, Manchester.

Hill, C.R. (1996), *Olympic Politics*, 2nd edn., Manchester.

Himmelseher, V. (1981), *Die Entwicklung der Sportversicherung in der Bundesrepublik Deutschland*, Pulheim.

Hiskey, M. (1994), 'Cost is clear, but long-term effect is unknown', *The Atlanta Journal* (21 August), E6–E7.

Hoberman, J. (1986), *The Olympic Crisis. Sport, Politics and the Moral Order*, New Rochelle, NY.

Hochbrückner, A. (2001), 'Die Präsentation der Olympischen Spiele Sydney 2000 in Fernsehen und Fernsehwerbung – ein internationaler Vergleich', unpublished Diplomarbeit, Johannes Gutenberg-Universität, Mainz.

Hofmann, A. (2001), 'Der städtische Schrottplatz als Museum für tonnenschwere Erinnerungen', *Frankfurter Allgemeine Zeitung*, 53 14 September, (214), 48.

Höhler, G. (1997), 'Athen versöhnt sich mit Olympia', *Der Tagesspiegel* (7 September).

Holzweißig, G. (1981), *Diplomatie im Trainingsanzug. Sport als politisches Instrument der DDR*, Oldenburg.

Howard, D.R. and J.L. Crompton (1995), *Financing Sport*, Morgantown, WV.

Hubbard, A. (1993), 'Barnum and bullshine', *The Observer* (7 February).

Huberty, E. and B.W. Wange (1976), *Die Olympischen Spiele. Montreal-Innsbruck*, Munich.

Humphreys, J.M. and M.K. Plummer (1992), 'The economic impact on the state of Georgia of hosting the Olympic Games', Atlanta, typescript.

Humphreys, J.M. and M.K. Plummer (1996), 'The economic impact on the state of Georgia of hosting the Olympic Games', Atlanta, typescript.

Huntington, S.P. (1996), *Kampf der Kulturen. Die Neugestaltung der Weltpolitik im 21. Jahrhundert*. Munich and Vienna.

Huot, R. (1996), 'Olympic coins - collectibles with a mission', *Olympic Message - Sources of Financing Sports* (3), 99–102.

Hyun, J. (1998), 'The impact of the 1988 Seoul Olympics on inbound tourism to Korea', *Study on Tourism*, 235–45.

International Monetary Fund (IMF) (1996), *International Financial Statistics. Yearbook 1996*, Washington, DC.

International Monetary Fund (IMF) (1997), *International Financial Statistics. Yearbook 1997*, Washington, DC.

International Monetary Fund (IMF) (2000), *International Financial Statistics. Yearbook 2000*, Washington, DC.

International Olympic Committee (1993a), *Marketing Matters* (2), Lausanne.

International Olympic Committee (IOC) (1958), *Olympic Charter 1958*, Lausanne.

International Olympic Committee (IOC) (1966a) *Minutes of the 64th Session of the IOC*, Rome (25–28 April 1966).

International Olympic Committee (IOC) (1966b) *Minutes of the 72th Session der IOC-Exekutive*, Rome (21–24 April 1966).

International Olympic Committee (IOC) (1978a), *Olympic Charter 1978*, Lausanne.

International Olympic Committee (IOC) (1978b), 'Agreement between IOC and the City of Los Angeles' (27 October), typescript.

International Olympic Committee (IOC) (1979), 'Agreement between IOC, United States Olympic Committee and Organising Committee of Games' (1 March), typescript.

International Olympic Committee (IOC) (1983), *Minutes of the Meeting of the IOC Executive Board with the National Olympic Committees*, Los Angeles (20 January).

International Olympic Committee (IOC) (1984), *Olympic Charter 1984*, Lausanne.

International Olympic Committee (IOC) (1987), *Olympic Charter 1987*, Lausanne.

International Olympic Committee (IOC) (1989), *Olympic Charter 1989*, Lausanne.

International Olympic Committee (IOC) (1993b), *Report IOC Enquiry Commission for the Games of the XXVII Olympiad 2000*, Lausanne.

International Olympic Committee (IOC) (1994), *Marketing Matters* (5), Lausanne.

International Olympic Committee (IOC) (1994b), *Olympic Charter 1994*, Lausanne.

International Olympic Committee (IOC) (1995a), *Manual for Candidate Cities for the Games of the XXVIII Olympiad 2004*, Lausanne.

International Olympic Committee (IOC) (1995b), *1995 Olympic Marketing Fact File*, Lausanne (7 June).

International Olympic Committee (IOC) (1995c), *Olympic Charter 1995*, Lausanne.

International Olympic Committee (IOC) (1996a), *Marketing Matters* (9), Lausanne.

International Olympic Committee (IOC) (1996b), *Marketing Matters* (8), Lausanne.

International Olympic Committee (IOC) (1996c), *1996 Olympic Marketing Fact File*, Lausanne (5 July).

International Olympic Committee (IOC) (1997a), *Marketing Matters* (10), Lausanne.

International Olympic Committee (IOC) (1997b), *Olympic Broadcast Analysis Report. Centennial Olympic Games 1996*, Lausanne.

International Olympic Committee (IOC) (1997c), *Marketing Matters* (11), Lausanne.

International Olympic Committee (IOC) (1997d), 'Host City Contract for the Games of the XXVIII Olympiad in the Year 2004' Lausanne (17 June).

International Olympic Committee (IOC) (1997e), *Report of the IOC Evaluation Commission for the Games of the XXVIII Olympiad 2004*, Lausanne (20 January).

International Olympic Committee (IOC) (1998a), *The Modernization of the Olympic Movement 1980–1998*, Lausanne.

International Olympic Committee (IOC) (1998b), *Marketing Matters* (12), Lausanne.

International Olympic Committee (IOC) (1999a), *Ambush Prevention and Clean Venue Guidelines*, Lausanne.

International Olympic Committee (IOC) (1999c), *Manual for Candidate Cities for the Games of the XXIX Olympiad 2008*, Lausanne: IOC.

International Olympic Committee (IOC) (1999e), *Broadcasting the Olympics*, Lausanne.

International Olympic Committee (IOC) (1999f), *Olympic Movement Directory*, Lausanne.

International Olympic Committee (IOC) (2000c), *Candidature Acceptance Procedure Games of the XXIX Olympiad 2008*, report by the IOC Candidature Acceptance Working Group to the executive board of the International Olympic Committee (18 August), Lausanne.

International Olympic Committee (IOC) (2000d), *The Olympic Games. Fundamentals and Ceremonies*, Lausanne.

International Olympic Committee (IOC) (2000e), *Olympic Charter 2000*, Lausanne.

International Olympic Committee (IOC) (2001a), *Sydney 2000 Marketing Report*, Lausanne: IOC.

International Olympic Committee (IOC) (2001b), *Marketing Matters* (18), Lausanne.

International Olympic Committee (IOC) (2001c), *Marketing Matters* (19), Lausanne.

International Olympic Committee (IOC) (2001d), *Olympic Games and Architecture. The Future of Host Cities*, Lausanne.

International Olympic Committee (IOC) (2001e), *Host City Contract for the Games of the XXIX Olympiad in the Year 2008*, (27 June), Lausanne.

International Olympic Committee (IOC) (2002), *Olympic Marketing Fact File*, Lausanne.

International Olympic Committee (IOC) (2003a), *Report of the Olympic Study Commission*, Lausanne.

International Olympic Committee (IOC) (2003b), *Marketing Matters* (22), Lausanne.

International Olympic Committee (IOC) (2003d), *Olympic Charter 2003*, Lausanne.

International Olympic Committee (IOC) (2004), *Games fo the XXX Olympiad in 2012*, Report by the IOC Candidature Acceptance Working Group to the executive board of the International Olympic Committee (12 March), Lausanne.

International Olympic Committee (IOC) (2004a), European TV-Rights for 2012 and 2012. Olympic News, www.olympic.org, visited 20 July 2004.

International Olympic Committee (IOC) (2004b), *Fact File*, Lausanne.

ISL (International Sport Leisure Agency) (1985), *TOP – The Consumer View. An International Research Survey into Sponsorship of the Olympic Games* (7 June), Lucerne.

Jägemann, H. (1997), 'Die internationale Dimension. Interview mit Erika Dienstl', in Deutscher Sportbund (ed.), *Sport Schützt Umwelt*, Frankfurt/M, p. 5.

Jennings, A. and C. Sambrook (2000), *This Great Olympic Swindle. When the World Wanted its Games Back*, Sydney.

Jeong, G.-H. (1997), 'Residents' perceptions on the long-term impacts of the Seoul Olympics to the Chamsil area development in a tourism perspective', in Department of Tourism Studies (ed.), The Impact of Mega Events, papers of the Talk at the Top conference (7–8 July), typescript.

Kaiser, U. and H. Maegerlein (1984), *Los Angeles, Olympische Spiele 1984, Sarajevo*, München.

Kang, Y.-S. and S. Perdue (1994), 'Long-term impacts of a mega-event on international tourismto the host country. A conceptual model and the case of the 1988 Seoul Olympics', in M. Uysal (ed.), *Global Tourism Behaviour*, Binghampton, NY, 205–26.

Katalis K. (2002), Intégrer l'expérience des Jeux Olympiques à Sydney en 2000 à la préparation des Jeux Olympiques à Athènes en 2004', in IOC/IOA (eds), *Rapport de la Quarante et unième Session pour Jeunes Participants 2001*, Olympia.

Kearney, S. (2001), 'Games cost blows to $3.3 billion', *Sunday Mail* (28 October).

Keller, P. (2001), 'Introductory Report', *World Conference on Sport and Tourism*, Madrid.

Kidane, F. (1997), 'The Olympic Movement and the environment', in L. DaCosta (ed.), *Environment and Sport. An International Overview*, Porto, 246–54.

Killanin, M. (1983), *My Olympic Years*, London.

Kim, J.-G., S.W. Rhee, J.-Ch. Yu, K.M. Koo and J.Ch. Hong (1989), *Impact of the Seoul Olympic Games on National Development*, Seoul: Korea Development Institute.

Kim, U.-Y. (1990), *The Greatest Olympics – from Baden Baden to Seoul*, Seoul.

Kirchner, C. (1980), *Auswirkungen von internationalen Großveranstaltungen auf die regionale Entwicklung. Dargestellt am Beispiel der IX. und XII. Olympischen Winterspiele Innsbruck 1964 und 1976*, Innsbruck.

Kistner, T. and J. Weinreich (1996), *Muskelspiele. Ein Abgesang auf Olympia*, Berlin.

Klatell, D.A. and N. Marcus (1988), *Sports for Sale. Television, Money, and the Fans*, Oxford.

Klink, B. (1996), 'Marketer sind im Olympiafieber', *Horizont* (12), 17.

Kloth, M. (1996), *Ausverkauf des Nachlasses: Geld zählt nichts gegen die fünf Ringe*, AGSFA news agency (25 August).

Klotz, G. (1996), 'Größer, Teurer, Klotziger: In der Hitze von Atlanta schmelzen die Rekorde', *Saarbrücker Zeitung* (10 July).

Koar, J. (1993), 'Los Angeles trägt die Goldmedaille für finanziellen Gewinn', *Stuttgarter Zeitung* (24 May).

Kotler, P. and F. Bliemel (1992), *Marketing – Management. Analyse, Planung, Umsetzung und Steuerung*, 7th completely revised edn., Stuttgart, pp. 917–60.

KPMG Peat Marwick (1993), 'Sydney Olympics 2000 economic impact study', typescript.

Krajasits, C. (1995), 'Olympische Winterspiele als Impuls für den Tourismus', in M. Steiner and E. Thöni (eds), *Sport und Ökonomie*, Graz, pp. 111–39.

Kramar, M.A. (1994), 'Development of East European and Soviet direct trade relations with South Korea, 1970–91', dissertation Florida State University, Tallahassee.

Krämer, W. (1996), 'Beim IOC rangiert der Sport also doch vor Geld', *NOK-Report* (3), 18–20.

Krause, M. (1993), *Erlös aus Olympia TV-Rechten gewichtiges Argument für Berlin*, AGSPORT news agency (13 July).

Krüger, A. (1996), 'The masses are much more sensitive to the perfection of the whole than to any separate details: the influence of John Ruskin's Political economy on Pierre de Coubertin', in the International Center for Olympic Studies (ed.), *Olympika*, London, ON (5), pp. 25–43.

Kühner, H. (1994), 'Entwicklung der Olympischen Spiele unter Berücksichtigung der Kommerzialisierung des Sports', unpublished Magisterarbeit, University of Stuttgart, Stuttgart.

Kühnle, D. (1996), 'Wir müssen die Olympische Einheit bewahren', in *Lufthansa Bordbuch* (4), 33–34.

Kwag, D.-H. (1988), 'Post-Olympic prospects of the Korean economy', Korea Exchange Bank, *Monthly Review* (September), 3–10.

Kynge, J., R. McGregor and D. Owen (2001), 'Jubel und Kritik nach IOC-Votum für China', *Financial Times Deutschland* (16 June), 13.

Lager, C. (1995), 'Volkswirtschaftliche Wirkungen 'OWS Graz 2002' – Simulation mittels eines multisektoralen dynamischen Modells', in M. Steiner, and E. Thöni (eds), *Sport und Ökonomie*, Graz, pp. 23–70.

Landry, F. (1987), 'Pierre de Coubertin, the modern Olympic Games and the Arts', in O. Szymiczek and Internatioanl Olympic Academy (eds), *Report of the Twenty-Sixth Session in 1986*, Lausanne, pp. 93–103.

Landry, F. and M. Yerlès (1996), *The International Olympic Committee. One Hundred Years. The Idea – The Presidents – The Achievements*, vol. 3, Lausanne.

Lee, C. (1988a), 'From wartime rubble to Olympic host', *Far Eastern Economic Revie*, (36), 60–5.

Lee, C. (1988c), 'Business boom causes hunger for space', *Far Eastern Economic Review*, (23), 72–3.

Lee, D.-W. (1989), *How to prepare Olympics and its task*, Seoul.

Lenk, H. (1972), *Werte Ziele Wirklichkeit der modernen Olympischen Spiele*, Beiträge zur Lehre und Forschung der Leibeserziehung, (17/18), Schorndorf.

Lennartz, K., W. Borgers and A. Höfer (eds) (2000), *Olympische Siege: Medaillen - Diplome - Ehrungen*, Berlin.

Lenskyj, H.J. (1996), 'When Winners are Losers. Toronto and Sydney Bids for the Summer Olympics', *Journal of Sport & Social Issues*, **20** (4), 392–410.

Lenskyj, H.J. (2000), *Inside the Olympic Industry. Power, Politics, and Activism*, New York.

Lenskyj, H.J. (2002), *The Best Olympics Ever? Social Impacts of Sydney 2000*, Albany.

Levesque, K. (2001), 'Il y a 25 ans les Jeux: une monstrueuse aventure financière', *Le Devoir* (7 July).

Lewis, R. (2004), 'The big picture', *Olympic Review*, 49 (4), 54–9.

Lillehammer OCOG (1994), *The Official Report of the Organizing Committee for the Games of the XVII Winter Games, Lillehammer 1994*, Lillehammer.

Liwocha, S. (1996), 'Nike will der Sportwelt sein Brandzeichen aufdrücken', *Stuttgarter Zeitung* (4 July) 152, 11.

Llinés, M. (1996), 'The history of Olympic ceremonies. From Athens (1896) to Los Angeles (1984). An overview', in M. Moragas Spà, J. MacAloon and M. Llinés (eds), *Olympic Ceremonies Historical Continuity and Cultural Exchange*, Lausanne, pp. 63–79.

Los Angeles OCOG (1979), 'Financial Plan. LAOOC. Planning, Box 194', Los Angeles (10 September), typescript.

Los Angeles OCOG (1981), *Second Official Report of the Organizing Committee for the XXIII Olympiad submitted to the members of the International Olympic Committee in Baden Baden* (1 October), Los Angeles.

Los Angeles OCOG (1984), *Official Report of the Organising Committee of the Games of Los Angeles 1984*, vol. 1, Los Angeles.

Lyberg, W. (s.t.), The IOC Sessions 1956–88, vol. 2, Lausanne, typescript.

Madden, J., M. Crowe and R. Cow (1997), *The Economic Impact of the Sydney Olympic Games, Final Report*, NSW Treasury and the Centre for Regional Economic, Economic Analysis University of Tasmania.

Mädler, H.-H. and J. Hetzger (1996), 'Topsponsor eröffnet seine eigenen Spiele', *Kölner Rundschau* (3 July).

Maennig, W. (1992), 'Kosten und Erlöse Olympischer Spiele in Berlin 2000', Berlin, typescript.

Maennig, W. (1997), 'Olympische Spiele und Wirtschaft. Weitverbreitete Mißverständnisse und achtzehn (Gegen-) Thesen', in O. Gruppe (ed.), *Olympischer Sport*, Schorndorf, 157–79.

Magnay, J. (1999), 'When big money gets into the Games', *The Sydney Morning Herald* (11 December), 46.

Marr, R. and A. Picot (1991), 'Absatzwirtschaft', in E. Heinen (ed.), *Industriebetriebslehre. Entscheidungen im Industriebetrieb*, 9th ed., Wiesbaden, 623–728.

Masterman, G. (2003), 'The event planning process: strategies and successful legacies', in M. Moragas, C. Kennett and N. Puig (eds), *The Legacy of Olympic Games (1984–2000)*, Lausanne, 457–64.

Maurer, M. (1996), 'Wessen Spiele?', *Stuttgarter Zeitung* (20 July).

Mayer, O. (1957a), Letter to A. Brundage (31 July), Brundage Collection, Box 114.

Mayer, O. (1957b), Letter to A. Brundage (21 December), Brundage Collection, Box 114.

McBeth, J. (1988a), 'Sporting Seoul awaits the five-ring circus', *Far Eastern Economic Review* (7 April), (14), 42–6.

McBeth, J. (1988b), 'Games: good news and bad', *Far Eastern Economic Review* (36), 62.

McBeth, J. (1988c), 'Anti-terrorism forces trained to Olympic pitch', *Far Eastern Economic Review* (36), 65–8.

McBeth, J. (1988d), 'Peking-Seoul link is out of the closet', *Far Eastern Economic Review* (36), 83–5.

McCay, M. and C. Plumb (2001), 'Reaching beyond the gold: the impact of the Olympic Games on real estate markets', *Global Insights*, (1).

McDowell, C.E. (1950), Letter to Arthur Smith (6 April), Brundage Collection, Box 225.

McGovern, T. (1950), Letter to A. Brundage (2 October), Brundage Collection, Box 225.

Medialdea, F. (1993), *Ein Jahr nach den Spielen, Olympischer Geist kehrt nach Barcelona zurück*, AGSPORT news agency (23 July).

Meffert, H. (1998), *Marketing*, 8th edn, Wiesbaden.

Meisl, W. (1928), 'Die Krise der Olympischen Idee', in W. Richter (ed.), *Die Olympischen Spiele von Amsterdam 1928*, Leipzig.

Mensah, E.A. (1996), 'The example of Africa', *Olympic Message – the Olympic Movement and the Mass Media* (1), 49–51.

Messing, M. (1993), 'Opinions on young people on the Olympic idea through cultural manifestations', in Panagiotopoulos (ed.), *The Institution of the Olympic Games. A Multidisciplinary Approach*. Athens, pp. 431–35.

Messing, M. (1998), 'The Cultural Olympiads of Barcelona and Atlanta from German tourists' point of view', in IOC and N. Müller (eds), *Coubertin and Olympism, Questions for the Future. Le Havre 1897–1997*, Niedernhausen, Strassburg, Sydney, pp. 276–80.

Messing, M. and D. Voigt (1981), 'Exkurs: Die Olympischen Spiele in Montreal und Moskau in der Berichterstattung der Medien', in G. Holzweißig (ed.), *Diplomatie im Trainingsanzug. Sport als politisches Instrument der DDR*, Oldenburg, pp. 131–86.

Messing, M. and N. Müller (1995), 'Werte, Programm und Organisation Olympischer Spiele im Urteil deutscher Sporttouristen in Barcelona 1992', *Forschungsmagazin der Johannes Gutenberg-Universität Mainz*, (2), 27–41.

Messing, M. and N. Müller (1996), 'Veranstaltungsbesuch und sportpolitische Polarisation deutscher Olympia-Touristen in Barcelona 1992', in Müller, N. and M. Messing (eds), *Auf der Suche nach der Olympischen Idee. Facetten der Forschung von Athen bis Atlanta*, Kassel, pp. 219–50.

Messing, M. and N. Müller (2001), 'Dataenauswertung der Befragung von Touristen während der Spiele in Sydney 2000', unveröffentlicher Forschungsbericht, Mainz.

Mexico OCOG (1969), *Official Report, Mexico 1968*, Mexico City.

Meyer-Künzel, M. (1999), 'Städtebau der Weltausstellungen und Olympischen Spiele. Stadtentwicklung der Veranstaltungsorte', Dissertation Technische Universität Carolo-Wilhemina, Braunschweig.

Meyer-Künzel, M. (2001), *Der planbare Nutzen. Stadtentwicklung durch Weltausstellung und Olympische Spiele*, Hamburg.

Miller, D. (1993), 'Manchester starts fund to help poor relations', *The Times* (22 May).

Millet, L. (1995), 'The Games of the city', in M. Moragas Spà and M. Botella (eds), *The Keys to Success*, Barcelona, pp. 188–202.

Minister of Industry, Trade and Commerce (ed.) (1977), *Canada Year Book 1976–77*, Ottawa.

Minister of Industry, Trade and Commerce (ed.) (1981), *Canada Year Book 1980–81*, Ottawa.

Minister of Industry, Trade and Commerce (ed.) (1985), *Canada Year Book 1985*, Ottawa.

Ministerio de Economía y Hacienda. Instituto Nacional de Estadística (1988), *Anuario Estadístico de España 1988*, Madrid.

Ministerio de Economía y Hacienda. Instituto Nacional de Estadística (1991), *Anuario Estadístico de España 1992*, Madrid.

Ministerio de Economía y Hacienda. Instituto Nacional de Estadística (1992), *Anuario Estadístico de España 1992*, Madrid.

Ministerio de Economía y Hacienda. Instituto Nacional de Estadística (1993), *Anuario Estadístico de España 1992*, Madrid.

Ministerio de Economía y Hacienda. Instituto Nacional de Estadística (1996), *Anuario Estadístico de España 1996*, Madrid.

Ministerio de Industria (1990), Anuario de Estadística, Madrid.

Montreal OCOG (1974), *Appendices to the Report by the Organizing Committee of the 1976 Olympic Games. Presented to the Executive Board of the IOC*, Vienna (22 October).

Montreal OCOG (1976), *Games of the XXI. Olympiad, Montreal 1976, Official Report*, vol. 1, Montreal.

Moragas Spà, M. (1991), 'Communication and culture, a single project: Barcelona 1992', in Centre d'Éstudis Olímpics i de l'Esport (ed.), *Olympic Games Media and Cultural Exchanges*, Barcelona, pp. 69–83.

Moragas Spà, M., A. Belén Moreno and R. Paniagua (2000), 'The evolution of volunteers at the Olympic Games', in M. Moragas, A.B. Moreno and N. Puig (eds), *Volunteers, Global Society and the Olympic Movement*, 24–26 November 1999, Lausanne, pp. 133–154.

Moragas Spà, M., N. Rivenburgh and J.F. Larson (1995), *Television in the Olympics*, London.

Morin, A. (1981), 'Olympia-Münzen – ein Markt', in Nationales Olympisches Komitee für Deutschland (ed.), *Die Zukunft der Olympischen Spiele*, Bulletin 6, Olympischer Kongress, Baden-Baden, pp. 54–60.

Morse, J. (2001), 'The Olympic Games and Australian tourism', paper presented at the World Conference on Sport and Tourism, Barcelona.

Moscow OCOG (1980), *Games of the XXII. Olympiad, Moscow 1980, Official Report of the Organising Committee of the Games*, Moscow.

Mount, M.C. (1985), 'OCOG responsibilities for broadcaster facilities', *Olympic Message*, (9), 45–51.

MRB/Research International/VPRC consortium (2004), *The image of the Olympic Games – Greek national survey*, Athens.

Müller, N. (1998), 'Kann die Olympische Idee überleben?', *Olympisches Feuer* (1), 11–13.

Müller, N. and IOC (eds) (1986), *Pierre de Coubertin. Textes Choisis, Vol. 2, Olympisme*. Zürich, Hildesheim and New York.

Müller, N. and M. Messing (1992), 'Unveröffentlichter tabellarischer Bericht zur Befragung deutscher Olympiatouristen in Barcelona 1992', Fachbereich Sport der Universität Mainz, Mainz.

Müller, N. and M. Messing (1997a), 'Unpublished tables to report on the survey among German Olympic tourists in Atlanta '96', Sports Faculty of the Johannes Gutenberg University, Mainz.

Müller, N. and M. Messing (1997b), 'Unveröffentlichter tabellarischer Bericht zur Befragung im Olympischen Jugendlager Nordrhein-Westfalen in Atlanta 1996', Fachbereich Sport der Universität Mainz, Mainz.

Müller, N. and S. Gieseler (1996), 'Olympische Spiele im Schatten des 1. Weltkrieges', in N. Müller and M. Messing (eds), *Auf der Suche nach der Olympischen Idee. Facetten der Forschung von Athen bis Atlanta*, Kassel, pp. 135–56.

Münchner Olympiapark GmbH (1991), *Geschäftsbericht 1991*, Munich.

Münchner Olympiapark GmbH (1992), *Geschäftsbericht 1992*, Munich.

Münchner Olympiapark GmbH (1993), *Geschäftsbericht 1993*, Munich.

Münchner Olympiapark GmbH (1994a), *Geschäftsbericht 1994*, Munich.

Münchner Olympiapark GmbH (1994b), *Der Olympiapark im Zahlenspiegel*, Munich.

Münchner Olympiapark GmbH (1995), *Geschäftsbericht 1995*, Munich.

Münchner Olympiapark GmbH (1996), *Geschäftsbericht 1996*, Munich.

Münchner Olympiapark GmbH (1997), *Geschäftsbericht 1997*, Munich.

Münchner Olympiapark GmbH (1998), *Geschäftsbericht 1998*, Munich.

Münchner Olympiapark GmbH (1999), *Geschäftsbericht 1999*, Munich.

Münchner Olympiapark GmbH (2000), *Geschäftsbericht 2000*, Munich.

Münchner Olympiapark GmbH (2001), *Geschäftsbericht 2001*, Munich.

Muñoz, F.M. (1996), 'Historic Evolution and Urban Planning Typology of Olympic Villages', Moragas Spà, M., M. Llinés M. and B. Kidd (eds), *Olympic Villages. Hundred Years of Urban Planning and Shared Experiences*. International Symposium on Olympic Villages. Lausanne, 27-51.

Müssig, K. et al. (eds) (1988), *Banklexikon*, 10th ed., Wiesbaden.

Nagano OCOG (1997), 'Olympic Coin agreement' (15 July), typescript

Nahr, G. (1972), 'Mit olympischer Schubkraft in die Krise', in H.-H. Henschen and R. Wetter, *Anti-Olympia. Ein Beitrag zur mutwilligen Defamierung und öffentlichen Destruktion der Olympischen Spiele und anderer Narreteien*, Munich, pp. 98–106.

Nederlands Olympisch Comité (ed.) (1930), *Officieel Gedenkbook van de Spielen der IXe Olympiade Amsterdam,1928*, Amsterdam.

Netzle, S. (1996), 'Ambush Marketing, die neue unfaire Marketing-Maßnahme im Sport', *SpuRt Zeitschrift für Sport und Recht* (3), 86–7.

New South Wales (NSW) (2001), *Budget Statement 2001–2002*, Sydney.

New Unity Movement (ed.) (1997), 'The 2004 Olympics: the Games we cannot win', *The Worker*, (13), Kenwyn, typoscript.

Newman, H.K. (1999*), Southern Hospitality: Tourism and the Growth of Atlanta*, Tuscaloosa.

Newman, R. (1999), 'Design', in R. Cashman and A. Hughes (eds), *Staging the Olympics. The Event and Its Impact*, Sydney, pp. 46–55.

Nieschlag, R., E. Dichtl and H. Hörschgen (1994), *Marketing*, 17th edn., Berlin.

NN (1972a), 'Täglich auf drei Kanälen', *Der Spiegel*, **26** (3), 32–6.

NN (1972b), 'Sieg – Tor – uff – geschafft', *Der Spiegel*, **26** (3), 26–31.

NN (1972c), 'Knall, Schuß, bumms, raus, weg', *Der Spiegel*, **26** (28 August) (36), 24–38.

NN (1984a), 'A gold for belt-tightening', *The Economist* (12 May), 41–2.

NN (1984c), '88 Games to cost 7 times as much as L.A. Olympics', *The Korean Herald* (25 August).

NN (1984d), 'Seoul to fully guarantee safety for '88 Olympians', *The Korean Herald* (29 August).

NN (1987), 'ABC and the Olympics – producing and selling the Games', in R. Jackson and T.L. Mc Phail (eds), *The Olympic Movement and the Mass Media. Past, Present and Future*, International Conference Proceedings, Calgary, pp. 8-3–8-11.

NN (1988a), 'Swim federation moves to preserve Olympic facilities', *Montreal Gazette* (31 May), E1.

NN (1988b), 'Insurance compensation for Olympic athletes, officials record $ 18, 000', *The Korean Herald* (10 August).

NN (1988c), 'Temporary slowdown expected in post-Olympic economy', *Newsreview* (13 August), 11.

NN (1988d), 'Seoul-Moscow direct sealane in negotiation', *Newsreview* (20 August), 11.

NN (1988e), 'Economy slows down in second quarter', *Newsreview* (27 August), 8.

NN (1988h), 'Olympic souvenir makers enjoy Seoul days of gold', *The Korean Herald* (16 October).

NN (1988i), 'SLOOC delivers $2 mil. Olympic profits to IOC', The Korean Herald (21 December).

NN (1989), 'SLOOC made net profit of 121, 7 mil. during '88 Olympics', *The Korean Herald* (20 August).

NN (1992), 'Gehört das Fernsehn zu den Verlierern?', *Stuttgarter Zeitung* (6 February).

NN (1993) 'China insists it has right to host Games', *The Examiner* (22 September).

NN (1994), 'Coca-Cola "To Sponsor is to Believe"', *Olympic Magazine of the Olympic Museum*, (1994) 4, 28–31.

NN (1995a), *Keine griechischen Einwände gegen Coca Cola als Sponsor des Feuers*, dpa (18 February).

NN (1995c), *Eintrittskarten für Olympia 1996 im Schnitt für 39, 72 Dollar*, AGNACH agency (14 March).

NN (1995d), *Elf Millionen Olympia-Tickets*, AGNACH news agency (15 March).

NN (1995e), *60 US-Städte helfen Atlanta mit insgesamt 2000 Bussen aus*, AGNACH news agency (15 March).

NN (1995f), 'Sponsorships of the Future and the Future of Sponsorship', International Events Group, IEG Sponsorship Report (May 27), pp. 1, 4–6, Typescript.

NN (1996a), 'Vor Terror darf ich keine Angst haben', *Der Spiegel*, 50 (32), 179–80.

NN (1996c), 'Unfair und illegal. Ambush-Marketer schaden sich selbst', *DSM, Marketing News* (3), 2.

NN (1996d), 'Kurze Meldungen', *Frankfurter Allgemeine Zeitung*, **48** (25 January), 25.

NN (1996e), 'OBI bleibt TOP-Sponsor auch für die nächste Olympiade', *DSM, Marketing News* (1), 3.

NN (1996f), 'Bankgesellschaft Berlin: Image und Bekanntheit durch das Team Olympia', *DSM, Marketing News* (4), 6.

NN (1996g), 'IOC entscheidet sich für EBU-Angebot', *Frankfurter Allgemeine Zeitung* (31 January), 26.

NN (1996h), 'Olympics 2004', *Argus (South Africa)* (14 February).

NN (1996i), 'Welcome on board', *Der Spiegel*, 50 (32), 126–27.

NN (1996j), 'Olympische Spiele in Atlanta: Die Sponsoren laufen sich warm', *Frankfurter Allgemeine Zeitung*, **48** (18 April), 17.

NN (1996k), 'Atlanta's high jump', *The Economist* (May 4), 25–6.

NN (1996l), 'Das Geschäft des Jahrhunderts', *General-Anzeiger* (17 July).

NN (1996m), 'Eine neue Dimension der Gewalt erreicht', *Frankfurter Allgemeine Zeitung*, **48** (29 July), (174), 32.

NN (1996n), 'Olympia für Sponsoren immer teurer', *Frankfurter Allgemeine Zeitung*, **48** (6 November), 21.

NN (1996o), 'Trotz Vermarktungsrekorden leere Kassen beim Olympia-Veranstalter', *Frankfurter Allgemeine Zeitung*, **48** (July 13), 36.

NN (1996p), 'IOC entscheidet sich für EBU-Angebot', *Frankfurter Allgemeine Zeitung*, **48** (31 January), 26.

NN (1997a), 'Coca-Cola steigert den Gewinn um 17 Prozent', *Frankfurter Allgemeine Zeitung*, **49** (3 Februar), 18.

NN (1997b), 'Wilder Markt in Goldgräberstimmung', *Sponsors*, **2** (8), 10–2.

NN (1997c), 'Olympiastadion gefährdet', *Sponsors*, **2** (11), 33.

NN (1997d), 'Große Sportereignisse sind für alle da', *Frankfurter Allgemeine Zeitung* (6 February), 18.

NN (1997e), *Atlanta mit ausgeglichener Abschlußbilanz*, AGSPORT news agency (1 July).

NN (1997f), 'Samaranchs Favoritin', *Frankfurter Allgemeine Zeitung*, **49** (8 September), 34.

NN (1997g), 'Kurze Meldungen', *Frankfurter Allgemeine Zeitung*, **49** (28 October), 42.

NN (1999a), 'Das IOC kauft Sydney die Olympia-Anleitung ab', *Frankfurter Allgemeine Zeitung*, **50** (22 September), (220), 47.

NN (1999b), 'Die Locke des Sportlers entlarvt Fälschungen', *Frankfurter Allgemeine Zeitung*, **50** (8 October), (234), 39.

NN (1999c), *Olympia-Organisatoren entschuldigen sich für Ticket-Skandal – Organisatoren beugen sich dem Druck von Verbraucherschützern*, dpa (29 October).

NN (2000a), 'Finanzen gedeckt: Die Bürger zahlen drauf', *Frankfurter Allgemeine Zeitung*, **51** (4 February), 40.

NN (2000b) 'Sydney gives NBC their lowest ratings since Tokyo in '64', *The Sydney Morning Herald*, (1 October), Internet.

NN (2001a), 'Ein weltrekordtauglicher Plastik-Pool', *Frankfurter Allgemeine Zeitung*, **52** (24 July), 43.

NN (2001b), 'Die Olympiastadt Peking [...]', *Frankfurter Allgemeine Zeitung*, **52** (26 July), (171), 42.

NN (2003), 'Sicherheit', *Frankfurter Allgemeine Zeitung*, **54** (26 November), 1–2.

NN (2004), 'EBU überbietet sich selbst für Olympia', *Frankfurter Allgemeine Zeitung*, **55** (19 Juni), 31.

NN (s.t.c), 'Sieben Argumente gegen Olympia', in H. Baum (ed.), *Nolympia Express. Ost/West-Bündnis gegen Olympia*, Berlin, p. 1.

NN (s.t.d), 'Barcelona in der Pleite', in H. Baum (ed.), *Nolympia Express. Ost/West-Bündnis gegen Olympia*, Berlin, p. 2.

Oanda, http://www.oanda.com, visited 2002.

Olympic Co-ordination Authority (2002), *Annual Report 2002*, Sydney.

Olympic Games Study Commission (2003), *Report to the 115th IOC Session, Prague*, (July), Lausanne.

Onesti, G. (1960), Letter to A. Brundage (6 May), Brundage Collection, Box 168.

Organisation for Economic Co-operation and Development (OECD) (1996), *National Accounts*, vol. 1, Paris.

Organisation for Economic Co-operation and Development (OECD) (2003), *Main Economic Indicators*, Paris.

Organisationskomitee München (1974a), *Die Spiele – Die Organisation*, Munich.

Organisationskomitee München (1974b), *Die Spiele – Die Bauten*, Munich.

Pabst, U. (ed.) (1986), *Kunst + Design Kultur Olympia. Willi Daume. Preisträger der Stankowski-Stiftung 1986*, Kassel.

Papanikos, G. (1999), *The Olympic Games of 2004 and its Impact on Greek Tourism*, working paper of the Tourism Research Institute, study series, (5), Athens.

Parc Olympique Montreal (2001), *Régie des Installations Olympiques, Rapport Annual 1997*, Montreal.

Park, S.-J. (1991), *The Seoul Olympics – the Inside Story*, London.

Parker, L. (2001), 'Business lands', *Clayton UTZ Magazine*, 7–9.

Parliament of the Commonwealth of Australia (1995), *Olympics 2000 ... and the Winner is?* Report by the House of Representatives Standing Committee on Industry, Science and Technology, Canberra.

Parsons, T. (1976), 'Zur Theorie sozialer Systeme', *Studienbücher zur Sozialwissenschaft*, vol. 14, Opladen.

Patterson, K. (1994), 'Who owns whom', *Dun & Bradstreet International*, (2).

Payne, M. (1989), 'Sport and industry', *Olympic Message – Marketing and Olympism* (24 July), 37–43.

Payne, M. (1996), 'Olympic marketing in the next millennium', *Olympic Message – Sources of Financing Sports*, (3), 19–24.

Payne, M. (1998), 'The sponsoring and marketing of the Atlanta Olympic Games', in IOC/IOA (eds), *Report of the Thirty-Seventh Session in 1997*, Lausanne, pp. 58–64.

Payne, M. (2001), *Interview in Australia Tourist Commission, Australia's Olympics, Special Post Games Tourism Report*, Sydney.

Perelman, R.B. (1985), *Olympic Retrospective the Games of Los Angeles 1984*, Los Angeles.

Persson, Ch. (2000), *The Olympic Host Selection Process*, Lulea.

Peto, R. (1989), *Grundlagen der Makroökonomie*, 9th edn, München.

Philemon, T.J. (1996 [1896]), *Official Report*, reprint, Athens, pp. 111–21.

Phillips, R. (1989), 'Cyclists gearing for fight over future of Velodrome', *Montreal Gazette* (23 March), P9–F5.

Plath, F. (1973), *Ökonomische Bewertung öffentlicher Investitionen*, Göttingen.

Plessis, M. du (1997), 'Rings of deception. The cost: You haven't heard the half of it!', *Cape Times* (21 August), 3–4.

Pound, R.W. (1996a), 'The importance of commercialism for the Olympic Movement', *Olympic Message – Sources of Financing Sports*, (3), 10–13.

Pound, R.W. (1996b), 'Es ist unkreativ, [...]', *DSM, Marketing News*, (3), 1.

Pouret, H. (1976), 'Olympic ceremonies', in M. Killanin and J. Rodda (eds), *The Olympic Games. 80 Years of People, Events and Records*, London, pp. 160–61.

Prasad, D. (1999), 'Environment', in R. Cashman and A. Hughes (eds), *Staging the Olympics. The Event and Its Impact*, Sydney, pp. 83–92.

Preuss, H. (1993), 'Die Kosten-Nutzen-Analysen Olympischer Spiele des Jahres 2000 in Berlin, unpublished Diplomarbeit, Georg-August-University Göttingen, Göttingen.

Preuss, H. (1998b), 'Problemizing arguments of the opponents of Olympic Games', in R.K. Barney, K.G. Wamsley, S.G. Martyn and G.H. MacDonald (eds), *Global and Cultural Critique: Problematizing the Olympic Games*, London, ON, 197–218.

Preuss, H. (1999), *Ökonomische Implikationen der Ausrichtung Olympischer Spiele von München 1972 bis Atlanta 1996*, Kassel.

Preuss, H. (2000a), *Economics of the Olympic Games. Hosting the Games 1972–2000*, Sydney.

Preuss, H. (2000b), 'Electing an Olympic City – a Multidimensional Decision', in K.B. Wamsley, S.G. Martyn, G.H. MacDonald, H. Gordon and R.K. Barney (eds), *Bridging*

Three Centuries: Intellectual Crossroads and the Modern Olympic Movement, London ON, pp. 89–104.

Preuss, H. (2000c), 'Globalization and its economic impact on the Olympic Games', in IOC/IOA (eds), *Report of the Thirty-Ninth Session in 1999*, Lausanne, pp. 123–42.

Preuss, H. (2001a), 'Legacy of the Games of the XXVII Olympiad – Sydney 2000', paper presented at the 2001 National Olympic Academy of the British Olympic Foundation, 27–29 April, Lilleshall.

Preuss, H. (2001b), 'Olympic ticket pricing', *European Journal for Sport Management, Special Issue 2001*, **8**, 37–62.

Preuss, H. (2002c), 'The economic and social impact of the Sydney Olympic Games', in IOC/IOA (eds), *Report of the Forty-First Session 2001*, Lausanne, pp. 94–109.

Preuss, H. (2002d), 'About the dialectic of traditional and legal ruling of the IOC against the background of commercialisation', *Annual of CESH* (European Committee for the History of Sport), pp. 111–124.

Preuss, H. (2002e), 'Olympische Spiele 2012 in Deutschland. Der stärkste Bewerbungswettbewerb in der Olympischen Geschichte', paper presented at the 3rd German Sport Economics Congress in Cologne, 22 November, in press.

Preuss, H. (2003a), 'Rarely considered economic legacies of Olympic Games', in M. Moragas Spà, M.C. Kennett and N. Puig (eds), *The Legacy of Olympic Games (1984–2000)*, Lausanne, pp. 243–52.

Preuss, H. (2003b), 'The economics of the Olympic Games: winners and losers', in B. Houlihan, B. (ed.), *Sport & Society*, London, Thousand Oaks, CA and New Dehli, pp. 252–271.

Preuss, H. and B. Kebernik (2000), 'Social structure, recruitment and opinions of the volunteers in Nagano 1998', in in M. Moragas, A.B. Moreno and N. Puig (eds), *Volunteers, Global Society and the Olympic Movement*, 24–26 November 1999, Lausanne, pp. 315–24.

Preuss, H. and H.-J. Weiss (2003), *Torchholder value added. Der ökonomische Nutzen der Olympischen Spiele 2012 in Frankfurt Rhein/Main*, Eschborn.

Preuß, H. and M. Messing (2002), 'Auslandstouristen bei den Olympischen Spielen in Sydney 2000', in A. Dreyer (ed.), *Tourismus im Sport*, Wiesbaden, pp. 223–41.

Preuss', H. (1996), 'Olympiabriefmarken bringen seit 1896 Gewinn', *Frankfurter Allgemeine Zeitung*, **48** (22 March) (70), 37.

PricewaterhouseCoopers (2002), 'Business and economic benefits of the Sydney 2000 Olympics: a collation of evidence', typeskript.

Pyrgiotis, Y. (2001), 'The Games in the XXIst century', in IOC (ed.), *Olympic Games and Architecture. The Future for Host Cities*, Lausanne, pp. 25–9.

Rademacher, H. (1996a), 'Kaltluft für Samaranch und ein bleibendes Geschenk für die Baseballfans', *Frankfurter Allgemeine Zeitung*, **48** (17 May), 34.

Rademacher, H. (1996b), 'Das kühne Spiel des Billy Payne', *Frankfurter Allgemeine Zeitung*, **48** (3 August), 15.

Rademacher, H. (1996c), 'Vorbereitung auf Olympia im Disney-Vergnügungspark', *Frankfurter Allgemeine Zeitung*, **48** (5 August), 3.

Rahmann, B. and M. Kurscheidt (2002), 'The soccer World Cup 2006 in Germany: choosing match locations by applying a modified cost–benefit model', in C.P. Barros, M. Ibrahímo, S. and Szymanski, S. (eds), *Transatlantic Sport. The Comparative Economics of North American and European Sports*. Cheltenham, UK and Northampton MA, USA: Edward Elgar, pp. 171–203

Rahmann, B., W. Weber, Y. Groening, M. Kurscheidt, H.-G. Napp and M. Pauli (1998), *Sozioökonomische Analyse der Fußball-WM 2006 in Deutschland*, Köln.

Reich, K. (1986), *Making It Happen: Peter Ueberroth and the 1984 Olympics*, Santa Barbara, CA.

Reth, I. (1993), 'Barcelona ein Jahr nach den Spielen', *Frankfurter Allgemeine Zeitung* , **45** (23 July), 35.

Rich, J. (2000), 'Are the Green Games really golden?', *Living Ethics. Newsletter of the St. James Ethics Centre*, **41**, 10.

Ricquart, V.J. (1988), *The Games within the Games. The Story Behind the 1988 Seoul Olympics*, Seoul.

Rigaud, A. (1997), 'Olympia 2004 als Arbeitsbeschaffungsmaßnahme', *NOK-Report* (3), 22.

Riordan, J. (1996), 'Olympic ceremonies in history (1980 to 1994). A pilgrimage to the past and a gesture of faith in the future', in M. Moragas Spà, J. MacAloon, and M. Llinés (eds), *Olympic Ceremonies Historical Continuity and Cultural Exchange*, Lausanne, pp. 145–52.

Ritchie, B.J.R. (2000), 'Turning 16 days into 16 years through Olympic Legacy', *Event Management*, 6, 155–65.

Ritchie, B.J.R. and B.H. Smith (1991), 'The impact of a mega-Event on host region awareness: a longitudinal study', *Journal of Travel Research*, **30** (1), 3–10.

Roaf, V., K. Deventer and C. Houston (1996), *The Olympics and Development. Lessons and Suggestions*, Observatory.

Röder, W. (1997), 'Rückkehr zu den Wurzeln?', *Kölner Stadt-Anzeiger* (6 September).

Rome OCOG (1960), *The Games of the XVII Olympiad, Rome 1960, The Official Report of the Organizing Committee*, Rome.

Rønningen, A. (1995), 'Analyse de l'impact économique des XVIIes Jeux Olympiques d'hiver à Lillehammer en 1994', Lausanne, typescript.

Roughton Jr, B. (1994), 'Some Georgians may find Games a bit too pricey', *The Atlanta Journal* (17 February), C1.

Roulac, S.E. (1993), 'Place wars and the Olympic Games', *Futurist* (6), 18–19.

Rozin, S. (1996), 'Empowering the Olympic Movement', reprinted from the 1996 *Fortune 500 Issue. Time Inc.*, n.p.

Ruffenach, G. (1996a), 'Money', *The Wall Street Journal* (19 July), R1, R6.

Ruffenach, G. (1996b), 'Sell, sell, sell', *The Wall Street Journal* (19 July), R15.

Rutheiser, D. (1996), *Imagineering Atlanta*, New York.

Saltzman, A. (1996), 'If not the gold, how about a paycheck?', *US News & World Report*, 120 (18), 72.

Sassen, S. (1996), *Metropolen des Weltmarktes. Die neue Rolle der Global Cities*, Frankfurt and New York.

Savoie, J.A.C. (1996), 'Lotteries: sport generates more wealth than it receives', *Olympic Message – Sources of Financing Sports*, (3), 111–13.

Schantz, O. (1995), 'The presidency of Avery Brundage (1952–1972)', in O. Schantz and K. Lennartz (eds), *The International Olympic Committee one Hundred Years. The Idea – The Presidents – The Achievements*, vol. 2, Lausanne, pp. 77–200.

Schänzer, W. (2000), 'Die medizinische Revolution. Über die Effizienz von Dopingkontrollen und die Nebenwirkungen verbotener Substanzen', in M. Gamper, J. Mühlethaler and F. Reidhaar (eds), *Doping. Spitzensport als gesellschaftliches Problem*. Zürich, 191-218.

Scheibe-Jaeger, A. (1996), *Finanzierungs-Handbuch für Non-Profit-Organisationen.*, Regensburg and Bonn.

Scherer, K.A. (1995), *100 Jahre Olympische Spiele Idee, Analyse und Bilanz*, Dortmund.

Schlossberg, H. (1996), *Sports Marketing*, Oxford.

Schlumberger, M. (1987), *Die Bewertung von Beschäftigungswirkungen öffentlicher Projekte im Rahmen der Kosten-Nutzen-Analyse*, Krefeld.

Schmidt, Th. (2003), 'Olympic stadiums of the 20th century. Typology and lines of development in architectual history', *Sportstätten- und bäderbau*, 37 (5), 18–21.

Schneider, F. (1991), *Corporate-Identity-orientierte Unternehmenspolitik: Eine Untersuchung unter besonderer Berücksichtigung von Corporate Design und Corporate Advertising*, Heidelberg.

Schneppen, A. (1998), 'In der Wirtschaftskrise soll Olympia die Stimmung verbessern', *Frankfurter Allgemeine Zeitung*, **50** (30 January), 36.

Schollmeier, P. (2001), *Bewerbungen um Olympische Spiele. Von Athen 1896 bis Athen 2004*, Germany: Books on Demand GmbH.

Schöps, H.J. (1983), 'Unglaublich mißbraucht, kaltblütig mißbraucht', *Der Spiegel*, **37** (32), 112–122.

Schweikle, J. (1996), 'Die Flasche und die Fackel', *Die Zeit* (12 January), 67.

Scott, J. (2002), 'Going for gold', *Good Title, Property News* (62), 6–7.

Scott, S. (1989), 'Velodrome to become "living science museum" as Bourassa, Doré unveil $40-million Biodrome', *Montreal Gazette* (18 August), A1.

Séguin, B. (2003), 'Olympic Games and Marketing Strategies: Relationships between stakeholders' unpublished doctorate thesis, Université des Sciences Humaines, Strasbourg.

Seifart, H. (1984), 'Sport and economy: the commercialization of Olympic sport by media', *International Review for Sociology of Sport*, **19** (3+4), 305–16.

Sellien, R. and H. Sellien (1997), *Gablers Wirtschaftslexikon*, 14th edn., Wiesbaden.

Seoul OCOG (1988), *Official Report of the Organising Committee of the Games of Seoul 1988*, vol. 1, Seoul.

Shani, D. and D. Sandler (1989), 'Olympic sponsorship versus ambush marketing', *Journal of Advertising Research*, **29** (August/September), 11.

Siebel, W. (1994), 'Was macht eine Stadt urban?', in F.W. Busch and H. Havekost (eds), *Oldenburger Universitätsreden – Ansprachen, Aufsätze, Vorträge* (61), Oldenburg.

Simson, V. and A. Jennings (1992), *Geld, Macht und Doping*, Munich.

Snyder, C. R., M.A. Lassegard and C.E. Ford (1986) 'Distancing after group success and failure: basking in reflected glory and cutting off reflected failure', *Journal of Personality and Social Psychology*, **51** (2), 382–8.

Southgate, L. (2001), 'Hotels run bad last in Games', *Australian* (11 May), 41.

Spilling, O.R. (1997), 'Long-term impacts of mega events – the case of Lillehammer 1994', in Department of Tourism Studies (ed.), *The Impact of Mega Events* papers of the Talk at the Top Conference (7–8 July), typescript.

State Chamber of Commerce (NSW) (2001), *Sydney 2000. A Report on the Olympic Impact on Business in a Host City*, Sydney.

Statistisches Landesamt Berlin (1996), *Statistisches Jahrbuch 1996*, Berlin.

Statistisches Landesamt München (1969), *Statistisches Jahrbuch der Landeshauptstadt München Berichtsjahr 1968*, Munich.

Statistisches Landesamt München (1970), *Statistisches Jahrbuch der Landeshauptstadt München Berichtsjahr 1969*, Munich.

Statistisches Landesamt München (1971), *Statistisches Jahrbuch der Landeshauptstadt München Berichtsjahr 1970*, Munich.

Statistisches Landesamt München (1972), *Statistisches Jahrbuch der Landeshauptstadt München Berichtsjahr 1971*, Munich.

Statistisches Landesamt München (1973), *Statistisches Jahrbuch der Landeshauptstadt München Berichtsjahr 1972*, Munich.

Statistisches Landesamt München (1974), *1875–1975 100 Jahre Städtestatistik in München*, Munich.

Statistisches Landesamt München (1976), *Statistisches Jahrbuch der Landeshauptstadt München Berichtsjahr 1974/1975*, Munich.

Stockholm OCOG (1912), *The Official Report of the Organizing Committee for the Games of Stockholm 1912*, vol. 1, Stockholm.

Strauss, J. (1993), *Das tägliche T-Shirt bringt in Lillehammer Millionen*, AGSPORT news agency (23 March).

Strauss, R. (1992), *Olympische Spiele im Jahr 2000 – Prüfung einer im Auftrag der Berlin 2000 Olympia GmbH erarbeiteten Rechnung von Prof. Maennig, Abgeordnetenhaus of Berlin*, Berlin, unpublished typescript.

Streltsova, E (1987), 'Cultural events in the programme of the 1980 Olympic Games in Moscow', in O. Szymiczek and International Olympic Academy (eds), *Report of the Twent-Sixth Session in 1986*, Lausanne, pp. 235–43.

Stupp, H.M. (1996), 'Sponsorship and television', *Olympic Message – Sources of Financing Sports*, (3), 25–34.

Sydney OCOG (1997), 'Olympic Coin Agreement' (1 September), typescript.

Sydney OCOG (2000), *The Games of the XXVII Olympiad. Sports Commission Report 1996–2000*, Sydney.

Sydney OCOG (2001), *Official Report of the XXVII Olympiad. Preparing for the Games*, vol. 1, Sydney.

Taylor, P. and C. Gratton (1988), 'The Olympic Games, an economic Analysis', *Leisure Management*, **8** (3), 32–4.

Telex Dienst Tourismus (1992), 'Vergrault Olympia die Touristen', *Süddeutsche Zeitung*, **44** (28 July), 29.

The Audit Office (1999), *Performance Audit Report. The Sydney 2000 Olympic and Paralympic Games. Review of Estimates*, Sydney.

Thompson, A. (1999), 'Security', in R. Cashman and A. Hughes (eds), *Staging the Olympics. The Event and Its Impact*, Sydney, pp. 106–20.

Thurow, R. (1996), 'Lord of the Rings', *The Wall Street Journal* (19 July), R14.

Tillier, A. (1994), 'Barcelona: An elegant, hardworking Euro-city', *Europe* (Nov), 341, 32–4.

Tokyo OCOG (1964), *The Games of the XVIII Olympiad Tokyo 1964, The Official Report of the Organizing Committee*, Tokyo.

Toohey, Ch. and A. Veal (2000), *The Olympic Games: a social science perspective*, Oxon.

Tourism Forecasting Council (TFC) (1998), *The Olympic Effect*, Canberra.

Trumpp, E. (1991), 'Die Olympischen Spiele 1932 in Los Angeles. Eine Neubewertung unter besonderer Berücksichtigung zeitgenössischer Publikationen und Quellenmaterials aus dem Stadtarchiv Los Angeles', Staatsexamensarbeit, Johannes Gutenberg-University Mainz.

Ueberroth, P., R. Levin and A. Quinn (1985), *Made in America. His Own Story*, New York.

United States Olympic Committee (USOC) 1995 (1995), *Annual Report 1995*, Colorado Springs CO.

Vall, J.B. (1995), 'The technological image of the Barcelona Olympic Games', in M. Moragas Spà and M. Botella (eds), *The Keys to Success*, Barcelona, pp. 254–60.

Vegara, J.M. and M. Salvador (1992), 'The Economic Impact of the Barcelona'92 Olympic Games', Ajuntamento de Barcelona (ed.) (May), typescript.

Veblen, T. (1981 [1899]), *Theorie der feinen Leute. Eine ökonomische Untersuchung der Institutionen*, Munich.

Voigt, B. (1999), 'Das neue Herz schlägt nur für 17 Tage', *Der Tagesspiegel* (7 July), 25.

Waldbröl, H.J. (1996a), 'Atlantas Ambiente billig, geschmacklos, unwürdig', *Frankfurter Allgemeine Zeitung*, **48** (13 November), 40.

Waldbröl, H.J. (1996b), 'Was hätte die Welt gesagt, wenn ich Atlanta gepriesen hätte?', *Frankfurter Allgemeine Zeitung*, **48** (14 November), 40.

Weber, C. (1994), 'Elemente einer wissenschaftlichen Kosten-Nutzen-Analyse am Beispiel der Olympischen Sommerspiele in München 1972', Diplomarbeit Georg-August-University Göttingen.

Weber, M. (1988 [1922]): *Gesammelte Aufsätze zur Wissenschaftslehre*. Winckelmann, J. (ed.), 7th ed., Tübingen.

Weirick, J. (1999), 'Urban design', in R. Cashman and A. Hughes (eds), *Staging the Olympics. The Event and Its Impact*, Sydney, pp. 70–82.

Weissenberg, P. (1996), 'Sponsorenjäger', *Werben & verkaufen*, 28, 59–61.

Wenn, St. (1993), 'A History of the International Olympic Committee and Television, 1936–1980', dissertation, Pennsylvania State University.

Westerloo, E. van (1996), 'Sportrechte: Preisskala nach oben offen?', *Media Perspektiven*, **10** (October), 514–20.

Wetter, R. (1972), 'Olympia als Fehlinvestition', in H.-H. Henschen and R. Wetter, *Anti-Olympia. Ein Beitrag zur mutwilligen Diffamierung und öffentlichen Destruktion der Olympischen Spiele und anderer Narreteien*, München, pp. 60–97.

Wilcox, D.A. (1994), 'THC '94 Lessons for the tourism industries from the 1984 Olympics at Los Angeles', Sydney, typescript.

Will, van de (1989), 'Montreal's Olympic velodrome to become a science museum', *Montreal Gazette* (18 August), A19.

Wimmer, M. (1975), *Bauten der Olympischen Spiele*, Leipzig.

Windlin, S. (1998), 'Wenn dem Hahn der Kamm blaßrosa schwillt', *Frankfurter Allgemeine Zeitung*, **50** (29 June) (147), 38.

Woo, K.-S. (1988), 'The long-term impact of the Seoul Olympic village. Seoul International Conference Jun 13–16, 1988. Hosting the Olympics', *The Long Term Impact – Report of the Conference*, Seoul, pp. 281–87.

World Bank (1987), *World Development Report 1987*, Washington, DC.

World Bank (1996), *World Development Report 1996*, Washington, DC.

Wright, G. (1978), 'The political economy of the Montreal Olympic Games', *Journal of Sport and Social Issues*, 2 (1), 13–18.

Xianpeng, L. (2003), 'The economic analysis of Beijing 2008 Olympic Games', in M. Moragas Spà, M.C. Kennett and N. Puig (eds), *The Legacy of Olympic Games (1984–2000)*, Lausanne, 227–28.

Xu, D., C. He and X. Ping (2003), 'Beijing 2008. Planning and organising the Olympic legacy', in M. Moragas Spà, M.C. Kennett and N. Puig (eds), *The Legacy of Olympic Games (1984–2000)*, Lausanne, pp. 422–5.

Zils, O. (2001), 'Mit Sicherheit teurer', *Horizont Sport Business*, 14–18.

Zollinger, H. (1994), 'Sponsoring-Markt Definition, Ist-Zustand, Potential', in Zollinger + Partner AG (ed.), *Sponsoring – Wer gräbt wem das Wasser ab? Zahlen, Fakten, Trends und aktuelle Marktstudie*, Zürich.

Interviews

Achten, A., Chief Executive Officer of the Deutsche Sport-Marketing GmbH (Frankfurt, 12 January 2004).

Arnold, T., NOC for Germany (Finances) (Frankfurt, 20 January 2004).

Arrington, M., OCOG Atlanta – Director Youth and Education (Atlanta, 1 August 1996).

Battle, C.H., OCOG Atlanta – Managing Director of International Relations and Vice president OCOG Atlanta (Olympia, 18 July 1997; letter 19 January 1998, phone, 22 February 1998).

Birch, R., Director of Ceremonies in Los Angeles '84, Barcelona '92, Atlanta '96 and Sydney 2000 (Olympia, 17 July 1997, letter 18 August 1997).

Brown, K., OCOG Sydney – Program Manager Cultural Olympiad (Sydney, 7 December 1999).

Cameron, A., OCOG Sydney – Manager Olympic Youth Camp (letter 29 October 1999; Sydney, 3 December 1999).

Chalkias, A., OCOG Athens 2004 – Marketing and Sponsoring Department (Athens, 26 November 2003).

DeFrantz, A., Member of IOC Executive Board – USA (Los Angeles, 4 September 1994; Olympia, 12 July 1997).

Demba, J., Bündnis 90/Grüne (AL) group in parliament, Head of Anti-Berlin Committee (Berlin 22 August 1993).

Diamantidis, H., OCOG Athens 2004 – Licensing Manager (Athens, 26 November 2003).

Eleftheriou, M., Section Manager Olympic Youth Camp (Athens, 15 December 2003).

Elphinston, B., OCOG Sydney – General Manager Sports (Olympia, 1 August 1999; Sydney, 6 December 1999).

Exarchos, Y., Vice-President of AOB Athens Olympic Broadcasting (Athens, October 2003).

Feldhoff, U., President of the International Canoe Federation (ICF) (phone, 28 January 2004).

Goldberg, D. J., Producer of the Olympic ceremonies in Atlanta 1996, D. Mischer Productions, Inc. (Olympia, 17 July 1997; letter, 23 August 1997).

Greib, G., Attorney of Himmelseher Sportversicherungen (phone, 2 July 1996 and 24 September 1997).

Hattig, F., Member of Bidding Committee Munich 1972 (Mainz, 14 February 2001).

Heine, Product Manager MDM, coins (phone, 17 June 1997 and 9 July 1997).

Jourdan, K., Head of Strategic Planning, Young and Rubicam (20 January 2004).

Kühner, H., Journalist at the Olympic Games of Atlanta 1996 (numerous interviews).

Loth, H., Stamps and coins dealer, Mainz (numerous interviews).

Mamangakis, G., OCOG Athens 2004 – Section Manager, Financial Planning and Budgeting (Athens, 16 December 2003).

Messing, M., Professor for Sports Sociology at the Johannes Gutenberg University Mainz (Mainz, numerous interviews).

Moragas Spà, M., Director – Centre d'Estudis Olímpics i de Esport, Barcelona (Olympia, 15 July 1997).

Müller, N., Professor for Sports History at the Johannes Gutenberg University Mainz, Commission member for Culture and Olympic education of the IOC and president of the International Pierre de Coubertin Committee. (Mainz, numerous interviews).

Navacelle de Coubertin, G. de, Greatnephew of Pierre de Coubertin (Mirville, 19 August 1997).

Papapetropoulos, T., OCOG Athens 2004 – General Manager, Financial Service (Athens, November 2003).

Payne, M.R., IOC Marketing Director (Olympia, 10 July 1997) and (Lausanne, 5 January 2004)

Pound, R., Member of the IOC Executive Board, Vice-President of the IOC (Montreal, 13 October 1998).

Price, R., Chairman of the Paralympics England (Olympia, 21 July 1997).

Protopsaltis, P.K., OCOG Athens – General Manager, Transport (Athens, July 2003).

Rodichenko, V., Vice-President of the Russian NOC (1 August 1999).

Roth, W., NOC for Germany (Finances) (Frankfurt, 26 June 1997).

Sauer, M., Sendeleiter of the television station (ZDF) (Mainz, 2 September 1997).

Schormann, K., President of the International Pentathlon Federation (UIPM) (Darmstadt, 19 January 2004).

Schröder, J., Personal adviser of W. Daume at the Olympic Games of Munich 1972 (phone, 28 June 1997).

Scott, Sir R., President of the Manchester 2000 Bid Committee (Olympia, 8 July 1997).

Simitsek, M., OCOG Athens 2004 – Executive Director and Chief Operating Officer (Athens, October 2003).

Slagel, T., OCOG – Director of Planning, Budgeting and Management Systems (Atlanta, 14 September 1994).

Tröger, W., President of the NOC for Germany, IOC Member (Frankfurt, 20 April 1998).

Volk, H., Philatelist, specialized in Olympic stamps (phone, 5 March 1996).

Wilson, R., OCOG Atlanta – stadium announcer of the Georgia Dome (Atlanta, 24 July 1996).

Correspondence

Bergman, M., IOC – Coordinator, Olympic Collectors Commission (15 September 1999 and 28 September 1999).

Bosiljevac, J., OCOG Sydney – Ticket Operations Manager (6 February 2000).

Hendricks, H., Provided information on the campaign against the bid of Cape Town 2004 (16 January 1998, and 19 January 1998).

Huot, R., IOC Advisor for coins, Vice-President of the International Olympic Numismatic Federation (20 June 1997).

Kidd, B., Professor and Director of the School of Physical and Health Education, University of Toronto (18 July 1997).

Lippert, T., Olympic Philatelist (14 January 2000).

Neuhöfer, F., Deutsche Sportjugend (German Sport Youth) (20 January 2004).

Rogge, J., President of the IOC (speech, Athens, 26 November 2003).

Sohn, S.-Y., Director of the Dept. Business Development – Seoul Olympic Sports Promotion Foundation (10 March 1996).

Spilling, O., Centre for Industrial Development and Entrepreneurship Norwegian School of Management (23 May 2001).

Sun, B., Professor at the Beijing University of Physical Education, Member of the Beijing Bidding Committee (18 January 2004).

Wheeler, J., IOC headquarters (2001).

Index